BRAIN
DUMP

BRAIN DUMP

Become a GENIUS on the Loo

GEOFF TIBBALLS

POP PRESS

3 5 7 9 10 8 6 4 2

Pop Press, an imprint of Ebury Publishing,
20 Vauxhall Bridge Road, London SW1V 2SA

Pop Press is part of the Penguin Random House group of companies
whose addresses can be found at global.penguinrandomhouse.com

Penguin
Random House
UK

Copyright © Pop Press 2019
Written and compiled by Geoff Tibballs
Internal illustrations from Shutterstock.com. By Natalie Adams /
Natasha Pankina / natrot / puruan / vectorsicon.com /
Visual Generation

Pop Press has asserted their right to be identified
as the author of this Work in accordance with the
Copyright, Designs and Patents Act 1988

First published in the United Kingdom by Pop Press in 2019
www.penguin.co.uk

A CIP catalogue record for this book is
available from the British Library

ISBN 9781529102574

Project editor: Liz Marvin
Typesetter: seagulls.net

Printed and bound in Great Britain by Clays Ltd, Elcograf S.p.A.

Penguin Random House is committed to a sustainable future
for our business, our readers and our planet. This book is made
from Forest Stewardship Council® certified paper.

MIX
Paper from
responsible sources
FSC® C018179

CONTENTS

INTRODUCTION

In our hectic daily lives, a trip to the bathroom is often the only time we have to ourselves – unless, of course, we have forgotten to lock the door and end up with unexpected company. It is a time for reflection, for contemplating the meaning of life, for dreaming of warm, sunny climes and now, thanks to this book, for acquiring new nuggets of knowledge. The length of time you spend in the bathroom each day probably depends on how much fibre there is in your diet, but with *Brain Dump* you will be able to learn at least one item of factual trivia with which to impress your friends and family in the time to takes you to do a poo – even if your last meal was a hot vindaloo washed down by half a dozen beers and an overripe pineapple. So, if you've ever sat there wondering what animal defecates cubes, how to say 'cheers' in Estonian, who was the first person to vomit in space, the sport whose terms include 'dump', 'wipe' and 'floater', or the rock 'n' roll classic that was described by its record label at the time as a 'novelty foxtrot', this book is as essential to your bathroom as a roll of toilet paper. And in case you run out of that, the pages are thick and soft, too.

PEOPLE

FROM HERE TO MATERNITY

BIRTHS

Queen Anne (1665–1714) was pregnant 18 times, but none of her children survived her.

Klara Pölzi and Alois Hitler had four sons. Gustav, Otto and Edmund all died young, leaving just Adolf to survive into adulthood.

American playwright Eugene O'Neill was both born in and died in a hotel room. He was born in New York's Barrett House Hotel in 1888 and died in room 401 of the Sheraton Hotel, Boston, in 1953. He is said to have remarked about the symmetry on his deathbed.

Frank Sinatra weighed an enormous 13.5 pounds at birth, and the difficult delivery meant that his mother Dolly was unable to have any more children. It also left Sinatra himself with a perforated eardrum for the rest of his life.

Jack Lemmon was born in an elevator at Newton-Wellesley Hospital, Massachusetts.

Prince Philip, Duke of Edinburgh, was born on the kitchen table of his family's villa in Corfu.

As a baby, Henry VIII had two official cradle rockers — Margaret Draughton and Frideswide Puttenham — who were each paid £3 a year to perform their duties.

At royal births, there was always the fear that an imposter baby might be smuggled into the bedchamber, concealed inside a warming pan or similar receptacle. So government ministers were required to act as witnesses and even as recently as 1926, the Duchess of York ensured that the Home Secretary attended the birth of the future Queen Elizabeth II to prevent any skulduggery.

Until the 1920s, babies in Finland were often delivered in saunas because it was believed that the heat helped keep infection at bay.

SEPARATED AT BIRTH

FAMOUS PEOPLE BORN
ON THE SAME DAY

Abraham Lincoln and Charles Darwin (12 February 1809)

Hubert Humphrey and Vincent Price (27 May 1911)

Karl Malden and Wilfrid Brambell (22 March 1912)

Pol Pot and Malcolm X (19 May 1925)

Margaret Thatcher and Lenny Bruce (13 October 1925)

Ariel Sharon and Fats Domino (26 February 1928)

Yoko Ono and Bobby Robson (18 February 1933)

Michael Caine and Quincy Jones (14 March 1933)

Albert Finney and Glenda Jackson (9 May 1936)

Vanessa Redgrave and Boris Spassky (30 January 1937)

Natalie Wood and Diana Rigg (20 July 1938)

Francis Ford Coppola and David Frost (7 April 1939)

Manfred Mann and Geoffrey Boycott (21 October 1940)

Aretha Franklin and Richard O'Brien (25 March 1942)

Eric Idle and John Major (29 March 1943)

John Denver and Ben Kingsley (31 December 1943)

Rudy Giuliani and Gladys Knight (28 May 1944)

Tyne Daly and Alan Rickman (21 February 1946)

George W. Bush and Sylvester Stallone (6 July 1946)

Stephen King and Don Felder (21 September 1947)

Marc Bolan and Rula Lenska (30 September 1947)

Rhea Perlman and Al Gore (31 March 1948)

Margot Kidder and George Wendt (17 October 1948)

George Foreman and Linda Lovelace (10 January 1949)

Lindsay Wagner and Meryl Streep (22 June 1949)

Steve Jobs and Alain Prost (24 February 1955)

Kate Bush and Daley Thompson (30 July 1958)

Lenny Henry and Michael Jackson (29 August 1958)

Princess Diana and Carl Lewis (1 July 1961)

Prince Edward and Neneh Cherry (10 March 1964)

Helena Bonham Carter and Zola Budd (26 May 1966)

Andre Agassi and Uma Thurman (29 April 1970)

Eva Longoria and will.i.am (15 March 1975)

Angelina Jolie and Russell Brand (4 June 1975)

Cat Deeley and Ryan Reynolds (23 October 1976)

BORN ON CHRISTMAS DAY

Isaac Newton (1642)

Dorothy Wordsworth (1771)

Helena Rubinstein (1872)

Conrad Hilton (1887)

Humphrey Bogart (1899)

Lew Grade (1906)

Quentin Crisp (1908)

Kenny Everett (1944)

Sissy Spacek (1949)

Annie Lennox (1954)

Chris Kamara (1957)

Shane MacGowan (1957)

Helena Christensen (1968)

Dido (1971)

Justin Trudeau (1971)

Marcus Trescothick (1975)

Alastair Cook (1984)

Georgia Moffett (1984)

FAMOUS PEOPLE WHO WERE ADOPTED

Truman Capote

Bo Diddley

Gerald Ford

Jamie Foxx

Michael Gove

Debbie Harry

Faith Hill

Steve Jobs

Eartha Kitt

Lee Majors

Nelson Mandela

Marilyn Monroe

Edgar Allan Poe

Nicole Richie

Babe Ruth

KT Tunstall

Fatima Whitbread

WHAT WERE THEY THINKING?

DISTINCTIVE CELEBRITY CHILD NAMES

Ace Knute (son of Jessica Simpson)

Apollo Bowie (son of Gwen Stefani)

Apple (daughter of Gwyneth Paltrow and Chris Martin)

Audio Science (son of Shannyn Sossamon)

Blue Ivy (daughter of Beyoncé and Jay-Z)

Bluebell Madonna (daughter of Geri Halliwell)

Bronx Mowgli (son of Ashlee Simpson)

Buddy Bear (son of Jamie Oliver)

Daisy Boo (daughter of Jamie Oliver)

Denim Cole (son of Toni Braxton)

Diva Thin Muffin (daughter of Frank Zappa)

Dweezil (son of Frank Zappa)

Elsie Otter (daughter of Zooey Deschanel)

Fifi Trixibelle (daughter of Paula Yates and Bob Geldof)

Heavenly Hiraani Tiger Lily
(daughter of Paula Yates and Michael Hutchence)

Jagger Snow (daughter of Ashlee Simpson)

Jermajesty (son of Jermaine Jackson)

Kal-El (son of Nicolas Cage)

Kyd (son of Téa Leoni and David Duchovny)

Mirabella Bunny (daughter of Bryan Adams)

Moon Unit (daughter of Frank Zappa)

Moroccan (son of Mariah Carey)

Moxie Crimefighter (daughter of Penn Jillette)

Ode Mountain (son of Jena Malone)

Petal Blossom Rainbow (daughter of Jamie Oliver)

Pilot Inspektor (son of Jason Lee)

Poppy Honey (daughter of Jamie Oliver)

River Rocket (son of Jamie Oliver)

Rumer (daughter of Demi Moore and Bruce Willis)

Satchel (daughter of Spike Lee)

Shiloh Nouvel (daughter of Angelina Jolie and Brad Pitt)

Zuma Nesta Rock (son of Gwen Stefani)

EXCLUDED
FROM SCHOOL

Adele (for fighting with a classmate over the relative merits of Will Young and Gareth Gates)

Lily Allen (for smoking and drinking)

Marlon Brando (for riding his motorcycle through the school halls)

Jackie Collins (for smoking and truancy)

Willem Dafoe (for making a pornographic film)

Roger Daltrey (for bringing an airgun to school)

Albert Einstein (for his rebellious attitude)

Gustave Flaubert (for leading a protest against a replacement teacher)

Salma Hayek (for playing pranks on the nuns at her Catholic school)

Elizabeth Hurley (for poor grades)

Courtney Love (for smoking and truancy)

Robert Pattinson (for stealing pornographic magazines and selling them at school)

Richard Pryor (for punching his science teacher)

Charlie Sheen (for poor grades and poor attendance)

CELEBRITIES' SCHOOL YEARBOOK AWARDS

Gillian Anderson was voted 'Most Likely to be Arrested' by her City High School classmates at Grand Rapids, Michigan.

Sandra Bullock, future star of *Miss Congeniality*, was voted 'Most Likely to Brighten Your Day' by her classmates at Washington-Lee High School, Virginia.

Tom Cruise was voted 'Least Likely to Succeed' by his classmates in high school.

Kevin Federline was named 'Most Likely to Be on *America's Most Wanted*' by his classmates in middle school.

Teri Hatcher was voted by her 1982 high school class as 'Girl Most Likely to Become a *Solid Gold* Dancer' (*Solid Gold* was an American music TV show of the 1980s).

Dennis Hopper was voted 'Most Likely to Succeed' by his classmates at Helix High School, La Mesa, California.

Even though he was already a star with The Jackson 5, Michael Jackson was named as the shyest in his class at California Preparatory High School in 1976.

Jennifer Lawrence was voted 'Most Talkative' in middle school for two years in a row.

Matthew McConaughey was named 'Most Handsome' during his senior year at Longview High School, Texas.

Jack Nicholson was voted 'Class Clown of 1954' at Manasquan High School, New Jersey.

Rosie O'Donnell was voted 'Most Popular' and 'Class Clown' by her peers at Commack High School, New York, before she graduated in 1980.

Brad Pitt was voted 'Best Dressed' at Kickapoo High School in Springfield, Missouri.

Natalie Portman was voted 'Most Likely to Be a Contestant On *Jeopardy!*' in her senior yearbook.

Diana Ross was named 'Best Dressed' in her 1962 high school yearbook.

Amy Schumer was voted 'Class Comedian' at South Side High School, Long Island, New York.

Cybill Shepherd was voted 'Most Attractive' in her senior year at high school.

Sylvester Stallone was voted 'Most Likely to End Up in the Electric Chair' by his peers at the Notre Dame Academy, Pennsylvania.

Robin Williams was voted 'Least Likely to Succeed' by his senior year classmates at Redwood High School, California, in 1969.

Bruce Willis was awarded the title of 'Most School Spirit' when he graduated from Penns Grove Regional High School, New Jersey, in 1973.

Oprah Winfrey's classmates at East Nashville High School, Tennessee, voted her the most popular student.

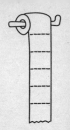

CELEBRITIES
WITH DEGREES

Rowan Atkinson (Electrical Engineering)

Dennis Bergkamp (Mechanical Engineering)

Steve Carell (History)

Gloria Estefan (Psychology)

Will Ferrell (Sports Broadcasting)

Art Garfunkel (Art History and Mathematics)

Ricky Gervais (Philosophy)

Hugh Grant (English Literature)

John Grisham (Accounting)

Hugh Hefner (Psychology)

Michael Jordan (Geography)

Lisa Kudrow (Psychobiology)

Eva Longoria (Kinesiology – the study
of human movement)

Chris Martin, Coldplay (Ancient Greek and Latin)

Brian May (Physics and Mathematics)

Bob Mortimer (Law)

Lionel Richie (Economics)

Arnold Schwarzenegger
(Business and International Economics)

Brooke Shields (French Literature)

Emma Watson (English Literature)

Nicky Wire, Manic Street Preachers (Politics)

Weird Al Yankovic (Architecture)

EARLY JOBS OF THE FAMOUS

Russ Abbot – hearse driver

Jennifer Aniston – bicycle messenger

Jeffrey Archer – deckchair attendant

Shirley Bassey – worker in a chamber pot factory

Warren Beatty – rat-catcher

Beyoncé – floor sweeper in her mum's hair salon

Orlando Bloom – clay pigeon trapper

Jon Bon Jovi – Christmas decoration maker

Marlon Brando – sewage worker

Raymond Burr – shepherd

Steve Buscemi – firefighter

Gerard Butler – lawyer

Michael Caine – meat porter

Jim Carrey – security guard

Chubby Checker – chicken packer

Kurt Cobain – school janitor

Jarvis Cocker – crab scrubber in a fishmonger's

Sean Connery – coffin polisher

Les Dawson – lavatory brush salesman

Eminem – dishwasher

Brandon Flowers – bellhop in a Las Vegas hotel

Errol Flynn – sheep castrator

Pope Francis – chemical technician

Peter Gabriel – milliner

Bob Geldof – pea canner

Whoopi Goldberg – mortuary beautician

Rock Hudson – vacuum cleaner salesman

Hugh Jackman – children's party clown

Glenda Jackson – shop assistant at Boots

Mick Jagger – porter at a psychiatric hospital

Tom Jones – apprentice glove cutter

Michelle Keegan – check-in clerk at Manchester Airport

Nicole Kidman – massage therapist

Burt Lancaster – lingerie salesman

Cyndi Lauper – dog kennel cleaner

Annie Lennox – fish factory worker

John Major – builder's labourer

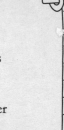

Meghan Markle – sales clerk at a Los Angeles yoghurt store called Humphrey Yogart

Matthew McConaughey – chicken coop cleaner

Steve McQueen – towel boy in a brothel

Bette Midler – pineapple chunker

Demi Moore – debt collector

Bill Murray – chestnut salesman

Liam Neeson – fork-lift operator at Guinness

Barack Obama – ice cream parlour worker

Ozzy Osbourne – slaughterhouse labourer

Michelle Pfeiffer – supermarket worker

Edith Piaf – wreath maker

Brad Pitt – fast food restaurant mascot (dressed as a giant chicken)

Terry Pratchett – West Country press officer for the Central Electricity Generating Board

Keanu Reeves – pasta shop manager

Keith Richards – ball boy at a tennis club

Phillip Schofield – candy floss seller

Captain Sensible – toilet cleaner

Sylvester Stallone – lion cage cleaner

Rod Stewart – gravedigger

Quentin Tarantino – usher at an adult cinema called the Pussycat Theatre

Tina Turner – cotton picker

Christopher Walken – assistant lion tamer

Kanye West – sales assistant in Gap

Bill Withers – aircraft toilet seat manufacturer

Malcolm Young of AC/DC – sewing machine mechanic in a bra factory

CELEBRITY SACKINGS

Walt Disney was fired as an aspiring cartoonist on the *Kansas City Star* because his editor said he 'lacked imagination and had no good ideas'.

Thomas Edison was fired from Western Union because, while conducting experiments during the night shift, he spilled sulphuric acid on the floor and it leaked through the floorboards and onto his boss's desk in the room below.

Boy George was sacked from his job as a shelf-stacker at Tesco for wearing the store's carrier bags. Tesco deemed his appearance 'disturbing'.

Madonna was sacked from New York fast-food restaurant Dunkin' Donuts for squirting jam at a customer.

Barry Manilow was sacked from a New York brewery for failing to shut the rolltop doors of the delivery truck. As the truck turned a corner, crates and bottles flew everywhere, turning the street into a river of beer.

Robert Mitchum lost his job at a Toledo car factory because he refused to wear socks to work.

Vic Reeves was sacked from his job on a pig farm partly because of his erratic tractor-driving. He once accidentally demolished 100 yards of fencing and on another occasion reversed into a pigsty.

J.K. Rowling was fired from her job as a secretary at Amnesty International because she kept daydreaming about her ideas for a story about a boy wizard.

Alexei Sayle lost his job as an assistant caretaker at a school for dodging off home early. He was shopped by the school's lollipop man.

Eric Sykes was sacked from a cotton mill for singing Bing Crosby's 'Where the Blue of the Night' with an empty bucket on his head.

MOST STRESSFUL JOBS IN THE WORLD

Enlisted military personnel

Surgeon

Firefighter

Airline pilot

Police officer

Nurse

Emergency dispatcher

Newspaper reporter

Events coordinator

Senior corporate executive

Public relations executive

Broadcaster

Teacher

Taxi driver

Social worker

FAMOUS PEOPLE
WHO ONCE HAD
THE SAME JOB

Matt LeBlanc and Harrison Ford (carpenters)

Harry Hill and Anton Chekhov (doctors)

David Jason and George Harrison (electricians)

Danny DeVito and Twiggy (hair stylists)

George Clooney and Jasper Carrott
(door-to-door insurance salesmen)

Mark Knopfler and Peter O'Toole (journalists)

Sharon Stone and Shania Twain (McDonald's workers)

Benny Hill and Sean Connery (milkmen)

Abraham Lincoln and Eric Clapton (postmen)

Dusty Springfield and Imelda Marcos (record shop clerks)

Sheryl Crow and Vincent van Gogh (schoolteachers)

Johnny Depp and Jerry Seinfeld (telemarketers)

FORMER
SCHOOLTEACHERS

Sir John Betjeman (English)

Dan Brown (English and Spanish)

Billy Crystal (substitute teacher)

Greg Davies (English and drama)

Roberta Flack (music and English)

Dawn French (drama)

Art Garfunkel (maths)

William Golding (English and philosophy)

Roy Hodgson (PE)

Hugh Jackman (PE)

Lyndon B. Johnson (school principal)

Stephen King (English)

D.H. Lawrence (general)

Brian May (maths and science)

Benito Mussolini (substitute teacher at a primary school)

George Orwell (biology and general subjects)

Romesh Ranganathan (maths)

J.K. Rowling (English)

Franz Schubert (primary school)

Gene Simmons (primary school)

Sting (English)

Mr T (PE)

PEOPLE WHOSE NAME REFLECTS THEIR JOB

Ronald Reagan's White House press spokesman Larry Speakes

Belgian footballer Mark De Man

TV gardener Bob Flowerdew

Nineteenth-century sanitary engineer Thomas Crapper

The Amazing Spider-Man film director Marc Webb

Church of England minister Randy Vickers

Poet William Wordsworth

2003 world poker champion Chris Moneymaker

BBC East Midlands weather presenter Sara Blizzard

Dutch architect Rem Koolhaas

British neurologist Russell Brain

American novelist Francine Prose

Detroit Tigers baseball player Cecil Fielder

Lord Chief Justice of England and Wales, Igor Judge

Professor of Psychiatry at Zurich University, Jules Angst

Russian hurdler Marina Stepanova

YE OLDE OCCUPATIONS

An ankle beater was a young person who helped drive cattle to market.

An antigropelos maker was someone who made waterproof leggings.

An armiger was a squire who carried a knight's armour.

A back-boy was a kitchen servant.

A back tenter was someone employed at the back of the weaving looms to clear away debris. Children were usually entrusted with this dangerous job as they were small enough to work underneath the machines while they were in operation.

A badgy fiddler was a military boy trumpeter.

A baller was a potter's assistant who made and weighed the balls of clay.

A basil worker used to make leather to bind books.

A belly builder built the interiors of pianos.

A bender was a leather cutter.

A bloomer produced iron from iron ore.

A bottom knocker made the base of the saggar (a fireclay container) in the pottery industry. The saggar is used to protect pottery from marking by flames and smoke while it is being fired.

A catchpole was a bailiff or sheriff's assistant.

A chair bodger was an itinerant craftsman who made chair legs.

A delver was a ditch digger.

An ellerman sold lamp oil.

A fagetter sold firewood.

A fripper or fripperer bought and sold old clothes.

A gong farmer or gong scourer emptied human excrement from cesspits and outside toilets.

A grimgribber was another name for a lawyer.

A hooker was a textile mill worker who operated the machinery that laid out fabric to the required length.

A huffler worked on canals to help boats and barges through locks.

A hurrier was a child or a woman employed to haul coal underground.

An iron puddler made wrought iron.

A jagger was a fish seller.

A knacker was a harness maker.

A knocker-up awoke factory workers by tapping on their bedroom windows with a long stick.

A lorimer made the metal mounting for horse bridles.

A matchet mounter worked in the cutlery industry, mounting knife blades to the handles, which were often made of bone.

A mewer made cages for hawks.

A mugger sold crockery, sometimes door-to-door.

A necessary woman was a servant who emptied and cleaned the chamber pots.

A necker fed the cardboard into machines that made boxes.

A nob thatcher was another term for a wig maker.

An ostiary was the doorkeeper at a monastery.

A paling man was an eel seller.

A pee dee was a boy employed by the captain of a boat carrying coal down river to port.

A powder monkey was the young boy – or occasionally girl – whose job it was to carry powder to a ship's guns.

A pugger trod the clay in the manufacture of bricks.

A quarrel picker was another term for a glazier.

A riddler purchased and graded wool.

A scavelman maintained waterways and ditches.

A scavenger was a child employed in a spinning mill to collect loose cotton from the floor under machinery.

A sewer rat was a bricklayer who repaired damaged sewers and tunnels.

A skepper made and sold woven beehives.

A slubber doffer removed the empty bobbins from the loom spindles in the weaving industry.

A swingler beat flax to remove the coarse parts.

A tarboy applied tar (antiseptic) to sheep that had been nicked by shearers.

A toe rag worked in the docks as a corn carrier.

A tranqueter made barrel hoops.

A whacker drove a team of horses or oxen.

A whipping boy was appointed by royal courts in the fifteenth and sixteenth centuries to be whipped in place of naughty princes.

RARELY INVOKED PATRON SAINTS

St Agatha of Sicily – bell makers and volcanic eruptions

St Apollonia – toothache

St Balthasar – playing card manufacturers

St Basilissa – chilblains

St Bernardine of Siena – advertising and public relations

St Bibiana – hangovers

St Bona of Pisa – flight attendants

St Catherine of Alexandria – spinsters and knife sharpeners

St Clotilde – disappointing children

St Dominic Savio – choirboys and young offenders

St Drogo of Sebourg – coffeehouses and unattractive people

St Dymphna – sleepwalkers

St Eligius – gas station workers

St Erasmus – appendicitis

St Fiacre – sexually transmitted disease

St Friard – fear of wasps

St Genesius – torture victims and clowns

St Gertrude of Nivelles – fear of mice

St Giles of Edinburgh – breastfeeding

St Gummarus of Belgium – lumberjacks
and troubled marriages

St Hubert of Liege – mad dogs

St Joseph of Arimathea – funeral directors

St Julian the Hospitaller – fiddle players and murderers

St Lidwina of Schiedam – ice skaters

St Martin of Tours – geese and reformed alcoholics

St Maturinus – plumbers

St Nicholas of Myra – broadcasters and the wrongly accused

St Roch – second-hand dealers

St Servatius – rheumatism

St Teresa of Ávila – chess

St Tryphon of Campsada – infestations of bedbugs

St Vitus – oversleeping

EVEN THE CAKE
WAS IN TIERS

EMOTIONAL WEDDING DAYS

On his wedding night in 1193, Philip II Augustus, King of France, discovered that his Danish bride Ingeborg had bad breath. He tried to send her back to Denmark the next day but she fled to a convent instead and spent the next 20 years as a virtual prisoner in various French castles.

Drowning his sorrows on his wedding day to Caroline of Brunswick in 1795, George IV got hopelessly drunk. He had to be carried to the altar, sobbed through the ceremony and spent his wedding night asleep in the fireplace.

Critic John Ruskin was apparently so repulsed by the sight of his wife Effie Gray's pubic hair on their wedding night in 1848 that their six-year marriage was never consummated.

Leopold II, King of the Belgians, was too ill to attend his own wedding to Austrian Archduchess Marie Henriette in 1853. So he sent his brother-in-law, Archduke Charles, to stand in for him.

Tracy and John O'Donnell of Westport, Connecticut, brawled on their wedding day in 1994 following a row over the traditional insertion of a piece of wedding cake into the bride's mouth. She accused her new husband of performing the ritual too forcefully.

A French bride was arrested at her wedding reception in 1995 for stabbing her new husband with the knife they had just used to cut the wedding cake.

Minutes before he was due to conduct a wedding at Normanton Parish Church, West Yorkshire, in 1996, Father Rodney Chapman tripped over a Bible, crashed into the aisle and broke his foot. Despite blood pouring down his face, he managed to marry Scott Niesyty and Paula Dunn before going to hospital.

When Romanian bride Manuela Voicu went into labour at her 2002 wedding, the best man, Ion Vidican, put on her dress and stood in for her.

Freddie Prinze Jr and Sarah Michelle Gellar had planned an outdoor ceremony in Mexico in 2002 but on their wedding day, a hurricane forced them indoors. Then the next day, when guests were making their way home, a 4.6 magnitude earthquake rocked the area.

Sixteen-year-old Carly O'Brien, from Gloucester, England, wanted a really big dress for her 2006 wedding to Michael Coffey but the gown designed by a family friend weighed 25 stone, was eight foot wide and had a 60-foot-long train, making it so enormous that the bride became wedged in the church door and had to be pushed up the aisle by 20 guests.

A groom was so drunk when he arrived for his 2007 wedding at an Indian village that the teenage bride married his brother instead.

A bride was arrested at her wedding reception in Port Chester, New York, in 2008 after getting involved in an argument with the band. She was accused of trashing a set of conga drums.

Dan and Jackie Anderson's entire wedding party fell into a lake in Crosslake, Minnesota, in 2014 when the jetty on which they were posing for photos suddenly collapsed beneath them.

Kelsey and Andy Schneck's 2018 wedding in Ohio was thrown into doubt the night before the ceremony when their officiant broke her ankle during the rehearsal dinner – only for the catering manager, Manny Morales, to step in and take her place.

FAMOUS PEOPLE WHO MARRIED THEIR FIRST COUSIN

Charles Darwin

Albert Einstein

Sir Vivian Fuchs

Carlo Gambino

André Gide

Saddam Hussein

Jesse James

Samuel Morse

Edgar Allan Poe

Sergei Rachmaninoff

Igor Stravinsky

Queen Victoria

Josiah Wedgwood

H.G. Wells

UNIQUE UNIONS

In 1979, a Swedish woman, Eija-Riita Eklöf, married the Berlin Wall and changed her surname to Berliner-Mauer, which means 'Berlin Wall' in German. When the wall was demolished in 1989, she complained: 'They mutilated my husband.'

To appease the spirit of his dead wife, a Taiwanese man, Chang Hsi-hsum, married an 11-inch, plastic Barbie doll at an elaborate ceremony at a Buddhist temple in 1999.

At a 2006 ceremony in Eilat, Israel, British woman Sharon Tendler married Cindy, a 35-year-old bottlenose dolphin. The union was sealed with a kiss and a piece of herring.

A Chinese man, Liu Ye, married a life-sized foam cut-out of himself in 2007 and admitted that he was 'maybe a bit narcissistic'.

Erika LaBrie, an ex-US Army soldier from San Francisco, married the Eiffel Tower in 2007 and changed her name to Erika La Tour Eiffel. She vowed eternal love to the 1,000-foot iron structure, despite claiming that she was also romantically attached to the Golden Gate Bridge.

Australian artist Jodi Rose married the fourteenth-century Pont du Diable bridge in southern France in 2013. After the ceremony, she said her stone husband was special because 'he understands that I love other bridges.'

Linda Ducharme married a Florida theme park Ferris wheel named Bruce in 2013. At the ceremony, the priest declared: 'I tie you flesh to steel.'

British divorcee Amanda Rodgers married her dog Sheba in a special ceremony attended by 200 people in Split, Croatia, in 2014. Sheba wore a traditional white bridal gown.

Claiming to have been in love with the building for 36 years, a San Diego woman married Santa Fe train station in 2015 and changed her name accordingly to Carol Santa Fe.

Amanda Teague from Northern Ireland married the ghost of a 300-year-old Haitian pirate in 2016, but two years later she announced that they had split up.

In 2018, at a Tokyo ceremony attended by 40 guests, Akihiko Kondo married an anime pop star hologram named Hatsune Miku because he doesn't trust real women.

MARRIAGE LINES

The term 'best man' dates back to the sixteenth century when the Germanic Goths kidnapped their future brides. Since it was invariably a two-man job, the friend of the groom who ably assisted the abduction was declared to be the best man.

Nineteenth-century British Prime Minister Viscount Palmerston was cited as co-respondent in a divorce case at the ripe old age of 78.

Louis XVI and Marie Antoinette did not consummate their marriage until seven years after the wedding.

In Anglo-Saxon times, the groom symbolically struck the bride on the head with a shoe to establish his authority in the relationship.

When Russian ruler Peter the Great learned that his wife Catherine had been unfaithful, he had the head of her lover, his own chamberlain William Mons, chopped off and inserted in a jar of alcohol, which was then placed on Catherine's bedside table to remind her of her infidelity.

Brides among the Tujia people of China are encouraged to cry for an hour a day for a whole month before the wedding.

Britain's Beverley Redman finally agreed to marry partner Keith in 2000 – after 8,500 proposals and 24 years of candlelit meals.

Each time actress Joan Crawford remarried, she also changed all the toilet seats in her house.

After the wedding ceremony, newly married couples from the Tidong people of northern Borneo are required to be confined to their house while neither emptying their bowels nor urinating for three days and nights.

SHORT-LIVED CELEBRITY MARRIAGES

Six hours: Actress Jean Acker locked Rudolph Valentino out of their hotel bedroom on their wedding night in 1919 and the marriage was never consummated. Valentino quickly filed for divorce.

One day: Zsa Zsa Gabor and Felipe de Alba, 1983

55 hours: Britney Spears and Jason Alexander, 2004

Eight days: Dennis Hopper and Michelle Phillips, 1970

Nine days: Dennis Rodman and Carmen Electra, 1998

14 days: Mario Lopez and Ali Landry, 2004

32 days: Ethel Merman and Ernest Borgnine, 1964

39 days: Drew Barrymore and Jeremy Thomas, 1994

72 days: Kim Kardashian and Kris Humphries, 2011

107 days: Nicolas Cage and Lisa Marie Presley, 2002

122 days: Pamela Anderson and Kid Rock, 2006

PEOPLE WHO HAVE BEEN MARRIED FIVE TIMES OR MORE

(AT TIME OF WRITING)

Nine times: Zsa Zsa Gabor, Jennifer O'Neill

Eight times: Larry King, Mickey Rooney, Artie Shaw, Elizabeth Taylor, Lana Turner

Seven times: Gregg Allmann, Jerry Lee Lewis, Richard Pryor, Martha Raye

Six times: Josephine Baker, Tony Curtis, Mel Harris, Rex Harrison, Henry VIII, Boris Karloff, Hedy Lamarr, Norman Mailer, Rue McClanahan, Claude Rains, Gloria Swanson, Billy Bob Thornton, Johnny Weissmuller, Jacob Zuma

Five times: Idi Amin, Eva Bartok, Sean Bean, Ingmar Bergman, Fred Berry, Ernest Borgnine, Richard Burton, James Cameron, David Carradine, Joan Collins, Mel Ferrer, Eddie Fisher, Ric Flair, Henry Fonda, George Foreman, Clark Gable, Judy Garland, Cary Grant, Buddy Greco, Rita Hayworth, Dennis Hopper, John Huston, Stan Laurel, Victor Mature, Brigitte Nielsen, Gary Oldman, Ginger Rogers, Kenny Rogers, Martin Scorsese, George C. Scott, Danielle Steel, Jane Wyman, Tammy Wynette

FAMOUS ACTORS
WHO MARRIED
NON-CELEBRITIES

Rowan Atkinson married makeup artist Sunetra Sastry.

Alec Baldwin married yoga instructor Hilaria Thomas.

Drew Barrymore married art consultant Will Kopelman.

Jeff Bridges met Susan Geston while
she was working as a waitress.

George Clooney married lawyer Amal Alamuddin.

Benedict Cumberbatch married theatre
director Sophie Hunter.

Matt Damon met wife Luciana Barroso
while she was working as a bartender.

Suranne Jones married magazine editor Laurence Akers.

Lisa Kudrow married advertising executive Michel Stern.

Tobey Maguire married jewellery designer Jennifer Meyer.

Chris O'Donnell married his college sweetheart,
Caroline Fentress, who became a schoolteacher.

Eddie Redmayne married financial
publicist Hannah Bagshawe.

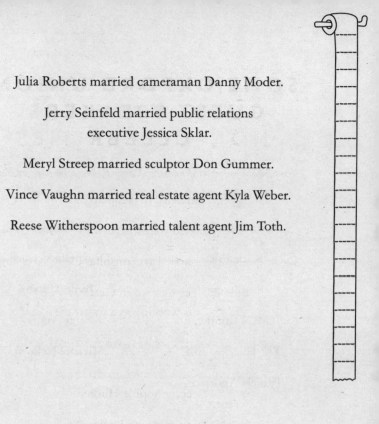

Julia Roberts married cameraman Danny Moder.

Jerry Seinfeld married public relations
executive Jessica Sklar.

Meryl Streep married sculptor Don Gummer.

Vince Vaughn married real estate agent Kyla Weber.

Reese Witherspoon married talent agent Jim Toth.

SOME OXFORD UNION GUEST SPEAKERS

These perhaps unexpected names are among those who have addressed the prestigious debating society at Oxford University

Kermit the Frog

Katie Price

Ron Jeremy

MC Hammer

The Cheeky Girls

Pamela Anderson

OJ Simpson

Donatella Versace

Jodie Marsh

Peter Andre

Michael Jackson

WHAT'S IN A NAME?

SOME FAMOUS PEOPLE
AND THEIR REAL NAMES

Alan Alda – Alphonso Joseph d'Abruzzo

Woody Allen – Allen Stewart Konigsberg

Adam Ant – Stuart Goddard

Elizabeth Arden – Florence Nightingale Graham

Bea Arthur – Bernice Frankel

Fred Astaire – Frederick Austerlitz

Iggy Azalea – Amethyst Amelia Kelly

Marc Bolan – Mark Feld

Bono – Paul Hewson

Elkie Brooks – Elaine Bookbinder

Michael Caine – Maurice Micklewhite

Jasper Carrott – Bob Davis

Butch Cassidy – Robert Leroy Parker

Coco Chanel – Gabrielle Bonheur Chanel

Alice Cooper – Vince Furnier

Elvis Costello – Declan McManus

Joan Crawford – Lucille LeSueur

Michael Crawford – Michael Dumble-Smith (he took his stage name from a passing Crawford's biscuit lorry)

Doris Day – Doris Mary Kapelhoff

Lana Del Rey – Elizabeth Woolridge Grant

Vin Diesel – Mark Sinclair

Kirk Douglas – Issur Danielovitch Demsky

Bob Dylan – Robert Zimmerman

The Edge – David Howell Evans

Carmen Electra – Tara Leigh Patrick

David Essex – David Cook

Example – Elliot Gleave (his stage name comes from his initials: e.g.)

Adam Faith – Terry Nelhams

50 Cent – Curtis James Jackson III

Flea – Michael Peter Balzary

Wayne Fontana – Glyn Ellis

Jamie Foxx – Eric Bishop

Billy Fury – Ronald Wycherley

Lady Gaga – Stefani Joanne Angelina Germanotta

Judy Garland – Frances Gumm

Whoopi Goldberg – Caryn Elaine Johnson

Cary Grant – Archibald Leach

Cee Lo Green – Thomas DeCarlo Callaway

Professor Green – Stephen Paul Manderson

Mata Hari – Margaretha Geertruida MacLeod

Calvin Harris – Adam Richard Wiles

Harry Houdini – Ehrich Weiss

Rock Hudson – Roy Scherer

Billy Idol – William Broad

Jay Z – Shawn Carter

Jessie J – Jessica Ellen Cornish

Elton John – Reginald Dwight

Alicia Keys – Alicia Augello Cook

Ben Kingsley – Krishna Pandit Bhanji

Billy J. Kramer – William Ashton

Estée Lauder – Josephine Esther Mentzer

Stan Laurel – Arthur Stanley Jefferson

Le Corbusier – Charles-Édouard Jeanneret

Lulu – Marie McDonald McLaughlin Lawrie

Elle MacPherson – Eleanor Gow

Marilyn Manson – Brian Hugh Warner

Bruno Mars – Peter Gene Hernandez

Meat Loaf – Marvin Lee Aday

Freddie Mercury – Farrokh Bulsara

George Michael – Georgios Kyriacos Panayiotou

Nicki Minaj – Onika Maraj

Helen Mirren – Helen Lydia Mironoff

Marilyn Monroe – Norma Jeane Mortenson

Demi Moore – Demetria Gene Guynes

Baby Face Nelson – Lester Joseph Gillis

Nena – Gabriele Kerner

Billy Ocean – Leslie Charles

Colonel Tom Parker – Andreas Cornelis van Kuijk

Katy Perry – Katheryn Hudson

Pink – Alecia Beth Moore

Plan B – Benjamin Paul Ballance-Drew

Iggy Pop – James Newell Osterberg

Pol Pot – Saloth Sar

P.J. Proby – James Marcus Smith

Paco Rabanne – Francisco Rabaneda Cuervo

Rag 'n' Bone Man – Rory Graham

The Red Baron – Manfred von Richthofen

Cliff Richard – Harry Rodger Webb

Rihanna – Robyn Fenty

Sugar Ray Robinson – Walker Smith Jr

Meg Ryan – Margaret Hyra

Rat Scabies – Christopher John Millar

Captain Sensible – Ray Burns

Del Shannon – Charles Westover

Omar Sharif – Michel Dimitri Chalhoub

Martin Sheen – Ramón Gerard Antonio Estévez

Gene Simmons – Chaim Witz

Slash – Saul Hudson

Anna Nicole Smith – Vickie Lynn Hogan

Snoop Dogg – Calvin Cordozar Broadus Jr

Dusty Springfield – Mary O'Brien

Sting – Gordon Sumner

Stormzy – Michael Omari

Tinie Tempah – Patrick Chukwuemeka Okogwu

Mother Teresa – Anjezë Gonxhe Bojaxhiu

Tintoretto – Jacopo Comin

Titian – Tiziano Vecelli

Tina Turner – Anna Mae Bullock

Shania Twain – Eilleen Regina Edwards

Twiggy – Lesley Hornby

Conway Twitty – Harold Jenkins

Bonnie Tyler – Gaynor Hopkins

Sid Vicious – Simon John Ritchie

John Wayne – Marion Morrison

Marty Wilde – Reg Smith

Shelley Winters – Shirley Schrift

Stevie Wonder – Stevland Hardaway Judkins

Bill Wyman – William Perks

FAMOUS PEOPLE KNOWN BY THEIR MIDDLE NAME

Henry Warren Beatty

Troyal Garth Brooks

James Gordon Brown

Arthur Neville Chamberlain

Stephen Grover Cleveland

Edward Montgomery Clift

Thomas Sean Connery

John Calvin Coolidge

Achille-Claude Debussy

Dorothy Faye Dunaway

Hannah Dakota Fanning

John William Ferrell

Elizabeth Stamatina Fey

William Clark Gable

Samuel Dashiell Hammett

Joseph Rudyard Kipling

Christopher Ashton Kutcher

James Hugh Calum Laurie

David Jude Heyworth Law

Patricia Rooney Mara

James Paul McCartney

Terence Steven McQueen

Keith Rupert Murdoch

James David Niven

Charles Patrick Ryan O'Neal

Olive Marie Osmond

Eldred Gregory Peck

William Bradley Pitt

Helen Beatrix Potter

Charles Robert Redford

Robert Oliver Reed

Ernestine Jane Russell

Marvin Neil Simon

Michael Sylvester Gardenzio Stallone

Marie Dionne Warwick

George Orson Welles

Walter Bruce Willis

James Harold Wilson

Mary Debra Winger

Laura Jeanne Reese Witherspoon

PEOPLE WITH MEMORABLE MIDDLE NAMES

Adele Laurie Blue Adkins

Ben Géza Affleck

Dido Florian Cloud de Bounevialle O'Malley Armstrong

Kevin Norwood Bacon

Orlando Jonathan Blanchard Bloom

Kobe Bean Bryant

John Marwood Cleese

James Kimberley Corden

Courteney Bass Cox

Daniel Wroughton Craig

Matt Paige Damon

Hilary Erhard Duff

Ralph Nathaniel Twisleton-Wykeham Fiennes

Richard Tiffany Gere

Mel Colmcille Gerard Gibson

Hugh John Mungo Grant

Robson Golightly Green

Nicholas Caradoc Hoult

Kate Garry Hudson

Quincy Delight Jones

Nick Simon Augustine Knowles

Jennifer Shrader Lawrence

Damian Watcyn Lewis

Andy Barron Murray

Jeremy Dickson Paxman

Alex Aristides Reid

Arnold Alois Schwarzenegger

Emma Charlotte Duerre Watson

Robert Primrose Wilson
(former Arsenal goalkeeper Bob Wilson)

INITIALLY INTERESTING

W.H. Auden – Wystan Hugh Auden

J.M. Barrie – James Matthew Barrie

G.K. Chesterton – Gilbert Keith Chesterton

E.E. Cummings – Edward Estlin Cummings

T.S. Eliot – Thomas Stearns Eliot

A.P. Herbert – Alan Patrick Herbert

k.d. lang – Kathryn Dawn Lang

D.H. Lawrence – David Herbert Lawrence

V.V.S. Laxman – Vangipurapu Venkata Sai Laxman

C.S. Lewis – Clive Staples Lewis

H.P. Lovecraft – Howard Phillips Lovecraft

George R.R. Martin – George Raymond Richard Martin

A.A. Milne – Alan Alexander Milne

P.J. O'Rourke – Patrick Jake O'Rourke

J.D. Salinger – Jerome David Salinger

A.J.P. Taylor – Alan John Percivale Taylor

J.R.R. Tolkien – John Ronald Reuel Tolkien

P.L. Travers – Pamela Lyndon Travers

J.M.W. Turner – Joseph Mallord William Turner

H.G. Wells – Herbert George Wells

J.P.R. Williams – John Peter Rhys Williams

P.G. Wodehouse – Pelham Grenville Wodehouse

UNLUCKY FOR SOME

SUPERSTITIOUS PEOPLE

Tiger Woods always wears a red shirt for the final round of every golf tournament he plays.

Jennifer Aniston always walks into an aeroplane with her right foot first and taps the outside of the aircraft for extra good luck.

French footballer Laurent Blanc used to kiss the bald pate of goalkeeper Fabien Barthez before each international match.

Axl Rose tries to avoid playing in cities that start with the letter 'M' because he hates the letter and thinks it will bring bad luck.

Charles Dickens always slept facing north because he believed it improved his creativity.

Michael Jordan wore the same old blue North Carolina shorts from his college days underneath his Chicago Bulls uniform for every single NBA game he played.

Irish nationalist leader Charles Parnell never signed a legislative bill that contained 13 clauses. He would refuse to put his name to it until a fourteenth was added.

Keith Richards loves eating shepherd's pie before concerts – and he has to be the one that breaks the crust.

Salvador Dali carried around a small piece of Spanish driftwood to ward off evil spirits.

Edward VII refused to have his bed linen changed on a Friday.

Dutch footballer Johan Cruyff used to spit his chewing gum into the opponent's half of the pitch just before kick-off.

Dr Seuss would overcome writer's block by going to his secret closet and putting on one of his 300 hats for inspiration.

Megan Fox listens to Britney Spears music while she is flying because she believes that it is not her destiny to die while listening to Britney.

James McAvoy says 'white rabbit' to the first person he sees on the first of every month – a superstition he has inherited from his grandmother.

Swimmer Rebecca Adlington always has to set her alarm clock – and the volume on the TV – on an even number.

Heidi Klum carries around with her a bag containing her own baby teeth for good luck.

George V kept the many clocks at Sandringham 30 minutes fast so that he would never be late for an appointment.

Coldplay singer Chris Martin always has to brush his teeth immediately before he goes on stage because he is afraid that if he doesn't, he won't be able to hit a note.

Tchaikovsky, while conducting, used to hold his chin with his left hand and conduct with his right because he was afraid his head would roll off his shoulders.

Serena Williams habitually bounces the ball five times before her first serve and twice before her second.

Hans Christian Andersen always turned back twice after leaving a room to ensure that all candles were extinguished. When staying in hotels, he carried with him a coil of rope in case he had to escape from a window due to fire.

Steven Tyler wears the teeth of a raccoon he caught as a child around his neck.

Arnold Schoenberg was superstitious about the number 13. Fittingly, the composer died on Friday the thirteenth at 13 minutes to midnight in his seventy-sixth year (7+6=13).

FAMOUS PEOPLE FROM BASINGSTOKE, HAMPSHIRE

John Arlott, cricket commentator

Jane Austen, author

Tom Cleverley, footballer

Mark Griffin, Trojan in the TV series *Gladiators*

Elizabeth Hurley, actress

Hilary Jones, TV doctor

Steve Lamacq, DJ

Tara Palmer-Tomkinson, socialite

Tanita Tikaram, singer/songwriter

Thomas Warton, eighteenthth-century poet laureate

CELEBRITIES WHO MAY HAVE SEEN A UFO

Muhammad Ali: 'A cigar-shaped ship hovered briefly over a car I was a passenger in one night driving north on the New Jersey Turnpike.'

Dan Aykroyd said that one night in the 1980s he felt a calling from aliens and at the same time people in his upstate New York neighbourhood reported seeing a large pink spiral suspended on the skyline.

Russell Crowe filmed a video of what he claimed could be a UFO from his Sydney apartment in 2013. He was filming fruit bats but instead saw two bright orange objects moving in tandem across the night sky.

Billy Ray Cyrus saw something in 2011 that 'looked like five or six disc-like shapes hovering'.

Danny Dyer said in 2011: 'I've seen UFOs. It wasn't an aeroplane, it certainly wasn't a balloon, it wasn't a Chinese lantern.'

Mick Jagger said he saw a mysterious, luminous craft lighting up the sky at the 1968 Glastonbury Festival.

John Lennon was in New York in 1975 when he spotted something in the sky that 'had light bulbs just going off, on, off, on. It went down the river, turned right at the United Nations.'

Shaun Ryder: 'I was a fifteen-year-old lad in Salford when I saw a ball of light whizzing about in the night sky as I stood at a bus stop.'

MAD MONARCHS AND ECCENTRIC EMPERORS

Babylonian ruler Nebuchadnezzar II (605–562 BC) believed he was a goat and accordingly ate vast amounts of grass.

Roman Emperor Caligula (AD 37–41) wanted to make his beloved horse, Incitatus, a consul.

Pedro I, King of Portugal (1357–67), issued instructions that his second wife Inez should be crowned with full pomp and ceremony – even though she had been dead for five years. He ordered her corpse to be placed on a throne next to him while noblemen lined up to kiss her withered hand.

Charles VI of France (1380–1422) was convinced that he was made of glass and refused to travel by coach in case the vibration caused him to shatter into a thousand pieces. He also demanded that iron rods by inserted into his clothes to stop him from breaking.

Queen Juana I of Castile (1504–55) was so devastated by the death of her husband Philip that she refused to allow him to be buried and had his coffin accompany her wherever she went. Occasionally she would lift the coffin lid and hold a conversation with his decaying remains.

Ibrahim I, Sultan of Turkey (1640–48), was so impressed by the spectacle of a cow's udder that he instructed his agents to scour the land for a woman of similarly bovine proportions.

He also liked to behave like a stallion at stud, neighing as he galloped among his large harem. The women in turn were expected to behave like mares, kicking and bucking at his every fumble.

Philip V of Spain (1700–46) commanded the Italian singer Farinelli to sing the same four arias in his presence every night for the last ten years of his life.

Frederick William I, King of Prussia (1713–40), was determined to recruit the tallest men in Europe for his army, even to the extent of having them kidnapped. A tall monk was snatched in Rome while he knelt in prayer and a lanky Dutch preacher was hauled off in mid-sermon, along with four of his congregation.

George II of Great Britain (1727–60) performed a curious nightly ritual. He used to stand outside his mistress's bedroom at precisely one minute to nine and on the stroke of nine o'clock he would enter the room, pull down his breeches and have sex, often without removing his hat.

During one of his many strange turns, George III of Great Britain (1760–1820) took to ending every sentence with the word 'peacock'. He also issued orders to people who were long since dead and imagined that his pillow was his dead son Octavius. It is said that he once shook hands with an oak tree in Windsor Great Park and talked to it for some minutes in the belief that it was the King of Prussia.

Ferdinand II of Sicily (1830–59) was so vain that he refused to allow his portrait on his country's postage stamps to be spoilt by an unsightly franking mark.

Throughout her life, Princess Alexandra of Bavaria, was convinced that as a child she had swallowed a full-sized grand piano – and nothing could shake her from that belief. She may have talked a lot of nonsense but she made a lovely tune.

Alexandra's nephew, Ludwig II of Bavaria (1864–86), decided to reverse night and day. He woke at 7pm and dined in the early hours of the morning. He had a moon painted on his bedroom ceiling and started going on long drives in the middle of the night on his golden sleigh. He also insisted that his staff had to approach him on all fours – like dogs.

Ludwig's brother, Otto of Bavaria (1886–1913), concluded that the only way to preserve his own sanity was to shoot a peasant every morning. So he started taking pot shots at workers in the royal garden, prompting his servants to load his pistol with blanks. To keep the king happy, they then arranged for a guard disguised as a peasant to stand beneath Otto's bedroom window and, when 'shot', pretend to be dead. Otto also frequently barked like a dog.

Emperor Menelik II of Abyssinia (1889–1913) firmly believed that the cure for any disease was to chew a few pages of the bible. Recovering from a stroke in 1913, he is said to have devoured the entire Book of Kings and dropped dead.

SHORT REIGNS

Louis XIX was king of France for 20 minutes on 2 August 1830, quickly abdicating in favour of his nephew, Henri V, who in turn lasted only a week.

Crown Prince Luis Filipe of Portugal technically ruled as Dom Luis III for 20 minutes on 1 February 1908 – the time between his father's assassination and his own death, having been shot in the same attack.

Sultan Sayyid Khalid bin Barghash ruled Zanzibar for two days from 25–27 August 1896. Britain refused to recognise his claim to the throne, resulting in the 38-minute Anglo-Zanzibar War, after which Khalid fled.

Chinese King Xioawen of Qin ruled for two days from 13–15 September 250 BC before dying suddenly.

Dipendra Bir Bikram Shah Dev ruled Nepal for around 56 hours from 1–4 June 2001. He succeeded to the throne after murdering his father during a massacre in which he also inflicted fatal wounds upon himself. He thus spent the duration of his reign in a coma.

King Inayatullah Khan Seraj ruled Afghanistan for three days from 14–17 January 1929 before abdicating.

ROTTEN RULERS

Roman Emperor Nero (AD 54–68) used to delight in serving his guests human excrement and then forcing them to lick the plates clean.

Roman Emperor Elagabalus (AD 218–222) once ordered a servant to find him 1,000 pounds of cobwebs. When the poor man returned without success, he was thrown into a cage where he was eaten alive by hundreds of hungry rats.

Vlad the Impaler, Prince of Wallachia (1448, 1456–62 and 1476), had up to 500,000 men, women and children murdered in the course of his three reigns, mostly by brutal impalement. Afterwards, he would often roast the bodies and boil their heads in a kettle. Although he was the inspiration for Dracula, there is no evidence that he drank the blood of his victims or ate the flesh of murdered dissidents, perhaps because he didn't want to eat something that might disagree with him.

Henry VII of England (1485–1509) employed a groom whose job it was to wipe the royal bottom.

Ivan IV, Tsar of Russia (1547–84), was so pleased with the newly built St Basil's Church in Moscow that he had the architects blinded so that they would never be able to design anything better. Having fallen out with the Archbishop of Novgorod, Ivan arranged for the cleric to be sewn into a bearskin and hunted to his death by a pack of hounds.

Murad IV, Sultan of Turkey (1623–40), ordered that anyone drinking coffee or smoking should be executed. He killed for fun, setting himself a personal target of ten murders a day, and once had a party of female picnickers drowned because they were making too much noise.

Anna, Empress of Russia (1730–40), punished two errant noblemen by ordering them to live like hens for a week. They were dressed in feathered costumes, made to sit on a straw nest and instructed to cluck away for seven days for the amusement of the royal court.

Catherine the Great of Russia (1762–96) was so outraged to discover the presence of dandruff on her collar that she had her hairdresser imprisoned in an iron cage for three years to stop the news spreading.

Queen Ranavalona I of Madagascar (1828–61) executed any of her subjects who appeared in her dreams.

US PRESIDENTS' AVERAGE APPROVAL RATINGS

(AS OF JANUARY 2019)

John F. Kennedy 70.1%

Dwight D. Eisenhower 65%

Franklin D. Roosevelt 63%

George Bush 60.9%

Bill Clinton 55.1%

Lyndon B. Johnson 55.1%

Ronald Reagan 52.8%

George W. Bush 49.4%

Richard Nixon 49.1%

Barack Obama 47.9%

Gerald Ford 47.2%

Jimmy Carter 45.5%

Harry S. Truman 45.4%

Donald Trump 39.0%

PRESIDENTIAL FACTS

Almost every member of Theodore Roosevelt's family owned a pair of wooden stilts, including the President and the First Lady.

Before becoming US President, Grover Cleveland was a hangman. As sheriff of Erie County, New York, he twice had to spring the trap at a hanging.

The 'S' in Harry S. Truman doesn't stand for anything.

John Tyler had 15 children from his two marriages. His last child, Pearl, was born when he was 70.

Thomas Jefferson soaked his feet in a bucket of cold water every day in the belief that it would prevent him catching a cold.

James Monroe once chased his Secretary of State, William H. Crawford, from the White House with a pair of fire tongs.

Richard Nixon met his future wife Pat when both auditioned for an amateur dramatics production of *The Dark Tower* in Whittier, California.

Ulysses S. Grant smoked at least 20 cigars a day, and once the public discovered how much he liked them, he received more than 20,000 as gifts. He died of throat cancer.

John Quincy Adams used to go skinny dipping in Tiber Creek, a tributary of the Potomac River.

Martin Van Buren's near-800-page autobiography did not contain a single mention of Hannah, who had been his wife for 12 years.

James Garfield could simultaneously write Latin with one hand and Greek with the other.

Gerald Ford worked as a male model in his twenties and was featured on the cover of *Cosmopolitan* in April 1942 wearing his Navy uniform.

Warren G. Harding was a keen poker player who once gambled away on a single hand an entire set of priceless White House china.

William Henry Harrison's inauguration speech went on for one hour and 40 minutes. Unfortunately, he delivered it on a cold, wet day in March 1841 and a month later he was dead from pneumonia, making his the shortest presidency to date.

Donald Trump was a registered Democrat from 2001 to 2009.

Five Presidents were elected despite losing the popular vote – John Quincy Adams (1824), Rutherford B. Hayes (1876), Benjamin Harrison (1888), George W. Bush (2000) and Donald Trump (2016).

STARS BEHIND BARS

CELEBRITIES WHO WENT TO PRISON

Tim Allen, the voice of Buzz Lightyear in the *Toy Story* films, served two years in jail from 1979 for drug trafficking.

Chuck Berry spent 20 months in jail from 1962 after being convicted of transporting a 14-year-old girl across state lines for immoral purposes.

James Brown was jailed at the age of 16 for stealing clothes from parked cars and again in 1988 after carrying a shotgun into an office building he owned and demanding to know who had used his private toilet.

Glen Campbell was sentenced to ten days in jail in 2003 on charges of extreme drunken driving and kicking a police officer.

David Crosby spent nine months in prison after being convicted of drugs and weapons offences in 1982.

Robert Downey Jr spent six months in jail in 1997 after missing a court-ordered drug test while already on probation. His offences had included drug possession and trespassing in a neighbour's home and then falling asleep on his bed while under the influence.

Errol Flynn served a number of jail sentences in the 1920s and 1930s, chiefly for assault.

Stephen Fry spent three months in prison on remand after being arrested at a Swindon hotel at the age of 18 for credit card fraud.

Zsa Zsa Gabor spent three days in jail in 1990 following an incident when she slapped a police officer who had pulled her over in her Rolls-Royce. An unrepentant Gabor said later: 'He deserved the slap.'

Merle Haggard was jailed in 1957 for attempting to rob a tavern in Bakersfield, California.

Paris Hilton was sentenced to 45 days in prison in 2007 for violating her probation after being arrested for driving offences, but ended up spending just three days inside.

Sophia Loren spent 17 days in jail in 1982 over alleged income tax irregularities. In 2013, she was finally cleared of any wrongdoing.

Paul McCartney was locked up for nine days in 1980 after being caught with almost half a pound of marijuana in his luggage at Tokyo airport.

Steve McQueen, then 15, spent two years at a California reform school in the mid 1940s after committing a number of petty crimes, including the theft of car hubcaps.

George Michael was sentenced to eight weeks in jail in 2010 after he crashed his Range Rover into a Hampstead photography shop while he was under the influence of drugs.

Robert Mitchum served 59 days in a California prison in 1948 for possession of marijuana.

Ivor Novello served a month in Wormwood Scrubs in 1944 for illegal use of petrol coupons in his Rolls-Royce car. Petrol was strictly rationed during the Second World War.

Ozzy Osbourne spent six weeks in jail because he was unable to pay a fine after being arrested for stealing clothes from a shop when he was 17. To teach him a lesson, his father had refused to pay the fine.

Jane Russell was jailed for four days for drunk driving in 1978.

Frank Sinatra, then 23, spent 16 hours in a New Jersey jail in 1938 after it was claimed that on two occasions 'under the promise of marriage' he'd had sex with a woman complainant 'who was then and there a single female of good repute'. He was initially charged with seduction, which was illegal at the time, but the complaint was dropped when it emerged that the lady in question was married. He was instead charged with adultery, but that, too, was dismissed.

Wesley Snipes was sentenced to three years in jail from 2010 for tax evasion.

Mae West was sentenced to ten days in prison in 1926 after her Broadway stage play *Sex* was deemed guilty of 'obscenity and corrupting the morals of youth'. Her sentence was subsequently reduced by one day for good behaviour.

Barry White spent four months in jail as a 17-year-old after being arrested for stealing $30,000 worth of Cadillac tyres.

PEOPLE WHO
SURVIVED THEIR
OWN EXECUTION

Having been impregnated by her master's grandson, Oxfordshire domestic servant Anne Greene was found guilty of infanticide in 1650 because the child was stillborn and she had tried to conceal it. After the hanging, Greene was found to have a pulse and doctors brought her back to life by giving her a tobacco smoke enema. She was granted a full pardon and even kept her coffin as a souvenir.

In 1705, one John Smith was sentenced to hang at Tyburn in London after being convicted of housebreaking, which was then a capital offence. As he dangled from the noose by the traditional method of slow strangulation, some of his friends tugged at his legs to shorten his suffering while others held his feet up in the hope that he wouldn't die. It worked, and after 15 minutes he was still very much alive, which was enough to earn him a reprieve.

Maggie Dickson was hanged in Edinburgh in 1721 for killing her own child but on the way to the cemetery she suddenly woke up and started banging on the inside of the coffin. The strange occurrence was viewed as God's will and she was freed to become known forever as Half-Hangit Maggie. A pub on the site still bears her name 300 years later.

Convicted of murder, 17-year-old William Duell was duly hanged in London in 1740. His body was cut down from the scaffold after the required 20 minutes (the drop method, which breaks the neck, was not introduced until the late nineteenth century) and then taken for dissection to a medical institute, where, to the alarm of all present, he was seen to be breathing quite healthily just as the surgeon's knife was about to slice into his stomach. The authorities decided to reprieve him and have him transported for life instead.

In 1803, Joseph Samuel was convicted of murdering a policeman in Australia and was taken for execution, only to survive because the rope broke three times, leaving him with nothing worse than a sprained ankle.

John Lee, a 19-year-old footman, was sentenced to hang at Exeter Prison in 1885 after being found guilty of murdering his employer, Emma Keyse. But three times the trapdoor failed to open, so the sentence was reduced to life imprisonment. Unsurprisingly Lee became known as 'the man they could not hang'.

Wenseslao Moguel was sentenced to death by firing squad in 1915 for his role in the Mexican Revolution. He was charged without trial and lined up to face nine bullets aimed at his body plus a final coup de grace to the head from close range. Amazingly, he survived and was found unconscious among the dead bodies of his comrades the next day. He was given medical attention and recovered.

Sixteen-year-old Willie Francis was sent to the electric chair in 1946 for murdering a Louisiana pharmacy owner but survived the supposedly lethal surge of electricity through his body because the chair, known as 'Gruesome Gertie', had been set up incorrectly by a drunken prison guard. Francis's reprieve was short-lived, however, and, despite a campaign to spare him a second ordeal, he was electrocuted successfully the following year.

In 2009, convicted murderer Romell Broom became the first person to survive an execution by lethal injection. Prison officers struggled for two hours to find a suitable vein for an IV line even though Broom actively tried to help them. Finally he was sent back to his cell and granted a week's reprieve by the Ohio governor, during which time his lawyers argued that he had already suffered enough. Nevertheless, he is currently due to go for a second execution in 2020.

FASHION
VICTIMS

Philip, Prince of Calabria (1747–77), was obsessed with gloves and would wear as many as 16 pairs at a time.

Jimmy Choo made his first pair of shoes when he was 11 years old – a pair of leather slippers for his mother's birthday.

In the eighteenth century, it was considered the height of fashion to wear false eyebrows made from mouse skin.

Ancient Egyptians used to wear scented wax cones on their heads. In the course of the day, the wax would melt and coat the wearer in perfume.

Before Crown Prince Sado of Korea (1735–62) travelled anywhere, his servants had to prepare as many as 30 silk outfits from which he would make his final choice.

The elastic bra strap clasp was based on an 1871 invention by Mark Twain.

The fashion for square-toed men's shoes in the late fifteenth century was inspired by Charles VIII of France to hide the fact that he had six toes on one foot.

The first hair perm in 1906 required the client to sit with six brass curlers in her hair. Each curler weighed almost two pounds, making it the equivalent of wearing 48 large potatoes on her head.

English dandy Beau Brummell (1778–1840) said that it took him five hours a day to get dressed and recommended that boots be polished with champagne. He would never raise his hat to a lady for fear that he would be unable to replace it at precisely the same optimum angle.

The first pair of Doc Martens shoes were made from old tyres after Munich doctor Klaus Maertens injured his foot while skiing in the Bavarian Alps in 1945.

The French philosopher Voltaire owned 80 canes.

Louis XIV of France (1643–1715) decreed that only members of the royal court were permitted to wear shoes with red heels in order to distinguish them from commoners.

Victorian men used to wear locks of their lover's pubic hair in their hats as mementos.

False eyelashes were invented solely for Hollywood. Producer D.W. Griffith wanted to enhance actress Seena Owen's eyes for the 1916 film *Intolerance* and had a wigmaker weave human hair through a fine gauze.

In Tudor England, the teeth of the wealthy often went black from sugar, leading to a fashion among the lower classes to blacken their teeth to show that they, too, could afford to buy it.

Filipino politician Imelda Marcos owned 500 black bras, one of which was bulletproof, and about 3,000 pairs of shoes.

Men wore high heels before women because when riding horses they needed a heel on their boot so that they could stand in the stirrups and shoot their bow and arrow effectively.

When Clark Gable removed his shirt during a scene in the 1934 film *It Happened One Night* and revealed that he was wearing nothing underneath, sales of vests reportedly dropped by more than 40 per cent.

After receiving a Brett Favre Green Bay Packers' football jersey for Christmas 2003, Connecticut schoolboy David Witthoft wore it every day for the next 1,581 days, finally shunning it on his twelfth birthday because by then it was too small for him.

In the eighteenth and nineteenth centuries, men's hats were often made using rabbit fur, which was then brushed with toxic mercury to form felt. Milliners inhaling the mercury could experience a trembling sensation known as the 'Danbury shakes' (after the hat-making town of Danbury, Connecticut), followed by an early death.

Marie Antoinette was so modest that she always wore a gown buttoned right up to her neck – even in the bath.

MR BLACKWELL'S WORST DRESSED LIST WINNERS

Until his death in 2008, acerbic Hollywood fashion critic Richard Sylvan Selzer (aka Mr Blackwell) issued an annual 'award' for whom he considered to be the worst dressed public figure that year.

1960: Anna Magnani

1961: Debbie Reynolds

1962: Zsa Zsa Gabor

1963: Zsa Zsa Gabor

1964: Barbra Streisand

1965: Princess Margaret

1966: Mia Farrow

1967: Barbra Streisand

1968: Julie Andrews

1969: Queen Elizabeth II

1970: Sophia Loren

1971: Ali MacGraw

1972: Raquel Welch

1973: Bette Midler

1974: Helen Reddy

1975: Caroline Kennedy

1976: Louise Lasser

1977: Farrah Fawcett

1978: Dolly Parton

1979: Bo Derek

1980: Brooke Shields

1981: Barbara Mandrell

1982: Princess Diana

1983: Joan Collins

1984: Cher

1985: Princess Stephanie of Monaco

1986: Meryl Streep

1987: Lisa Bonet

1988: Sarah Ferguson

1989: La Toya Jackson

1990: Sinead O'Connor

1991: Julia Roberts

1992: Madonna

1993: Glenn Close

1994: Camilla Parker-Bowles

1995: Howard Stern

1996: Dennis Rodman

1997: The Spice Girls

1998: Linda Tripp

1999: Cher

2000: Britney Spears

2001: Anne Robinson

2002: Anna Nicole Smith

2003: Paris Hilton

2004: Nicollette Sheridan

2005: Britney Spears

2006: Britney Spears and Paris Hilton

2007: Victoria Beckham

HIDDEN TALENTS

Rowan Atkinson – HGV driver

Justin Bieber – Rubik's Cube solver

Pierce Brosnan – fire eater

George W. Bush – painter

Victoria Coren Mitchell – poker player

Tom Cruise – fencer

Steve Davis – DJ

Colin Farrell – line dancer

Flea, Red Hot Chili Peppers – beekeeper

Harrison Ford – pilot

Jennifer Garner – clog dancer

Christina Hendricks – accordion player

Kendall Jenner – bird impressionist

Angelina Jolie – knife thrower

Eva Longoria – clarinet player

Steve Martin – banjo player

Ellen Page – juggler

Margot Robbie – tattoo artist

Mark Ruffalo – unicyclist

Susan Sarandon – ping pong player

Taylor Swift – jam maker

Jack White – furniture upholsterer

Bruce Willis – harmonica player

CRAZY COLLECTORS

Graham Barker, from Perth, Western Australia, has been collecting his own belly button fluff in glass jars since 1984.

Kevin Cook, from Colorado Springs, has a collection of around 50,000 dice.

Ronnie Crossland, from West Yorkshire, has collected over 1,000 photographs of cement mixers.

Brent Dixon, from Valdosta, Georgia, has collected over 41,000 non-duplicate key chains since 2001.

Edeltraud Dreier, from Berlin, Germany, has collected more than 1,300 kitchen timers.

Marianne Dumjahn, from Mainz, Germany, has collected around 400,000 international sugar packets since 1982.

Candace Frazee keeps 29,000 items of rabbit-related memorabilia at her home in Pasadena, California.

Bob Gibbins, from Herefordshire, has collected over 240 life-sized, anatomically correct, love dolls – rubber, silicone and inflatable.

Richard Gibson, of Lafayette, Louisiana, has been collecting his fingernail and toenail clippings since 1978.

Movie star Tom Hanks has a collection of hundreds of vintage typewriters.

Manfred Klauda, from Munich, Germany, has collected more than 9,400 chamber pots.

Dentist Val Kolpakov, from Marietta, Georgia, has collected 2,200 tubes and tins of toothpaste, including flavours such as chocolate, champagne and curry.

Demetra Koutsouridou, of Greece, has over 8,500 pencil sharpeners.

Antonia Kozakova, from Slovakia, has collected more than 63,000 napkins.

Charlotte Lee, from Seattle, Washington, has a collection of over 5,600 rubber ducks.

Paul Luke, from Essex, has collected over 11,000 different milk bottles.

Todd Mannebach, of Des Moines, Iowa, has collected 24 million pull tabs from aluminium cans.

Dave Mannix, from Cheshire, spent 20 years building up his collection of 100,000 National Lottery scratchcards.

Becky Martz, from Houston, Texas, has collected more than 14,600 banana labels.

Sam McCarthy-Fox, from Worthing, West Sussex, has built up a collection of over 50,000 glass marbles.

Martin Mihál, from the Czech Republic, has more than 120,000 empty chocolate wrappers from around the world.

David Morgan, from Burford, Oxfordshire, has a collection of more than 550 traffic cones.

John Reznikoff, from Westport, Connecticut, has collected the hair of over 120 dead celebrities, including John F. Kennedy, Ludwig van Beethoven and Elvis Presley.

Dr Manny Rothstein, a dermatologist from Fayetteville, North Carolina, has a collection of 675 back scratchers from over 70 different countries.

Gail Santos, from Tijuana, Mexico, has collected over 15,000 bars of soap in 200 fragrances.

Ladislav Sejnoha, of the Czech Republic, has built up a collection of over 200,000 used bus tickets – each one different.

Steven Smith, from Great Yarmouth, Norfolk, has collected over a million matchbox labels.

Maryly Snow, from Oakland, California, has a collection of over 2,000 toothbrushes.

New Yorker Harry Spiller has built up a collection of more than 5,000 Chinese restaurant menus, the oldest dating back to 1879.

Angelika Unverhau, from Dinslaken, Germany, has more than 220,000 ballpoint pens.

Niek Vermeulen, from Wormerveer in the Netherlands, has collected over 6,000 airline sick bags.

Rainer Weichert, from Moers, Germany, has built up a collection of 11,570 hotel 'Do Not Disturb' signs, dating back to 1910.

Scott Wiener's Brooklyn apartment is home to his collection of 750 empty pizza boxes.

PASSING
THE TIME

Gayadhar Parida spent more than 50 years living up a tree in India following a minor disagreement with his wife.

Jay Cochrane, from Toronto, Canada, spent 21 days on a high wire in 1981.

Toimi Soini forced himself to stay awake for 11 and a half days in Hamina, Finland, in 1964.

In 2004, Zdenek Zahradka, from the Czech Republic, survived ten days voluntarily buried underground in a coffin without food or water.

In 1986, Barry Kirk, from Port Talbot, South Wales, spent 100 hours sitting in a bathtub of baked beans.

Gareth Sanders ironed continuously for 100 hours in a Bristol supermarket in 2015, pressing about 2,000 items.

An Indian man, Mahendra Singh Rajat, tossed two coins alternately for 58 hours and five minutes in 1991.

In 2011, Dustin Barker, from Clinton, Iowa, kept the big toe of his right foot in his mouth for one minute 49 seconds while simultaneously hopping on his left foot.

WOULD YOU BELIEVE IT?

AMAZING COINCIDENCES

Mark Twain was born on 30 November 1835, 20 days after Halley's Comet passed close to Earth. He later remarked that, just as he had come into the world with the comet, he would also 'go out' with it. Halley's Comet next passed near Earth on 20 April 1910 and Twain died the following day.

A Frenchman, Jean Marie Dubarry, was executed on 13 February 1746 for the murder of his father. A hundred years later to the day, another Frenchman named Jean Marie Dubarry was also executed for killing his father.

Swindon Town Football Club's James Dunne was sent off after clashing with Accrington Stanley's James Dunne in an English League Division Two football match on 5 May 2018.

Separated at the age of four weeks, identical twin brothers Jim Lewis and Jim Springer grew up without knowing much about one another until they were reunited in 1979 at the age of 39. They discovered that both had childhood dogs that they named 'Toy'; both had been married twice – first to a Linda, then to a Betty; both drove light blue Chevrolets; both chain-smoked; both chewed their fingernails and suffered from migraines; both took holidays at the same Florida beach; Lewis had a son named James Alan while Springer had a son named James Allan, and both had held part-time posts as sheriffs in Ohio.

In 1990, a 15-year-old schoolboy named James Bond sat his GCSE examinations at Argoed High School in Flintshire, North Wales. The reference number on his exam paper was 007.

In July 1975, Erskine Lawrence Ebbin was knocked off his moped and killed by a taxi in Hamilton, Bermuda. It was the same taxi with the same driver, carrying the same passenger, that had killed Ebbin's brother Neville in July the previous year. Both brothers were 17 when they died, and had been riding the same moped in the same street.

Although they were not related, Joe Cocker sometimes used to babysit Jarvis Cocker in their home city of Sheffield. Before both found fame as musicians, Joe worked as a gas fitter and fitted the gas fire in Jarvis's mum's flat.

A total of 112 men died during the Hoover Dam project. The first, on 20 December 1922, was surveyor J.G. Tierney; the last on 20 December 1935, was his son Patrick.

French playwright Molière died in 1673 after collapsing on stage while playing a hypochondriac in his own play, *Le Malade Imaginaire*.

Four of the first six US Presidents – George Washington, Thomas Jefferson, James Madison and John Quincy Adams – were aged 57 at the time of their inauguration.

In 1938, playwright A.J. Talbot penned a one-act comedy, *Chez Boguskovsky*, in which a man named Boguskovsky steals a painting from the Louvre in Paris. The following year, on 15 August 1939, a painting was stolen from the Louvre, and the culprit turned out to be a man named Boguskovsky.

Browsing through a Parisian bookstore in the 1920s, American novelist Anne Parrish came across one of her childhood favourites, *Jack Frost and Other Stories*. She looked inside and read the inscription on the flyleaf: 'Anne Parrish, 209 N. Weber Street, Colorado Springs'. It was her own book!

On 6 March 2018, Millwall midfielder George Saville scored after just 51 seconds of the English Championship football match against Hull City – and four days later he repeated the feat, scoring in the fifty-first second of a game against Brentford.

Twins John and Arthur Mowforth, who had led almost identical RAF careers, died from heart attacks on the same day in 1975 – 90 miles apart. John died in Bristol and Arthur died in Windsor.

In 1974, former British Prime Minister Edward Heath, a keen sailor, learned that his yacht *Morning Cloud III* had been lost at sea. The previous week, he had posed for a photo with author John Dyson at the launch of his thriller *The Prime Minister's Boat Is Missing*.

While on a business trip in the late 1950s, George D. Bryson stayed at a hotel in Louisville, Kentucky. Given his key to room 307, he asked if there was any mail for him, and learned that there was indeed a letter for George D. Bryson in room 307. However, it turned out that it was not for him but for the room's previous occupant, another man named George D. Bryson.

In 1953, US TV reporter Irv Kupcinet was in London to cover the coronation of Elizabeth II. In a drawer of his room at the Savoy Hotel, Kupcinet found items that belonged to his friend, basketball player Harry Hannin. Two days later, before he could tell Hannin about his chance find, Kupcinet received a letter from Hannin who said that while staying at a hotel in Paris, he had found in a drawer a tie with Kupcinet's name on it.

On Christmas Eve 1994, 31-year-old twin sisters Lorraine and Levinia Christmas decided on the spur of the moment to drive to one another's houses to deliver presents ... only to crash into each other on an icy country road in Norfolk. They ended up spending Christmas Day in the same hospital as their father (Father Christmas), who was recovering from surgery.

Allman Brothers Band members Duane Allman and Berry Oakley died in separate motorcycle accidents almost exactly a year apart (on 29 October 1971 and 11 November 1972) and just three blocks away from each other in their hometown of Macon, Georgia. Both men were 24.

On 1 July 2014, two twins were fined for speeding on the same road, on the same morning, at the same speed. Dave and Paul Dooley, both retired military driving instructors, fell foul of the law for doing 35mph in a 30mph zone on Winwick Road, Warrington.

In 1664, when a ship sank in the Menai Strait off North Wales, 81 people died and the only survivor was Hugh Williams. In 1785, another ship sank at the same spot with 60 people on board, and the only survivor was a Hugh Williams. In 1820, a third vessel sank in the Menai Strait, and all 25 aboard were drowned except for a survivor named Hugh Williams.

For three successive seasons between 1956 and 1958, Leeds United were drawn at home to Cardiff City in the third round of the FA Cup. Each time, Cardiff won 2–1.

When Helen MacGregor was sent a 21-year-old postcard of Otley, Yorkshire, where she grew up, she was amazed to see her young self in the centre of the photo. A friend had sent it to her, unaware that the child in the street scene was Miss MacGregor, then aged three.

In 1838, Edgar Allan Poe wrote a novel titled *The Narrative of Arthur Gordon Pym of Nantucket* about four shipwreck survivors who, after days at sea, decide to kill and eat the cabin boy, Richard Parker. In 1884, the ship *Mignonette* foundered off Trinidad, leaving only four survivors drifting in the open sea. Eventually the senior crew members decided to kill and eat the cabin boy ... whose name was Richard Parker.

DUMB CRIMINALS

Two burglars stole TV sets from a house in Tallahassee, Florida, but were arrested when they decided to return to the crime scene shortly afterwards because they had forgotten to steal the remotes.

A robber who held up a Colorado Springs store ordered the clerk to fill a bag with cash and a bottle of whiskey. However the clerk refused to give him the alcohol because he didn't think he was 21. To prove that he was, the robber showed his driving licence, bearing his full name and address.

A thief who fled from a Tokyo museum in 1998 with a valuable 600-year-old Chinese platter accidentally dropped it while making his escape and saw his haul shatter into hundreds of pieces.

In 1992, robbers in Las Vegas held up a van thought to contain gambling chips, only to discover that it was carrying potato chips instead.

Fleeing from Hastings District Court in New Zealand in 2009, two prisoners who were handcuffed together made the mistake of running around opposite sides of a lamppost, as a result of which they promptly slammed into one another and crashed to the ground.

Two men who raided a Rhode Island gas station only remembered to put on ski masks after grabbing money from the cash register. One also forgot to take the cigarette out of his mouth first and burned his face.

Six would-be robbers walked into a shop in Charleroi, Belgium, in 2018 and told the owner to open the till, but he said it was almost empty and that if they wanted more money they should come back at closing time. So they did ... and found police officers waiting for them.

A Sunderland man used a manhole cover to smash a shop window but then stepped back, fell down the open hole and had to be rescued by fire crews.

James Newsome might have got away with robbing an Arkansas convenience store – had he not carried out the raid while wearing an orange hard hat with his name on it.

A man who tried to steal a cash machine in California was apprehended when his prosthetic leg fell off while he was making his getaway.

Six schoolboys from Queensland, Australia, went to great lengths to produce fake driving licences so that they could gain underage entry into pubs and clubs – but forgot to change out of their school uniforms for the photos.

A man who tried to rob a pharmacy in Beaver, West Virginia, in 2015 had to leave empty-handed after accidentally pepper-spraying himself.

Needing to change clothes quickly after robbing a bank in Hermiston, Oregon, a man climbed into the boot of his getaway car, but inadvertently locked himself in. To add insult to injury, it was a passing police officer who heard his cries for help.

A Dutch woman who stole a pair of jeans from a store in a theft captured by surveillance cameras rang the shop later that day to ask if it would exchange them for a larger size. When she returned, she seemed surprised to be arrested.

When a witness at Dennis Newton's 1985 trial for armed robbery in Oklahoma City identified him in court, Newton accused her of lying and screamed: 'I should have blown your f***ing head off!' He then added as an afterthought: 'If I'd been the one that was there.' He was jailed for 30 years.

After he and five others burgled a Tesco store in Greater Manchester, Roland Tough took photos of the raid to show his friends in jail how well he was doing. His mistake was to drop the roll of film off to be developed two weeks later at the very same Tesco, where employees recognised some of the stolen items.

A gunman who raided a Portland, Oregon, branch of Burger King fled empty-handed when he heard what he thought was the sound of security alarms but was actually the timers on the microwave ovens.

A man walked into a Louisiana store, put a $20 bill on the counter and asked for change. When the cashier opened the till, the man pulled a gun and snatched the contents – $15. He then ran out, leaving his $20 bill on the counter, and thus finished the raid $5 out of pocket.

An opportunist thief in Texas stole two plastic bags from a parked pickup truck and found that they contained 25 pounds of dog poop.

A man was arrested in Modesto, California, in 2002 after trying to hold up a bank without a weapon. He used a thumb and a finger to simulate a gun but forgot to keep his hand in his pocket during the raid.

A would-be thief in Drogheda, Ireland, used a brick to try and smash a car window, but was knocked unconscious when the brick rebounded off the glass and hit him in the face.

A burglar in New Mexico was arrested after he phoned the homeowners to ask how the stereo system he had recently stolen from them worked.

A pair of Michigan robbers entered a record store in an agitated state. Nervously waving his gun, the first robber shouted: 'Nobody move!' When his accomplice then moved, the first bandit shot him.

A bank robber in Jacksonville, Florida, foolishly wrote his demand note on the back of a police report that contained full details of his previous arrest.

Fleeing from the scene of a failed carjacking in Reno, Nevada, the suspect ran into a building, where he was arrested after becoming stuck in a freshly poured concrete floor.

Angry at being arrested for shoplifting in Braunschweig, Germany, in 2006, a 70-year-old man attempted to bite a police officer – before realising that he had left his false teeth at home.

A Jacksonville, Florida, woman who struggled with her spelling was arrested as she tried to cash a forged cheque for $498.35 from the Frist Unoin bank.

Two burglars who broke into a house in Clarksville, Tennessee, in 2016 then tried to pawn the stolen goods – unaware that it was the pawn shop owner's house that they had robbed.

Thieves broke into a shop in Medellin, Colombia, in 1999 and made off with shoes valued at nearly $17,000 – without spotting that all 756 shoes were for right feet. The shop owner had taken the precaution of locking the matching left shoes in a storeroom.

When police in Madison, Wisconsin, found cocaine in Leonard Hodge's underwear during a routine search, his defence was that the underpants he was wearing weren't his.

UNUSUAL DISGUISES ADOPTED BY CRIMINALS

A robber held up a bank in Manchester, New Hampshire, in 2007 disguised as a tree, with branches and leaves taped to his body.

A man tried to rob a post office in Kalmar, Sweden, in 1998 while brandishing a baseball bat and wearing a yellow chicken costume.

Kasey Kazee robbed a liquor store in Ashland, Kentucky, with his entire head wrapped in duct tape apart from openings for his eyes and mouth.

A man carried out an armed robbery in Sweden dressed in a giant blue rabbit costume.

A masked robber held up a Manchester fish and chip shop in 2017 while waving a weapon concealed in a bag. He claimed it was a gun but was forced to leave empty-handed when staff correctly deduced that its bendy shape indicated a banana.

A robber dressed in a full Batman costume held up an Iowa convenience store in 2018.

Before trying to break into an apartment in Carroll, Iowa, a pair of burglars decided to disguise themselves by drawing masks on their faces with a black marker pen. Sadly, they chose a permanent marker and were arrested a few blocks away with, as the local police chief put it, 'guilt written all over their faces'.

A burglar who broke into a drug store in Huaibei, China, in 2017 wrapped his entire head in toilet paper to avoid being recognised, not realising that a security camera had already caught his face before he put on his strange disguise.

In 2010, a man robbed a bank in Setauket, New York, dressed as Darth Vader.

Two men held up a convenience store in Arvada, Colorado, in 2008 wearing skimpy women's thongs as masks.

After robbing a Polish cosmetics store, a thief hid from police by rolling himself up in a carpet and propping it against a balcony while police searched his aunt's Warsaw apartment. He was eventually arrested when one officer went out onto the balcony for a cigarette and noticed that the carpet was trembling.

In 2017, a man robbed a Henderson, Kentucky, restaurant dressed as a Coca-Cola bottle.

A thief painted his entire face green in an attempt to avoid being identified while stealing a woman's purse at a train station in Krasnodar, Russia. A 23-year-old man was quickly arrested because he was the only person in the vicinity with a green face.

In 2018, a burglar raided a business in Melbourne, Australia, wearing a full lion costume, complete with tail and frizzy dark mane.

Worried that the orange prison uniform would be a giveaway, a man who had just escaped from a Waco, Texas, jail in 2003 broke into a university theatre department and stole a leprechaun costume in the hope that he would blend in better with the crowds.

PERSONAL BELONGINGS SOLD AT AUCTION

A two-line handwritten note by Albert Einstein that explains the theory of happiness sold at auction for $1.3 million in 2017. Einstein gave the signed note to a worker at Tokyo's Imperial Hotel in 1922 in lieu of a tip.

The wooden chair on which J.K. Rowling sat while she wrote the first two Harry Potter books fetched $394,000 at a rare books auction in New York in 2016.

A wheelchair used by physicist Stephen Hawking sold for $386,240 in 2018.

A pair of John Lennon's iconic round glasses sold for $97,000 in 2009.

A bible belonging to Elvis Presley sold for $94,600 in 2012. But at the same auction, a pair of his old underpants failed to reach the reserve price of $11,000.

A shirt stained with John Lennon's blood from the night he was murdered sold for $45,000 in 2016. The shirt was being worn at the time by Jay Hastings, concierge at the Dakota building in New York, who rushed to Lennon's aid after the musician was shot by Mark Chapman.

A set of three chest X-rays of Marilyn Monroe, taken when she was 28, fetched $45,000 at auction in 2010.

A box containing Truman Capote's ashes was sold at auction for $45,000 in 2016, and, in accordance with the late author's wishes, the purchaser was required to take the cremated remains along to parties and other social events.

A rotten tooth that once belonged to John Lennon was bought by Canadian dentist Michael Zuk for $31,000 in 2011.

A single lock of Abraham Lincoln's hair, collected after his assassination, sold for $25,000 at a Dallas auction in 2015.

A set of Winston Churchill's false teeth sold for $23,000 in 2010.

A lock of David Bowie's hair sold for $18,750, a few months after his death in 2016.

A cheque signed by Marilyn Monroe for $228.80 to a furniture company on the day before she died in 1962 sold for $15,000 in 2012.

A pair of Queen Victoria's silk bloomers with a 50-inch waist fetched $14,950 at auction in 2011 – three times more than the estimate.

An engraved silver Tiffany and Co. dog bowl that was used by Joan Rivers' beloved Yorkshire terrier Spike sold for $13,750 in 2016.

An angry handwritten letter penned by Kurt Cobain to MTV fetched $12,800 in 2010.

A cigar half-smoked by Winston Churchill in 1947 sold for $12,000 in 2017. The four-inch stub had been retrieved from an ashtray by a British airman.

A pair of mint-green pyjamas worn by Elvis Presley during his stay at the Baptist Memorial Hospital, Memphis, in April 1977 – four months before his death – fetched $10,400 at auction in 2017.

The loincloth worn by Charlton Heston in *Ben Hur* sold for $10,000 in 1997.

The black Jean-Paul Gaultier bra that Madonna wore on her 1993 tour sold for $8,200 four years later.

A pair of 'secret' reading glasses owned by Adolf Hitler sold for $7,500 in 2011.

The body tag from the corpse of Lee Harvey Oswald fetched $7,000 at auction.

A pair of John F. Kennedy's Navy-issue, white boxer shorts sold for $5,000 in 2003.

The shrivelled penis of Napoleon Bonaparte was bought by American Dr John Lattimer for $3,000 in 1977. The surgeon performing the autopsy on Napoleon had apparently chopped it off and kept it as a memento.

Several strands of Michael Jackson's burnt hair – singed when it caught fire while he was making a 1984 Pepsi commercial – sold in 2009 for $1,600.

A record player that belonged to Cher in the 1970s sold for $1,400 in 2006.

A toupee, described as 'brown with a hint of grey', that was worn by John Wayne in the 1967 film *El Dorado*, sold for $1,244 at auction in 2010.

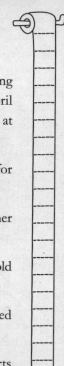

ONE OF THOSE DAYS

Duncan Robb, from Chesterfield, England, flew his girlfriend to Belfast for a romantic Valentine's Day weekend in 2018 with the promise of seeing her favourite rock band, the Red Hot Chili Peppers, only to discover that the bargain-price tickets he had bought online were for the Red Hot Chilli Pipers, 'the world's best bagpipe band'.

A 38-year-old woman from Galati, Romania, spent two days in hospital in 2007 after swallowing her lover's false teeth while experimenting with 'a special type of passionate kiss'.

Pensioner Joan Hiscock nearly burned down her Hampshire old people's home after putting her slippers under the grill to warm them up.

Actor Tony Randall, who had been appointed spokesperson for US National Sleep Disorder Month, overslept on 9 May 1995 and missed a guest spot on the TV show *Wake Up America*.

Georgia hunter Donnie Lamb shot a raccoon out of a tree, not realising that his friend, Brad Davis, was standing directly underneath. The 15-pound animal crashed 60 feet onto Davis's head, knocking him out, fracturing three of his vertebrae and putting him in a neck brace for weeks.

Francis Karnes, of Sacramento, California, was charged with reckless endangerment after he shot his lawnmower because it wouldn't start.

When 19-year-old barman Luke Woolston was asked to cash up and put the day's takings in a safe place, he decided to put the $2,000 in notes in a hot oven at the pub in Ormesby, Norfolk, and seemed surprised when they went up in smoke.

A man in Stravropol, Russia, got his penis frozen fast onto a metal bus shelter after urinating in the street in temperatures of minus 30 Celsius. He made the mistake of turning towards the shelter before zipping up his fly.

Katherine Gaydos of Lantana, Florida, had her left eye glued shut for several days in 2015 after mistaking super glue for eye drops.

In 1978, Bob Speca was preparing to break a world record by toppling 100,000 dominoes at New York's Manhattan Center. He had painstakingly positioned 97,499 over the course of several hours when a TV cameraman, on hand to capture the big moment, dropped his press badge and set off the whole wave prematurely.

A sign erected in 2009 on Interstate 39 near Rothschild and Schofield, Wisconsin, spelt only one word correctly – 'exit'. The sign read: 'Exit 185 Buisness 51 Rothschield Schofeild.'

To prove his love for his girlfriend, Hannes Pisek made a heart shape using 220 candles on the floor of his Austrian apartment. He then lit them and went to collect his sweetheart from work, but his hopes of a romantic evening were dashed when the flat caught fire in his absence. To make matters worse, she dumped him and moved back in with her parents.

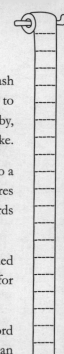

Firefighters in Baton Rouge, Louisiana, accidentally burned down their own fire station after leaving fish frying on the stove when they were called out to attend a blaze.

After 15 years of searching for a rare orchid, botanists Lionel Pucker and Tim Batty finally found a specimen in New Zealand – crushed beyond salvation beneath the groundsheet of their tent.

An abandoned cigarette burned a California mobile home to the ground, causing $200,000 worth of damage ... while its occupants were attending a meeting to help them quit smoking.

When Dorset teenager Charlene Williams asked a tattoo artist to ink the word 'mum' on her back in Chinese letters, she ended up with 'friend from hell' instead. Apparently the tattooist was unaware that Chinese letters change their meaning when put together.

Internet design consultant Raina Kumra sued a New York City bar in 2009 after suffering concussion when she was hit by a stuffed moose head falling off a wall.

While out for a walk in County Durham in 2009, 66-year-old George Stastny tripped on a narrow footpath and tumbled down a 20-foot cliff. His wife Mary managed to drag him semi-conscious back to the top before running to fetch help. No sooner had she left than he stood up, fainted, and fell back down the same cliff.

Trying to smoke out a nest of raccoons in his attic with a kerosene-soaked rag on a stick, Kansas City pensioner C.W. Roseburr merely succeeded in burning down his house instead.

Worried that burglars might target his home while he and his wife were away on a 2007 business trip, Mr Cui, of Qingdao, China, decided to hide his $6,000 of savings in the kitchen garbage bin. But when the couple returned, they forgot all about the secret stash and instinctively threw out the garbage because the bin was full. By the time they realised, it was too late.

After accidentally dropping his phone down a toilet on a train travelling between La Rochelle and Paris, a French passenger tried to fish it out but instead saw his arm trapped by the toilet's powerful suction system. The train was halted for two hours while fire crews cut through pipework. He eventually came out on a stretcher, with his hand still jammed in the toilet bowl.

Romanian pensioner Constantin Luican ran up a $1,400 bill on a telephone sex chat line because he fell asleep during the call.

CREATIVE DEATHS

Canadian lawyer Garry Hoy fell 24 storeys to his death in 1993 while attempting to demonstrate to a group of law students that the glass windows of the Toronto-Dominion Centre were unbreakable. He barged into a pane with his shoulder but the glass gave way and he ended up in the courtyard below. The head of his legal firm described him as 'one of the best and brightest' members.

Edward Archbold, of West Palm Beach, Florida, choked to death after winning a 2012 cockroach-eating contest. The inquest ruled that death was a result of 'anthropod body parts' blocking his airways.

In 2014, Peng Fan, a chef in Foshan, China, was fatally bitten by a cobra's severed head, which he had cut off 20 minutes earlier while preparing a soup.

A man in Kitwe, Zambia, was electrocuted in 2000 when, having run out of space on his clothes line, he decided to hang the remainder of his wet washing on a live power line.

After causing a disturbance in a 7-Eleven store in St Louis, Missouri, in 1994, Robert Puelo grabbed a hot dog, stuffed it defiantly down his throat, marched out without paying … and promptly choked to death.

One day in 1982, David Grundman thought it would be fun to shoot cacti in the Arizona Desert – until he shot repeatedly at a 26-foot-high specimen, causing a 500-pound arm to break off and crush him to death.

Li Xiao Meng, a 16-year-old business student from China, plunged to his death in 2005 while bouncing up and down on the bed of his Singapore hotel room and playing air guitar like a rock star. He got so carried away that he bounced straight out of the open window and fell three floors to his death.

In 2013, Joao Maria de Souza was crushed to death in his bed by a cow falling through the roof of his home in Caratinga, Brazil.

Paul G. Thomas, co-owner of a wool mill in Thompson, Connecticut, died in 1987 of suffocation after falling into a machine and becoming wrapped in 800 yards of wool.

Ector Rodriguez, the owner of a bowling alley in Florence, Colorado, died in 2018 after getting stuck in the pin setting machine.

In 1994, frustrated golfer Jeremy Brenno, from Gloversville, New York, lashed out at a bench with a number three wood, but the club shaft broke, bounced back at him and pierced his heart.

Dr Jacquelyn Katarac suffocated in 2010 while trying to break into the Bakersfield, California, home of her estranged boyfriend by descending feet first down the chimney. Her body was found three days later wedged about two feet above the fireplace after a house-sitter detected a strange smell in the room.

In 2013, Indian daredevil Sailendra Nath Roy suffered a fatal heart attack at a height of 60 feet above the Teesta River

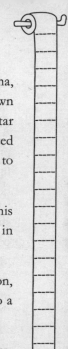

while breaking his own world record for the longest distance travelled along a zip wire by ponytail.

A chronic snorer, Londoner Mark Gleeson tried to cure the problem in 1996 by stuffing two of his girlfriend's tampons up his nose – one in each nostril – only to suffocate while he slept.

Ken Barger, of Newton, North Carolina, accidentally shot himself dead in 1992 while answering a call in the middle of the night. He went to pick up his bedside phone but, half asleep, grabbed his .38 Smith and Wesson special instead. The gun went off when he pulled it to his ear.

PEOPLE WHO DIED ON THE TOILET

American comedian Lenny Bruce died of a heroin overdose while sitting on the toilet in 1966.

Catherine the Great, Empress of Russia, died in 1796 after suffering a massive stroke while straining to overcome constipation on the toilet.

Judy Garland unintentionally overdosed on barbiturates in 1969 while using the toilet at a rented house in London.

Saxon king Edmund Ironside died in 1016, murdered, according to contemporary accounts, by nobleman Eadric Streona who hid in the privy pit below the wooden commode and stabbed the unsuspecting Edmund twice with a longsword while he was defecating, leaving the weapon impaled in the king's bowels.

Roman Emperor Elagabalus was hacked to death by the Praetorian Guard in AD 222 as he hid in the toilet. His body was thrown into one of the sewers that ran into the River Tiber.

George II, an enthusiastic farter, overexerted himself on the toilet in 1760 with such force that he fell off and fatally smashed his head on a bathroom cabinet. He was found slumped on the floor by his German valet who had feared that the crash he had heard was 'louder than the usual royal wind'.

Michael Anderson Godwin had just seen his death sentence for murder reduced to life imprisonment in 1989 when, attempting to fix the TV set in his South Carolina cell, he bit into a wire while sitting naked on a metal toilet and accidentally electrocuted himself.

Elvis Presley suffered a fatal heart attack while using the toilet at his Graceland home in 1977 and was found face down in the bathroom. According to his fiancée Ginger Alden: 'Elvis looked as if his entire body had completely frozen in a seated position while using the commode and then had fallen forward, in that fixed position.'

Conservative politician Christopher Shale was found dead in a portable toilet at the 2011 Glastonbury Festival, having suffered a heart attack.

English writer Evelyn Waugh died of heart failure in 1966 while sitting on the toilet after returning home from church.

King Wenceslaus III of Bohemia was assassinated with a spear in 1306 by an unknown assailant while sitting quietly on the toilet.

FAMOUS PEOPLE WHO DROWNED – BUT NOT IN THE TOILET

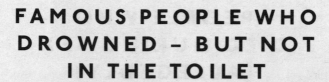

Jeff Buckley

Johnny Burnette

George, Duke of Clarence

Harold Holt

Whitney Houston

Brian Jones

King Louis II of Hungary

Robert Maxwell

Josef Mengele

Percy Bysshe Shelley

Dennis Wilson

Natalie Wood

Virginia Woolf

PEOPLE WHO DIED DURING SEX (ALLEGEDLY)

Pope John XII died on 14 May 964 while having sex with a woman named Stefanetta. Some say he died of a stroke at the height of passion, but other sources claim that His Holiness met his demise after Stefanetta's husband caught him in the act and bludgeoned him to death with a hammer.

French President Félix Faure died from apoplexy in the Élysée Palace in Paris on 16 February 1899 while engaged in sexual activities in his office with socialite Marguerite Steinheil who, at 30, was 28 years his junior. Contemporary reports suggest that Faure suffered his fatal seizure while she was performing oral sex on him.

Former US Vice-President Nelson Rockefeller died on 26 January 1979 of a heart attack at the age of 70, allegedly while having sex with an aide, 25-year-old Megan Marshack. The refusal of an autopsy and order of a hasty cremation further fuelled the rumours.

Brent Tyler and Chelsea Tumbleston were killed in 2007 after they fell 50 feet from the sloping roof of an office in Columbia, South Carolina, while having sex.

Australian politician Sir Billy Snedden died on 27 June 1987 after suffering a fatal heart attack at a Travelodge motel near Sydney while having sex with his son's ex-girlfriend.

A policeman told Melbourne's *The Truth* newspaper that Snedden had expired 'at the peak of physical congress'.

Jim McConaughey, father of actor Matthew McConaughey, died of a heart attack in 1992 during a regular early morning sex session with his wife Kay. She later described it as 'just the best way to go'.

Romanian First Division footballer Mario Bugeanu and Mirela Iancu died of carbon monoxide poisoning in 1999 while having sex in a car. They had parked in Bugeanu's garage but were in such a hurry that they had left the engine running.

Atlanta police officer William Martinez died on 12 March 2009 from heart disease while engaged in a threesome. His widow, who had not been present at the time, successfully sued her late husband's doctor for negligence on the grounds that he had failed to warn Martinez to avoid physical exertion.

Sharai Mawera was mauled to death by a lion in Zimbabwe in 2013 while having sex at a secluded spot in the bush with her married boyfriend, who fled the scene naked and wearing only a condom.

OTHER PEOPLE
WHO DIED IN 2016

So many truly famous people died in 2016 – David Bowie, George Michael, Muhammad Ali, Victoria Wood, Terry Wogan and Prince to name but a few – that it was easy for others to get overlooked. Here are some you may have missed:

Richard Adams (author of *Watership Down*), Edward Albee (playwright who wrote *Who's Afraid of Virginia Woolf?*), Chris Amon (former New Zealand Formula One driver), Sylvia Anderson (co-creator of *Thunderbirds*), Kenny Baker (little actor who played R2-D2 in *Star Wars*), Ken Barrie (voice of Postman Pat), Boutros Boutros-Ghali (former United Nations secretary-general), Pete Burns (flamboyant Dead or Alive singer), Prince Buster (Jamaican singer-songwriter), William Christopher (actor who played Father Mulcahy in the TV version of *M*A*S*H*), Michael Cimino (director of *The Deer Hunter*), Patty Duke (US actress), Frank Finlay (actor), David Gest (reality TV star), AA Gill (restaurant critic), John Glenn (astronaut), Vivean Gray (actress who played Mrs Mangel in *Neighbours*), Dan Haggerty (star of *Grizzly Adams*), Robert Horton (star of *Wagon Train*), Barry Howard (actor who played Barry Stuart-Hargreaves in TV comedy *Hi-De-Hi!*), Gordie Howe (Canadian ice hockey legend), Burt Kwouk (Cato in the Pink Panther films), Carla Lane (creator of TV comedies *The Liver Birds* and *Bread*), Harper Lee (author of *To Kill a Mockingbird*), Garry Marshall (producer of *Happy Days*), Ian McCaskill (UK TV weatherman), Scotty Moore (Elvis

Presley's backing guitarist), Gordon Murray (creator of *Trumpton*), Hugh O'Brian (US actor who played Wyatt Earp on TV), Billy Paul (soul singer who had 1973 hit with 'Me and Mrs Jones'), Shimon Peres (former Israeli Prime Minister and President), Jimmy Perry (co-creator of *Dad's Army*), Janet Reno (former US attorney general), Denise Robertson (agony aunt on TV Show *This Morning*), Leon Russell (US songwriter), Garry Shandling (comedian), Raine Spencer (stepmother of Princess Diana), Dave Swarbrick (singer with folk band Fairport Convention), Walter Swinburn (jockey), Peter Vaughan (actor who played Grouty in *Porridge*), Bobby Vee (US pop singer), Tony Warren (creator of *Coronation Street*), Arnold Wesker (playwright), Maurice White (founder of Earth, Wind & Fire), Douglas Wilmer (actor who played Sherlock Holmes on TV), Alan Young (human straight man to TV talking horse Mister Ed).

DIED ON THE
SAME DAY

John Adams and Thomas Jefferson (4 July 1826)

Sergei Prokofiev and Joseph Stalin (5 March 1953)

Jean Cocteau and Edith Piaf (11 October 1963)

Aldous Huxley, John F. Kennedy and C.S. Lewis
(22 November 1963)

Marc Bolan and Maria Callas (16 September 1977)

Orson Welles and Yul Brynner (10 October 1985)

Christopher Isherwood and Phil Lynott (4 January 1986)

Sammy Davis Jr and Jim Henson (16 May 1990)

Dizzy Gillespie and Rudolf Nureyev (6 January 1993)

Federico Fellini and River Phoenix (31 October 1993)

Georg Solti and Mother Teresa (5 September 1997)

Milton Berle, Dudley Moore and Billy Wilder
(27 March 2002)

Anita Roddick and Jane Wyman (10 September 2007)

Arthur C. Clarke and Paul Scofield (19 March 2008)

Farrah Fawcett and Michael Jackson (25 June 2009)

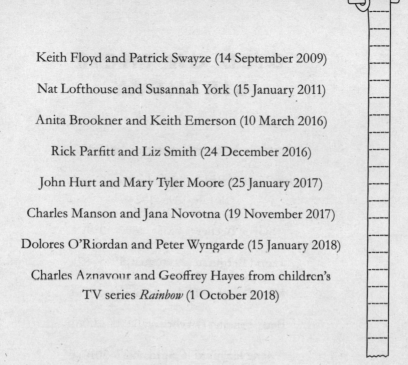

Keith Floyd and Patrick Swayze (14 September 2009)

Nat Lofthouse and Susannah York (15 January 2011)

Anita Brookner and Keith Emerson (10 March 2016)

Rick Parfitt and Liz Smith (24 December 2016)

John Hurt and Mary Tyler Moore (25 January 2017)

Charles Manson and Jana Novotna (19 November 2017)

Dolores O'Riordan and Peter Wyngarde (15 January 2018)

Charles Aznavour and Geoffrey Hayes from children's TV series *Rainbow* (1 October 2018)

DIED ON THEIR BIRTHDAY

Gertrude Astor (9 November, 1887–1977)

George Francis Barnes (aka Machine Gun Kelly)
(18 July, 1895–1954)

Sidney Bechet (14 May, 1897–1959)

Ingrid Bergman (29 August, 1915–82)

Mike Douglas (11 August, 1920–2006)

Betty Friedan (4 February, 1921–2006)

Merle Haggard (6 April, 1937–2016)

Raphael (6 April, 1483–1520)

Franklin D. Roosevelt Jr (17 August, 1914–88)

William Shakespeare (23 April, 1564–1616)

FAMOUS LAST WORDS

Johnny Ace (while playing Russian roulette): 'It's okay! Gun's not loaded. See?'

John Quincy Adams: 'This is the last of Earth. I am content.'

Marie Antoinette: 'Pardon me, sir. I meant not to do it.'

Johann Sebastian Bach: 'Don't cry for me, for where I go music is born.'

John Barrymore: 'Die, I should say not, dear fellow. No Barrymore would allow such a conventional thing to happen to him.'

James Brown: 'I'm going away tonight.'

Winston Churchill: 'I'm so bored with it all.'

Joan Crawford: 'Damn it! Don't you dare ask God to help me!'

Bing Crosby: 'That was a great game of golf, fellas … Let's get a Coke.'

Joe DiMaggio: 'I'll finally get to see Marilyn.'

Douglas Fairbanks Sr: 'I've never felt better.'

Adam Faith: 'Channel 5 is all shit, isn't it? Christ, the crap they put on there. It's a waste of space.'

W.C. Fields (to his longtime mistress Carlotta Monti): 'God damn the whole friggin' world and everyone in it but you, Carlotta.'

Ian Fleming (to the ambulance drivers rushing him to hospital): 'I am sorry to trouble you chaps. I don't know how you get along so fast with the traffic on the roads these days.'

James French, convicted murderer (to members of the press as he sat in the electric chair awaiting execution): 'Hey, fellas! How about this for a headline for tomorrow's paper? French Fries!'

Edmund Gwenn, actor (when a friend said that dying must be terribly difficult): 'Not nearly as difficult as playing comedy.'

Steve Jobs (looking at his family): 'Oh wow. Oh wow. Oh wow.'

John Le Mesurier: 'It's all been rather lovely.'

Groucho Marx: 'This is no way to live!'

Karl Marx: 'Go on, get out! Last words are for fools who haven't said enough.'

Wolfgang Amadeus Mozart: 'The taste of death is upon my lips. I feel something, that is not of this earth.'

Donald O'Connor: 'I would like to thank the Academy for my lifetime achievement award that I will eventually get.'

Edith Piaf: 'Every damn fool thing you do in this life you pay for.'

Buddy Rich (asked by a nurse if there was anything he couldn't take): 'Yeah, country music.'

General John Sedgwick (seconds before being shot in the face by a Confederate sharpshooter at the Battle of Spotsylvania): 'They couldn't hit an elephant at this distance.'

Frank Sinatra: 'I'm losing it.'

Rudolph Valentino: 'Don't pull down the blinds. I feel fine. I want the sunlight to greet me.'

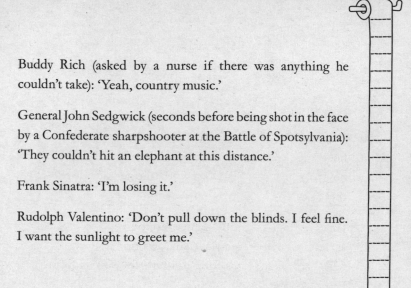

THE
NATURAL
WORLD

HAVE EWE HERD?

FASCINATING FACTS
ABOUT SHEEP

Sheep can recognise up to 50 other sheep faces and remember them for two years.

Tests have shown that around eight per cent of male sheep are gay.

Thanks to their large, rectangular pupils, sheep have excellent peripheral vision and can see nearly 360 degrees without turning their head.

There are approximately 900 different breeds of sheep around the world.

A castrated male sheep is called a wether.

The ancient Egyptians believed that sheep were sacred and had their favourite rams mummified when they died, just like humans.

The history of wool manufacture in Britain dates back to around 1900 BC.

Spain placed so much value on its Merino sheep that until 1786 exporting sheep was an offence punishable by death.

Tallow, the fat extracted from sheep, is used to make soap and candles.

The small intestines from 11 sheep are needed to make one tennis racket.

SOME COUNTRIES WHERE SHEEP OUTNUMBER PEOPLE

Falkland Islands (312 to 1)

Mongolia (8 to 1)

Uruguay (7 to 1)

New Zealand (6 to 1)

Namibia (5 to 1)

Australia (3 to 1)

Iceland (3 to 1)

Wales (3 to 1)

Turkmenistan (2.2 to 1)

Mauritania (2 to 1)

Somalia (2 to 1)

Ireland (1.7 to 1)

Libya (1.5 to 1)

Scotland (1.2 to 1)

COMPARATIVE SPEEDS

270mph: peregrine falcon (diving)

106mph: spine-tailed swift

100mph: racing pigeon

70mph: cheetah

68mph: sailfish

64mph: dolphin

61mph: pronghorn

60mph: mako shark

50mph: lion

48mph: killer whale

43mph: greyhound, ostrich

39mph: thoroughbred racehorse

36mph: Australian dragonfly

33mph: hawk moth

30mph: grizzly bear

23mph: human sprinting

21mph: spiny-tailed iguana

12mph: black mamba

3.1mph: human walking

0.23mph: giant tortoise

0.1mph: three-toed sloth

0.03mph: garden snail

SPIDERS
TO AVOID

The Sydney funnel web spider has been responsible for several human deaths in Australia over the past 100 years. It is highly aggressive and likes to deliver a series of bites with needle-sharp fangs that are longer than those in some snakes while it clings to its victim. It is said to be able to bite through shoe leather and even fingernails. Victims suffer muscle spasms, palpitations, vomiting, confusion and swelling of the brain and, before an effective anti-venom was introduced in 1981, death could be expected in as little as 15 minutes.

The venom of the aggressive Brazilian wandering spider (also known as the banana spider because it is often found on banana leaves) can cause irregular heartbeat and eventually complete respiratory paralysis. In men, it can also bring about prolonged, painful erections, or priapism. It is nearly 20 times more poisonous than a black widow.

The redback spider's venom can produce sweating, a rapid heartbeat and swollen lymph nodes. More than 250 redback bites are treated each year in Australia. Bites often occur when the redback climbs into shoes or clothing.

The bite of a black widow spider is said to be 15 times more potent than a rattlesnake's, but luckily they prefer to scurry away when confronted and so rarely trouble humans. Instead the female, which is twice the size of the male, reserves her aggression for her partner, often eating him straight after mating. A widow bite initially feels like a small pinprick but the victim soon experiences muscle pain, cramping, nausea and difficulty with breathing.

The brown widow spider is considered even more dangerous than the black widow, but it only injects a small amount of venom when it bites. Even so, a brown widow bite caused the deaths of two people in Madagascar in the 1990s.

A bite from a brown recluse spider can cause a large skin ulcer that may take months to heal and even require skin grafts. In extreme cases, the wound may become infected, leading to amputation or eventually death. They do not take kindly to being sprayed with bug repellent either, as it only makes them angrier and more toxic.

Found throughout the United States, the yellow sac spider has a venom that can damage or destroy human cell functions, causing lesions and swellings.

The fast-moving wolf spider of Europe and the United States usually only bites in self-defence. However, a nip from its large fangs can cause victims to suffer dizziness, nausea and an increased heart rate.

The tarantula takes its name from the Italian town of Taranto. Its bite was once thought to be fatal unless victims danced furiously until they dropped from exhaustion. Tarantella dancing is still popular in Italy, although in truth, a tarantula's bite usually causes nothing worse than a sharp pain, because its venom is milder than a bee's. There are more than 850 species of tarantula, ranging in size from as small as a fingernail to as large as a dinner plate when the legs are fully extended.

A BUG'S LIFE

At least 80 per cent of the planet's species are insects.

The larva of the polyphemus moth of North America eats 86,000 times its own birth weight in the first two months of its life.

A rhinoceros beetle is able to support 100 times its own weight on its back. It can also walk for an hour carrying 30 times its weight without showing distress, the equivalent of a man walking for an hour with a car on his head and not feeling tired.

A ladybird will eat more than 5,000 insects in its lifetime.

Only female mosquitoes bite animals and humans and drink their blood. They can drink up to three times their own body weight in blood during a single feed. The male prefers flower nectar.

Mosquitoes prefer blondes to brunettes.

A cockroach can live for weeks after its head has been cut off.

Cockroaches have lived on Earth for 250 million years without changing in any way.

Despite their name, centipedes do not have exactly 100 legs. The number of legs can range from 30 to 354, but it is always an odd number of pairs, so they can never have 100.

An ancient dragonfly called *Meganeuropsis*, or the griffinfly, had a wingspan of up to 2.5 feet and was capable of eating small frogs.

A dung beetle can drag 1,141 times its weight – like a human pulling six double-decker buses.

Crickets chirp more frequently the higher the temperature, averaging around 62 per minute at 55 Fahrenheit. According to Dolbear's Law, calculated by American physicist Amos Dolbear in 1897, if you count the number of chirps produced in 14 seconds by the snowy tree cricket and add 40, you will get the approximate temperature in degrees Fahrenheit.

Crickets hear through their knees because their hearing organs are located on their front legs.

Butterflies taste with their feet.

Millions of North American monarch butterflies migrate up to 3,000 miles each winter to California and Mexico. They make only one round trip before dying, but their descendants instinctively know the way, following the same route that their ancestors took and sometimes even landing on the very same tree.

The caterpillar of the king page butterfly camouflages itself as bird droppings.

A caterpillar has some 4,000 muscles – around six times more than a human.

An 1874 locust swarm in Nebraska covered around 198,600 square miles – almost double the size of Colorado – and contained an estimated 12.5 trillion insects.

A small swarm of 40 million locusts eats the same amount of food per day as 35,000 people.

Ironically, ants can be found on every single continent except Antarctica.

There are 1.4 million ants to every human on the planet.

A trap-jaw ant can close its jaws at 140mph.

A supercolony of Argentine ants found in 2002 weaved its way for 3,700 miles along the coast of the Mediterranean from northern Italy to Spain's Atlantic coast and contained millions of individual nests.

Soldier ants use their heads to plug the entrances to their nests and keep intruders at bay, like a cork in a bottle.

A fly can react to something it sees and change direction in 30 milliseconds.

A housefly can transport germs up to 15 miles from the original source of contamination.

The lesser water boatman swims upside down on ponds, using two long legs as paddles. Although only two millimetres long, it can produce 99.2 decibels of noise, which is like listening to an orchestra playing at full volume from the front row.

Before laying eggs, a female tick will, in a single feed, drink up to 600 times her own body weight in blood.

A bite from the lone star tick can stop you enjoying burgers or steak. The tick carries a substance called alpha-gal that makes people allergic to red meat.

As part of their camouflage, stick insects have fake buds and leaf scars on their body.

Earwigs got their name because it was once widely believed that they liked to burrow into human ears to lay their eggs.

The meadow froghopper can jump 100 times its own height – up to about 28 inches – the equivalent of an adult human being able to jump over a 50-storey building.

Termite queens can produce 7,000 eggs in a single day.

Although many insects live for only a few days, a termite queen can reign for half a century.

THE BUZZWORD
ON BEES

A bee's wings beat 190 times a second – that's 11,400 times a minute.

Bees fly about 55,000 miles and visit some two million flowers to bring in enough nectar to make one pound of honey.

Only female honey bees sting; the males are harmless.

Male bees die after mating with the queen. Sex takes place in mid-air and the drone ejaculates with such force that the tip of his penis is left behind inside her and his abdomen ruptures, causing him to fall to the ground, where he dies soon after.

The average worker bee produces only about one-twelfth of a teaspoon of honey in her lifetime.

Different bees have different jobs. Scout bees devote their life to finding new food sources, soldier bees guard the nest, and 1 per cent of all middle-aged bees become undertakers – their brains wired in such a way that they feel compelled to remove dead bees from the hive.

Despite their tiny brains, bees can be trained to recognise individual human faces.

Africanised honey bees, or killer bees, were created by cross-breeding African honey bees with European bees. Since being accidentally released in Brazil in 1957, they have killed more than 1,000 people as well as horses and other animals. Victims receive ten times more stings than from European honey bees.

SCHMIDT STING
PAIN INDEX

Arizona entomologist Justin O. Schmidt has ranked the sting of over 80 species of insect based on his personal suffering, usually accidental, but occasionally induced:

Pain level

0.5 – Club-horned wasp ('Disappointing. A paper clip falls on your bare foot')

1.0 – Anthophorid bee ('Almost pleasant, a lover just bit your earlobe a little too hard')

1.0 – Mud dauber wasp ('Sharp with a flare of heat; jalapeno cheese when you were expecting Havarti')

1.0 – Sweat bee ('Light, ephemeral, almost fruity. A tiny spark has singed a single hair on your arm')

1.2 – Fire ant ('Sharp, mildly alarming. Like walking across a shag carpet and reaching for the light switch')

1.5 – Western cicada killer wasp ('Pain at first sight. Like poison oak, the more you rub, the worse it gets')

1.8 – Bullhorn acacia ant ('A rare, piercing, elevated sort of pain. Someone has fired a staple into your cheek')

2.0 – Bald-faced hornet ('Similar to getting your hand mashed in a revolving door')

2.0 – European hornet/honey bee ('Burning, corrosive, but you can handle it. Like a match head that flips off and burns on your skin')

2.0 – Matabele ant ('The debilitating pain of a migraine contained in the tip of your finger')

2.0 – Yellowjacket ('Hot and smoky. Imagine W.C. Fields extinguishing a cigar on your tongue')

2.5 – Fierce black polybia wasp ('A ritual gone wrong, satanic. The gas lamp in the old church explodes in your face when you light it')

2.5 – Golden paper wasp ('Sharp, piercing and immediate. You know what cattle feel when they are branded')

3.0 – Maricopa harvester ant ('After eight unrelenting hours of drilling into that ingrown toenail, you find the drill wedged into the toe')

3.0 – Red-headed paper wasp ('The closest you will come to seeing the blue of a flame from within the fire')

3.0 – Southern paper wasp ('Caustic and burning, like spilling a beaker of hydrochloric acid on a paper cut')

3.0 – Velvet ant ('Explosive and long-lasting, you sound insane as you scream. Hot oil from a deep fryer spilling over your entire hand')

4.0 – Tarantula hawk ('Blinding, fierce, shockingly electric. Like a running hairdryer has just been dropped into your bubble bath')

4.0 – Warrior wasp ('Torture. You are chained in the flow of an active volcano')

4.0-plus – Bullet ant ('Pure, intense, brilliant pain … like walking over flaming charcoal with a three-inch nail embedded in your heel')

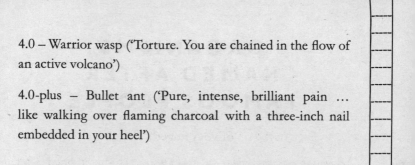

ORGANISMS NAMED AFTER FAMOUS PEOPLE

Zaglossus attenboroughi – a species of echidna named after David Attenborough

Bursina borisbeckeri – a species of sea snail named after Boris Becker

Heteropoda davidbowie – a species of huntsman spider named after David Bowie

Funkotriplogynium iagobadius – a species of mite named after James Brown (*Iago* is 'James' and *badius* is 'Brown' in Latin)

Agathidium bushi – a species of beetle named after George W. Bush

Pristimantis jamescameroni – a species of frog named after James Cameron

Aphonopelma johnnycashi – a species of tarantula named after Johnny Cash

Hyloscirtus princecharlesi – a species of tree frog named after Prince Charles

Avahi cleesei – a species of woolly lemur named after John Cleese

Etheostoma clinton – a species of fish named after Bill Clinton

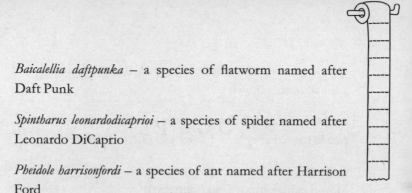

Baicalellia daftpunka – a species of flatworm named after Daft Punk

Spintharus leonardodicaprioi – a species of spider named after Leonardo DiCaprio

Pheidole harrisonfordi – a species of ant named after Harrison Ford

Saepocephalum stephenfryii – a species of bird louse named after Stephen Fry

Aleiodes gaga – a species of wasp named after Lady Gaga

Rostropria garbo – a species of solitary wasp named after Greta Garbo

Cryptocercus garciai – a species of cockroach named after Jerry Garcia

Eristalis gatesi – a species of Costa Rican fly named after Bill Gates

Albunea groeningi – a species of mole crab named after *Simpsons* creator Matt Groening

Sylvilagus palustris hefneri – a subspecies of marsh rabbit named after Hugh Hefner

Elseya irwini – a species of turtle named after Steve Irwin

Jaggermeryx – an extinct hippo-like species named after Mick Jagger

Aptostichus angelinajolieae – a species of trapdoor spider named after Angelina Jolie

Scaptia beyonceae – a species of fly with a colourful rear named after Beyoncé Knowles

Baeturia laureli and *Baeturia hardyi* – two similar species of cicada named after Stan Laurel and Oliver Hardy

Kalloprion kilmisteri – a species of bristle worm named after Motorhead's Lemmy (Ian Kilmister)

Bumba lennoni – a species of tarantula named after John Lennon

Litarachna lopezae – a species of aquatic mite named after Jennifer Lopez

Mandelia mirocornata – a species of sea slug named after Nelson Mandela

Gnathia marleyi – a species of parasitic crustacean named after Bob Marley

Heteragrion brianmayi – a species of damselfly named after Brian May

Cirolana mercuryi – a species of isopod named after Freddie Mercury

Barbaturex morrisoni – an extinct lizard named after Jim Morrison

Rubus mussolinii – a hybrid blackberry named after Benito Mussolini

Caloplaca obamae – a species of lichen named after Barack Obama

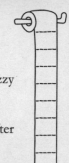

Dendropsophus ozzyi – a species of frog named after Ozzy Osbourne

Synalpheus pinkfloydi – a species of pistol shrimp named after Pink Floyd

Anelosimus pratchetti – a species of Australian spider named after Terry Pratchett

Heterospilus reagani – a species of wasp named after Ronald Reagan

Cervus roosevelti – a subspecies of elk named after Theodore Roosevelt

Agra schwarzeneggeri – a species of beetle named after Arnold Schwarzenegger

Hyla stingi – a species of Colombian frog named after Sting

Alviniconcha strummeri – a species of sea snail named after Joe Strummer

Tetragramma donaldtrumpi – a fossil species of sea urchin named after Donald Trump

Agra katewinsletae – a species of beetle named after Kate Winslet

Myrmekiaphila neilyoungi – a species of spider named after Neil Young

Phialella zappai – a species of jellyfish named after Frank Zappa

DEADLIEST CREATURES

BY AVERAGE HUMAN DEATHS GLOBALLY PER YEAR

1. Mosquito: 750,000

2. Snake: 100,000

3. Dog: 25,000

4. Freshwater snail: 20,000
(carries parasitic worms that can infect
people with deadly disease)

5= Tsetse fly: 10,000

5 = Assassin bug: 10,000
(carries Chagas disease)

7. Scorpion: 3,000

8. Ascaris roundworm: 2,500

9. Tapeworm: 2,000

10. Crocodile: 1,000

11. Hippopotamus: 500

12. Elephant: 400

13. Cape buffalo: 200

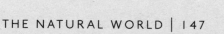

14. Lion: 200

15. Jellyfish: 100

16. Bee: 90

17. Tiger: 40

18. Shark: 12

19. Wolf: 10

20. Bear: 8

ANIMAL CRACKERS

Because they are equipped with a powerful barrier between the stomach and the oesophagus, rats are unable to vomit. They can't burp either.

When the first duck-billed platypus arrived at the British Museum in 1799, incredulous scientist George Shaw thought it was a hoax – the beak of a duck glued on to the body of a beaver-like animal. He even cut the pelt with scissors to try and find the stitches that attached the bill to the pelt. The museum's oldest preserved platypus specimen still has those scissor marks.

If a giant panda is really hungry, it will eat upwards of 84 pounds of bamboo shoots in a single day.

Camels can lose up to 30 per cent of their body weight in perspiration and still survive. Humans would die of heat shock after sweating away only 12 per cent of their body weight.

The tiny rock hyrax – a rat-like creature from central Africa – is the closest living relative of the elephant.

Nine-banded armadillos almost always give birth to identical quadruplets. This is because the female only produces a single egg, which separates into four parts after fertilisation.

Armadillos can walk underwater, holding their breath for up to six minutes at a time.

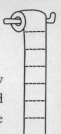

Big Norm, a domestic pig that lived in Hubbardsville, New York, weighed a whopping 1,600 pounds when he died in 2008 — making him over eight times heavier than the average man.

Giant anteaters can eat 30,000 ants a day.

During summer, a moose's antlers can grow by up to an inch every day.

Although polar bears appear white, their fur is actually transparent. It only looks white because it reflects visible light. Beneath their fur, polar bear skin is actually black.

A bite from a grizzly bear can crush a bowling ball.

Grey squirrels can fall 100 feet from a tree without injuring themselves, because their bushy tail acts as a parachute.

Sloths move so slowly that algae grows on their fur. But they are surprisingly good swimmers and, like humans, can do the breaststroke with ease.

Beavers have been known to build dams over 2,750 feet long — that's more than half a mile.

A kinkajou's tail is twice as long as its body. While sleeping high in the forest canopy, it often wraps itself up in its tail and uses it as a pillow.

Like humans, cows form close friendships and choose to spend much of their time with two to four preferred individuals. They also hold grudges for years and may dislike certain other cows.

The backbone of the tiny hero shrew from Africa is so strong that it can support the weight of a fully-grown man.

A skunk is able to spray a distance of 10 feet with accuracy. The foul smell can linger for weeks and can be detected for anywhere up to a mile downwind.

All domestic golden hamsters are descended from a single female found in Syria in 1930.

WILDLIFE HOMES

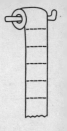

Aardvark – burrow

Alligator – nest

Badger – sett

Beaver – lodge

Eagle – eyrie

Fox – den or earth

Hare – form

Lion – den

Mole – tunnel

Otter – holt

Rabbit – burrow or warren

Tiger – lair

Squirrel – drey

Wolf – lair or den

BABY CREATURES

Badger – kit or cub

Beaver – kitten

Boar – shoat or farrow

Coyote – whelp

Deer – fawn

Eagle – eaglet

Echidna – puggle

Eel – elver

Elephant – calf

Falcon – eyas

Ferret – kit

Fish – fry

Fox – cub

Gerbil – pup

Goat – kid

Goose – gosling

Hare – leveret

Hedgehog – hoglet

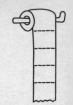

Hippopotamus – calf

Horse – foal

Jellyfish – planula or ephyra

Kangaroo – joey

Llama – cria

Mole – pup

Otter – pup, cub, kit or whelp

Owl – owlet

Oyster – spat

Partridge – cheeper

Pigeon – squab

Porcupine – porcupette

Rabbit – kitten

Seal – calf

Sheep – lamb

Spider – spiderling

Swan – cygnet

Turkey – poult

Whale – calf

MALES AND
FEMALES

Alligator – bull and cow

Badger – boar and sow

Deer – stag or buck and doe or hind

Donkey – jack and jenny

Duck – drake and duck or hen

Elephant – bull and cow

Falcon – tiercel and formel

Ferret – hob and jill

Fox – dog and vixen

Gerbil – buck and doe

Giraffe – bull and cow

Goat – billy and nanny

Hare – buck and doe

Hippopotamus – bull and cow

Horse – stallion and mare

Kangaroo – boomer and flyer

Mole – boar and sow

Pig – boar and sow

Rabbit – buck and doe

Seal – bull and cow

Sheep – ram and ewe

Swan – cob and pen

Whale – bull and cow

Zebra – stallion and mare

SPECIES WHERE THE FEMALE IS MUCH BIGGER

Blanket octopus – 10,000:1

Bone-eating marine worm – 57:1

Green spoon worm – 50:1

Anglerfish – 40:1

Golden orb-weaver spider – 10:1

Limpet – 10:1

Burrowing barnacle – 8:1

Great bustard – 3:1

Black widow spider – 2:1

Praying mantis – 2:1

LONG
MIGRATIONS

Arctic tern – 44,375 miles

Sooty shearwater – 40,625 miles

Alaskan bar-tailed godwit – 15,500 miles

Grey whale – 14,000 miles

Northern elephant seal – 13,125 miles

Leatherback turtle – 12,500 miles

Humpback whale – 11,700 miles

Globe skimmer dragonfly – 10,625 miles

Adélie penguin – 8,000 miles

Caribou – 3,125 miles

Monarch butterfly – 3,000 miles

Great white shark – 2,500 miles

Salmon – 2,375 miles

Wildebeest – 1,000 miles

CREATURES THAT MATE FOR LIFE

Albatross

Bald eagle

Barn owl

Beaver

Black vulture

California mouse

Condor

Coyote

French angelfish

Gentoo penguin

Gibbon

Golden eagle

Grey goose

Jackdaw

Kirk's dik-dik
(an African antelope)

Lovebird

Malagasy giant rat

Prairie vole

Sandhill crane

Shingleback skink

Swan

Termite

Turtle dove

Wolf

WILD SEX

A pair of Indian pythons were once observed copulating for 180 days.

Since the female bedbug has no sexual opening, the male drills a vagina, using his penis as a drill, before inserting his sperm.

Female porcupines are interested in sex for only about ten hours a year. To woo a partner, the male stands on his hind legs and sprays her with a huge jet of urine from about six feet away.

The seahorse is the only creature where the male becomes pregnant.

The male moth mite is born as a mature insect and at birth helps his mother by using his hind legs to drag his sisters out of the sexual cavity. He then mates with them and continues to hover around his mother's birth passage ready to pounce on the next crop of sisters.

Snow leopards can mate up to 36 times a day.

After mating, the male garter snake from North America seals up the female's sexual opening with a mucous plug to ensure that no other male can mate with her.

Female dragonflies will sometimes fake their own deaths to avoid mating.

Bonobos (pygmy chimpanzees) and dolphins are the only animals other than humans that are known to engage in sex for pleasure rather than for the purpose of fertilisation.

Water mites employ bondage techniques during reproduction. While mating, the male pins the female to the ground with tiny hooks so that she can hardly move. He also glues himself to her with a special secretion to ensure there is no escape.

The male orb-web spider has detachable genitalia, allowing him to flee while simultaneously completing intercourse before the larger female eats him.

Adélie penguins have been seen to indulge in necrophilia.

The testes of a species of fruit fly, *Drosophila bifurca*, make up 11 per cent of its body mass. When straightened out, its coiled sperm are more than two inches long – over 1,000 times bigger than human sperm.

A male rhinoceros has been known to mount a female for an hour, ejaculating every ten minutes.

A small Australian marsupial, the antechinus, mates itself to death. During the mating season, the males have sex with as many females as possible – in robust romps that can last for 14 hours – but the exertion proves too much for them, and their bodies fail shortly afterwards, leading to death.

Stick insects have been known to mate for 79 days.

The female praying mantis eats her partner after – and sometimes during – sex. But his sex drive is so strong that he can carry on regardless even while she is munching away at him.

The Argentine lake duck has a penis that is 17 inches long – more than twice the length of the bird's body. He sometimes uses it to lasso a female that is trying to escape.

ANIMALS THAT MASTURBATE ... AND HAVE BEEN CAUGHT IN THE ACT

Adélie penguin	Horse
Cape ground squirrel	Japanese macaque
Cat	Lemur
Chimpanzee	Marine iguana
Dog	Moose
Dolphin	Porcupine
Elephant	Turtle
Ferret	Vampire bat
Gorilla	Walrus

AVERAGE ERECT PENIS LENGTHS FOR DIFFERENT ANIMALS

Blue whale – 8ft

Elephant – 6ft

Bull – 3ft

Horse – 2ft 6in

Rhinoceros – 2ft

Donkey – 1ft 8in

Pig – 1ft 6in

Man – 5.2in

Chimpanzee – 3¼in

Gorilla – 1¼in

Cat – ¾in

Mosquito – one-hundredth of an inch

AVERAGE
LIFE SPANS

Quahog clam – 220 years

Giant tortoise – 150 years

Whale – 90 years

Crocodile – 80 years

Tuatara – 70 years

Elephant – 60 years

Koi carp – 55 years

Alligator – 45 years

Orangutan – 45 years

Hippopotamus – 43 years

African grey parrot – 40 years

Camel – 40 years

Chimpanzee – 40 years

Dogfish – 35 years

Gorilla – 35 years

Grizzly bear – 32 years

Horse – 28 years

Giraffe – 25 years

King cobra – 18 years

Cat – 17 years

Lion – 14 years

Frog – 7 years

Earthworm – 6 years

Robin – 1.1 years

Worker bee – 5 weeks

Mayfly – 12 hours

MONKEY (AND APE) BUSINESS

The nose of a proboscis monkey can be seven inches long.

Gorillas share 98.3 per cent of their DNA with humans.

Koko, a captive gorilla in the United States, was taught sign language and eventually learned 1,000 signs and could understand 2,000 words of English.

Each gorilla has a unique noseprint.

The scientific name of the western lowland gorilla is *Gorilla gorilla gorilla*.

The scream of a howler monkey can be heard up to three miles away.

Patas monkeys can run at speeds of 35mph – almost as fast as a racehorse.

Although chimpanzees mainly eat fruits and leaves, they do also eat meat, their favourite being red colobus monkey. In the late 1990s, chimps living in a national park in Uganda were killing up to half the local red colobus monkey population every year.

A pygmy marmoset is no bigger than a banana.

Mandrill monkeys have fangs that are longer than a lion's.

Adult male orangutans spend 90 per cent of their time alone.

Mother orangutans carry their offspring for the first five years, and may suckle them for as long as seven years.

White-faced capuchin monkeys smear their fur with giant millipedes, which act as insect repellent.

A spider monkey's tail can pick up items as small as a peanut.

A male baboon can kill a leopard.

MOST POWERUL BITES

(MEASURED IN POUNDS
PER SQUARE INCH)

1. Nile crocodile – 5,000psi

2. Saltwater crocodile – 3,690psi

3. American alligator – 2,125psi

4. Jaguar – 2,000psi

5. Hippopotamus – 1,825psi

6. Bull shark – 1,350psi

7. Gorilla – 1,300psi

8. Polar bear – 1,235psi

9. Grizzly bear – 1,200psi

10. Spotted hyena – 1,100psi

11. Tiger – 1,050psi

12. Alligator snapping turtle – 1,004psi

13. Kodiak bear – 930psi

14. Great white shark – 669psi

15. Lion – 650psi

WHAT'S DUNG
IS DUNG

Wombat poo is cube-shaped so that it can mark its territory. Its distinctive shape allows the wombat to differentiate it from other animals' poos. Also, because wombats tend to poo on rocks and other precarious places, cube-shaped poo is less likely to roll off. A single animal can produce up to 100 cubes in a night.

Black vultures deliberately poo on their own legs, probably to help eliminate the bacteria they acquire from standing in rotting meat.

During the First World War, bat droppings were used to make explosives, because bat guano consists chiefly of saltpeter (potassium nitrate), a key ingredient in fireworks.

Parrotfish feed on coral and then excrete the digestible parts as tiny grains of sand, creating new beaches and islands. One humphead parrotfish can poo 200 pounds of sand each year. Almost every grain of sand on Hawaii's stunning white beaches is fish poo.

Giant pandas produce up to 48 pounds of poo every day.

Kopi luwak, one of the world's most expensive types of coffee, is made from beans collected from the poo of the palm civet, a small, cat-like creature from Asia.

Sloths only poo once a week, an event that requires them to come down from their treetop homes and perform what is

known as the 'poo dance'. Immediately before the moment of excretion, they wiggle their bottoms and sway rhythmically from side to side, possibly to get rid of irritating parasites in their fur.

Because elephants only digest 45 per cent of their food and their waste is mostly made up of fibre, companies in India and Thailand have developed a method for converting elephant poo into paper. Every day, an elephant can produce enough dung to make 100 pages of paper.

Hippos spin their tails to launch their poo, torpedo-like, under water, sending pieces flying a distance of several feet. This is believed to be attractive to a potential mate. Large herds of hippos can produce more than nine tons of excrement each day, the sheer volume killing off fish that have the misfortune to live downstream.

MARSUPIALS

Koala fingerprints are so similar to humans' that they have hindered crime scene investigations in Australia.

Koalas hardly ever drink water. Instead they rely on eating eucalyptus leaves, which contain 55 per cent water.

Koala bears sleep for up to 22 hours a day.

About 70 per cent of koalas have chlamydia.

Numbats eat as many as 20,000 termites a day.

Female kangaroos have three vaginas.

Female red kangaroos are able to simultaneously produce two different types of milk from adjacent teats to feed joeys at different stages of development.

Kangaroos are excellent swimmers and have been found swimming a mile out to sea.

Marsupial moles have upside-down pouches to keep sand and dirt out when digging.

Tasmanian devils scare away predators and rivals by sneezing loudly.

Gilbert's potoroo, or the 'rat-kangaroo' is one of the most endangered animals in the world today, with a population of about 100.

When threatened, opossums play dead ('playing possum'), but they're not playing at all – they simply faint from fear. Their lips are drawn back, the teeth are bared, saliva forms around the mouth, the eyes close, and a foul-smelling fluid is secreted from the anal glands. The stiff, curled body can be prodded or even carried away without showing any sign of life, and it can remain in this state for four hours before regaining consciousness.

When baby opossums are born, they are so tiny that an entire litter can fit in a teaspoon.

GESTATION PERIODS

Elephant – 645 days

Killer whale – 510 days

Walrus – 456 days

Rhinoceros – 450 days

Giraffe – 430 days

Donkey – 365 days

Alpaca – 345 days

Horse – 336 days

Seal – 330 days

Cow – 286 days

Human – 270 days

Red deer – 260 days

Gorilla – 250 days

Moose – 245 days

Hippopotamus – 240 days

Black bear – 220 days

Porcupine – 202 days

Baboon – 187 days

Rhesus monkey – 164 days

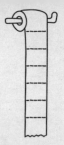

Goat – 150 days

Sheep – 147 days

Beaver – 128 days

Pig – 113 days

Lion – 108 days

Otter – 73 days

Guinea pig – 65 days

Domestic cat – 64 days

Wolf – 64 days

Dog – 61 days

Red fox – 52 days

Kangaroo – 42 days

Mole – 40 days

Grey squirrel – 35 days

Hedgehog – 35 days

Rabbit – 31 days

Wombat – 27 days

Gerbil – 25 days

Mouse – 21 days

Hamster – 20 days

Opossum – 12 days

SUPER SENSES

Camels can see with their eyes closed. They have three eyelids, two of which have lashes to protect their eyes during sandstorms. The third works like a windscreen wiper to clean sand from their eyes but is thin enough to see through even when their eyes are shut.

Shrimps are able to see five times more colours than humans, because some species have 15 different types of colour photoreceptors, compared to our three.

Reindeer change their eyesight in winter, extending their vision into ultraviolet so that the lichen they feed on glows purple against the white snow.

Peregrine falcons can spot prey from over a mile away.

A dragonfly's eyesight is so good that it catches 95 per cent of its prey, compared to a lion's 40 per cent.

A Cuban boa can capture a bat in a pitch-black cave as it can see infrared heat, which is invisible to human eyes. The snake does not even need to use its eyes to detect the infrared, because it has a line of heat-sensitive pits along the bottom of its jaw.

The bodies of catfish are covered in taste receptors so they can tell when a tasty meal is close by.

Polar bears can sniff out a seal on ice 20 miles away.

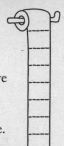

A dog's sense of smell is about 100,000 times more effective than a human's.

A barn owl's ears allow it to pinpoint prey to the millimetre.

Elephants can hear thunderstorms from over 300 miles away, the equivalent of someone in London hearing a storm in Edinburgh.

Elephants can hear even better by lifting one leg off the ground.

HIGH AND MIGHTY

Even though a giraffe's neck can be seven feet long, it only possesses the same number of bones — seven — as a human neck.

A single kick from a giraffe can kill a lion.

Giraffes sleep for as little as four hours a day and usually in the form of a number of power naps lasting no longer than a few minutes.

Elephants can't jump, because their leg muscles are relatively weak for their body size.

An elephant's trunk contains more than 40,000 muscles and is sensitive enough to pick up a single blade of grass but strong enough to rip branches off a tree.

Elephants will drink up to 50 gallons of water a day — enough to fill a bathtub, or more than 900 glasses of water.

Rhinoceros skin is over ten times thicker than human skin.

Hippopotamus sweat is red. The red pigment not only acts as a sunscreen, it also kills bacteria on the hippo's skin.

Despite possessing a 10-foot-long stomach, a hippopotamus can run faster than a man.

Although hippos spend most of their time in the water, they're too bulky to swim or even float. They move around under water by pushing off from the riverbed or trotting along it.

A hippo can open its mouth wide enough for a four-foot-tall child to stand inside, although it's probably not a good idea.

TV WESTERN STEEDS

AND THEIR RIDERS

Beauty (Adam Cartwright in *Bonanza*)

Brandy (Cheyenne Bodie)

Buck (Trampas in *The Virginian*)

Chub (Hoss Cartwright in *Bonanza*)

Cochise (Little Joe Cartwright in *Bonanza*)

Diablo (the Cisco Kid)

Buttermilk (Dale Evans)

Jouster (Rowdy Yates in *Rawhide*)

Jubilee (Jim Hardie in *Tales of Wells Fargo*)

Little Buck (Flint McCullough in *Wagon Train*)

Loco (Pancho in *The Cisco Kid*)

Lucky (Dick West in *The Range Rider*)

Marshall (Matt Dillon in *Gunsmoke*)

Midnight (Gil Favor in *Rawhide*)

Rafter (Paladin in *Have Gun – Will Travel*)

Rawhide (Range Rider)

Rebel (Buck Cannon in *The High Chaparral*)

Scout (Tonto)

Silver (the Lone Ranger)

Target (Annie Oakley)

Topper (Hopalong Cassidy)

Tornado (Zorro)

Trigger (Roy Rogers)

HARD TO FATHOM

WEIRD FACTS FROM THE DEEP

Most sharks never sleep because they must constantly pump water through their mouth and over their gills to breathe or they will die.

Because their fins are so stiff, sharks can't swim backwards.

Sharks lose teeth regularly and can go through 30,000 in a lifetime.

Sharks do not have vocal cords, so they make no sound, which is why they are known as 'silent killers'.

Of over 250 species of shark, only 18 are known to be dangerous to humans.

The smallest shark is the dwarf lantern at just six inches long. The largest, the whale shark, can reach over 41 feet in length.

Sharks have been living in Earth's oceans for 450 million years. The oldest known species of shark still in existence today is the goblin shark, which has been around for 120 million years.

Items found inside sharks' stomachs include torpedoes, bicycle parts, car number plates, a horse's head, a porcupine, bottles of wine, petrol cans and even a suit of armour.

Electric eels can produce a discharge of 650 volts – enough to stun, or even kill, a small horse.

The ovaries of a female oarfish can measure more than seven feet long.

A jellyfish is 95 per cent water.

A recently dead jellyfish can still sting. In an incident on a New Hampshire beach, a single washed up lion's mane jellyfish broke up and the fragmented tentacles stung 150 people.

The tentacles of a lion's mane jellyfish can stretch for over 100 feet – considerably longer than a tennis court.

The sting from the Australian sea wasp, a species of box jellyfish, can kill a human in four minutes.

The venom of the Irukandji jellyfish that lives off the northern coast of Australia is 100 times more powerful than that of a cobra.

Despite being the largest animal on Earth, the blue whale can't swallow anything larger than a beach ball.

The blue whale's heart beats only nine times a minute. Its heartbeat can be heard over two miles away. Its heart can weigh in excess of 1,300 pounds and is about the size of a Volkswagen Beetle.

The arteries of a blue whale are so large that a four-year-old child could swim through them.

The clicking noise made by a sperm whale is loud enough to burst a diver's eardrums.

Some piranhas are vegetarians, feeding solely off river weeds.

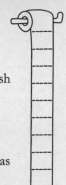

Single shoals of herring can contain tens of millions of fish and stretch for over six miles.

A stressed octopus will sometimes eat its own arms.

Black sea bass spend the first few years of their lives as females before changing into males.

A starfish can turn its stomach inside out to eat food that is too large to fit through its small mouth.

The climbing perch can leave the water and shin up trees in pursuit of insects.

The giant spider crab of Japan measures 12 feet wide from the tips of its claws. If it felt so inclined, it could hug a hippo.

The eyes of a giant squid are larger than a human head, yet its eyesight is much worse than a human's.

ANIMAL STARS
AND THEIR MOST
FAMOUS ROLES

Andre the seal, subject of the 1994 film *Andre*, was played by a seal named Tory.

Beethoven, the lovable St Bernard in the 1992 film of the same name and its sequel *Beethoven 2*, was played by Chris.

Benji was originally played by a mixed breed dog named Higgins.

Cheeta in the Tarzan movies of the early 1930s was played by a trained chimp named Jiggs.

Clyde, who starred alongside Clint Eastwood in the 1978 film *Every Which Way But Loose*, was played by an orangutan named Manis.

Eddie, the Jack Russell terrier in *Frasier*, was played by Moose, who was noted for his ability to stare long and hard at actor Kelsey Grammer. At the height of his fame, Moose, who was reportedly paid $10,000 per episode, received more fan mail than his human co-stars. As Moose aged, he shared the part with his son Enzo.

Flipper was played at first by a dolphin named Susie and then primarily by another called Kathy.

Hooch, the canine co-star of *Turner and Hooch*, was played by Beasley, a French mastiff. It was his only movie role.

Fury was played by a horse named Highland Dale.

Lassie was originally played by Pal, who was a male collie even though Lassie was female.

Mister Ed, the talking horse, was played by Bamboo Harvester.

Toto in *The Wizard of Oz* was played by a female Cairn terrier named Terry.

Trigger, Roy Rogers' equine sidekick, was played by Golden Cloud, although Rogers renamed him Trigger. When the horse died in 1965, Rogers had him stuffed and mounted by a taxidermist.

Wellard, Robbie Jackson's dog in *EastEnders*, was played by three different Belgian Tervuren dogs – Zenna, her daughter Chancer, and her granddaughter Kyte.

Willy, the star of the 1993 film *Free Willy*, was played by a male orca named Keiko.

FEATHERED AND FURRED FELONS

In 2015, officials in India arrested a pigeon that was suspected of being a spy. The bird's body was stamped with what appeared to be a Pakistani phone number.

A German Shepherd dog was arrested in the Spanish city of Seville in 1983 for snatching handbags from shoppers.

In Basel, Switzerland in 1474, a rooster was put on trial for 'the heinous and unnatural crime of laying an egg', which the townspeople were concerned was spawned by Satan.

A donkey named Blacky was jailed in Chiapas, Mexico, in 2008 after biting a man in the chest and kicking a second man.

A pig was arrested in 2018 for stalking Ryan Singley as he walked home from the train station in Elyria, Ohio, in the early hours of the morning.

Police in India's Maharashtra state arrested a foul-mouthed parrot named Hariyal in 2015 for hurling abuse at an elderly woman whenever she walked past the house. The parrot had been taught to swear by the woman's stepson who was involved in a bitter property dispute with her.

In 1740, a cow in France was hanged after being found guilty of sorcery.

In 2009, police in Nigeria detained a goat on suspicion of attempted armed robbery. Vigilantes took the animal to the police, claiming that it was an armed robber who had used black magic to transform himself into a goat to evade arrest after trying to steal a car.

Eight donkeys were imprisoned in Orai, India, for four days in 2017 for eating $1,000 worth of plants.

A pig was publicly hanged in Falaise, France, in 1386 for causing the death of a three-month-old baby.

A chicken was fined $60 for illegally crossing the road in Johannesburg, California, in 2005. Ophelia, a black Polish hen, strayed onto the street in violation of state law which bans livestock from highways. Her owners, Linc and Helena Moore, successfully appealed by arguing that the chicken was domesticated and could not therefore be considered as livestock.

BIZARRE BIRDS

It takes 90 minutes to hard boil an ostrich egg. The shell is so strong that it can support the weight of a clinically obese person.

An ostrich's eye is bigger than its brain.

When a bald eagle loses the feathers on one wing, it moults them on the other wing to remain balanced.

Woodpeckers bang their heads into trees at 15mph, 12,000 times a day.

A woodpecker's tongue can be up to four inches long and when retracted it wraps around the inside of the bird's head.

If a turkey vulture feels threatened but has eaten too much to be able to fly, it regurgitates its food to empty its stomach so that it can take to the skies. It can propel vomit over a distance of 10 feet.

Chickens communicate using over 200 distinct noises.

A pelican can hold three gallons of water in its pouch. The capacity of a pelican's pouch is three times greater than that of its stomach.

All 17 species of penguin are found exclusively in the southern hemisphere.

In some species of penguin – such as the king and the emperor – the male incubates the eggs while the female goes off hunting.

If a female emperor penguin loses a chick, she will often kidnap another penguin's baby.

Owls have fringes on the trailing edges of their wing feathers that allow them to fly in silence, approaching prey undetected.

Up to 988 million birds die each year from crashing into windows in the United States alone.

Starlings were introduced to the United States in the late nineteenth century by the American Acclimatization Society, a group that wanted to bring to America every species of bird mentioned in Shakespeare's works.

The wandering albatross can fly up to 600 miles in a single day without once flapping its wings.

A hummingbird's wings beat 80 times per second.

The tail of the quetzal from Central America is so long that it has to take off from a branch by launching itself backwards into space like a skydiver.

A pair of swifts with chicks to feed can catch up to 20,000 insects and spiders in a single day.

A young swift may fly non-stop for over 300,000 miles between leaving the nest and making its first landing. Swifts even sleep and mate on the wing.

In the two weeks it spends in the nest, a baby robin will eat about 14 feet of earthworms.

Flamingos aren't naturally pink. They get their distinctive colour from eating pigments found in algae and invertebrates.

The shrike gets its common name of 'butcher bird' because it impales its victims – usually mice, lizards or small birds – on sharp thorns while it eats them.

A puffin can carry as many as ten fish in its beak at a time.

Although the kiwi is only about the same size as a chicken, it lays an egg that is ten times larger than a hen's. The kiwi's egg is nearly a quarter of its body weight.

ANIMALS
BEHAVING BADLY

In 1997, Carmen LaBrecque was chased home through the streets of Salem, Massachusetts, for more than 15 minutes by a crazed skunk.

A giraffe was the brains behind a mass escape from a travelling Dutch circus in 2008. It kicked a hole in the cage, allowing 15 camels, two zebras and an unspecified number of llamas and pot-bellied pigs to make a break for freedom.

A black bear passed out on the lawn of a resort in Washington state in 2004 after drinking 36 cans of beer.

Chippy, an 11-year-old chimpanzee, made nuisance calls to workers at Scotland's Blair Drummond Safari Park for three days and nights in 2001 after stealing a mobile phone from a keeper's pocket. The chimp kept pressing numbers stored in the phone's memory and hitting the redial button. Staff were about to call the police when they recognised the shriek of a chimp on the other end of the line.

Ed Stuardi, from Mobile, Alabama, was stalked by a lovelorn, 150-pound emu over a period of several days in 1998 before animal rescuers took the bird away.

An octopus stole a $700 camera from a diver off the coast of New Zealand in 2010. The octopus prised the camera from Victor Huang's grasp but after a five-minute chase, Huang managed to snatch it back.

A goat put three people in hospital after rampaging through a Melbourne nursing home in 2010.

A herd of hungry cows ate through the fuselage of a light aeroplane that had landed in a field near Hereford in 2004, causing $15,000 of damage and leaving the plane grounded.

In 2004, a moose stole a bicycle that Bjorn and Monica Helamb had placed in their garden in Vuoggatjalme, Sweden, to stop the animal eating their rose bushes. The determined moose, a frequent visitor to the garden, leaned through the bicycle frame to reach the flowers and then wandered off with it hanging around her neck. The bicycle was found 500 yards away, mangled beyond repair.

MOST VENOMOUS SNAKES

(BY TOXICITY)

1. Inland taipan or fierce snake (Australia)

2. Eastern brown snake (Australia/Indonesia)

3. Coastal taipan (Australia)

4. Beaked sea snake (Australia)

5. Black mamba (Africa)

6. Belcher's sea snake (Australia)

7. Tiger snake (Australia)

8. Philippine cobra (Philippines)

9. Common krait (India)

10. Death adder (Australia)

IN COLD BLOOD

REPTILES AND AMPHIBIANS

Chameleon spit is 400 times thicker than human spit.

Many chameleons have tongues that are twice the length of their bodies.

Some lizards have detachable tails which they use to escape an attack. In many cases, the disguarded tail will continue to wriggle to distract the predator while the lizard makes its getaway.

The tuatara lizard, which lives off the coast of New Zealand, has a third eye. Located on top of the lizard's head, the parietal eye has no iris and therefore cannot focus on an image, but it can differentiate between light and shade, helping the tuatara to determine the time of year for giving birth.

The basilisk lizard of Central America can run on water. It moves quickly at five feet per second so that its long, fringed toes barely break the surface of the water and its feet create an air pocket that prevents it from sinking. Its long tail also acts as a rudder.

Each time a rattlesnake sheds its skin, it adds another segment to its rattle.

The most venomous snake in the world hardly ever kills anyone. One bite from the inland taipan, or fierce snake, of central Australia contains enough lethal venom to kill at least 100 men, but, despite its name, it has a placid nature and because it lives in the arid outback it rarely comes into contact with people. Only one fatality has ever been recorded from an inland taipan bite.

Australia is home to 20 of the world's 25 most venomous snakes.

A reticulated python can survive for almost two years without food.

The male Darwin's frog, found on the southern coast of Chile, swallows the eggs his mate lays and keeps them in a sac under his chin. When the tadpoles are big enough, he opens his mouth and releases them.

The paradoxical frog of South America shrinks as it grows. It is smaller as an adult than it is as a tadpole. Whereas the tadpole can reach a length of 10 inches, the adult frog never exceeds three inches.

The two inch-long golden poison frog has enough venom to kill ten adult humans.

When toads vomit, they not only bring up the contents of the stomach but the stomach itself. The entire stomach hangs inside out from the toad's mouth for a few moments before being swallowed again.

Only one out of every 100 eggs laid by a female sea turtle lives for a year and only one out of every 1,000 eggs reaches adulthood.

A sea turtle increases its weight by 6,000 times as it grows from hatchling to adult.

Loggerhead turtles are able to eat poisonous Portuguese man o' wars without coming to any harm.

Due to a restrictive membrane, crocodiles can't stick their tongues out. But alligators can.

Crocodiles can't chew either. They clamp their prey in their jaws and twist a lump off by writhing around in the water.

To prevent indigestion, crocodiles always carry about five pounds of pebbles in their stomach.

Although a crocodile's jaw can bite through a human leg, it has very little opening strength and its mouth can be held shut with a rubber band.

SOME ANIMALS AND BIRDS THAT HAVE BECOME EXTINCT SINCE 1900

East Greenland reindeer (Greenland, 1900)

Long-tailed hopping mouse (Australia, 1901)

Martinique giant rice rat (Martinique, 1902)

Bulldog rat (Christmas Island, 1903)

Japanese wolf (Japan, 1905)

Merriam's elk (United States, 1906)

Black mamo or hoa (Hawaii, 1907)

Huia (New Zealand, 1907)

Dawson's caribou (Canada, 1908)

Slender-billed grackle (Mexico, 1910)

Newfoundland wolf (Newfoundland, 1911)

Laughing owl (New Zealand, 1914)

Passenger pigeon (North America, 1914)

Rodrigues day gecko (Mauritius, 1917)

Carolina parakeet (United States, 1918)

Norfolk Island starling (Australia, 1925)

Bubal hartebeest (Algeria, 1925)

Paradise parrot (Australia, 1927)

Syrian wild ass or Syrian onager (Jordan, 1927)

Thylacine (Australia, 1930)

Schomburgk's deer (Thailand, 1932)

Desert rat-kangaroo (Australia, 1935)

Bali tiger (Bali, 1937)

Grand Cayman thrush (Cayman Islands, 1938)

Toolache wallaby (Australia, 1939)

Caribbean monk seal (Caribbean, 1952)

Pig-footed bandicoot (Australia, 1950s)

Barbados raccoon (Barbados, 1964)

Mexican grizzly bear (Mexico, 1964)

Guam flying fox (Guam, 1968)

New Zealand bush wren (New Zealand, 1972)

Round Island burrowing boa (Mauritius, 1975)

Colombian grebe (Colombia, 1977)

Dusky seaside sparrow (Florida, 1987)

Golden toad (Costa Rica, 1989)

Pyrenean ibex (Spain, 2000)

Eastern cougar (North America, 2011)

Western black rhinoceros (Cameroon, 2011)

Pinta Island tortoise (Ecuador, 2012)

Formosan clouded leopard (Taiwan, 2013)

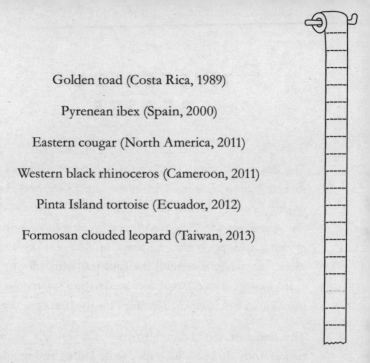

MYSTERIOUS
BEASTS

The Beast of Bodmin is a large, black panther-like cat said to have roamed Cornwall from the late 1970s, occasionally slaying livestock. There have been over 60 sightings down the years, but a 1995 government investigation found no evidence to support the existence of a big cat on Bodmin Moor. Just when it seemed the fuss was dying down, 1998 video footage showed what appeared to be a mysterious large black cat in the distance. The hunt for the beast goes on.

The Beast of Gévaudan terrorised the French mountain region from 1764 to 1767, supposedly killing and mutilating more than 100 adults and children. It was described as having short red hair, a large, dog-like head and huge teeth. The killings finally stopped when a nobleman shot it dead with a gun loaded with silver bullets. Some said it was a very large wolf, others insisted that it was a werewolf, while recent speculation suggests the culprit was an escaped lion.

The Beast of Truro supposedly preyed on pet cats and livestock around the Cape Cod area of Massachusetts in the early 1980s. A mountain lion was widely held responsible, even though they are not native to the region.

The Flathead Lake Monster is a Nessie-type creature that is rumoured to inhabit the depths of Flathead Lake, Montana. It was first spotted in 1889 when passengers on a boat saw a large, whale-like object in the water. Although a 1950s reward for anyone who could catch the monster went unclaimed, sightings persist, with about 13 in 1993 alone, most describing a dark, eel-like creature between 20 and 40 feet long.

The Gloucester Sea Serpent was active off the coast of Massachusetts around 1817. When a small black creature with humps was later found on a local beach, this was declared to be an offspring of the serpent and a new species was named. However, a naturalist who examined it said it was just a snake with tumours on its spine.

The Kongamato is a huge bird-like creature, said to resemble a prehistoric pterosaur, that has been seen from time to time in parts of Africa. In 1956, an engineer in northern Rhodesia described seeing two such beasts flying overhead. The following year, a man said his serious chest wound was caused by an attack from a large, bird-like creature. When asked to draw it, he apparently drew a pterosaur.

Old Yellow Top was a seven-foot-tall, Big Foot-like animal sighted several times around Cobalt, Ontario, between 1906 and 1970. Canadians named it after its light-coloured mane and the blonde patch of hair on its head.

The Surrey Puma is the name given to the legendary big cat that has been seen occasionally in rural locations to the south of London since 1959. At the height of its fame in the 1960s, Godalming police station received 362 reported sightings in a two-year period. Nevertheless, the Surrey Puma remains elusive and has yet to help police with their enquiries.

DOG TALES

Dogs wag their tail to the right when they're happy and to the left when they're frightened.

Dogs sweat mainly through their paws.

Dogs can shake 70 per cent of water out of their fur in four seconds, generating more G-force than Formula One drivers experience in sharp corners.

The average dog is as intelligent as a two-year-old child.

Small dogs have more dreams than big dogs. A toy poodle may dream once every ten minutes whereas a great dane may have an hour between each dream.

The basenji, a breed of African hunting dog, can't bark due its unusually-shaped larynx. Instead it makes a strange yodelling sound.

Dalmatians are born with almost pure white coats. Their first spots usually appear about four weeks after birth.

As many as 30 per cent of Dalmatians are partially deaf and about five per cent are deaf in both ears.

The Doberman Pinscher takes its name from a nineteenth-century German tax collector, Karl Friedrich Dobermann, who bred the animals to help him put the frighteners on his clients.

Poodles were originally bred to retrieve game from water and the reason the fur on the lower half of their bodies was clipped was to make them better swimmers.

Surveys suggest that the Afghan hound is the most stupid breed of dog and the Border collie the most intelligent.

The Dandie Dinmont terrier, named after a character created by Sir Walter Scott in his 1815 novel *Guy Mannering*, is now considered rarer than the giant panda.

In Croatia, scientists discovered that lampposts were falling down because a chemical in the urine of male dogs was rotting the metal.

One-third of dog owners admit that they talk to their dogs on the phone or leave messages for them on answering machines while they are away.

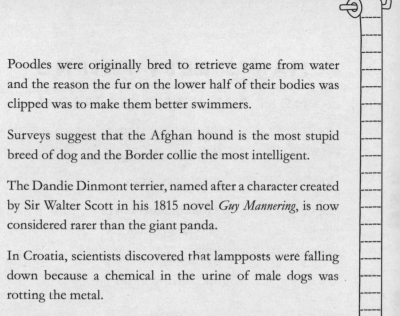

MAN'S BEST FRIEND

MOST POPULAR DOG BREEDS

Labrador retriever

German shepherd

Golden retriever

Bulldog

Beagle

French bulldog

Poodle

Rottweiller

Yorkshire terrier

Boxer

German shorthaired pointer

Siberian husky

Dachshund

Great Dane

Doberman pinscher

Australian shepherd

Miniature schnauzer

Pembroke Welsh corgi

Shih tzu

Cavalier King Charles spaniel

CAT NIPS

Cats can make over 100 different vocal sounds compared to a dog's ten.

The domestic cat is the only species of cat that holds its tail vertically while walking. Wild cats hold their tails horizontally or between their legs when on the move.

All tortoiseshell cats are female except for the occasional sterile male.

Cats are unable to taste anything sweet.

A cat can jump up to five times its own height in a single leap.

Cats usually have 18 toes – five on each front paw and four on each back paw. However, polydactyl cats have been reported with as many as 28 toes in total.

Cats rarely meow at each other, only at humans. Typically they purr, hiss or spit at other cats.

There are an estimated 100 million feral cats worldwide.

In ancient Egypt, people used to shave their eyebrows to mourn the death of their cat.

A tabby cat named Dusty, born in Texas in 1935, gave birth to 420 kittens during her life. She produced her last kitten in 1952.

A wooden casket containing the ashes of Frisky, the cat that appeared in the opening titles of *Coronation Street* for more than 1,000 episodes, sold at auction for $1,000 in 2010.

A bronze statue was built at a Scottish distillery in honour of a cat named Towser who caught nearly 30,000 mice in his 24-year lifetime.

The cheetah is the only big cat that can't retract its claws.

Although the lion is known as the 'king of the jungle', almost all lions live on grasslands. Only one population of wild forest-dwelling lions remains – in Gir Forest National Park, India.

A male lion's roar can be heard five miles away.

PET PROJECTS

Artist Salvador Dali kept a pet ocelot named Babou, who would join him in high-class restaurants. He also had a fondness for anteaters and was pictured walking one on a leash through the streets of Paris in 1969.

American novelist Patricia Highsmith kept 300 snails as pets, even taking them in her handbag to dinner parties.

When Lord Byron was told that his dog was not allowed to accompany him to Trinity College, Cambridge, he took along a tame bear instead. The college authorities had no legal basis for complaint, and the bear, which he walked on a chain, stayed with him until he graduated.

French poet Gérard de Nerval used to walk his pet lobster, Thibault, on a long blue ribbon through the gardens of the Palais-Royal in Paris.

Norwegian playwright Henrik Ibsen kept a live scorpion in an empty glass on his writing desk.

The Marquis de Lafayette owned a pet alligator, which he took with him on an 1825 visit to the White House, when John Quincy Adams was US President. The reptile was housed in a bath tub in the East Room.

American-born French entertainer Josephine Baker had a pet cheetah, Chiquita.

Silent movie star Clara Bow had the fur of her two chow dogs dyed red to match the colour of her own hair.

Virginia Woolf kept a pet marmoset named Mitz.

A young Elvis Presley had a pet kangaroo that was given to him by a booking agent. Presley later donated the animal to Memphis Zoo.

Wolfgang Amadeus Mozart kept a pet starling for three years, and when the bird died he arranged a funeral and even composed an epitaph for it.

George Orwell owned a pet goat named Muriel.

Michael Jackson's pet chimpanzee Bubbles accompanied him almost everywhere, and together they once drank tea with the mayor of Osaka in Japan.

American First Lady Grace Coolidge kept a pet raccoon, Rebecca.

English actor Sir Ralph Richardson used to take his parrot Jose for rides on his motorcycle, often arriving at the theatre with the bird perched on his shoulder.

Florence Nightingale often kept a small owl in her pocket.

Paris Hilton had to visit hospital in 2006 after being bitten by her pet kinkajou, Baby Luv.

Napoleon Bonaparte's wife Josephine owned a female orangutan, which, immaculately dressed in a white cotton chemise, would join her at the dinner table.

George Clooney used to own a pot-bellied pig named Max.

Mary, Queen of Scots and Charles I were both accompanied to their executions by their faithful dogs.

HEROIC PETS

Priscilla, a pig owned by Victoria Herberta, of Houston, Texas, hit the headlines in 1984 when she saved 11-year-old Anthony Melton from drowning in Lake Somerville. After swimming to the boy's assistance, Priscilla used her snout to keep his head above water until he could hold on to her collar and then dragged him ashore.

Toby, a two-year-old golden retriever, performed the Heimlich manoeuvre to save his owner, Debbie Parkhurst, in Maryland in 2007 when she was choking on a piece of apple. As she struggled for breath, Toby pushed her to the ground by putting his front paws on her shoulders and then jumped up and down on her chest, eventually dislodging the apple from her windpipe.

In 1989, Adam McGuire was surfing near Sydney when he was attacked by a shark. As the shark moved in for the kill, it was distracted by a school of dolphins thrashing around in the water. The dolphins then kept the shark at bay by circling McGuire until his friends were able to rescue him.

Max the Labrador saved the life of a stranger who got lost in 2010 during an expedition in Mexico's Sierra Madre Oriental mountains. After 14-year-old Juan Heriberto Trevino became detached from the rest of his group and fell down a ravine, Max appeared on the scene and stayed by the boy's side for the next two days – keeping him warm at night – until rescuers showed up.

When Simon Steggall slipped into a diabetic coma while watching television at his Cambridgeshire home in 2004, his life was saved by his one-and-a-half-stone rabbit, Dory, who jumped up onto his chest and started digging at it furiously. The rabbit's strange behaviour alerted Mrs Steggall, who thought her husband had simply nodded off. 'I work for the ambulance service,' she said afterwards, 'and I'm embarrassed that the rabbit spotted it before I did.'

Gizmo the cat saved owner Ron Perkins from a 2017 fire at his home in Bartow, Florida, by meowing persistently to wake him up as smoke filled the room.

Khan, a Doberman Pinscher, saved 17-month-old Charlotte Svillcic from an attack by a deadly king brown snake in 2007. Charlotte was playing in the garden of the family's home in Adelaide, Australia, when Khan, spotting the snake, grabbed her by the nappy and threw her out of the way. Khan was bitten on the nose by the snake but recovered after an injection of anti-venom.

Seeing a young deer drowning in New York's Long Island Sound in 2017, Storm the golden retriever swam out to the fawn, grabbed it by the neck and then swam back to shore with it. Once on dry land, he started nudging the deer with his nose and pawing it to make sure it was okay.

THE LASSIE SYNDROME

PETS THAT CAME HOME

Geoff Hancock's fox terrier, Whisky, returned to the family home in Melbourne, Australia, in 1973 after making a nine-month, 1,800-mile journey from Darwin.

In 2012, Bucky, a black Labrador, apparently walked 500 miles from Winchester, Virginia, to Myrtle Beach, South Carolina, where his owner, Mark Wessells, had moved to work.

In 1983, Spot, a cross-breed sheepdog, jumped on board a London-bound National Express coach in Cardiff and refused to move. The dog got off at London's Victoria coach station and then, 30 minutes later, just as the coach was about to set off on the return journey, Spot jumped back on, occupied the same seat and completed a 310-mile round trip.

Barbara Paule's cat, Muddy Water White, disappeared in Dayton, Ohio, in 1985 – but returned home to Pennsylvania three years later at the end of a 450-mile trek.

In 2016, Pero the sheepdog walked 240 miles back to his birthplace in Wales after escaping from his new owners in Cumbria. The journey took him 12 days and included crossing two motorways and countless other main roads.

In 1924, Bobbie the Wonder Dog made a journey of 2,550 miles over six months from Indiana to Oregon – across desert and mountains – after becoming separated from his owners on a road trip.

TALENTED PETS

Twiggy, a grey squirrel, was taught to water-ski by Chuck and Lou Ann Best, of Deltona, Florida.

Twinkie, a Jack Russell owned by Doree Sitterly from California, can burst 100 balloons in 39 seconds.

Nora, a grey tabby rescue cat owned by Betsy Alexander and Burnell Yow of Philadelphia, attracted 17 million hits in two years on YouTube with her accomplished piano playing, which *The Times* described as 'halfway between Philip Glass and free jazz'.

Happie, a Nigerian dwarf goat owned by Melody Cooke of Fort Myers, Florida, could ride a skateboard.

Feather, a greyhound owned by Samantha Valle from Frederick, Maryland, can jump a height of 75.5 inches.

Congo, a chimpanzee at London Zoo, painted or drew more than 400 artworks. In 2005, three of his paintings sold for $26,000.

Norman, a French sheepdog owned by Karen Cobb from Canton, Georgia, could ride a scooter.

Bibi, a Congo African grey parrot owned by American Greg Moss, can say 'hello' in over 20 languages.

Otis, a pug owned by Will DaSilva of California, has completed more than 60 tandem skydiving jumps.

PLANTS AND THEIR MEANINGS

Amaryllis: pride

Anemone: frailty

Azalea: temperance

Barberry: sourness

Basil: hatred

Bilberry: treachery

Bindweed: humility

Bluebell: constancy

Buttercup: ingratitude

Cactus: endurance

Dahlia: dignity

Daisy: innocence

Delphinium: haughtiness

Fern: sincerity

Fuchsia: taste

Helenium: tears

Hellebore: scandal

Holly: domestic happiness

Hollyhock: fecundity

Jonquil: desire

Lettuce: cold-heartedness

Lily (white): purity

Loosestrife: pretension

Marigold (French): jealousy

Marjoram: delusion

Mint: virtue

Nettle: slander

Peony (pink): shame

Peony (red): devotion

Phlox: unanimity

Rose (yellow): infidelity

Rudbeckia: justice

St. John's Wort: animosity

Saxifrage: affection

Venus Fly Trap: deceit

ROSES NAMED AFTER FAMOUS PEOPLE

Marie Antoinette, Charles Aznavour, Ingrid Bergman, Captain Bligh, Marc Bolan, Anne Boleyn (easy to dead-head), George Burns, Lord Byron, Maria Callas, Bobby Charlton, Agatha Christie, Christopher Columbus, Bing Crosby, Leonardo da Vinci, Abraham Darby, Edgar Degas, Charles Dickens, Amelia Earhart, Chris Evert, Henry Fonda, Henry Ford, James Galway, Cary Grant, Jimmy Greaves, Audrey Hepburn, Thora Hird, Bob Hope, Victor Hugo, Penelope Keith, Felicity Kendal, Toulouse Lautrec, Sue Lawley, Maureen Lipman, Gina Lollobrigida, Henri Matisse, Freddie Mercury, Claude Monet, Olivia Newton-John, Florence Nightingale, Rosie O'Donnell, Dolly Parton, Anna Pavlova, Samuel Pepys, Marco Polo, Charlotte Rampling, Nancy Reagan, Auguste Renoir, Angela Rippon, Ginger Rogers, Mrs Franklin D. Roosevelt, Gabriela Sabatini, Arthur Scargill, William Shakespeare, Barbra Streisand, Elizabeth Taylor, Liv Tyler, Richard Wagner, June Whitfield.

ARMED SHRUBBERY

DANGEROUS PLANTS

The grapple tree of South Africa produces a fearsome fruit called the Devil's Claw, which is covered in lethal hooks that latch on to passing animals. If the animal touches the fruit with its mouth, the fruit attaches itself to the animal's jaw, preventing it from eating. Lions have starved to death following an encounter with the Devil's Claw.

The pitcher plant of Malaysia is capable of eating rats, lizards and frogs. Lured inside by the plant's brightly coloured rim and nectar-secreting walls, they fall foul of the slippery surface and plunge 20 inches to the bottom of the pitcher, where they die slowly in a lethal cocktail of rainwater and digestive acids.

Just brushing against a New Zealand tree nettle can be dangerous for humans, causing nausea, paralysis and even death.

The Venus fly trap takes half an hour to squash and kill a fly, and then ten days to digest it. The plant can also digest human flesh.

Abraham Lincoln's mother, Nancy, was killed by milk sickness, a condition that affects people who consume milk or meat from a cow that has grazed on the highly toxic plant, white snakeroot.

GREEN FINGERS

The rare *Puya raimondii* of Bolivia can take up to 150 years to bloom – and as soon as it does, it dies.

The six-foot-wide leaves of the giant Amazon water lily are strong enough to support the weight of a child.

The fast-growing lady in the veil mushroom from Africa takes just 20 minutes to reach its full height of eight inches.

An orange tree brought to France in 1421 bore fruit for 473 years.

The giant rafflesia of Borneo attracts carrion-loving insects by looking and smelling like a lump of rotting meat.

A bristlecone pine tree living in California's White Mountains is over 5,000 years old.

The combined length of the roots of a Finnish pine tree can stretch over 30 miles.

Seeds of the lotus plant have been known to germinate 1,300 years after being dispersed.

In 2005, a single, laboratory-grown Shenzhen Nongke orchid was sold at auction for $202,000.

TRANSPORT
AND TRAVEL

SOME PASSENGERS WHO MISSED THE *TITANIC*

At least 55 passengers cancelled their booking on the Titanic's *maiden and only voyage at very short notice. They included:*

John Pierpont Morgan, owner of the *Titanic* – prior engagement

Edward W. Bill – wife had a premonition of impending doom

Henry C. Frick, US steel magnate – wife sprained her ankle

Milton S. Hershey, inventor of the Hershey bar – returned to New York three days earlier on urgent business

Rev. J. Stuart Holden, London clergyman – wife taken ill on eve of voyage

Mr and Mrs J. Horace Harding – preferred the faster *Mauretania*

Frank Carlson – car broke down and he missed the boat

Robert Bacon, US ambassador to France – extended business in Paris

Edgar Selwyn, US film producer – stayed in the UK for another week to hear Arnold Bennett give a reading from his latest novel

James V. O'Brien – delayed by a court case in Ireland

Colonel J. Warren Hitchens – unhappy with cabin

George W. Vanderbilt, US railroad baron – mother-in-law was worried about maiden voyages

Bertram Slade, crew member – just missed the ship after being held up at a Southampton level crossing by a passing freight train

UK SHIPPING FORECAST AREAS

(Clockwise from the north)

Viking, North Utsire, South Utsire, Forties, Cromarty, Forth, Tyne, Dogger, Fisher, German Bight, Humber, Thames, Dover, Wight, Portland, Plymouth, Biscay, Trafalgar, FitzRoy, Sole, Lundy, Fastnet, Irish Sea, Shannon, Rockall, Malin, Hebrides, Bailey, Fair Isle, Faroes, Southeast Iceland.

LIFE ON THE OCEAN WAVES

Whistling was a sign of mutiny in the British Royal Navy. Traditionally, the only crew member aboard the ship allowed to whistle was the chef, because it meant he wasn't eating the food.

All gondolas in Venice must be painted black.

Despite having received no naval training, having no previous combat experience and being outnumbered by 133 ships to 13, Korean Admiral Yi Sun-sin still defeated the Japanese at the Battle of Myeongnyang in 1597.

A party barge capsized on Lake Travis in 2004 when dozens of passengers on board moved to one side of the boat as it approached the only nudist beach in Texas.

Canadian seaman Joshua Slocum, who, in 1898, became the first person to sail solo around the world, couldn't swim.

During the Second World War, the Dutch warship *Abraham Crijnssen* was disguised as a tropical island to escape detection by the Japanese. It was the only ship of its class in the Javanese region to survive.

Quarantine comes from the Latin word for 40, which was the number of days a ship had to wait to dock at Venice in the fourteenth century because of the plague.

When the *Royal Adelaide* was wrecked on Dorset's Chesil Beach in 1872, her cargo of spirits was washed ashore. Seven people drowned in the wreck, but another four died on the beach that night from drinking too much of the washed-up cargo.

Even though it is landlocked, Paraguay has its own navy, employing around 1,800 personnel.

Royal Caribbean's *Harmony of the Seas* cruise liner has 37 main bars, for which 110,231 pounds of ice cubes are made every day.

The anchor of the *Titanic* weighed over 15 tons and it needed a team of 20 horses to deliver it.

During the First World War, the *RMS Carmania* sank a German ship, *SMS Cap Trafalgar*, which was disguised as the *RMS Carmania*.

Modern cruise ships have morgues – with capacity for up to four bodies – because so many of their passengers are elderly.

All gun salutes in the US Navy are fired in odd numbers at five-second intervals.

In 1784, Chunosuke Matsuyama, a Japanese sailor, sent a message in a bottle to report that his boat had been shipwrecked. The bottle washed ashore 151 years later in Hiraturemura, the village where he was born.

SOME CARS
THAT ARE NAMED
AFTER PEOPLE

Aston Martin (Lionel Martin, who competed in hill climbs near Aston Clinton, Buckinghamshire)

Bugatti (Ettore Bugatti)

Buick (David Dunbar Buick)

Chevrolet (Louis Chevrolet)

Chrysler (Walter Chrysler)

Citröen (André-Gustave Citröen)

Daimler (Gottfried Daimler)

Dodge (John and Horace Dodge)

Hillman (William Hillman)

Honda (Soichiro Honda)

Lancia (Vincenzo Lancia)

Mercedes (Mercédès Jellinek, ten-year-old daughter of Austrian entrepreneur Emil Jellinek)

Opel (Adam Opel)

Peugeot (Armand Peugeot)

Porsche (Ferdinand Porsche)

Rolls-Royce (Charles Rolls and Henry Royce)

Skoda (Emil Skoda)

Toyota (Sakichi Toyoda – his family changed their name to Toyota since it needs ten strokes to write 'Toyoda' in Japanese but only eight for 'Toyota' – and eight is a lucky number in Japan)

FAMOUS PEOPLE (IN THE MOTORING ERA) WHO NEVER HAD A DRIVER'S LICENCE

Kate Beckinsale

Ray Bradbury

Lena Dunham

Albert Einstein

Noel Gallagher

Ricky Gervais

Quincy Jones

Jack Kerouac, author of *On the Road*

Spike Lee

Vladimir Nabokov

Barbara Walters

Charlie Watts

Mae West

Robbie Williams

And Nicholas Winding Refn, Danish director of the 2011 movie *Drive*, who failed his driving test eight times.

COUNTRIES AND TERRITORIES THAT DRIVE ON THE LEFT

Anguilla, Antigua and Barbuda, Australia, Bahamas, Bangladesh, Barbados, Bermuda, Bhutan, Botswana, British Virgin Islands, Brunei, Cayman Islands, Channel Islands, Christmas Island, Cocos Islands, Cook Islands, Dominica, Falkland Islands, Fiji, Grenada, Guyana, Hong Kong, India, Indonesia, Ireland, Isle of Man, Jamaica, Japan, Kenya, Kiribati, Lesotho, Macau, Malawi, Malaysia, Maldives, Malta, Mauritius, Montserrat, Mozambique, Namibia, Nauru, Nepal, New Zealand, Niue, Norfolk Island, Northern Cyprus, Pakistan, Papua New Guinea, Pitcairn Islands, Saint Helena, Saint Kitts and Nevis, Saint Lucia, Saint Vincent and the Grenadines, Samoa, Seychelles, Singapore, Solomon Islands, South Africa, Sri Lanka, Suriname, Swaziland, Tanzania, Thailand, Timor-Leste, Tokelau, Tonga, Trinidad and Tobago, Turks and Caicos Islands, Tuvalu, Uganda, United Kingdom, United States Virgin Islands, Zambia, Zimbabwe.

MOTORING
MISHAPS

Stan Caddell thought he would save money on a car wash by using the Mississippi River instead. So he carefully reversed his Chevrolet into a foot of water at Hannibal, Missouri, but as soon as he climbed out, the vehicle floated away and had to be retrieved by police some distance downstream.

Jozef Cene, a German police officer, left a pub in Wiltshire in 2007 and drove straight into a canal after mistaking it for a wet road.

A driver on a 2001 shopping trip to Hamburg, Germany, wrecked six cars (plus her own) and caused an estimated $15,000 worth of damage while trying to park.

Ninety-one-year-old Betty Borowski, from Milwaukee, Wisconsin, was trapped under her car for two days after crawling beneath the vehicle to look for her keys.

Two English football fans who travelled to Cologne, Germany, for a game in 2006 parked their car and made a note of what they thought was the street name, 'Einbahn Strasse'. But when they tried to find it later, they learned that 'Einbahn Strasse' means 'one-way street' in German, and that every other street in the city centre bore that sign.

An Italian driver was literally stuck in traffic near Milan in 2001 after the truck in front of him crashed into a tree and shed its load of glue across the highway. The car driver got out to investigate, and his feet immediately stuck to the tarmac, where he remained for several hours until rescue workers turned up.

Arriving by car at a hair salon in Soldotna, Alaska, 73-year-old Della Miller skidded on snow and crashed through the front window of the salon, causing $15,000 damage and sending a customer flying six feet across the room. Although shaken by the incident, Mrs Miller proceeded with her hair appointment.

Ljubomir Ivanov, a 35-year-old Macedonian, drove for six hours across Italy and into Germany in 2005 before discovering that he had accidentally left his wife at a gas station near Pesaro in central Italy.

On a visit to Bury St Edmunds, Suffolk, in 2006, Eric King parked his black Ford Focus in a residential street and walked into the town centre but then forgot where he had left the vehicle. It took him ten return visits and seven months before he was eventually reunited with it.

On his second day as a Glasgow bus driver, Barry Bean got hopelessly lost and wedged his bus under a low bridge. In attempting to release the vehicle, he crashed into a parked car, hit a lamppost and demolished several garden fences. Nobody was surprised to learn that his name was Mr Bean.

Andrea Zimmer was rescued by police officers in 2009 after completing at least 50 circuits of a roundabout in Braunschweig, Germany, in an unsuccessful attempt to find an exit.

At the end of her driving test in Portage, Indiana, Jessica Krasek crashed the car into the examiners' office while trying to park. She failed the test.

Setting off on the short journey to buy a newspaper from a store in Yass, New South Wales, 81-year-old Eric Seward took a wrong turn and ended up driving for nine hours and 370 miles to Melbourne.

In 2007, a Polish man named Prawo Jazdy had clocked up 50 separate traffic offences but had always managed to escape with a ticket by giving Irish police a different home address each time. Their quest to bring the elusive Mr Jazdy to justice was complicated when a bilingual officer pointed out that Prawo Jazdy means 'driving licence' in Polish.

MAJOR INTERNATIONAL VEHICLE REGISTRATION CODES

Algeria (DZ), Argentina (RA), Australia (AUS), Austria (A), Bahamas (BS), Barbados (BDS), Belgium (B), Bolivia (BOL), Bosnia and Herzegovina (BIH), Botswana (BW), Brazil (BR), Bulgaria (BG), Cambodia (K), Canada (CDN), Chile (RCH), Colombia (CO), Costa Rica (CR), Croatia (HR), Cuba (C), Cyprus (CY), Czech Republic (CZ), Denmark (DK), Ecuador (EC), Egypt (ET), Estonia (EST), Faroe Islands (FO), Finland (FIN), France (F), Georgia (GE), Germany (D), Ghana (GH), Greece (GR), Guatemala (GCA), Honduras (HN), Hungary (H), Iceland (IS), India (IND), Indonesia (RI), Ireland (IRL), Israel (IL), Italy (I), Ivory Coast (CI), Jamaica (JA), Japan (J), Jordan (HKJ), Kenya (EAK), Latvia (LV), Libya (LAR), Liechtenstein (FL), Lithuania (LT), Luxembourg (L), Macedonia (MK), Malaysia (MAL), Malta (M), Mexico (MEX), Moldova (MD), Montenegro (MNE), Morocco (MA), Netherlands (NL), New Zealand (NZ), Nigeria (WAN), Norway (N), Pakistan (PK), Paraguay (PY), Peru (PE), Poland (PL), Portugal (P), Romania (RO), Russia (RUS), Saudi Arabia (KSA), Senegal (SN), Serbia (SRB), Slovakia (SK), Slovenia (SLO), South Africa (ZA), South Korea (ROK), Spain (E), Sri Lanka (CL), Sweden (S), Switzerland (CH), Thailand (T), Trinidad and Tobago (TT), Tunisia (TN), Turkey (TR), Uganda (EAU), Ukraine (UA), United Kingdom (GB), United States (USA), Uruguay (UY), Venezuela (YV), Vietnam (VN), Zambia (Z), Zimbabwe (ZW).

AUTO FACTS

Traffic lights were introduced 18 years before the car was invented. In 1868, a set of revolving red and green gas lanterns, manually operated by the police, was installed in London's Parliament Square to regulate horse drawn carriages. The apparatus was removed four years later after it exploded, injuring the officer on duty.

By 1908, the poo from 120,000 horses in New York City was causing so much mess that horseless carriages – i.e. cars – were seen as the environmentally friendly alternative.

In 1916, 55 per cent of all the cars in the world were Model T Fords.

Until 1976, London taxi cabs were legally required to carry a bale of hay and a stack of oats – a relic from the days of horse-drawn cabs.

Over half of the world's roundabouts – more than 30,000 – are in France.

In Finland, taxi drivers must pay royalties for the music they play in their cars while transporting customers.

There are more than 140,000 taxi cabs in Mexico City.

Counting every nut, bolt and screw, each car contains about 30,000 individual parts.

The dashboard was originally a piece of wood attached to the front of a horse-drawn carriage that prevented the carriage driver getting splattered with mud thrown up by the horses' hooves.

Early cars didn't have windscreen wipers. Instead drivers rubbed a potato over the glass.

Every year in Sweden, there are 6,000 road accidents involving moose.

The first car to have a rear-view mirror was driven by inaugural Indianapolis 500 winner Ray Harroun in 1911, who used it to see the cars that were chasing him.

Hong Kong has more Rolls-Royces per head of population than any city in the world.

Around 65 per cent of all the cars ever produced by Rolls-Royce are still on the road.

As a perk for playing James Bond, actor Daniel Craig gets free Aston Martins for the rest of his life.

A 2010 traffic jam in China stretched for more than 60 miles. It lasted for two weeks and some drivers reported being stuck in it for five days.

Traffic is so bad in Bangkok that the police have a special unit for delivering babies who don't make it to hospital in time.

A car is stolen somewhere in the United States every 43 seconds.

The 1,400-mile-long Alaska Highway was built in just seven months.

South African residents can legally attach small flamethrowers to the side of their cars to thwart carjackers.

Residents of Churchill, Canada, leave their cars unlocked on Main Street to offer a refuge for pedestrians who come face to face with polar bears.

Ralph Teetor, the American engineer who invented cruise control, was blind.

There are more cars than people in Los Angeles.

In Somalia, 200 times as many camels are used for transport as cars.

All driving tests in Britain were suspended for six months from November 1956 during the Suez crisis. Learners were allowed to drive unaccompanied and examiners helped to administer petrol rations.

When James Dean showed fellow actor Alec Guinness his new Porsche Spyder, Guinness warned him: 'If you get in that car, you will be found dead in it by this time next week.' The encounter took place on 23 September 1955. Seven days later, Dean was killed after crashing the Spyder.

WORLD'S TOP SELLING CARS (2018)

1. Toyota Corolla*
2. Ford F-Series
3. Volkswagen Golf
4. Honda Civic
5. Toyota RAV4
6. Volkswagen Tiguan
7. Volkswagen Polo
8. Honda CR-V
9. Toyota Camry
10. Chevrolet Silverado
11. Hyundai Elantra
12. Ram Pick-up
13. Hyundai Tucson
14. Nissan Qashqai
15. Toyota Hilux
16. Ford Focus
17. Volkswagen Passat
18. Mercedes C-Class
19. Honda Accord
20. Volkswagen Lavida

*A Toyota Corolla is sold somewhere
in the world every 40 seconds.

FAMOUS HARLEY-DAVIDSON OWNERS

Bryan Adams, Muhammad Ali, Pamela Anderson, Ann-Margret, Dan Aykroyd, David Beckham, Jon Bon Jovi, Pat Boone, Marlon Brando, Eric Cantona, Cher, Eric Clapton, George Clooney, Jasper Conran, David Copperfield, Elvis Costello, Jack Dempsey, Neil Diamond, Bob Dylan, Clint Eastwood, Chris Eubank, Michael Flatley, Andrew Flintoff, Peter Fonda, Harrison Ford, Clark Gable, Larry Hagman, Richard Hammond, Woody Harrelson, Jimi Hendrix, Buddy Holly, Michael Hutchence, Billy Idol, Michael Jackson, Billy Joel, Don Johnson, John Kerry, Evel Knievel, k.d. lang, Jay Leno, Adam Levine, Charles Lindbergh, Jodie Marsh, Ewan McGregor, Steve McQueen, George Michael, Liam Neeson, Crown Prince Olaf of Norway, Pink, Brad Pitt, Robert Plant, Elvis Presley, Lou Reed, Keanu Reeves, Roy Rogers, Mickey Rourke, Arnold Schwarzenegger, William Shatner, Nancy Sinatra, Bruce Springsteen, Sylvester Stallone, Elizabeth Taylor, Justin Timberlake, John Travolta, Bruce Willis, Ian Wright.

COUNTRIES WITH MOST
CYCLISTS PER HEAD

(WITH PERCENTAGE OF
POPULATION THAT CYCLES)

1. Netherlands (99%)

2. Denmark (80%)

3. Germany (76%)

4. Sweden (64%)

5. Norway (61%)

6. Finland (60%)

7. Japan (57%)

8. Switzerland (49%)

9. Belgium (48%)

10. China (37%)

CYCLING SHORTS

From 1888 until the law was abolished in 1930, every cyclist in Britain had to ring the bell on his bicycle continuously while in motion.

Of all journeys made in the Netherlands, 27 per cent are by bicycle, compared to 5 per cent in the UK and just 1 per cent in the United States.

Every year, as many as 15,000 bicycles are pulled out of the canals in Amsterdam.

An Englishman named Mr Trinden invented the Balloon Velocipede in 1869 because he hated cycling up hills. He attached his bicycle to a giant balloon in the hope that the balloon would pull him up the hill without him falling off.

In 2015, a team of enthusiasts from South Australia built a rideable bicycle that measured over 135 feet long – roughly twice the length of a bowling lane.

There are more than nine million bicycles in Shanghai.

At the 1904 Tour de France, 12 riders were disqualified, chiefly for travelling part of the way by train or car. As a result, the fifth-placed finisher, 19-year-old Henri Cornet, was eventually crowned the winner four months after the race.

PIONEERING
AVIATORS

One of the first recorded attempts to fly was made around 1020 AD by Oliver of Malmesbury, an English Benedictine monk, who tried to fly from his abbey using wings. He broke both legs.

In 1709, Father Bartolomeu de Gusmão demonstrated a model hot-air balloon to King John V of Portugal in a large drawing-room in Lisbon. The balloon rose to a height of 12 feet before being destroyed to prevent it setting the curtains on fire.

In 1742, intrepid French nobleman the Marquis de Bacqueville attempted to fly across the River Seine in Paris with paddles fitted to his arms and legs. He leaped from a window ledge on the top floor of his house and began flapping furiously, only to drop to the ground like a stone. Fortunately he landed in a pile of old clothes in a washerwoman's boat and escaped with nothing worse than a broken leg.

In 1783, Jacques Alexandre César Charles released a 12-foot-diameter, unmanned balloon to fly 45 minutes from Paris to Gonesse, where it was attacked and destroyed by villagers who thought it was a monster.

In 1785, Frenchman Jean-Pierre Blanchard and his American backer, Dr John Jeffries, set off to fly their balloon across the English Channel. Flying perilously low, they were forced to remove almost all their clothes to lighten the load so that by the time they landed safely in France, both men were wearing only their underpants.

In 1848, Englishman John Stringfellow built an aeroplane powered by a steam engine. He launched the unmanned monoplane by running it down a slope before releasing it. According to contemporary reports, his machine demonstrated genuine powered flight by climbing a little before hitting a wall.

In 1874, Belgian shoemaker Vincent de Groof planned to fly over London in 'a device with bat-like wings'. He was raised to an altitude of 1,000 feet by balloon and then released over the River Thames. Alas, the wing structure failed disastrously and his flying machine crashed down into a street in Chelsea, killing him.

In the 1900s, Parisian Count de Guiseux, tested his Aeroplane Bicycle, a contraption that consisted of a pair of large wings attached to a bicycle. The count had to pedal furiously to have any hope of elevation, making any form of sustained flight an exhausting prospect, and his craft was said to have achieved little more than modest hops.

AIR MILES
FROM LONDON

Manchester – 163

Plymouth – 192

Brussels – 200

Paris – 214

Amsterdam – 223

Dublin – 289

Belfast – 322

Glasgow – 345

Berlin – 580

Monaco – 642

Prague – 644

Vienna – 770

Madrid – 785

Rome – 892

Stockholm – 893

Warsaw – 903

Budapest – 904

Lisbon – 984

Belgrade – 1,050

Tallinn – 1,111

Helsinki – 1,135

Reykjavik – 1,177

Athens – 1,489

Istanbul – 1,557

Moscow – 1,559

Cairo – 2,183

Dubai – 3,403

New York – 3,471

Karachi – 3,927

Chicago – 3,958

Miami – 4,433

Vancouver – 4,715

Mumbai – 4,477

Beijing – 5,080

Los Angeles – 5,454

Seoul – 5,518

Mexico City – 5,557

Johannesburg – 5,617

Rio de Janeiro – 5,753

Tokyo – 5,954

Hong Kong – 5,991

Sydney – 10,558

Auckland – 11,405

UP, UP, AND AWAY

At peak season in July or August, there are more than 16,000 flights in the air worldwide at the same time.

The shortest scheduled passenger flight in the world is the daily Loganair flight between the Orkney islands of Westray and Papa Westray off the coast of Scotland. The distance is 1.7 miles and the flight time is just over a minute. Until he retired in 2013, pilot Stuart Linklater flew the island hop more than 12,000 times.

The wingspan of a Boeing 747 (195 feet) is longer than the Wright Brothers' maiden flight (120 feet).

The average 747 has up to 175 miles of wiring.

The cockpit windshield of a Boeing 747-400 costs as much as an entire new BMW car.

American Airlines saved an estimated $40,000 in 1987 by removing one olive from every salad served in first class.

Singapore Airlines spends approximately $700 million on food every year and $16 million on wine.

The emblem of the Royal New Zealand Air Force is the kiwi, a flightless bird.

The changing air pressure in an aeroplane cabin numbs about one-third of a person's taste buds.

The first airline to offer online check in was Alaska Airlines in 1999.

John F. Kennedy International Airport in New York City used to be known as Idlewild Airport. The name was changed on 24 December 1963, just over a month after Kennedy was assassinated.

Pilots and co-pilots are required to eat different meals in case of food poisoning.

Studies show that 80 per cent of all plane crashes occur in the three minutes after takeoff and in the last eight minutes before landing.

According to *Popular Mechanics* magazine, sitting near the tail section of an aeroplane improves your chances of surviving an accident by 40 per cent.

Plane exhaust kills more people than plane crashes. Around 10,000 people are killed annually by toxic pollutants from aeroplanes – ten times more than are killed each year in plane crashes.

Only about five per cent of the world's total population has ever been on an aeroplane.

WE APOLOGISE FOR THE DELAY TO YOUR FLIGHT

On 2 July 1982, all flights in and out of Los Angeles International Airport were disrupted when Larry Walters (aka Lawn Chair Larry) attached helium-filled balloons to a garden chair and floated across controlled airspace at 16,000 feet.

A 2018 flight from Orlando to Cleveland was delayed for two hours when a passenger tried to take an emotional support squirrel with her onto the plane. She said the animal would keep her calm during the flight, but although Frontier Airlines does allow certain emotional support pets, all rodents are banned.

A 2017 flight from Liverpool to Malaga was delayed when a passenger spilled some orange juice after boarding, causing an electrical fault that grounded the plane.

A Spirit Airlines flight was delayed after landing at Orlando International Airport in 2018 when a huge alligator was spotted lumbering across the runway.

A 2013 Jet2 flight from Milas, Turkey, to Manchester was cancelled because the aeroplane had spent too long in the sun.

In 2011, passengers on a Scandinavian Airlines flight from Stockholm to Chicago were delayed for over three hours after a mouse was spotted by the cabin crew.

A 2016 flight from Cancun, Mexico, to London Stansted was delayed because of missing cutlery.

Flights were suspended from Milan's Linate Airport in 2007 when 60 hares invaded the runway.

A 2009 flight from Houston's George Bush Intercontinental Airport was delayed for 45 minutes when two otters escaped from their holding cages and bolted across the tarmac.

A 2014 flight from Los Angeles to Melbourne had to turn back when the toilet exploded.

A 2015 American Airlines flight from Dallas/Fort Worth to Frankfurt, Germany, was delayed after a swarm of 10,000 bees made a nest under the aeroplane's wing.

A 2018 Finnair flight from Helsinki to Rome was delayed for 90 minutes because the pilot turned up drunk.

BUSIEST AIRPORTS

BY PASSENGER NUMBERS PER YEAR

1. Hartsfield-Jackson Atlanta International Airport, USA (103.9 million)

2. Beijing Capital International Airport, China (95.7 million)

3. Dubai International Airport, United Arab Emirates (88.2 million)

4. Tokyo Haneda Airport, Japan (85.4 million)

5. Los Angeles International Airport, USA (84.5 million)

6. O'Hare International Airport, Chicago, USA (79.8 million)

7. London Heathrow Airport, England (78.0 million)

8. Hong Kong International Airport (72.6 million)

9. Shanghai Pudong International Airport, China (70.0 million)

10. Paris-Charles de Gaulle Airport, France (69.4 million)

11. Amsterdam Airport Schiphol, Netherlands (68.5 million)

12. Dallas/Fort Worth International Airport, USA (67.0 million)

13. Guangzhou Baiyun International Airport, China (65.8 million)

14. Frankfurt Airport, Germany (64.5 million)

15. Istanbul Ataturk Airport, Turkey (63.8 million)

16. Indira Gandhi International Airport, Delhi, India (63.4 million)

17. Soekarno-Hatta International Airport, Tangerang, Indonesia (63.0 million)

18. Singapore Changi Airport (62.2 million)

19. Seoul Incheon International Airport, South Korea (62.1 million)

20. Denver International Airport, USA (61.3 million)

AIRPORTS THAT ARE NEAREST TO THE CITIES THEY SERVE

1. Gibraltar (1.4 miles)

2. Jeju, South Korea (1.6 miles)

3. Heraklion, Crete (1.8 miles)

4. Tallinn, Estonia (2.5 miles)

5= Lisbon, Portugal (3.7 miles)

5= Southampton, England (3.7 miles)

7. Nice, France (3.8 miles)

8. Wellington International, New Zealand (4.4 miles)

9. Ho Chi Minh City, Vietnam (4.6 miles)

10. Sofia, Bulgaria (4.7 miles)

11. Mexico City International, Mexico (4.9 miles)

12. Taipei, Taiwan (5.1 miles)

AIRPORTS THAT ARE FURTHEST FROM THE CITIES THEY SERVE

1. Paris Vatry, France (91 miles)

2. Frankfurt Hahn, Germany (75 miles)

3. Oslo Torp, Norway (68 miles)

4= Barcelona Reus, Spain (66 miles)

4= Stockholm Skavsta, Sweden (66 miles)

6. Stockholm Vasteras, Sweden (65 miles)

7. Barcelona Girona, Spain (64 miles)

8. Paris Beauvais Tillé (63 miles)

9. Hamburg Lubeck, Germany (45 miles)

10= Kuala Lumpur, Malaysia (42 miles)

10= London Southend, England (42 miles)

12. London Stansted, England (41 miles)

TRAINSPOTTING

The line between Lima and Huancayo in the Peruvian Andes reaches altitudes of over 15,000 feet. The air is so thin that nurses travel on the train to provide oxygen to any passengers who are feeling faint.

The longest stretch of straight railway track in the world is the one crossing the Nullarbor Plain on the Trans-Australian Railway. Between a point west of Ooldea, South Australia, and a spot near Loongana in Western Australia it runs for 297 miles without a curve.

When trains were first introduced in the United States in the 1830s, many people believed that women's bodies were not built to travel at 50mph and that their uteruses would fly out if they reached such a speed.

In India, train drivers are paid more than software engineers.

The length of the Indian rail network would circle the equator nearly one and a half times.

Indian Railways' Guwahati-Trivandrum Express has the reputation for being one of the world's most unreliable trains, arriving at its destination on average between 10 and 12 hours late.

Every day, Indian Railways transports more passengers than the entire population of Australia.

The longest passenger journey that can be made without changing trains is from Moscow to Vladivostok on the Trans-Siberian Railway – some 5,800 miles, nearly a quarter of the way around the globe.

In 1896, US military cadets from Auburn, Alabama, greased the local railroad tracks the night before a football game with Georgia Tech. When the visiting team's train arrived it was unable to stop and slid halfway to the next town, forcing the Tech players to walk five miles back to the game and probably contributing to their subsequent 45-0 defeat.

In the nineteenth century, women travelling alone on trains in Britain would often place sharp pins between their lips when entering tunnels in case strange men tried to kiss them in the dark.

New York City's Grand Central station has 44 platforms.

Japanese trains are so punctual that apologies are issued to passengers even if there is a one-minute delay.

The Beijing Subway employs professional pushers who physically squeeze commuters into packed train carriages at peak times.

In 1919, when there was a shortage of coal in Russian Turkestan, dried fish was used as locomotive fuel.

On a branch of the Arica-La Paz Railway in Chile, engines were once powered by llama dung.

In late nineteenth-century South Africa, a baboon named Jack acted as an official assistant to disabled signalman James Wide and was paid 20 cents a day for his work by the Cape Town–Port Elizabeth Railway.

In 1971, Mr and Mrs William Farmer, from Margate, Kent, travelled to Wales for their summer holiday. At the start of the week, they joined a British Rail mystery tour, which promptly took them straight back to Margate.

LONDON UNDERGROUND TRIVIA

When the first London Underground escalators were installed at Earl's Court station in 1911, a man with a wooden leg, 'Bumper' Harris, was hired to ride up and down them to reassure the public that they were safe to use.

Mansion House and South Ealing are the only London Underground stations with every vowel in their name.

The distance between Leicester Square and Covent Garden on the Piccadilly Line is only 260 metres and the journey takes just 20 seconds.

Covent Garden station is said to be haunted by the ghost of actor William Terriss who was stabbed to death nearby in 1897.

In 1926, suicide pits were installed beneath tracks due to an increasing number of passengers throwing themselves in front of trains. Today, the most common time for Tube suicides is around 11am.

Only 45 per cent of the Underground is actually in tunnels.

Aldgate station is built on a huge plague pit, where more than 1,000 bodies are buried.

Draughtsman Harry Beck was paid 10 guineas (£10.50) for designing the iconic London Underground map in 1931.

The 'mind the gap' announcement at Tube stations was introduced in 1969.

The total length of the London Underground network is 250 miles – equal to travelling from London to Middlesbrough.

US talk show host Jerry Springer was born at Highgate station in 1944 after his mother had taken shelter there during a German air raid.

An estimated half a million mice live in the London Underground system.

LONDON UNDERGROUND STATIONS THAT HAVE CHANGED THEIR NAME

Acton Town (Mill Hill Park until 1910)

Arsenal (Gillespie Road until 1932)

Bank (City until 1940)

Barbican (Aldersgate until 1968)

Boston Manor (Boston Road until 1911)

Chalfont & Latimer (Chalfont Road until 1915)

Chiswick Park (Acton Green until 1887)

Clapham North (Clapham Road until 1926)

Euston Square (Gower Street until 1909)

Fulham Broadway (Walham Green until 1952)

Gloucester Road (Brompton (Gloucester Road) until 1907)

Goodge Street (Tottenham Court Road until 1908)

Great Portland Street (Portland Road until 1917)

Green Park (Dover Street until 1933)

Hounslow Central (Heston Hounslow until 1925)

Hounslow East (Hounslow Town until 1925)

Hounslow West (Hounslow Barracks until 1925)

Kensington (Olympia) (Kensington (Addison Road) until 1946)

Ladbroke Grove (Notting Hill until 1880)

Lambeth North (Westminster Bridge Road until 1917)

Liverpool Street (Bishopsgate until 1909)

Marylebone (Great Central until 1917)

Monument (Eastcheap until 1884)

Moor Park (Sandy Lodge until 1923)

Oakwood (Enfield West until 1934)

Queensway (Queen's Road until 1946)

Ravenscourt Park (Shaftesbury Road until 1888)

St. Paul's (Post Office until 1937)

Tooting Bec (Trinity Road (Tooting Bec) until 1950)

Tottenham Court Road (Oxford Street until 1908)

Tower Hill (Mark Lane until 1946)

Warren Street (Euston Road until 1908)

West Kensington (North End (Fulham) until 1877)

Westminster (Westminster Bridge until 1907)

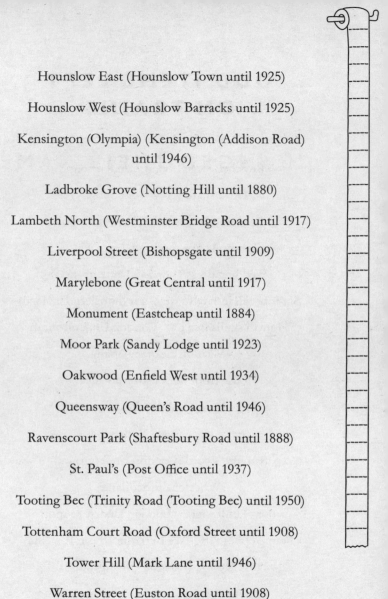

ODD ITEMS LEFT ON TRAINS

Prosthetic leg (London Underground)

Dead shark (New York Subway)

Lawnmower (London Underground)

Tarantula in a sandwich box (Wales)

Wedding dress (London Underground)

Six-foot-tall inflatable dinosaur (northern England)

Human skulls in a bag (London Underground)

Vacuum cleaner (Japan)

House front door (eastern England)

Judge's wig (London Underground)

False teeth (New York Subway)

Samurai sword (London Underground)

Wheelchair (Scotland)

Jar of bull sperm (London Underground)

Framed photo of Mary Berry (northern England)

Stuffed fox (London Underground)

Breast implants (London Underground)

Urn containing ashes (London Underground)

Life-sized carboard cut-out of Donald Trump
(East Midlands Trains, England)

WORLD'S OLDEST METRO SYSTEMS

1. London, England (1863)

2. Budapest, Hungary (May 1896)

3. Glasgow, Scotland (December 1896)

4. Chicago, United States (1897)

5. Paris, France (1900)

6. Boston, United States (1901)

7. Berlin, Germany (1902)

8. Athens, Greece (1904)

9. New York City, United States (1904)

10. Philadelphia, United States (1907)

11. Hamburg, Germany (1912)

12. Buenos Aires, Argentina (1913)

13. Madrid, Spain (1919)

14. Barcelona, Spain (1924)

15. Tokyo, Japan (1927)

16. Osaka, Japan (1933)

17. Moscow, Russia (1935)

18. Stockholm, Sweden (1950)

19. Toronto, Canada (1954)

20. Rome, Italy (February 1955)

EUROPE'S BUSIEST
TRAIN STATIONS

BY PASSENGER NUMBERS PER YEAR

1. Gare du Nord, Paris, France (206.7 million)

2. Châtelet-Les-Halles, Paris, France (179.9 million)

3. Hamburg Hauptbahnhof, Germany (175 million)

4. Frankfurt (main) Hauptbahnhof, Germany
(164.3 million)

5. Zurich Hauptbahnhof, Switzerland (153.6 million)

6. Roma Termini, Rome, Italy (150 million)

7. München Hauptbahnhof, Munich, Germany
(127.8 million)

8. Milano Centrale, Milan, Italy (120 million)

9. Berlin Hauptbahnhof, Berlin, Germany (110 million)

10. Madrid Atocha, Spain (108.6 million)

11. Paris Saint-Lazare, France (107.9 million)

12. Köln Hauptbahnhof, Cologne, Germany (102 million)

13. Gare de Lyon, Paris, France (100.4 million)

14. London Waterloo, England (99.4 million)

15. Wien Mitte, Vienna, Austria (97.8 million)

EPIC JOURNEYS

Leaving Portland, Maine, in 2000, Gary Hatter drove 14,594 miles on a lawnmower in nine months, travelling through all 48 contiguous US states, plus forays into Canada and Mexico, before reaching his destination of Daytona Beach, Florida.

In 2009, 65-year-old Englishman David Baird pushed a wheelbarrow 2,557 miles across Australia in 122 days.

In 2005, Vasilii Hazkevich drove a tractor 13,172 miles on a three-month journey that started and finished in Vladimir, Russia.

In 1930, American James B. Hargis and his mechanic, Charles Creighton, drove a car in reverse from New York to Los Angeles and all the way back again without once stopping the engine – a round trip of 7,180 miles in 42 days.

Lars Clausen rode 9,126 miles across the United States on a unicycle in 2002.

In 1977, Clem Jones, Lutz Frankenfield and Paul Harding sailed 2,400 miles from Darwin, Australia, to Singapore on a boat made from 15,000 beer cans.

In 2006, South Africans Adriaan Marais and Marinus Du Plessis travelled 13,000 miles from Anchorage, Alaska, to Miami, Florida, on jet skis.

In 2004, Josh Caldwell and Hunter Weeks rode a Segway with a top speed of 10mph for 4,064 miles across America. The journey required over 100 days and 400 battery charges.

Cheng Yanhua paddled 1,500 miles down China's Yangtze River in 2007 on the inner tube of a tyre.

In 2002, 'Rusty' Moncrieff made the 2,595-mile crossing of the USA from Florida to California on roller skates. It took him 69 days.

Departing from London in 2012, Surrey schoolteachers Richard Sears and Nick Gough drove 26,325 miles through 39 countries in a tuk-tuk (an open-sided, three-wheeled auto rickshaw), arriving in Buenos Aires 16 months later.

Jack Sexty jumped the 26.2 miles of the 2014 Manchester marathon course on a pogo stick.

In 2005, Tim FitzHigham became the first person to row across the English Channel in a bathtub.

For 60 days in 2008, Robert G. Davis rode a snowmobile for 12,163 miles through Maine and Canada.

In 2013, Dmitri Galitzine took 1 hour 56 minutes to complete the three-mile crossing of the Solent, off the south coast of England, in a hollowed out, motorised pumpkin.

In 2006, Welshman Dave Cornthwaite skateboarded 3,618 miles across Australia in 90 days.

In 1999, Hank Harp drove a three-wheeled motorised toilet from Land's End, Cornwall, to John O'Groats, Scotland, in 30 days.

In 2007, Christian Adam from Germany cycled for over 37 miles backwards while playing the violin.

PUSHING
THE LIMITS

In 2004, Billy Baxter rode a 1200cc motorbike at 164.9mph in Wiltshire … while blindfolded.

In 2014, Piers Ward drove a lawnmower at 116.5mph at a testing ground in Spain.

In 2014, Rev. Ray Biddiss from Yorkshire reached a speed of 114mph on his motorcycle hearse.

In 2010, Perry Watkins drove a high-powered dining table (with six chairs) at 113.8mph at Santa Pod raceway in Northamptonshire.

In 2014 on the Isle of Man, Matthew Hine drove a souped-up mobility scooter at 107.6mph.

In 2018, Kevin Nicks drove a garden shed at 105mph in Wales.

In 2011, Australian Glenn Suter clocked 101mph while driving a sofa that was powered by a motorcycle engine.

In 2016, Sweden's Erik Lundberg achieved a speed of 81.1mph while riding a skateboard downhill in Quebec.

In 2013, Matt McKeown from Plymouth rode a jet-propelled shopping trolley at 70.4mph.

In 2007, American Paul Stender reached a speed of 70mph on his jet-powered outhouse, the Port-o-Jet.

In 2008, Englishman Edd China drove a motorised bed on wheels at 69mph.

In 2013, Colin Furze from Lincolnshire drove a motorised toilet bowl (complete with functioning flushing mechanism) at 55mph.

THE ARTS

NATIONAL ANTHEMS

Albania: 'Hymn to the Flag'

Algeria: 'We Pledge'

Andorra: 'The Great Charlemagne'

Angola: 'Forward Angola'

Antigua and Barbuda: 'Fair Antigua, We Salute Thee'

Armenia: 'Our Fatherland'

Aruba: 'Aruba Precious Country'

Australia: 'Advance Australia Fair'

Austria: 'Land of Mountains, Land on the River'

Bahamas: 'March On, Bahamaland'

Bahrain: 'Our Bahrain'

Bangladesh: 'My Golden Bengal'

Barbados: 'In Plenty and in Time of Need'

Belarus: 'We, the Belarusians'

Belgium: 'The Brabançonne (The Song of Brabant)'

Belize: 'Land of the Free'

Benin: 'The Dawn of a New Day'

Bhutan: 'The Thunder Dragon Kingdom'

Bolivia: 'Bolivians, A Most Favourable Destiny'

Botswana: 'Blessed Be This Noble Land'

Brunei: 'God Bless the Sultan'

Bulgaria: 'Dear Motherland'

Burkina Faso: 'One Single Night'

Burundi: 'Beloved Burundi'

Cameroon: 'O Cameroon, Cradle of Our Forefathers'

Canada: 'O Canada'

Central African Republic: 'The Rebirth'

Chad: 'People of Chad'

China: 'March of the Volunteers'

Colombia: 'Oh Unfading Glory'

Costa Rica: 'Noble Fatherland, Your Beautiful Flag'

Croatia: 'Our Beautiful Homeland'

Cuba: 'The Anthem of Bayamo'

Czech Republic: 'Where My Home Is'

Denmark: 'There Is a Lovely Land/King Christian
Stood by the Lofty Mast'

Dominica: 'Isle of Beauty, Isle of Splendour'

Ecuador: 'We Salute You Our Homeland'

Egypt: 'My Homeland, My Homeland, My Homeland'

El Salvador: 'Proudly Salute the Fatherland'

Equatorial Guinea: 'Let Us Tread the Path of
Our Immense Happiness'

Eritrea: 'Eritrea, Eritrea, Eritrea'

Estonia: 'My Native Land, My Pride and Joy'

Ethiopia: 'March Forward, Dear Mother Ethiopia'

Faroe Islands: 'O Faroe Islands, My Deepest Treasure'

Finland: 'Our Land'

France: 'The Marseillaise (The Song of Marseille)'

Georgia: 'Freedom'

Germany: 'Song of the Germans'

Ghana: 'God Bless Our Homeland Ghana'

Greece: 'Hymn to Freedom'

Grenada: 'Hail Grenada'

Guinea-Bissau: 'This Is Our Beloved Country'

Guyana: 'Dear Land of Guyana, of Rivers and Plains'

Honduras: 'Your Flag Is a Heavenly Light'

Hungary: 'God Bless the Hungarians'

India: 'Hail the Ruler of All Minds'

Ireland: 'The Soldier's Song'

Israel: 'The Hope'

Italy: 'The Song of the Italians'

Jamaica: 'Jamaica, Land We Love'

Japan: 'May a Thousand Years of Happy Reign Be Yours'

Kazakhstan: 'My Kazakhstan'

Kenya: 'Oh God of All Creation'

Kiribati: 'Stand Up, Kiribati'

Latvia: 'God Bless Latvia'

Lebanon: 'All of Us! For Our Country,
For Our Flag and Glory'

Liberia: 'All Hail, Liberia, Hail!'

Liechtenstein: 'High Above the Young Rhine'

Macedonia: 'Today Over Macedonia'

Madagascar: 'Oh Beloved Land of Our Ancestors'

Malawi: 'Oh God Bless Our Land of Malawi'

Maldives: 'In National Unity Do We Salute Our Nation'

Mali: 'For Africa and For You, Mali'

Marshall Islands: 'Forever Marshall Islands'

Moldova: 'Our Tongue'

Myanmar: 'Till the End of the World'

Namibia: 'Namibia, Land of the Brave'

Nepal: 'A Garland of a Hundred Flowers'

Netherlands: 'The William'

New Zealand: 'God Defend New Zealand'

Nicaragua: 'Hail to Thee, Nicaragua'

Northern Ireland: 'Londonderry Air'

Norway: 'Yes, We Love This Country'

Pakistan: 'Blessed Be the Sacred Land'

Panama: 'Hymn of the Isthmus'

Paraguay: 'Paraguayans, the Republic or Death'

Peru: 'We Are Free, Let Us Remain So Forever'

Poland: 'Poland Is Not Yet Lost'

Portugal: 'The Portuguese'

Romania: 'Awaken Thee, Romanian'

Rwanda: 'Beautiful Rwanda'

Saint Kitts and Nevis: 'O Land of Beauty!'

Saint Lucia: 'Sons and Daughters of Saint Lucia'

Scotland: 'Scotland the Brave'

Senegal: 'Pluck Your Koras, Strike the Balafons'

Serbia and Montenegro: 'Hey, Slavs'

Seychelles: 'Join Together, All Seychellois'

Sierra Leone: 'High We Exalt Thee, Realm of the Free'

Slovakia: 'Lightning Over the Tatras'

Slovenia: 'Go Ahead, the Flag of Glory'

Spain: 'The Royal March'

Sweden: 'Thou Ancient, Thou Free'

Switzerland: 'Swiss Psalm'

Tajikistan: 'Happiness of the Nation'

Tanzania: 'God Bless Africa'

Trinidad and Tobago: 'Forged From the Love of Liberty'

Tunisia: 'Defenders of the Homeland'

Turkey: 'The March of Independence'

Tuvalu: 'Tuvalu for the Almighty'

Ukraine: 'Ukraine's Glory Has Not Perished'

United Kingdom: 'God Save the Queen'

United States: 'The Star-Spangled Banner'

Vanuatu: 'We, We, We'

Venezuela: 'Glory to the Brave People'

Vietnam: 'The March to the Front'

Wales: 'Land of My Fathers'

Zambia: 'Stand and Sing of Zambia, Proud and Free'

Zimbabwe: 'Lift High Zimbabwe's Banner'

LONG TOP 40
SONG TITLES

'You Can Make Me Dance Sing or Anything (Even Take the Dog For a Walk, Mend a Fuse, Fold Away the Ironing Board, or Any Other Domestic Short Comings)' – The Faces, 1974 (115 letters)

'Jeremiah Peabody's Poly Unsaturated Quick Dissolving Fast Acting Pleasant Tasting Green and Purple Pills' – Ray Stevens, 1961 (89 letters)

'Calling Occupants of Interplanetary Craft (The Recognised Anthem of World Contact Day)' – The Carpenters, 1977 (74 letters)

'Rachmaninoff's Eighteenth Variation on a Theme By Paganini (The Story of Three Loves)' – Winifred Atwell, 1954 (70 letters)

'I Don't Want Nobody to Give Me Nothing (Open Up the Door, I'll Get It Myself)' – James Brown, 1969 (57 letters)

'Indian Reservation (The Lament of the Cherokee Reservation Indian)' – The Raiders, 1971 (56 letters)

'Does Your Chewing Gum Lose Its Flavour (On the Bedpost Overnight?)' – Lonnie Donegan, 1959 (53 letters)

'Objects in the Rear View Mirror May Appear Closer Than They Are' – Meat Loaf, 1994 (52 letters)

'If I Said You Have a Beautiful Body Would You Hold It Against Me?' – The Bellamy Brothers, 1979 (51 letters)

'Gilly Gilly Ossenfeffer Katzenellen Bogen by the Sea' – Max Bygraves, 1954 (45 letters)

'San Francisco (Be Sure to Wear Some Flowers in Your Hair)' – Scott McKenzie, 1967 (45 letters)

NUL POINTERS AT THE EUROVISION SONG CONTEST

(SINCE CONTEST EXPANDED)

1978 Norway: 'Mil Etter Mil' – Jahn Teigen

1981 Norway: 'Aldri I Livet' – Finn Kalvik

1982 Finland: 'Nuku Pommiin' – Kojo

1983 Spain: 'Quién Maneja Mi Barca?' – Remedios Amaya;
Turkey: 'Opera' – Çetin Alp and the Short Waves

1987 Turkey: 'Şarkım Sevgi Üstüne'
– Seyyal Taner and Locomotif

1988 Austria: 'Lisa, Mona Lisa' – Wilfried

1989 Iceland: 'þad sem enginn ser'
– Daníel Agust Haraldsson

1991 Austria:, 'Venedig im Regen' – Thomas Forstner

1994 Lithuania: 'Lopsine mylimai' – Ovidijus Vyšniauskas

1997 Norway: 'San Francisco' – Tor Endresen; Portugal:,
'Antes Do Adeus' – Celia Lawson

1998 Switzerland: 'Lass' Ihn' – Gunvor

2003 United Kingdom: 'Cry Baby' – Jemini

2015 Austria: 'I Am Yours' – The Makemakes;
Germany: 'Black Smoke' – Ann Sophie

CATCHY EUROVISION SONG CONTEST TITLES

'Voi Voi' (Norway, 1960)

'La La La' (Spain, 1968)
(It contained 138 la's in a song lasting 2min 39sec,
thus averaging almost one la per second)

'Boom Bang-A-Bang' (United Kingdom, 1969)

'Baby Baby' (Belgium, 1973)

'Ding Dinge Dong' (Netherlands, 1975)

'Pump-Pump' (Finland, 1976)

'Djambo Djambo' (Switzerland, 1976)

'Boom Boom Boomerang' (Austria, 1977)

'A-Ba-Ni-Bi' (Israel, 1978)

'Diggi-Loo Diggi-Ley' (Sweden, 1984)

'Olé Olé' (Israel, 1985)

'Bana Bana' (Turkey, 1989)

'Yamma Yamma' (Finland, 1992)

'Ding Dong' (Israel, 2011)

'Waggle Your Bum' (Austria, 2012)

'Man Gewöhnt Sich so Schnell an das Schöne' (Germany, 1964)

BANDS AND THEIR ORIGINAL NAMES

The Beach Boys (The Pendletones)

The Bee Gees (The Rattlesnakes)

Black Sabbath (Polka Tulk Blues Band)

Blue Oyster Cult (Soft White Underbelly)

Blur (Seymour)

Coldplay (Starfish)

The Cure (The Obelisk)

Def Leppard (Atomic Mass)

Elbow (Mr Soft)

Green Day (Sweet Children)

Joy Division (Warsaw)

Kaiser Chiefs (Runston Parva)

Keane (The Lotus Eaters)

KISS (Wicked Lester)

Led Zeppelin (The New Yardbirds)

The Libertines (The Strand)

Madness (The North London Invaders)

Marmalade (Dean Ford and the Gaylords)

Maroon 5 (Kara's Flowers)

Muse (Rocket Baby Dolls)

Nickelback (The Village Idiots)

Nirvana (Pen Cap Chew)

Pearl Jam (Mookie Blaylock)

Pink Floyd (The Screaming Abdabs)

Procul Harum (The Paramounts)

Queen (Smile)

Radiohead (On a Friday)

Red Hot Chili Peppers (Tony Flow and the
Miraculously Majestic Masters of Mayhem)

Snow Patrol (Shrug)

Spandau Ballet (Gentry)

Status Quo (The Spectres)

Steely Dan (The Leather Canary)

Stereophonics (Tragic Love Company)

Talking Heads (The Artistics)

Tears for Fears (History of Headaches)

U2 (Feedback)

Van Halen (Rat Salad)

The Who (The High Numbers)

JOHN LENNON AND
THE NUMBER NINE

Lennon was convinced that throughout his life the number nine 'follows me around'. Here is the evidence:

He and his son Sean were both born on 9 October.

The first home he lived in was at 9 *Newcastle* Road, *Wavertree, Liverpool* – three words which each contain nine letters.

As a student, he took the number 72 bus (7+2=9) from home to Liverpool Art College.

The group became The Beatles in 1960 and Lennon left in 1969, nine years later.

The Beatles' first appearance at the Cavern Club in Liverpool was on 9 February 1961.

Future manager Brian Epstein first attended a Beatles concert at the Cavern exactly nine months later on 9 November 1961.

Epstein secured a recording contract for The Beatles with EMI on 9 May 1962.

The Beatles' first hit, 'Love Me Do', was on Parlophone disc R 4949.

Their record-breaking debut on America's *The Ed Sullivan Show* was on 9 February 1964.

From 1973 to his death in 1980, Lennon and Yoko Ono lived in the Dakota apartment building in New York City, located on the corner of 72nd Street (7+2=9).

Their first apartment in the Dakota building was number 72 (7+2=9).

His fixation with the number nine frequently manifested itself in his songs, which included titles such as 'Number 9 Dream', 'Revolution 9' and 'One After 909'.

When released as a single, 'Number 9 Dream' peaked at number nine on the Billboard Hot 100 chart.

The cover of his 1974 album *Walls and Bridges* features a painting done by Lennon when he was a boy. It depicts a footballer with a number nine on his back.

He was shot dead by Mark Chapman outside the Dakota building late on the evening of 8 December 1980 but the five-hour time difference meant that it was 9 December in his birthplace of Liverpool.

His body was taken to the Roosevelt Hospital on Ninth Avenue, Manhattan. Both 'Roosevelt' and 'Manhattan' have nine letters.

ROCK TRIVIA

Axl Rose used to earn $8 an hour by smoking cigarettes for a science experiment at UCLA.

Daryl Hall and John Oates met at a band competition in Philadelphia. When gun shots rang out between rival gangs, they both ran for the same elevator and got talking.

Foo Fighters' Dave Grohl has an alley named after him in his hometown of Warren, Ohio.

In 2015, Dave Grohl broke his leg after falling from the stage during a concert in Gothenburg, Sweden. After receiving medical treatment backstage, he played the rest of the concert sitting in a chair with his leg in a plaster cast.

When Decca Records first released 'Rock Around the Clock' by Bill Haley and His Comets in 1954, most people had never heard of the term 'rock and roll'. Struggling to describe the tune, the label on the record called it a 'novelty foxtrot'.

The Clash's 'Rock the Casbah' was written after rock music was banned in Iran in 1979.

The words 'mamma mia' spent 11 consecutive weeks topping the UK charts in 1975–76 – nine weeks as a prominent part of Queen's 'Bohemian Rhapsody', followed immediately by two weeks of Abba's 'Mamma Mia'.

Chevy Chase played drums for the college band that evolved into Steely Dan.

Elvis Presley never played a concert outside North America.

Ed Sheeran is a second cousin of Gordon Burns, presenter of the 1980s TV game show *The Krypton Factor*.

At a 1974 concert in New York's Central Park, Bruce Springsteen opened for Anne Murray.

When The Beatles visited India in 1968 to find inner peace, Ringo Starr took two suitcases – one packed with clothes and the other with tins of baked beans because he mistrusted spicy food.

Irritated by his record label, in 1984 Johnny Cash recorded a deliberately awful song, 'The Chicken in Black', in which he imagined his brain being transplanted into a performing chicken.

Two members of Jefferson Airplane – guitarist Paul Kantner and the band's original singer, Signe Toly Anderson – both died separately on the same day, 28 January 2016.

Ryan Adams and Bryan Adams were both born on November 5.

English folk rock singer Roy Harper once gave the kiss of life to a sheep.

The only member of ZZ Top who doesn't have a beard is drummer Frank Beard.

The video for Ultravox's 'Vienna' was partly filmed in London's Covent Garden.

Tom DeLonge left Blink-182 in 2015 so that he could devote more time to researching UFOs and aliens.

Icelandic singer Björk used to have a phobia about television sets because someone had convinced her that they made her susceptible to hypnosis.

Kings of Leon had to abandon a 2010 show in St Louis, Missouri, after they were repeatedly hit in the face by pigeon droppings from birds in the rafters.

Freddie Mercury had four extra teeth in his upper jaw.

Bono took his name from a Dublin hearing aid shop Bonavox, which translates from Latin as 'good voice'.

U2 guitarist The Edge fell off the edge of the stage at a concert in Vancouver in 2015.

PEOPLE MENTIONED IN BILLY JOEL'S 'WE DIDN'T START THE FIRE'

Harry Truman, Doris Day, Johnnie Ray, Walter Winchell, Joe DiMaggio, Joe McCarthy, Richard Nixon, Marilyn Monroe, Julius and Ethel Rosenberg, Sugar Ray Robinson, Marlon Brando, Dwight D. Eisenhower, Elizabeth II, Rocky Marciano, Liberace, George Santayana, Joseph Stalin, Georgy Malenkov, Abdel Nasser, Sergei Prokofiev, Nelson Rockfeller, Tommaso Campanella, Roy Cohn, Juan Peron, Arturo Toscanini, Albert Einstein, James Dean, Davy Crockett, Peter Pan, Elvis Presley, Brigitte Bardot, Nikita Khrushchev, Princess Grace of Monaco, Boris Pasternak, Mickey Mantle, Jack Kerouac, Chou En-Lai, Charles de Gaulle, Charles Starkweather, Buddy Holly, Fidel Castro, Syngman Rhee, John F. Kennedy, Chubby Checker, Ernest Hemingway, Adolf Eichmann, Bob Dylan, John Glenn, Sonny Liston, Floyd Patterson, Pope Paul VI, Malcolm X, Ho Chi Minh, Menachem Begin, Ronald Reagan, Ayatollah Khomeini, Sally Ride, Bernhard Goetz.

SONGS IN ENGLISH CONTAINING UN SOUPÇON OF FRENCH

'Voulez-Vous' – Abba

'Michelle' – The Beatles

'Denis' – Blondie

'Sunday Girl' – Blondie

'To the End' – Blur

'The Red Balloon' – The Dave Clark Five

'Jennifer Juniper' – Donovan

'Hold On Tight' – Electric Light Orchestra

'Games Without Frontiers' – Peter Gabriel

'It's a Beautiful World' – Noel Gallagher's
High Flying Birds

'Les Bicyclettes de Belsize' – Engelbert Humperdinck

'Eyes Without a Face' – Billy Idol

'Lady Marmalade' – Labelle

'What Have They Done to My Song Ma' – Melanie

'I Belong to You' – Muse

'Hungry For You' – The Police

'Monsieur Dupont' – Sandie Shaw

'Five Minutes' – The Stranglers

'Psycho Killer' – Talking Heads

'My Cherie Amour' – Stevie Wonder

MEMBERS OF
THE '27 CLUB'

A number of musicians have died at the age of 27. They include:

Dave Alexander (The Stooges), 1975

Kurt Cobain (Nirvana), 1994

Pete de Freitas (Echo and the Bunnymen), 1989

Richey Edwards (Manic Street Preachers)
disappeared and presumed dead, 1995

Pete Ham (Badfinger), 1975

Jimi Hendrix, 1970

Robert Johnson, 1938

Brian Jones (The Rolling Stones), 1969

Janis Joplin, 1970

Ron 'Pigpen' McKernan (The Grateful Dead), 1973

Jim Morrison (The Doors), 1971

Kristen Pfaff (Hole), 1994

Alan Wilson (Canned Heat), 1970

Amy Winehouse, 2011

COMPOSERS WHO DIED BEFORE REACHING FORTY

Vincenzo Bellini (33)

Georges Bizet (36)

Frédéric Chopin (39)

George Gershwin (38)

Felix Mendelssohn (38)

Wolfgang Amadeus Mozart (35)

Otto Nicolai (38)

Giovanni Pergolesi (26)

Henry Purcell (36)

Franz Schubert (31)

CLASSICAL GAS

Beethoven used to pour jugs of iced water over his head to stimulate his brain while composing.

There are two skulls in Joseph Haydn's tomb. After his head was stolen by grave robbers, a replacement skull was put in the tomb. When the original was restored in 1954, the replacement was not removed.

A single violin is made from over 70 separate pieces of wood.

Franz Liszt received so many requests for locks of his hair that he bought a dog and sent fur clippings instead.

The Fugue in G Minor by Domenico Scarlatti was inspired by his cat walking across the piano.

Mozart composed a piano piece for his friend Haydn that had to be played using two hands and the nose.

Robert Schumann tried to cure his injured hand by plunging it into the entrails of a slaughtered animal.

American baritone Leonard Warren died onstage at New York's Metropolitan Opera House in 1960 moments after singing Verdi's *'Morir, Tremenda Cosi'* ('To Die, a Momentous Thing').

I'LL BET YOU THINK THIS SONG IS ABOUT YOU

PEOPLE WHO ARE THE SUBJECT OF SONGS

Rosanna Arquette ('Rosanna' by Toto)

Syd Barrett ('Shine On You Crazy Diamond' by Pink Floyd)

Pattie Boyd ('Layla' and 'Wonderful Tonight'
by Eric Clapton)

Rita Coolidge ('Delta Lady' by Leon Russell)

Marvin Gaye and Jackie Wilson ('Nightshift'
by The Commodores)

Buddy Holly ('American Pie' by Don McLean)

Julian Lennon ('Hey Jude' by The Beatles)

Iggy Pop ('The Jean Genie' by David Bowie)

Andy Kaufman ('Man on the Moon' by R.E.M.)

Carole King ('Oh Carol' by Neil Sedaka)

Martin Luther King ('Pride (in the Name of Love)' by U2)

Elle Macpherson, Christie Brinkley and Whitney Houston
('Uptown Girl' by Billy Joel)

Linda McCartney ('Maybe I'm Amazed' by Paul McCartney)

Don McLean ('Killing Me Softly with His Song'
by Lori Lieberman/Roberta Flack)

Marilyn Monroe/Princess Diana ('Candle in the Wind'
by Elton John)

Vincent van Gogh ('Vincent' by Don McLean)

SOME SONGS
WHOSE TITLE IS
NOT IN THE LYRICS

'Pompeii' – Bastille

'A Day in The Life' – The Beatles

'Song For Whoever' – The Beautiful South

'Paranoid' – Black Sabbath

'Slight Return' – The Bluetones

'Song 2' – Blur

'Space Oddity' – David Bowie

'Cloudbusting' – Kate Bush

'Superstar' – The Carpenters

'Tubthumping' – Chumbawamba

'The Scientist' – Coldplay

'Badge' – Cream

'Annie's Song' – John Denver

'Sunshine Superman' – Donovan

'Positively 4th Street' – Bob Dylan

'Subterranean Homesick Blues' – Bob Dylan

'The Last Resort' – The Eagles

'What's Up' – 4 Non Blondes

'Whistle For The Choir' – The Fratellis

'Halcyon' – Ellie Goulding

'Goodnight Saigon' – Billy Joel

'The Riddle' – Nik Kershaw

'Immigrant Song' – Led Zeppelin

'Creeque Alley' – The Mamas and The Papas

'Weekend in New England' – Barry Manilow

'Alternate Title/Randy Scouse Git' – The Monkees

'Blue Monday' – New Order

'True Faith' – New Order

'Smells Like Teen Spirit' – Nirvana

'The Hindu Times' – Oasis

'Fairytale of New York' – The Pogues

'Bohemian Rhapsody' – Queen

'Night Owl' – Gerry Rafferty

'Unchained Melody' – The Righteous Brothers

'Sympathy For The Devil' – The Rolling Stones

'Pyjamarama' – Roxy Music

'How Soon Is Now?' – The Smiths

'Chocolate' – Snow Patrol

'Dakota' – Stereophonics

'Young Turks' – Rod Stewart

'A Lover's Concerto' – The Toys

'The Unforgettable Fire' – U2

'Christmas Wrapping' – The Waitresses

'After the Gold Rush' – Neil Young

BAND NAME ORIGINS

Backstreet Boys are named after a flea market, the Backstreet Market, in Orlando, Florida.

Bastille chose their name because singer Dan Smith's birthday is 14 July – Bastille Day.

Biffy Clyro take their name from a childhood game played by vocalist Simon Neil and drummer Ben Johnston in which they think up unlikely Cliff Richard merchandise. Apparently one of their spoof items was a ballpoint pen that they called a Cliffy Biro, which eventually became Biffy Clyro.

The Doors were named after Aldous Huxley's book *The Doors of Perception*.

Duran Duran took their name from Dr Durand Durand, the evil mad scientist in the 1968 Jane Fonda film *Barbarella*, as many of their early gigs were played at Barbarella's club in Birmingham.

Foo Fighters was the name that Allied airmen gave to UFOs during the Second World War.

Iron Maiden take their name from the torture device depicted in the 1939 film *The Man in the Iron Mask*.

Kasabian are named after Linda Kasabian, the member of Charles Manson's 'family' who eventually put him behind bars.

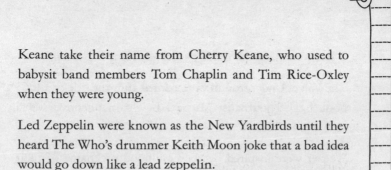

Keane take their name from Cherry Keane, who used to babysit band members Tom Chaplin and Tim Rice-Oxley when they were young.

Led Zeppelin were known as the New Yardbirds until they heard The Who's drummer Keith Moon joke that a bad idea would go down like a lead zeppelin.

Lynyrd Skynyrd named themselves after Leonard Skinner, a gym teacher at their Jacksonville, Florida, high school in the 1960s, who had a zero tolerance for students with long hair.

Nickelback took their name from band member Mike Kroeger saying, 'Here's your nickel back' when he worked on the tills at Starbucks.

The Pogues were originally called Pogue Mahone after 'Póg mo Thóin', Irish Gaelic for 'Kiss my arse'. When the BBC received complaints, the name was shortened to The Pogues.

Procul Harum was the name of a Siamese cat that belonged to a friend of Guy Stevens, the band's manager.

The Searchers were named after the 1956 John Ford western film, *The Searchers*.

Simple Minds took their name from a line in David Bowie's 'The Jean Genie'.

Steely Dan is the name of a strap-on dildo in the novel *Naked Lunch* by William Burroughs.

The Thompson Twins were the bumbling detectives in Hergé's comic strip *The Adventures of Tintin*.

T'Pau were named after the Vulcan heroine in *Star Trek*.

The Velvet Underground were named after the title of a 1963 book by US journalist Michael Leigh on unconventional sexual practices.

Weezer were inspired by the childhood nickname of their asthmatic frontman Rivers Cuomo.

EXCESS ALL AREAS

MUSICIANS' TOUR RIDERS

For their 1982 world tour, Van Halen stipulated that there should be no brown M&Ms in their candy dishes backstage.

Mary J. Blige used to request her own private toilet (with a new toilet seat) at every venue she played.

Mötley Crüe once asked for a 15-foot boa constrictor.

Before appearing at a festival in Northern Ireland, Eminem asked for a wooden pond to be constructed in his backstage area and filled with his favourite koi carp.

According to her former personal assistant, Lady Gaga requested 'a mannequin with puffy pink pubic hair' for her 2009 Monster Ball Tour.

Axl Rose demanded a square melon be placed in his dressing room in 2012.

Mariah Carey asked for 20 white kittens and 100 white doves on a 2009 visit to London, but concerns over health and safety eventually led to the idea being dropped.

Katy Perry's floral requests are for 'white and purple hydrangeas, pink and white roses, and peonies. ABSOLUTELY NO CARNATIONS.'

MOST POPULAR UK FUNERAL SONGS

1. 'Always Look on the Bright Side of Life'
   – Eric Idle/Monty Python

2. 'The Lord Is My Shepherd' (Psalm 23)

3. 'Abide With Me'

4. *Match of the Day* theme tune

5. 'My Way' – Frank Sinatra

6. 'All Things Bright and Beautiful'

7. 'Angels' – Robbie Williams

8. Elgar's 'Enigma Variations'

9. 'You'll Never Walk Alone' – Gerry and the Pacemakers

10. 'Soul Limbo' (theme to radio's *Test Match Special*)
    – Booker T and the MGs

11. Pachelbel's 'Canon in D'

12. 'My Heart Will Go On' – Celine Dion

13. *Last of the Summer Wine* theme tune

14. *Only Fools and Horses* theme tune

15. 'Time to Say Goodbye' – Sarah Brightman
    and Andrea Bocelli

16. Vivaldi's 'Four Seasons'

17. Schubert's 'Ave Maria'

18. *Coronation Street* theme tune

19. 'You Raise Me Up' – Westlife

20. 'Over the Rainbow' – Eva Cassidy

GUEST MUSICIANS

Marvin Gaye played the drums on The Marvelettes' 'Please Mr Postman'.

Duane Allman played guitar on Derek and the Dominos' 'Layla'.

Mick Jagger sang backing vocals on Carly Simon's 'You're So Vain'.

Elton John played piano on The Hollies' 'He Ain't Heavy, He's My Brother'.

John Lennon sang background vocals on David Bowie's 'Fame'.

Paul Weller played guitar on Oasis's 'Champagne Supernova'.

A young Cher sang background vocals on The Righteous Brothers' 'You've Lost That Lovin' Feelin''.

Stephen Stills played guitar on Bill Withers' 'Ain't No Sunshine'.

Stevie Wonder played harmonica on Eurythmics' 'There Must Be an Angel'.

Mick Fleetwood played drums on Warren Zevon's 'Werewolves of London'.

James Taylor and Linda Ronstadt sang backing vocals on Neil Young's 'Heart of Gold'.

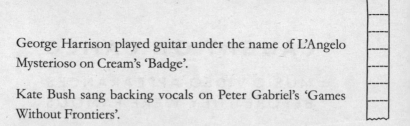

George Harrison played guitar under the name of L'Angelo Mysterioso on Cream's 'Badge'.

Kate Bush sang backing vocals on Peter Gabriel's 'Games Without Frontiers'.

Jimmy Page played guitar on the Tom Jones hit 'It's Not Unusual'.

Michael Jackson sang supporting vocals on Rockwell's 'Somebody's Watching Me'.

Rick Wakeman played Mellotron on David Bowie's 'Space Oddity'.

Michelle Phillips of The Mamas and The Papas sang backing vocals on Belinda Carlisle's 'Heaven Is a Place on Earth'.

Jeff Beck played guitar on Bon Jovi's 'Blaze of Glory'.

Phil Collins played drums on Adam Ant's 'Puss 'n Boots'.

Eric Clapton played guitar on The Beatles' 'While My Guitar Gently Weeps'.

Sting sang the line 'I want my MTV' on Dire Straits' 'Money For Nothing'.

Eddie Van Halen played guitar on Michael Jackson's 'Beat It'.

CAUGHT ON CAMEO

MUSIC VIDEO APPEARANCES
BEFORE THEY WERE FAMOUS

Twelve-year-old Naomi Campbell tap-danced in the 1982 video for Culture Club's 'I'll Tumble 4 Ya'.

Courteney Cox was the adoring fan in the 1984 video for Bruce Springsteen's 'Dancing in the Dark'.

In 1990, Tess Daly appeared in two Duran Duran videos for the songs 'Serious' and 'Violence of Summer (Love's Taking Over)'. Three years later she and other models appeared almost naked ('with nothing but Elastoplast to protect our modesty') in the video for The Beloved's track 'Sweet Harmony'.

Sixteen-year-old Claire Danes appeared in the video for Soul Asylum's 1995 song 'Just Like Anyone' as a college girl who grows angel wings.

A 21-year-old Keeley Hawes starred in the video for Suede's 1997 song 'Saturday Night', which was shot on a disused Piccadilly Line platform at Holborn station on the London Underground.

In 1993, Angelina Jolie played a teenage runaway in the video for Meat Loaf's 'Rock and Roll Dreams Come Through'.

Budding actor Matt LeBlanc starred in the 1990 video for Jon Bon Jovi's 'Miracle'.

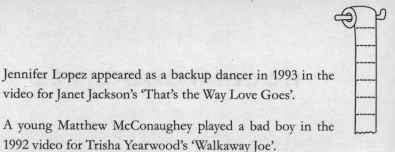

Jennifer Lopez appeared as a backup dancer in 1993 in the video for Janet Jackson's 'That's the Way Love Goes'.

A young Matthew McConaughey played a bad boy in the 1992 video for Trisha Yearwood's 'Walkaway Joe'.

Eva Mendes was seen driving a convertible in the 1998 video for Will Smith's 'Miami'.

Alicia Silverstone played a sullen teenager in the 1993 video for Aerosmith's 'Cryin''.

In 1982, Patrick Swayze was one of the dancers in the video for Toto's 'Rosanna'.

HOLLYWOOD LIVES

Sophia Loren's prize for winning her first beauty contest aged 14 included several rolls of wallpaper and a tablecloth with matching napkins.

Shirley Temple's hairdo always had exactly 56 curls.

When he was little, Jim Carrey used to wear his tap-dancing shoes to bed in case his parents needed cheering up in the middle of the night.

Clint Eastwood is allergic to horses.

Quintessential Englishman David Niven made his screen debut in 1934 as a Mexican bandit with a drooping moustache in a Hopalong Cassidy film.

James Cagney never said 'you dirty rat' in any of his films.

Ryan Gosling was asked to audition for the boy band Backstreet Boys but he turned it down.

Judy Garland was a first cousin three times removed of former US President Ulysses S. Grant.

In 1932, Broadway actress Peg Entwistle committed suicide by jumping off the letter H in the Hollywood sign.

Leonardo DiCaprio's mother named him Leonardo because she was pregnant and looking at a Da Vinci painting in Florence's Uffizi Gallery when he first kicked.

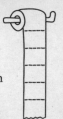

When horror star Bela Lugosi died, he was buried in Dracula's cloak.

Bruce Lee was the Hong Kong cha-cha champion of 1958.

Donald O'Connor made six films with Francis the Talking Mule in the 1950s but handed over his leading role to Mickey Rooney when he learned that the mule was receiving more fan mail than him.

Tom Cruise enrolled to become a priest at 14, but dropped out after a year.

Claudette Colbert insisted that sets were built and scenes directed in order to favour the left side of her face. She often refused to be filmed from the right unless it was a long shot.

Charles Bronson's family were so poor that he sometimes had to wear his sister's old dress to school.

Marilyn Monroe even used to bleach her pubic hair blonde.

Yul Brynner used to be a trapeze artist with a circus in France until he was injured in a fall.

Despite starring in *Charlie and the Chocolate Factory*, Johnny Depp was allergic to chocolate as a child.

At the start of Bing Crosby's career, the studio insisted on gluing his prominent ears back with spirit gum to make him look more photogenic.

When Ava Gardner died, she left her pet corgi Morgan a monthly salary plus his own limo and maid.

Maurice Chevalier's contract with Paramount, signed as talkies were being introduced, was rendered invalid if he ever lost his French accent.

Born in 1968, Daniel Craig was the first James Bond to have been born after the film franchise started and after the death of Bond's creator, Ian Fleming.

Young Marlon Brando wandered so much on his way to kindergarten that his older sister Jocelyn used to take him to school on a leash.

Clark Gable was mistakenly listed as a girl on his birth certificate.

MOVIE WALK-ONS

The real Frank Abagnale Jr appeared in *Catch Me If You Can* – the 2002 film based on his life as an impostor – as the French policeman who arrests Leonardo DiCaprio.

David Beckham played a KGB projectionist in *The Man from U.N.C.L.E* (2015).

Jaws author Peter Benchley appeared as a reporter in the 1975 movie version.

Richard Branson played a passenger going through airport security in *Casino Royale* (2006).

The Stone Roses' frontman Ian Brown was seen as a wizard in *Harry Potter and the Prisoner of Azkaban* (2004).

American footballer Brett Favre played himself in *There's Something About Mary* (1998).

George Harrison appeared as a background character in Monty Python's *The Life of Brian* (1979).

Hugh Hefner was seen as a pipe-smoking Roman in Mel Brooks' *History of the World – Part I* (1981).

Billy Idol played himself in *The Wedding Singer* (1998).

Lord of the Rings director Peter Jackson played a knife-wielding Santa in *Hot Fuzz* (2007).

Clive James appeared as one of Bazza's drunk mates in Barry Humphries' *Barry McKenzie Holds His Own* (1974).

Stephen King played a minister at a funeral in the 1989 adaptation of his novel *Pet Sematary*.

George Lucas was cast as a theme park attendant in *Beverly Hills Cop III* (1994).

Coldplay's Chris Martin played a bloodthirsty zombie in *Shaun of the Dead* (2004).

US basketball star Shaquille O'Neal appeared as an unorthodox policeman in *Grown Ups 2* (2013).

Ozzy Osbourne played anti-heavy metal evangelist Rev Aaron Gilstrom in *Trick or Treat* (1986).

Pablo Picasso appeared in a crowd scene in *The Testament of Orpheus* (1962).

Keith Richards played Jack Sparrow's drunken father in *Pirates of the Caribbean: At World's End* (2007) – an apt choice as Richards partly inspired Johnny Depp's portrayal of Sparrow.

Steven Spielberg played a clerk in a scene near the end of *The Blues Brothers* (1980).

Bruce Springsteen played himself in *High Fidelity* (2000).

Donald Trump played himself in *Ghosts Can't Do It* (1989). His performance earned him a Golden Raspberry award as Worst Supporting Actor.

Mike Tyson played himself in *The Hangover* (2009).

Future Australian Prime Minister Gough Whitlam appeared as 'man in nightclub' in *The Broken Melody* (1938).

OSCAR ODDITIES

Since 1950, Oscar winners cannot officially sell their statuette without first offering it back to the Academy for a dollar.

James Dean only made three movies and was nominated for Best Actor in two of them – both posthumously.

Liza Minnelli, who won Best Actress award for *Cabaret* in 1972, is the only Oscar winner whose parents were Oscar winners too. Her mother, Judy Garland, received an honorary award in 1939 and her father, Vincente Minnelli, won Best Director for *Gigi* in 1958.

Ethel and Lionel Barrymore are the only brother and sister to have won Academy Awards for acting.

Marlon Brando and Robert De Niro are the only actors to have won an Oscar for playing the same character, Vito Corleone, in *The Godfather* (1972) and *The Godfather Part II* (1974) respectively.

Beatrice Straight won Best Supporting Actress for *Network* in 1977 despite being on screen for only six minutes. Similarly, Judi Dench won Best Supporting Actress in 1999 for her eight minutes of total screen time as Queen Elizabeth I in *Shakespeare in Love*.

For playing the role of Katharine Hepburn in *The Aviator* (2004), Cate Blanchett became the first actress to win an Academy Award for playing another Academy Award winner.

Maggie Smith won an Academy Award for playing a failed Oscar nominee in *California Suite* (1978).

Shirley Temple won an honorary Oscar for her achievements in the movie industry in 1934 ... when she was just five years old.

American actor John Cazale only appeared in five films, but all five were nominated for the Academy Award for Best Picture – *The Godfather, The Conversation, The Godfather Part II, Dog Day Afternoon* and *The Deer Hunter.*

The only Oscar to win an Oscar was Oscar Hammerstein II who won an award for his song, 'The Last Time I Saw Paris', in the 1941 movie *Lady Be Good.*

I'LL PASS ON
THIS ONE

ACTORS WHO REJECTED
STAR ROLES

Kim Basinger turned down the part of Catherine Tramell in *Basic Instinct*, allowing it to go the virtually unknown Sharon Stone.

Michael Caine rejected the Oliver Reed role in *Women in Love* because of the nude wrestling scene with Alan Bates.

Sean Connery said no to Gandalf in *The Lord of the Rings* trilogy because he couldn't understand the script.

Gary Cooper turned down the role of Rhett Butler in *Gone with the Wind* because he was sure it would be a flop.

Joan Crawford backed out of *From Here to Eternity* because she didn't like the costumes.

Mel Gibson declined the Russell Crowe role of Maximus in *Gladiator*.

Anthony Hopkins passed up the offer to play the lead in *Gandhi*, for which Ben Kingsley won an Oscar.

Bette Midler feared that her fans wouldn't want to see her playing a nun and so rejected the *Sister Act* part that went to Whoopi Goldberg.

Anthony Newley turned down the title role of *Alfie* that made Michael Caine's career.

Jack Nicholson refused the role of Michael Corleone in *The Godfather* and it went to Al Pacino instead.

Al Pacino passed on the lead in *Die Hard*, clearing the way for Bruce Willis. Pacino also declined the role of Han Solo in *Star Wars* that went to Harrison Ford.

Michelle Pfeiffer rejected the Jodie Foster role in *The Silence of the Lambs* because she thought the film was too violent.

George Raft turned down the lead in *The Maltese Falcon* because he didn't think it was an important picture. Humphrey Bogart stepped in at short notice.

Robert Redford passed up the chance to play Dustin Hoffman's role in *The Graduate*.

Molly Ringwald rejected the role in *Pretty Woman* that made Julia Roberts a star. Ringwald also said no to playing Molly Jensen in *Ghost*, a part that eventually went to Demi Moore.

Will Smith passed on the role of Neo in *The Matrix*. His loss was Keanu Reeves' gain.

John Travolta has since admitted that he made a mistake in turning down the title role in *Forrest Gump*.

Henry Winkler, who had played the Fonz in *Happy Days*, declined the role of Danny Zuko in *Grease* for fear of being typecast.

DENTISTS
IN MOVIES

Cactus Flower, 1969: Walter Matthau plays Dr Julian Winston, a habitual liar who persuades his nurse to pose as his wife so that he can deceive his girlfriend.

Captives, 1994: Julia Ormond plays prison dentist Rachel Clifford who, following the break-up of her marriage, begins a relationship with a patient who is serving time for the murder of his wife.

Charlie and the Chocolate Factory, 2005: Christopher Lee plays Dr. Wilbur Wonka, dentist father of Willy, who, unlike his sweet-toothed son, is a fervent believer in flossing.

Consequence, 2003: Armand Assante plays Sam Tyler, a down-on-his-luck dentist who fakes his own death for an insurance scam.

Dark Command, 1940: Gabby Hayes plays travelling dentist Doc Grunch whose business partner deliberately starts fights so that he can knock loose his opponent's teeth, which the doc then offers to pull for a fee.

The Dentist, 1932: W.C. Fields plays an unorthodox dentist who prefers to remove teeth by wrestling his patients to the floor rather than using any form of pain relief.

The Dentist, 1996, and *The Dentist 2*, 1998: Corbin Bernsen plays Dr Alan Feinstone, a successful dentist who turns to murder after learning that his wife has been cheating on him.

Django Unchained, 2012: Christoph Waltz plays Dr. King Schultz who quits dentistry to become a bounty hunter.

Eversmile, New Jersey, 1989: Daniel Day-Lewis plays Fergus O'Connell, an American dentist whose mission in life is to spread the virtues of oral hygiene to the people of Argentina.

Ghost Town, 2008: Ricky Gervais plays Bertram Pincus, a British dentist who can see and communicate with the ghosts that haunt New York City.

Horrible Bosses, 2011: Jennifer Aniston plays the predatory Dr Julia Harris who sexually harasses her male assistant, making his life so miserable that he contemplates having her killed.

Inherent Vice, 2014: Martin Short plays libidinous, coke-sniffing dentist Dr Rudy Blatnoyd.

The In-Laws, 1979: Alan Arkin plays mild-mannered Manhattan dentist Dr Sheldon Kornpett who becomes involved in an international crime caper courtesy of his prospective son-in-law's father.

Little Shop of Horrors, 1986: Steve Martin plays evil dentist Dr Orin Scrivello who overdoses on nitrous oxide before his dismembered body is eaten by a carnivorous plant.

Marathon Man, 1976: Laurence Olivier plays Nazi war criminal Christian Szell who uses his drill as a weapon of torture to extract information.

MASH, 1970: John Schuck plays Captain Walter Koskiusczko 'Painless Pole' Waldowski, the army hospital dentist who wants to commit suicide.

Novocaine, 2002: Steve Martin plays Los Angeles dentist Dr Frank Sangster whose practice runs into difficulties after he has an affair with a seductive female patient seeking a root canal.

The Paleface, 1948: Bob Hope plays Dr 'Painless' Potter, a timid, hopeless dentist recruited by Calamity Jane to help uncover a gun smuggling operation in the Wild West.

The Strawberry Blonde, 1941: James Cagney plays volatile 1890s New York dentist Biff Grimes who faces stiff competition in landing the girl of his dreams.

MOVIE CLIPS

Brad Pitt injured his Achilles' tendon while playing Achilles in the 2004 movie *Troy*.

To please his daughters, George Lucas allowed the band members of NSYNC to make a cameo appearance in *Star Wars Episode II: Attack of the Clones*. The footage was then cut from the final version of the film.

1,400 actresses were interviewed to play Scarlett O'Hara in *Gone with the Wind*.

Joe Pesci really bit Macaulay Culkin during a scene in *Home Alone* – and Culkin still has the scar on his finger to prove it.

Sean Connery was 58 and Dustin Hoffman 51 when they played father and son in the 1989 film *Family Business*.

The costume designers for *The Lord of the Rings* trilogy pieced together so much chainmail armour that it rubbed away their fingerprints.

A young Simon Cowell worked as a runner on Stanley Kubrick's *The Shining*. He polished Jack Nicholson's axe.

Over 300,000 extras were used for the funeral scene in *Gandhi*.

Alfred Hitchcock's *Psycho* was the first American film to show a toilet flushing.

Bruce, the great white shark in *Finding Nemo*, was named after the mechanical shark used in *Jaws*, which itself was named 'Bruce' after director Steven Spielberg's lawyer.

Hitler's favourite movies included *King Kong*, *The Hound of the Baskervilles* and *Snow White and the Seven Dwarfs*.

Donald Pleasence, one of the stars of *The Great Escape*, was a genuine Second World War prisoner of war.

The sound of the velociraptors communicating with each other in *Jurassic Park* is actually the sound of tortoises mating.

The word 'actually' is spoken 22 times during *Love Actually*.

The creepy mask worn by killer Michael Myers in *Halloween* was originally a Captain Kirk mask from *Star Trek* and is really a likeness of William Shatner's face.

Mickey Mouse was banned in Romania in 1935 because it was feared that the sight of a 10-foot-tall rodent on screen would scare the nation's children.

Jimmy the raven (aka Jimmy the crow) appeared in more than 600 feature films from the 1930s onwards. He first appeared in *You Can't Take It with You* in 1938, after which director Frank Capra cast the bird in every movie he made, including *Arsenic and Old Lace* and *It's a Wonderful Life*.

The scene in *Pulp Fiction* where Vincent stabs Mia in the heart with a needle was shot in reverse. So in reality John Travolta was pulling the needle *out* of Uma Thurman's body.

One out of every 160 New Zealanders was involved in the making of *The Lord of the Rings*.

George Lucas owned an Alaskan malamute dog, Indiana, that not only inspired the name Indiana Jones but also the character of Chewbacca in *Star Wars*.

Alan Rickman was deliberately dropped a second before he was expecting it to get his true reaction to falling from a building in *Die Hard*.

The title of the Jack Nicholson movie *As Good As It Gets* translated into Chinese as 'Mr Cat Poop'.

FILM TAGLINES

Alien: 'In space, no one can hear you scream.'

Apollo 13: 'Houston, we have a problem.'

Arachnophobia: 'Eight legs, two fangs, and an attitude.'

Armageddon: 'Earth. It was fun while it lasted.'

The Blues Brothers: 'They'll never get caught. They're on a mission from God.'

Bonnie and Clyde: 'They're young … they're in love … they kill people.'

Casablanca: 'They had a date with fate in Casablanca.'

Catch Me If You Can: 'The true story of a real fake.'

Chicken Run: 'Escape, or die frying.'

Close Encounters of the Third Kind: 'We are not alone.'

Cocktail: 'When he pours, he reigns.'

Cool Runnings: 'One dream. Four Jamaicans. Twenty below zero.'

Deliverance: 'This is the weekend they didn't play golf.'

Dirty Harry: 'You don't assign him to murder cases. You just turn him loose.'

Dumb and Dumber: 'For Harry and Lloyd, every day is a no-brainer.'

Edward Scissorhands: 'His story will touch you, even though he can't.'

A Fish Called Wanda: 'A tale of murder, lust, greed, revenge, and seafood.'

The Fly: 'Be afraid. Be very afraid.'

Jaws 2: 'Just when you thought it was safe to go back in the water …'

Jurassic Park: 'An adventure 65 million years in the making.'

A Nightmare on Elm Street: 'If Nancy doesn't wake up screaming, she won't wake up at all.'

Pinocchio: 'For anyone who has ever wished upon a star.'

The Poseidon Adventure: 'Hell, upside down.'

Psycho (1998): 'Check in. Unpack. Relax. Take a shower.'

Quiz Show: 'Fifty million people watching but no one saw a thing.'

Revenge of the Nerds: 'It's time for the odd to get even.'

Rocky: 'His whole life was a million-to-one shot.'

Saving Private Ryan: 'The mission is a man.'

Shaun of the Dead: 'A romantic comedy. With zombies.'

Star Wars: 'A long time ago, in a galaxy far, far away.'

Superman: 'You'll believe a man can fly.'

There's Something About Mary: 'Love is in the hair.'

This Is Spinal Tap: 'Does for rock and roll what *The Sound of Music* did for hills.'

Volcano: 'The coast is toast.'

WHOSE LINE
IS IT ANYWAY?

VENTRILOQUISTS IN THE MOVIES

The Great Gabbo (Erich von Stroheim) and doll Otto, *The Great Gabbo* (1929)

Professor Echo (Lon Chaney), *The Unholy Three* (1930)

Edgar Bergen and doll Charlie McCarthy, *You Can't Cheat an Honest Man* (1939)

Maxwell Frere (Michael Redgrave) and doll Hugo, *Dead of Night* (1945)

Jerry Morgan (Danny Kaye) and doll Clarence, *Knock on Wood* (1954)

Hans (Massimo Serrato) and doll Grog, *Hypnosis* (1962)

The Great Vorelli (Bryant Haliday) and doll Hugo, *Devil Doll* (1964)

Corky Withers (Anthony Hopkins) and doll Fats, *Magic* (1978)

Barney Dunn (Herb Reynolds), *Broadway Danny Rose* (1984)

Joey (Joshua Morell) and doll Fletcher, *Making Contact* (1985)

Steven Schoichet (Adrien Brody), *Dummy* (2002)

Mary Shaw (Judith Roberts) and doll Billy and others, *Dead Silence* (2007)

The ventriloquist (Kevin Spacey), *The Ventriloquist* (2012)

REAL NAMES OF SUPERHEROES

Aquaman – Arthur Curry

Batgirl – Barbara Gordon

Batman – Bruce Wayne

Bionic Woman – Jaime Sommers

Black Widow – Natalia Alianova Romanova

Captain America – Steve Rogers

Catwoman – Selina Kyle

Green Arrow – Oliver Queen

The Hulk – Dr Bruce Banner

Iron Man – Tony Stark

Man from Atlantis – Mark Harris

Robin – Dick Grayson

Six Million Dollar Man – Steve Austin

Spider-Man – Peter Parker

Supergirl – Kara Zor-El

Superman – Clark Kent

Wolverine – James Howlett

Wonder Woman – Diana Prince

ACTORS'
SOBRIQUETS

America's Sweetheart – Mary Pickford

The Blonde Bombshell – Betty Hutton

The Brazilian Bombshell – Carmen Miranda

The Duke – John Wayne

The Girl with the Million Dollar Legs – Betty Grable

The Ice Maiden – Ursula Andress

The Iron Butterfly – Loretta Young

The It Girl – Clara Bow

The Italian Stallion – Sylvester Stallone

The King of Cool – Steve McQueen

The Look – Lauren Bacall

The Magnificent Wildcat – Pola Negri

The Man of a Thousand Faces – Lon Chaney

The Mexican Spitfire – Lupe Velez

The Muscles from Brussels – Jean-Claude Van Damme

The Platinum Blonde – Jean Harlow

The Professional Virgin – Doris Day

The Sex Kitten – Brigitte Bardot

The Singing Cowboy – Gene Autry

The Sweater Girl – Lana Turner

The Vagabond Lover – Rudy Vallee

INSURANCE
POLICIES

Double act Bud Abbott and Lou Costello took out a five-year, $250,000 insurance policy to protect themselves from having a career-ending argument. The policy expired long before they split up in 1957.

In the early 1930s, American vaudeville performer Roscoe Ates was insured against losing his trademark stutter.

Charlie Chaplin insured his famous feet for $150,000.

Harry Corbett, creator of glove puppet Sooty, used to pay £150 a year to insure his thumb and two fingers.

In the 1940s, Bette Davis insured her 28-inch waistline for $28,000.

Marlene Dietrich insured her smoky voice for $1 million.

Comedian Ken Dodd had his buck teeth insured for £5 million.

Comedian Jimmy 'Schnozzle' Durante had his bulbous nose insured for $100,000.

In 2007, *Ugly Betty* star America Ferrera had her smile insured for $10 million by Aquafresh.

Betty Grable had her long legs insured for $1.25 million.

Australian cricketer Merv Hughes had his handlebar moustache insured for $370,000 during his playing days.

In the 1970s, Dolly Parton insured her breasts for $600,000.

American footballer Troy Polamalu had his long, curly hair insured for $1 million by Head and Shoulders.

When Anthony Quinn had his head shaved for the 1968 film *The Magus*, he took out insurance to cover the risk of his hair not re-growing afterwards.

Guitarist Keith Richards has his hands insured for $1.6 million.

Food critic and restaurateur Egon Ronay insured his taste buds for £250,000.

In the 1980s, Bruce Springsteen insured his gravelly voice for $6 million.

When Shirley Temple was first insured, her contract stipulated that no money would be paid if the child star died or suffered injury while drunk.

Cross-eyed Ben Turpin was insured for $100,000 against the possibility of his eyes ever returning to normal.

SOME HOLLYWOOD CANADIANS

Pamela Anderson (Ladysmith, British Columbia)

Dan Aykroyd (Ottawa)

Jim Carrey (Newmarket, Ontario)

Deanna Durbin (Winnipeg)

Nathan Fillion (Edmonton)

Glenn Ford (Quebec)

Michael J. Fox (Edmonton)

Ryan Gosling (London, Ontario)

Stana Katic (Hamilton, Ontario)

Raymond Massey (Toronto)

Eric McCormack (Toronto)

Rick Moranis (Toronto)

Mike Myers (Scarborough, Ontario)

Ellen Page (Halifax, Nova Scotia)

Anna Paquin (Winnipeg)

Barbara Parkins (Vancouver)

Mary Pickford (Toronto)

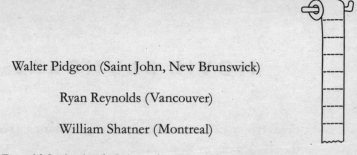

Walter Pidgeon (Saint John, New Brunswick)

Ryan Reynolds (Vancouver)

William Shatner (Montreal)

Donald Sutherland (Saint John, New Brunswick)

Fay Wray (Cardston, Alberta)

MOVIE BLUNDERS

Fresh tyre tracks are visible on the ground during a scene in the classic western *Stagecoach*.

TV aerials can be seen on the roofs of Victorian London in the 1966 black comedy *The Wrong Box*.

In *Pulp Fiction*, bullet holes appear in a wall before the scene in which the shots are fired.

A scene in the American Civil War film *Glory* shows a child wearing a digital wristwatch.

The Sound of Music is set in 1938, but in one scene an orange box can be seen stamped 'Produce of Israel', a nation that was not founded until ten years later.

In *Pirates of the Caribbean: The Curse of the Black Pearl,* just as Jack Sparrow (Johnny Depp) says 'On deck, you scabrous dogs', a crew member is visible in the background wearing a white T-shirt and sunglasses and gazing out to sea.

The heroine of the 1969 Swedish film *Adalen 31*, set in 1931, strips off in one scene to reveal bikini marks. But the bikini wasn't invented until 1946.

In Hitchcock's *North by Northwest*, a boy in the background in the Mount Rushmore cafeteria scene can be seen putting his fingers in his ears a few seconds before a gunshot rings out, presumably having learned when to protect his hearing from previous takes.

A corpse in a battle scene in the 1952 film *Son of Ali Baba* moves its arm just as someone is about to step on it.

A white van appears on screen during a battle scene in the thirteenthth-century epic *Braveheart*. In the same movie, a crew member can be seen in the background wearing a baseball cap.

A scene from *Gone with the Wind* shows a supposed oil lamp with an electrical cord hanging from it.

In James Cameron's *Titanic*, Jack Dawson (Leonardo DiCaprio) claims to have gone ice fishing on Lake Wissota, Wisconsin. But the man-made reservoir was not built until 1917 – five years after the *Titanic* sank.

During Judy Garland's performance of 'The Trolley Song' in *Meet Me in St Louis*, a voice can be heard calling out, 'Hi, Judy!' It was obviously a friend who had arrived on set and thought that Garland was only rehearsing.

Although the film is set in 1936, a scene from *Raiders of the Lost Ark* features an extra walking by dressed in modern-day T-shirt and jeans.

During a scene in *Gladiator*, a chariot hits a wall and flips over to reveal a gas canister hidden in the back.

AN INFINITE
DEAL OF NOTHING

CHOICE SHAKESPEAREAN INSULTS

'This woman's an easy glove, my lord; she goes off and on at pleasure' – Lafeu, *All's Well That Ends Well*

'I do desire we may be better strangers' – Orlando, *As You Like It*

'No longer from head to foot than from hip to hip, she is spherical, like a globe I could find out countries in her' – Dromio of Syracuse, *The Comedy of Errors*

'More of your conversation would infect my brain' – Menenius, *Coriolanus*

The tartness of his face sours ripe grapes – Menenius, *Coriolanus*

'There's no more faith in thee than in a stewed prune' – Falstaff, *Henry IV, Part I*

He was a man of an unbounded stomach – Queen Katharine, *Henry VIII*

'Where wilt thou find a cavern dark enough to mask thy monstrous visage?' – Brutus, *Julius Caesar*

'Sell your face for five pence and 'tis dear' – Bastard, *King John*

'Thou art a boil, a plague-sore, or embossed carbuncle, in my corrupted blood' – Lear, *King Lear*

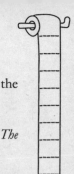

'They have been at a great feast of languages and stolen the scraps' – Moth, *Love's Labour's Lost*

'Gratiano speaks an infinite deal of nothing' – Bassanio, *The Merchant of Venice*

'The rankest compound of villainous smell that ever offended nostril' – Falstaff, *The Merry Wives of Windsor*

'Never hung poison on a fouler toad' – Anne, *Richard III*

'His complexion is perfect gallows' – Gonzalo, *The Tempest*

'Would thou wert clean enough to spit upon' – Timon, *Timon of Athens*

'He has not so much brain as ear-wax' – Thersites, *Troilus and Cressida*

'A coward, a most devout coward, religious in it' – Fabian, *Twelfth Night*

STAGE
WHISPERS

Ronald Reagan auditioned for the part of a president in Gore Vidal's 1960 play *The Best Man* but was turned down because the producers didn't think he looked sufficiently presidential.

All productions of *King Lear* were banned in Britain between 1788 and 1820 because the government deemed the play inappropriate in view of George III's supposedly deteriorating mental health.

John Gielgud was the fire warden for London's Theatre Royal Haymarket during the Blitz.

Samuel Beckett's play *Breath* is just 35 seconds long. No people are seen on stage and the 'dialogue' consists solely of two cries and the amplified sound of somebody slowly inhaling and exhaling.

Broadway runs for 33 miles, 18 of which are not even within New York City limits.

There is no longer a row with the letter I at theatres on Broadway, because people kept thinking it was a number one and that they had bought front row tickets. So they were disappointed to find themselves on row nine instead.

The complete works of William Shakespeare use a vocabulary of 17,677 words, of which around 1,700 are believed to have been invented by the Bard.

Shakespeare's Globe theatre is the only building in the centre of London permitted to have a thatched roof since the Great Fire of 1666.

In 1600, Shakespearean clown William Kempe morris danced all the way from London to Norwich. It took him nine days.

If a prompt desk is on stage right instead of stage left, it is known as a bastard prompt.

For 15 years and 6,240 performances between 1979 and 1994, actress Nancy Seabrooke attended a London theatre as understudy for the part of Mrs Boyle in Agatha Christie's *The Mousetrap*. In all that time, she only got to perform the role on 72 occasions.

London's Dominion Theatre stands on the site of the Great Beer Flood of 1814, when a nearby brewery burst open and caused a 15-foot-high wave of beer that killed eight people.

In 1960, when he was still plain Karol Wojtyla, the future Pope John Paul II wrote a play, *The Jeweller's Shop*, that was eventually staged at London's Westminster Theatre in 1982. It was also later turned into a film, starring Burt Lancaster and Olivia Hussey.

Billy Elliot the Musical toured in Durham, North Carolina, long before ever playing in County Durham, England, where the play is set.

On 4 May 2013, actress Helen Mirren, dressed as Queen Elizabeth II for her role in *The Audience*, left the stage of London's Gielgud Theatre to remonstrate in the street outside with a troupe of drummers who were disturbing her performance.

From 2001 to 2011, Danny the wheaten terrier made 1,400 appearances as Sandy on the UK tour of the musical *Annie*.

A West End production of Lord Lytton's play *The Lady of Lyons* opened and closed at London's Shaftesbury Theatre on 26 December 1888. After waiting for an hour, the audience was sent home because nobody could raise the safety curtain. Following that fiasco, the run was cancelled.

A 2017 Broadway production of *Cats* was marred when one of the cast's costumes proved so lifelike that she was chased off stage during the show's opening number by an audience member's guide dog.

POISON PENS

BITING REVIEWS FROM CRITICS

'When Mr Crane Wilbur calls his play *Halfway to Hell* he underestimates the distance' – Brooks Atkinson

[Of *Oh, Calcutta!*] 'The sort of show that gives pornography a bad name' – Clive Barnes

[On the revival of *Godspell*] 'For those who missed it the first time, this is your golden opportunity: you can miss it again' – Michael Billington

'Lillian Gish comes on stage as if she'd been sent for to sew rings on the new curtains' – Mrs Patrick Campbell

'The only moving thing about Charlton Heston's performance was his wig' – Michael Coveney

'Two things should be cut: the second act and the child's throat' – Noël Coward

'Mr [Creston] Clarke played the King [Lear] all evening as though under constant fear that someone else was about to play the ace' – Eugene Field

[Of *Dr Faustus*] 'Cedric Hardwicke conducted the soulselling transaction with the thoughtful dignity of a grocer selling a pound of cheese' – Hubert Griffith

'I have knocked everything in this play except the chorus girls' knees, and there God anticipated me' – Percy Hammond

'I don't like the play, but then I saw it under adverse conditions – the curtain was up' – George S. Kaufman

'I have seen stronger plots in a cemetery' – Stewart Klein

'*The House Beautiful* is play lousy' – Dorothy Parker

[On a 2000 revival of *Jesus Christ Superstar*] 'As Glenn Carter plays him [Jesus], he is practicing for a more important appearance at Madame Tussaud's wax museum' – John Simon

[Of *The Glorious Days*) 'There was a heated diversion of opinion in the lobbies during the interval but a small conservative majority took the view that it might be as well to remain in the theatre' – Kenneth Tynan

[Of *The Hero in Man*] 'Most of the heroes are in the audience' – Walter Winchell

'*Number Seven* opened last night. It was misnamed by five' – Alexander Woollcott

POSTMAN PAT
AROUND THE WORLD

Postbote Pat (Austria and Germany)

Postmand Per (Denmark)

Postimies Pate (Finland)

Pierre Martin (France)

Taxydromos Pat (Greece)

Posturinn Pall (Iceland)

Il Postino Pat (Italy)

Pieter Post (Netherlands)

Listonosz Pat (Poland)

O Carteiro Paulo (Portugal)

Padraig Post (Scottish Gaelic)

Pat el Cartero (Spain)

Postis-Per (Sweden)

REJECTED TITLES FOR MONTY PYTHON'S FLYING CIRCUS

Owl Stretching Time

The Toad Elevating Moment

A Horse, a Spoon and a Basin

Bunn, Wackett, Buzzard, Stubble and Boot

Vaseline Review

The Whizzo Easishow

The Venus De Milo Panic Show

Arthur Megapode's Cheap Show

Arthur Megapode's Zoo

Megapode's Atomic Circus

Arthur Megapode's Flying Circus

Gwen Dibley's Flying Circus

Cynthia Fellatio's Flying Circus

E.L. Moist's Flying Circus

Baron Von Took's Flying Circus

Julian Davidgor Python's Flying Circus

Bob Python's Flying Circus

Brian Python's Flying Circus

Keith Python's Flying Circus

Norman Python's Flying Circus

THINGS WE HAVE LEARNED FROM WATCHING TV SOAPS

Women always get pregnant after an inappropriate one-night stand.

Pregnancy testing kits are always left where other people can find them.

Women always fall down stairs during pregnancy.

Anyone caught semi-naked with someone else's partner will say, 'It's not what it looks like.'

The groom's car always breaks down on the way to the wedding venue.

Every wedding ceremony involves a fight.

It's easy to get married on Christmas Day.

There is a 75 per cent chance of being jilted at the altar.

People only ever date someone living on the same street.

It's easy to get a job – often without an interview.

Nobody ever has to commute to work.

Doctors are experts in every field of medicine.

Solicitors are experts in every area of law.

The police are useless and only ever arrest the wrong person.

The older and more innocent a person is, the greater the chance of them being sent to jail.

People only go into pubs to start a fight.

A surprise party always ends in tears.

Couples always choose to discuss their private problems in the most public place.

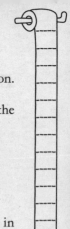

Anyone who says 'It's just a headache' will be on life support by the end of the week.

Small children can be left at home to look after themselves, often for several years.

Houses magically keep themselves clean.

Nobody ever watches TV.

Even the poorest families can afford to buy breakfast in the local café instead of making it themselves.

Every family has a supply of long-lost, never-previously-mentioned, relatives.

When someone says 'There's something I must tell you', the other person never lets them speak.

DEATHS IN NEIGHBOURS

Dan Fielding (heart attack) 1985

Bernie Sutton (hit by a car) 1985

Loretta Martin (car crash) 1985

Charles Durham (shot) 1985

Annabelle York (old age) 1986

Jean Richards (car crash) 1986

Jeremy Lord (car crash) 1987

Daphne Clarke (cardiac arrest) 1988

Rob Lewis (car crash) 1989

Kerry Bishop (shot at a duck hunt) 1990

Garth Kirby (overdose) 1992

Todd Landers (hit by a van) 1992

Jim Robinson (heart attack) 1993

Gary Briggs (car crash) 1994

Sally Gottlieb (cancer) 1994

Julie Martin (fall) 1994

Reuben White (heart condition) 1995

Cody Willis (accidentally shot during
a police drugs raid) 1996

Cheryl Stark (hit by a car) 1996

Helen Daniels (old age) 1997

Fred Parkes (old age) 1998

Lily Madigan (old age) 1998

Brendan Bell (heart attack) 2000

Madge Bishop (cancer) 2001

Barry Burke (car crash) 2001

Drew Kirk (fall from a horse) 2002

Dee Bliss (drowned – possibly) 2003

Charlie Cassidy (emphyscma) 2004

Gus Cleary (murdered by a blow to the head) 2004

David Bishop (plane crash) 2005

Liljana Bishop (plane crash) 2005

Serena Bishop (plane crash) 2005

Alex Kinski (leukaemia) 2005

Cameron Robinson (hit by a car) 2006

Stingray Timmins (aneurysm) 2007

Terrence Chesterton (blow to the head) 2007

Alan Napier (heart failure) 2007

Jessica Wallace (crushed by a falling roof) 2008

Richard Aaronow (renal failure) 2008

Chris Knight (head injuries) 2008

Marco Silvani (burned in a bush fire) 2008

Jill Ramsay (hit by a car) 2009

Bridget Parker (pulmonary embolism) 2009

Josh Burns (fall from a ladder) 2009

Ringo Brown (hit by a motorbike) 2010

Jim Dolan (skin cancer) 2011

Troy Miller (head injury) 2012

Rhys Lawson (blood clot) 2013

Priya Kapoor (crushed by a heavy pot plant) 2013

Robbo Slade (cardiac arrest following hit and run) 2013

Kate Ramsay (shot) 2014

Matt Turner (hit by a car) 2015

Josh Willis (crushed in an explosion at Lassiter's Hotel) 2016

Doug Willis (head injury) 2016

Father Guidotti (heart failure) 2016

Regan Davis (head injury) 2016

Kazuko Sano (pneumonia) 2016

Hamish Roche (drowned in a hot tub) 2017

Valerie Grundy (heart attack) 2018

Sonya Rebecchi (cancer) 2019

SOME PEOPLE
WHO HAVE PLAYED
THEMSELVES IN
THE SIMPSONS

Andre Agassi, Julian Assange, Buzz Aldrin, Kim Basinger, Tony Bennett, Halle Berry, Justin Bieber, Tony Blair, Richard Branson, Mel Brooks, James Brown, David Byrne, Elvis Costello, Cat Deeley, Ellen DeGeneres, Placido Domingo, Helen Fielding, Peter Frampton, Joe Frazier, Lady Gaga, Richard Gere, Mel Gibson, Rudy Giuliani, Wayne Gretzky, Melanie Griffith, Tom Hanks, George Harrison, Stephen Hawking, Hugh Hefner, Bob Hope, Mick Jagger, Elton John, Magic Johnson, Tom Jones, Larry King, Stephen King, Tom Kite, Eartha Kitt, Cyndi Lauper, Johnny Mathis, Paul McCartney, Ian McKellen, Rupert Murdoch, Elon Musk, Willie Nelson, Paul Newman, Leonard Nimoy, Nick Park, Dolly Parton, Katy Perry, Tom Petty, Gordon Ramsay, Little Richard, Keith Richards, Dennis Rodman, Ronaldo, Linda Ronstadt, J.K. Rowling, Susan Sarandon, Ryan Seacrest, Brooke Shields, Stephen Sondheim, Britney Spears, Jerry Springer, Ringo Starr, Sting, Elizabeth Taylor, Justin Timberlake, Pete Townshend, John Updike, Gore Vidal, Barry White, Pharrell Williams, Serena Williams, Tom Wolfe, Mark Zuckerberg.

MUPPET SHOW CHARACTERS YOU MAY HAVE FORGOTTEN

Annie Sue – young pig singer and Miss Piggy's rival for Kermit's affections

Beauregard – dim janitor at the Muppet Theatre

Camilla the Chicken – The Great Gonzo's love interest

Crazy Harry – wild-eyed pyrotechnic expert

Eric the Yodeling Clam – one of Gonzo's uniquely talented acts

Floyd Pepper – bass player for the Electric Mayhem

George the Janitor – Beauregard's predecessor

Gladys – cafeteria lady

Hilda – wardrobe mistress

Janice – guitar player with the Electric Mayhem

J.P. Grosse – feared owner of the Muppet Theatre and uncle of Scooter

Lew Zealand – entertainer whose act specialises in boomerang fish

Lubbock Lou – played jaw-harp in the band Lubbock Lou and His Jughuggers

Marvin Suggs – musician who played the Muppaphone, an instrument made of living balls of fluff

Mildred Huxtetter – aristocratic, purple lady who danced with guest Charles Aznavour

Pops – stage doorman for the Muppet Theatre

Wanda – one half of wholesome singing duo Wayne and Wanda

Winky Pinkerton – penguin who performs bird impressions

Zeke – shaggy, yellow-haired banjo player with Lubbock Lou and His Jughuggers

TV TIDBITS

Victoria Beckham once played a roller-skating sperm on a BBC sex education programme, *Body Matters*.

Fred and Wilma Flintstone were the first couple to be shown in bed together on American TV.

When Mel Blanc, who voiced Barney Rubble, was seriously injured in a 1961 car crash, the producers managed to record 40 episodes of *The Flintstones* from his hospital bed – even though he was wearing a full-body cast and was unable to sit up.

Meghan Markle appeared on 34 episodes of the US version of the game show *Deal or No Deal* as one of the briefcase girls.

Actor Kit Harington, who plays Jon Snow in the TV series *Game of Thrones*, is a descendant of Robert Catesby, one of the Gunpowder Plotters who tried unsuccessfully to blow up the English Parliament in 1605. Harington actually played Catesby in the UK TV series *Gunpowder*.

Patrick McGoohan turned down the offer to star as The Saint in the 1960s because he disapproved of Simon Templar having a new girlfriend every week.

Until 1987, no TV was broadcast in Iceland on a Thursday.

Marcel the monkey used to disgust the cast of *Friends* by vomiting up live worms on set.

In the ten seasons of *Friends*, the six main characters drank 1,154 cups of coffee.

Former Nazi Rudolf Hess was a big fan of *Dynasty*.

After breaking his ankle in a fall, actor Conrad Phillips, who played the swashbuckling Swiss folk hero in the 1950s TV series *The Adventures of William Tell*, had to perform an entire episode from a wheelchair.

It has been calculated that the average American child sees about 13,000 deaths on TV between the ages of five and 14.

James Doohan, who played Scotty in *Star Trek*, lost his right middle finger to friendly fire on D-Day. Another bullet to his chest was stopped by a silver cigarette case given to him by his brother. Following Doohan's death in 2005, some of his ashes were blasted into space on board a rocket.

More than 7,000 people in Britain still watch black and white TV.

In recent years, Norwegian television has devoted entire evenings to 'slow TV', where nothing much happens. Programmes have included 12 hours of logs burning on a fire, 18 hours of minute-by-minute salmon fishing, and a 12-hour live knitting marathon.

The Beatles were once the support act to TV ventriloquist's doll Lenny the Lion.

BAT VILLAINS

(FROM THE 1960S
BATMAN TV SERIES)

The Archer (Art Carney)

The Black Widow (Tallulah Bankhead)

The Bookworm (Roddy McDowall)

Catwoman (Julie Newmar/Eartha Kitt)

Chandell (Liberace)

Nora Clavicle (Barbara Rush)

The Clock King (Walter Slezak)

Colonel Gumm (Roger C. Carmel)

Dr Cassandra (Ida Lupino)

Egghead (Vincent Price)

False Face (Malachi Throne)

Lord Marmaduke Ffogg (Rudy Vallee)

Mr Freeze (George Sanders/Otto Preminger/Eli Wallach)

The Joker (Cesar Romero)

King Tut (Victor Buono)

Lola Lasagne (Ethel Merman)

Louie the Lilac (Milton Berle)

The Mad Hatter (David Wayne)

Marsha, Queen of Diamonds (Carolyn Jones)

Minerva (Zsa Zsa Gabor)

The Minstrel (Van Johnson)

Olga, Queen of the Cossacks (Anne Baxter)

Ma Parker (Shelley Winters)

Lady Penelope Peasoup (Glynis Johns)

The Penguin (Burgess Meredith)

The Puzzler (Maurice Evans)

The Riddler (Frank Gorshin/John Astin)

Sandman (Michael Rennie)

Shame (Cliff Robertson)

The Siren (Joan Collins)

Zelda the Great (Anne Baxter)

BRITISH SITCOM
TITLES OVERSEAS

Absolutely Fabulous became *Pour Me Another One* in Russia

Absolutely Fabulous became *Totally Hysterical* in Sweden

Are You Being Served? became *Beane's of Boston* in the US

Birds of a Feather became *Stand By Your Man* in the US

Coupling became *Sexy Six* in France

Dad's Army became *The Rear Guard* in the US

The Fall and Rise of Reginald Perrin became *Reggie* in the US

Fawlty Towers became *Snavely* in the US

Fawlty Towers became *Tall John's Inn* in Finland

The Good Life became *Good Neighbors* in the US

The IT Crowd became *Cube Heads* in Hungary

The Likely Lads became *Steubenville* in the US

Man About the House became *Three's Company* in the US

Mind Your Language became *What a Country!* in the US

On the Buses became *Lotsa Luck* in the US

Only Fools and Horses became *Shady Deals* in Croatia

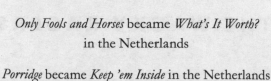

Only Fools and Horses became *What's It Worth?*
in the Netherlands

Porridge became *Keep 'em Inside* in the Netherlands

Porridge became *On the Rocks* in the US

Rising Damp became *Steam Heat* in the US

Steptoe and Son became *Albert and Herbert* in Sweden

Steptoe and Son became *Sanford and Son* in the US

Till Death Us Do Part became *All in the Family* in the US

The Vicar of Dibley became *The Vicar in Stilettos* in Poland

The Vicar of Dibley became *Minister of the Divine* in the US

The Young Ones became *Oh, No! Not THEM* in the US

THE WACKY RACERS

The full starting grid from the 1960s
Hanna-Barbera cartoon Wacky Races.

00. Dick Dastardly and Muttley in the Mean Machine

1. The Slag Brothers in the Bouldermobile

2. The Gruesome Twosome in the Creepy Coupe

3. Professor Pat Pending in the Convert-A-Car

4. Red Max in the Crimson Haybailer

5. Penelope Pitstop in the Compact Pussycat

6. Sergeant Blast and Private Meekley
in the Army Surplus Special

7. The Ant Hill Mob in the Bulletproof Bomb

8. Luke and Blubber in the Arkansas Chuggabug

9. Peter Perfect in the Turbo Terrific

10. Rufus Ruffcut and Sawtooth in the Buzz Wagon

DOCTOR WHO COMPANIONS

First Doctor (William Hartnell):

Susan Foreman (Carole Ann Ford)

Barbara Wright (Jacqueline Hill)

Ian Chesterton (William Russell)

Vicki (Maureen O'Brien)

Steven Taylor (Peter Purves)

Katarina (Adrienne Hill)

Sara Kingdom (Jean Marsh)

Dodo Chaplet (Jackie Lane)

Polly (Anneke Wills)

Ben Jackson (Michael Craze)

Second Doctor (Patrick Troughton):

Polly (Anneke Wills)

Ben Jackson (Michael Craze)

Jamie McCrimmon (Frazer Hines)

Victoria Waterfield (Deborah Watling)

Zoe Heriot (Wendy Padbury)

Brigadier Lethbridge-Stewart (Nicholas Courtney)

Third Doctor (Jon Pertwee):

Liz Shaw (Caroline John)

Jo Grant (Katy Manning)

Sarah Jane Smith (Elisabeth Sladen)

Fourth Doctor (Tom Baker):

Sarah Jane Smith (Elisabeth Sladen)

Harry Sullivan (Ian Marter)

Leela (Louise Jameson)

K-9

Romana I (Mary Tamm)

Romana II (Lalla Ward)

Adric (Matthew Waterhouse)

Nyssa (Sarah Sutton)

Tegan Jovanka (Janet Fielding)

Fifth Doctor (Peter Davison):

Adric (Matthew Waterhouse)

Nyssa (Sarah Sutton)

Tegan Jovanka (Janet Fielding)

Vislor Turlough (Mark Strickson)

Kamelion

Peri Brown (Nicola Bryant)

Sixth Doctor (Colin Baker):

Peri Brown (Nicola Bryant)

Mel Bush (Bonnie Langford)

Seventh Doctor (Sylvester McCoy):

Mel Bush (Bonnie Langford)

Ace (Sophie Aldred)

Eighth Doctor (Paul McGann):

Grace Holloway (Daphne Ashbrook)

Ninth Doctor (Christopher Eccleston):

Rose Tyler (Billie Piper)

Adam Mitchell (Bruno Langley)

Jack Harkness (John Barrowman)

Tenth Doctor (David Tennant):

Rose Tyler (Billie Piper)

Mickey Smith (Noel Clarke)

Donna Noble (Catherine Tate)

Martha Jones (Freema Agyeman)

Jack Harkness (John Barrowman)

Astrid Peth (Kylie Minogue)

Sarah Jane Smith (Elisabeth Sladen)

Jackson Lake (David Morrissey)

Lady Christina de Souza (Michelle Ryan)

Adelaide Brooke (Lindsay Duncan)

Wilfred Mott (Bernard Cribbins)

Eleventh Doctor (Matt Smith):

Amy Pond (Karen Gillan)

Rory Williams (Arthur Darvill)

River Song (Alex Kingston)

Craig Owens (James Corden)

Clara Oswald (Jenna Coleman)

Twelfth Doctor (Peter Capaldi):

Clara Oswald (Jenna Coleman)

River Song (Alex Kingston)

Nardole (Matt Lucas)

Bill Potts (Pearl Mackie)

Thirteenth Doctor (Jodie Whittaker):

Ryan Sinclair (Tosin Cole)

Yasmin Khan (Mandip Gill)

Graham O'Brien (Bradley Walsh)

STARS WHO BEGAN ON CHILDREN'S TV

Ben Affleck (*The Voyage of the Mimi*)

Christina Aguilera (*The All-New Mickey Mouse Club*)

Jessica Alba (*The Secret World of Alex Mack*)

Alan Arkin (*Sesame Street*)

Todd Carty (*Grange Hill*)

Miley Cyrus (*Hannah Montana*)

Jane Danson (*Children's Ward*)

Cat Deeley (*SMTV Live*)

Leonardo DiCaprio (*Romper Room*)

Anita Dobson (*Play Away*)

Mickey Dolenz (*Circus Boy*)

Hilary Duff (*Lizzie McGuire*)

Selena Gomez (*Barney and Friends*)

Ryan Gosling (*The All-New Mickey Mouse Club*)

Jennifer Love Hewitt (*Kids Incorporated*)

Jeremy Irons (*Play Away*)

David Jason (*Do Not Adjust Your Set*)

Demi Lovato (*Barney and Friends*)

Roger Moore (*Ivanhoe*)

Alanis Morissette (*You Can't Do That on Television*)

Tina O'Brien (*Children's Ward*)

Keri Russell (*The All-New Mickey Mouse Club*)

Phillip Schofield (*Going Live!*)

Robert Shaw (*The Buccaneers*)

Britney Spears (*The All-New Mickey Mouse Club*)

Justin Timberlake (*The All-New Mickey Mouse Club*)

Dennis Waterman (*Just William*)

Holly Willoughby (*S Club TV*)

BLINK AND
YOU'LL MISS THEM

CELEBRITY TV CAMEO ROLES

Wearing a commissionaire's uniform and top hat, John Lennon appeared as a lavatory attendant in a 1966 episode of the Peter Cook and Dudley Moore comedy series *Not Only … But Also*.

When running for President in 1968, Richard Nixon went on *Rowan and Martin's Laugh-In* just to say the show's catchphrase 'Sock it to me'. He needed six takes to get it right.

Former US President Gerald Ford and Secretary of State Henry Kissinger both guested on *Dynasty*.

Stephen Hawking appeared in an episode of *Star Trek: The Next Generation*, playing a game of poker with Albert Einstein, Sir Isaac Newton and Data.

The Beach Boys had a walk-on in *T.J. Hooker*.

John Cleese played an art gallery visitor in a 1979 episode of *Doctor Who*.

Little Richard and James Brown both guested on *Miami Vice*, but George Michael turned down the chance to play a waiter.

Michael Palin appeared as a surfer in an episode of Australian soap *Home and Away*.

Clive James played a postman in *Neighbours*.

Bob Hope, Burt Reynolds, Mickey Rooney, Dick Van Dyke and Julio Iglesias all had cameo roles in *The Golden Girls*.

Al Gore played an environmentally friendly janitor in a 2009 episode of comedy series *30 Rock*.

Robin Williams and Billy Crystal played two customers at coffee shop Central Perk in *Friends*.

David Crosby appeared on an episode of *Ellen*.

Prince Charles appeared in *Coronation Street* in a 2000 episode to mark the show's fortieth anniversary.

Frank Sinatra made a guest appearance on an episode of *Magnum P.I.* as a New York cop.

Sharon Osbourne played an uncompromising pool hall manager in an episode of *CSI*.

Taylor Swift played a murder victim in an episode of *CSI*.

SELECTED CALLERS
ON *FRASIER*

Gillian Anderson, Kevin Bacon, Halle Berry, Pat Boone, Matthew Broderick, Mel Brooks, Cindy Crawford, Billy Crystal, Macaulay Culkin, Jeff Daniels, David Duchovny, Hilary Duff, Gloria Estefan, Carrie Fisher, Jodie Foster, Art Garfunkel, Daryl Hannah, Tommy Hilfiger, Ron Howard, Eric Idle, Stephen King, Laura Linney, Ray Liotta, John Lithgow, Malcolm McDowell, John McEnroe, Helen Mirren, Bill Paxton, Christopher Reeve, Carly Simon, Neil Simon, Ben Stiller, Eddie Van Halen, Rufus Wainwright, Elijah Wood.

BEWILDERING TV QUIZ SHOW ANSWERS

Jamie Theakston: Where do you think Cambridge University is?
Contestant: Geography isn't my strong point.
Jamie Theakston: There's a clue in the title.
Contestant: Leicester?
— *Beg, Borrow or Steal*

Bob Holness: What 'L' do you make in the dark, when you don't consider the consequences?
Contestant: Love.
Bob Holness: No, I'm sorry. I'm afraid the actual answer was 'leap'.
— *Blockbusters*

Bradley Walsh: Complete the popular saying, 'Always the bridesmaid, never the …'
Contestant: Groom.
— *The Chase*

Ulrika Jonsson: Name the last thing you take off before going to bed.
Contestant: Your feet.
— *Dog Eat Dog*

Steve Harvey: Name something that follows the word 'pork'.
Contestant: Cupine.
— *Family Feud*

Grant Denyer: Name something France is famous for.

Contestant: Big Ben.

– *Family Feud* (Australia)

Les Dennis: Name a bird with a long neck.

Contestant: Naomi Campbell.

– *Family Fortunes*

Alexander Armstrong: Who was assassinated by Lee Harvey Oswald in Dallas?

Contestant: JR.

– *Pointless*

Gethin Jones: What is the more common name given to the aurora borealis?

Contestant: Hmm. I'm not really a plant person.

– *Sell Me the Answer*

Ben Shephard: What is the capital of the republic of Ecuador?

Contestant: Well, Ecuador's in Spain, so I'll say Barcelona.

– *Tipping Point*

Anne Robinson: Of which popular hot drink is 'eat' an anagram?

Contestant: Chocolate.

– *The Weakest Link*

Chris Tarrant: Which word specifically links a kind of mammal with an archbishop or high-ranking bishop? a) Carnivore b) Rodent c) Primate d) Marsupial.

Contestant: Marsupial.

– *Who Wants to Be a Millionaire*

EXAMPLES OF
TV CENSORSHIP

In 1957, CBS only allowed the pilot episode of *Leave It to Beaver* to be shown on condition that all shots of a toilet seat were cut.

Australian TV banned an episode of the children's cartoon series *Peppa Pig* in 2015 because the show suggested that spiders were nothing to be afraid of.

In keeping with the conservative broadcasting standards of the early 1960s, Dick Van Dyke and his onscreen wife Mary Tyler Moore always slept in separate beds on *The Dick Van Dyke Show*.

American network CBS banned the words 'breasts' and 'virgin' from *M*A*S*H*. Writer Larry Gelbart partly got round the ban by introducing a soldier from the Virgin Islands.

Myanmar banned *The Simpsons* on the grounds that the predominance of yellow and red was similar to the colour combination used by rebel groups in the country.

American network ABC refused to allow a fully-dressed Jeff Colby to kiss wife Fallon's foot in *The Colbys* for fear of encouraging foot fetishists.

Elvis Presley's act was considered so overtly sexual that when he appeared on *The Ed Sullivan Show* in 1957 he was only filmed from the waist up.

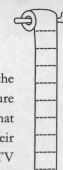

Jordanian TV refused to show Israel's performance at the 1978 Eurovision Song Contest and cut instead to a picture of a bunch of daffodils. When it then became apparent that Israel was going to win, most Arabic TV stations ended their broadcast early, claiming technical difficulties. Jordan's JTV went so far as to tell its viewers that Belgium had won, even though Belgium had finished a distant second.

Thirteen episodes of *Upstairs, Downstairs* were banned in the US for 17 years because they dealt with homosexuality and adultery.

The Muppet Show was banned in Saudi Arabia in 1979 because Miss Piggy was considered offensive on religious grounds.

The Sydney-based Australian soap *Number 96*, which began in 1972, contained such risqué bedroom scenes that for transmission in moralistic Melbourne a thick black band was often superimposed across the lower half of the screen.

Lucille Ball was never allowed to say the word 'pregnant' on *I Love Lucy*. It had to be 'expecting' or 'having a baby'.

In 1966, the BBC tried to postpone an episode of *Pinky and Perky*, which starred two singing puppet pigs, until after the forthcoming general election because it was afraid the show might contain political bias.

Chinese censors banned Winnie-the-Pooh from appearing on state-controlled TV in 2017 following suggestions that he bore an uncanny likeness to Chinese President Xi Jinping.

China also banned *Doctor Who* in 2011 because Chinese officials disapprove of any TV show portraying time travel.

ARTY FACTS

Vincent van Gogh sold only one painting in his lifetime.

Van Gogh painted *The Starry Night* while he was a patient at a psychiatric hospital in Saint-Rémy-de-Provence in southern France. Today, the hospital has a wing named after the painter.

In 1961, Henri Matisse's painting *Le Bateau* was hung upside down at New York's Museum of Modern Art for 46 days before anyone noticed.

Salvador Dali smeared himself with goat dung before meeting his wife for the first time.

Dali believed that he was the reincarnation of his dead brother.

When the *Mona Lisa* was stolen from the Louvre in Paris in 1911, the empty space it left on the wall attracted more visitors than the painting had. Among those questioned by police over the theft was Pablo Picasso.

Picasso's full name has 23 words. He was baptised Pablo Diego José Francisco de Paula Juan Nepomuceno Maria de los Remedios Cipriano de la Santisima Trinidad Martyr Patricio Clito Ruiz y Picasso.

In a career spanning 75 years, Picasso produced about 13,500 paintings, 100,000 prints and engravings, 34,000 book illustrations and 300 sculptures.

Paul Gauguin worked as a labourer on the construction of the Panama Canal.

Claude Monet's distinctive style was the result of cataracts that blurred his vision in later life.

L.S. Lowry worked as a full-time rent collector until his retirement in 1952, only painting in his spare time.

In 1652, while installing a doorway in the Milan convent where Leonardo da Vinci's *The Last Supper* is on display, builders cut into the bottom-centre part of the mural and removed Jesus's feet.

An unfinished horse statue by da Vinci was used for archery practice by invading French soldiers in 1499. In doing so, they destroyed it.

Damien Hirst directed the video for Blur's 'Country House'.

US artist Grant Wood wanted to use his mother Hattie as a model for his painting *American Gothic* but eventually decided that having to stand for so long would be too exhausting for her. So he persuaded his sister Nan to pose instead while wearing their mother's apron.

When J.M.W. Turner was 13, his father sold his best drawings for a few shillings by displaying them in his London barber shop.

Rembrandt was so poor that in 1662 he had to sell his late wife's grave. He died penniless seven years later.

Studio photographers used to ask their subjects to say 'prunes' instead of 'cheese' because it led to the desired tightening of the lips that was the fashion in the early 20th century. It was only when they realised it was possible to smile and look natural in photos that 'cheese' was introduced.

MOST EXPENSIVE PAINTINGS SOLD AT AUCTION

(AS OF JANUARY 2019)

1. *Salvator Mundi* by Leonardo da Vinci ($450.3 million)

2. *Les Femmes d'Alger* by Pablo Picasso ($185.2 million)

3. *Nu Couché* by Amedeo Modigliani ($175.9 million)

4. *Portrait of Dr Gachet* by Vincent van Gogh ($154.5 million)

5. *Three Studies of Lucian Freud* by Francis Bacon ($149.6 million)

6. *Bal du moulin de la Galette* by Pierre-Auguste Renoir ($146.3 million)

7. *Garçon à la pipe* by Pablo Picasso ($135 million)

8. *The Scream* by Edvard Munch ($127.8 million)

9. *Nude, Green Leaves and Bust* by Pablo Picasso ($119.5 million)

10. *Irises* by Vincent van Gogh ($116.1 million)

11. *Dora Maar au Chat* by Pablo Picasso ($115.6 million)

12. *Young Girl with a Flower Basket* by Pablo Picasso ($115 million)

TURNER PRIZE NOMINEES

Damien Hirst was nominated for, but did not win, the Turner Prize in 1992 for his infamous shark in formaldehyde. He had better luck three years later with a pickled, bisected cow and calf.

Rachel Whiteread won in 1993 with her concrete cast of the inside of a London house.

Gillian Wearing won in 1997 for a video of actors in police uniforms standing silently for an hour.

Chris Ofili won in 1998 for painting with elephant dung.

Tracey Emin's unmade bed, complete with stained sheets, condoms and soiled underwear, made the final shortlist of four in 1999.

Martin Creed won in 2001 for an empty room in which the lights switched on and off at five-second intervals.

Jake and Dinos Chapman were nominated in 2003 for a bronze sculpture designed to look like two cheap plastic blow-up sex dolls.

In 2005, Simon Starling won for a shed that was converted into a boat, sailed to the gallery, and was then erected again as a shed.

Mark Wallinger won in 2007 partly for a two-hour film of him wandering around an empty Berlin museum at night while dressed in a bear suit.

Cathy Wilkes was nominated in 2008 for a display that featured a female mannequin sitting naked on the toilet surrounded by leftover food.

Susan Philipsz won in 2010 for an installation under three bridges in Glasgow in which she sang the sea shanty 'Lowlands Away'.

James Richards was nominated in 2014 for a series of erotic photos found in a book in a Tokyo library, from which the genitals had been sandpapered away by Japanese censors.

Helen Marten won in 2016 for a series of sculptures made from everyday items such as cotton buds, marbles, shoe soles, snooker chalk and bicycle chains.

ART FAILS

A carefully crafted, avant-garde art exhibit at an Italian museum was destroyed in 2015 when it was thrown out by overzealous cleaners who mistook it for rubbish left over from a party.

A museum in Cleveland, Ohio, discovered in 2009 that an exhibit believed to be a lock of aviator Amelia Earhart's hair was instead a worthless piece of thread.

When English sculptor David Hensel submitted a laughing head on a wooden plinth for exhibition at London's Royal Academy in 2006, he was surprised to see only the plinth put on show. It transpired that the Academy had thought they were two separate works and much preferred the simple support to the elaborately sculpted head.

A 1997 exhibition of rotting fish in sealed bags by South Korean artist Lee Bul at New York's Museum of Modern Art was pulled after only a few hours when the ventilation equipment failed, making the stench unbearable.

A giant inflatable dog poo – an artwork by American Paul McCarthy – broke free from its moorings outside a museum in Berne, Switzerland, in 2008 and landed on a nearby children's home.

CATCHY BOOK TITLES

Knitting with Dog Hair: Better a Sweater from a Dog You Know and Love Than from a Sheep You'll Never Meet by Kendall Crolius and Anne Montgomery

Reusing Old Graves by Douglas Davies and Alastair Shaw

Penetrating Wagner's Ring by John L. DiGaetani

The Stray Shopping Carts of Eastern North America: A Guide to Field Identification by Julian Montague

The 2009–2014 World Outlook for 60-milligram Containers of Fromage Frais by Philip M. Parker

Highlights in the History of Concrete by Christopher Stanley

How to Avoid Huge Ships by John W. Trimmer

Greek Rural Postmen and Their Cancellation Numbers by Derek Willan

Developments in Dairy Cow Breeding and Management: And New Opportunities to Widen the Uses for Straw by Gareth Williams

The Book of Marmalade: Its Antecedents, Its History and Its Role in the World Today by C. Anne Wilson

Natural Bust Enlargement Total Power: How to Increase the Other 90% of Your Mind to Increase the Size of Your Breasts by Donald L. Wilson

BANNED BOOKS

Alice's Adventures in Wonderland by Lewis Carroll was banned in Hunan, China, from the 1930s because the censor thought that attributing human language to animals was insulting to humans.

Animal Farm by George Orwell was banned in schools in the United Arab Emirates in 2002 because it features a talking pig.

Brave New World by Aldous Huxley was removed from classrooms in Miller, Missouri, in 1980 for 'making promiscuous sex look like fun'.

The Diary of a Young Girl by Anne Frank was banned by the Alabama State Textbook Committee in 1983 for being too depressing.

Mary Shelley's *Frankenstein* was banned in South Africa in 1955 for containing 'obscene' and 'indecent' material.

The Grapes of Wrath by John Steinbeck was banned in parts of California for its unflattering portrait of the state's residents.

Little Red Riding Hood was banned in 1990 by school officials in Culver City, California, because one of the items in her basket is a bottle of wine, which was therefore likely to encourage underage drinking.

My Friend Flicka by Mary O'Hara was banned by some Florida schools in 1990 because it uses the word 'bitch' to describe a female dog.

Schindler's Ark by Thomas Keneally was banned in Lebanon for its positive depiction of Jews.

Uncle Tom's Cabin by Harriet Beecher Stowe was banned in the Confederate states during the American Civil War because of its anti-slavery content.

Where's Wally? was among the top 100 banned books in the 1990s because the original printing of the first book in the series featured a cartoon of a crowded beach scene that showed a side view of a woman with one uncovered breast.

The Wizard of Oz by L. Frank Baum was the subject of a 1986 lawsuit from seven Fundamentalist Christian families in Tennessee who objected to its depiction of benevolent witches.

FICTIONAL DETECTIVES
AND THEIR AUTHORS

Inspector Roderick Alleyn (Ngaio Marsh)

Lew Archer (Ross Macdonald)

Father Brown (G.K. Chesterton)

Brother Cadfael (Ellis Peters)

Albert Campion (Margery Allingham)

Charlie Chan (Earl Derr Biggers)

Nick and Nora Charles (Dashiell Hammett)

Adam Dalgliesh (P.D. James)

Nancy Drew (Edward Stratemeyer)

C. Auguste Dupin (Edgar Allan Poe)

Jack Frost (R.D. Wingfield)

Cordelia Gray (P.D. James)

Mike Hammer (Mickey Spillane)

Harry Hole (Jo Nesbø)

Sherlock Holmes (Arthur Conan Doyle)

Meyer Landsman (Michael Chabon)

Inspector Thomas Linley (Elizabeth George)

Jules Maigret (Georges Simenon)

Philip Marlowe (Raymond Chandler)

Jane Marple (Agatha Christie)

Kinsey Millhone (Sue Grafton)

Inspector Endeavour Morse (Colin Dexter)

Charlie Parker (John Connolly)

Hercule Poirot (Agatha Christie)

Agatha Raisin (M.C. Beaton)

John Rebus (Ian Rankin)

Arkady Renko (Martin Cruz Smith)

Matt Scudder (Lawrence Block)

Sam Spade (Dashiell Hammett)

Nick Stefanos (George Pelecanos)

Tom Thorne (Mark Billingham)

Dick Tracy (Chester Gould)

Kurt Wallander (Henning Mankell)

Chief Inspector Reg Wexford (Ruth Rendell)

Lord Peter Wimsey (Dorothy L. Sayers)

BOOKS YOU SHOULD HAVE READ CONDENSED INTO TWO LINES

The Catcher in the Rye: Expelled from school, troubled teenager Holden Caulfield tries to find himself in New York and encounters nuns, prostitutes, his former teachers, his sister and an old girlfriend along the way.

Don Quixote: A middle-aged man obsessed with chivalry decides he's a knight and, with his squire, roams Spain looking for dragons to slay. By the time he realises he's crazy, it's too late and he dies from a fever.

Great Expectations: Poor orphaned Pip. He thinks his benefactor is an old woman with an aversion to house-cleaning but it turns out to be a notorious convict whose secret daughter, Estella, repeatedly breaks Pip's heart.

The Great Gatsby: Party-loving millionaire Jay Gatsby is keen to hook up again with the now married Daisy Buchanan. They begin an affair that ends when Gatsby is shot dead by a love rival in a case of mistaken identity.

The Hound of the Baskervilles: Sherlock Holmes and Watson go to Dartmoor where a big dog is wreaking havoc. It is being unleashed by a local naturalist – a long-lost Baskerville hell-bent on seizing the family fortune.

Lady Chatterley's Lover: With a paralysed, impotent and distant husband, Lady Chatterley romps in the woods with her bit of rough, gamekeeper Mellors. She falls pregnant, he gets fired but hubby refuses to give her a divorce.

Lord of the Flies: Schoolboys stranded on a deserted tropical island turn feral. Amid a bitter power struggle and visions of monsters, some are slaughtered, the ordeal only ending with the arrival of a passing ship.

Pride and Prejudice: Feisty Elizabeth Bennet is wary of the rich, handsome and haughty Mr Darcy. Although she is beneath him socially, he eventually overcomes his pride and she her prejudice and the two marry.

To Kill a Mockingbird: Lawyer Atticus Finch upsets the locals in 1930s Alabama by defending a black man accused of rape. When the town drunk attacks Finch's children, their reclusive neighbour, Boo Radley, saves the day.

The Wind in the Willows: Ratty gets ratty with (and Badger badgers) reckless driver Toad whose car is towed away by police. Is Mole the informer? Released from jail, Toad finds Toad Hall has weasel squatters. Such is life.

NOMS DE PLUME

Richard Bachman (Stephen King)

Beachcomber (J.B. Morton)

M.C. Beaton (Marion Chesney)

Currer Bell (Charlotte Brontë)

Lewis Carroll (Charles Lutwidge Dodgson)

Leslie Charteris (Leslie Charles Bowyer-Yin)

George Eliot (Mary Anne Evans)

Ford Madox Ford (Ford Hermann Hueffer)

C.S. Forester (Cecil Louis Troughton Smith)

Nicci French (Nicci Gerard and Sean French)

Robert Galbraith (J.K. Rowling)

O. Henry (William Sydney Porter)

James Herriot (James Alfred Wight)

E.L. James (Erika Leonard)

John le Carré (David John Moore Cornwell)

Molière (Jean Baptiste Poquelin)

George Orwell (Eric Arthur Blair)

Ellis Peters (Edith Pargeter)

Anne Rice (Howard Allen Frances O'Brien)

Saki (Hector Hugh Munro)

George Sand (Amantine Lucile Aurore Dupin)

Lemony Snicket (Daniel Handler)

Stendhal (Marie-Henri Beyle)

Patience Strong (Winifred Emma May)

P.L. Travers (Helen Goff)

Mark Twain (Samuel Langhorne Clemens)

Voltaire (François-Marie Arouet)

FOOTNOTES

LITERARY TRIVIA

The only book in Latin ever to feature on the *New York Times* bestseller list was a 1960 translation of *Winnie-the-Pooh*.

L. Frank Baum, author of *The Wizard of Oz*, came up with the name after spotting that the filing cabinet in his study had a drawer labelled O-Z.

Due to his failing eyesight, James Joyce wrote much of his novel *Finnegans Wake* in coloured crayon on pieces of cardboard.

Beatrix Potter shot a squirrel out of a tree to provide a model for Squirrel Nutkin.

Evelyn Waugh's first wife was named Evelyn. They were known as 'He-Evelyn' and 'She-Evelyn'.

The first book on plastic surgery was written as early as 1597.

J.K. Rowling came up with the names for the Hogwarts houses in Harry Potter while she was on an aeroplane and jotted them down on a sickbag.

Sir Walter Scott had a salt cellar that was made from the fourth cervical vertebra of Charles I.

When Stephen King walked unannounced into a bookshop in Alice Springs, Australia, for an impromptu book signing session in 2007, customers thought he was a vandal defacing the books and reported him to staff.

Harriet Beecher Stowe, author of *Uncle Tom's Cabin*, lived next door to Mark Twain in Hartford, Connecticut.

When travelling, Charles Dickens kept a navigation compass with him to ensure that he always slept facing north because he believed it improved his writing.

Washington Irving, author of *Rip Van Winkle*, the man who slept for 20 years, suffered from insomnia.

John Steinbeck's original manuscript for *Of Mice and Men* was eaten by his puppy, Toby.

T.E. Lawrence lost his manuscript for *The Seven Pillars of Wisdom* at Reading railway station in 1919 and had to rewrite it from notes.

Gadsby, a 50,000-word novel written by American author Ernest Vincent Wright in 1939, contains no words with the letter 'e'.

When Alexandre Dumas, author of *The Count of Monte Cristo* and *The Three Musketeers*, fought his first duel his trousers fell down.

J.R.R. Tolkien's great granddaughter, Ruth Tolkien, is the only blind fencer competing in sighted contests in the UK.

After suffering a major stroke, French writer Jean-Dominique Bauby dictated his 1997 book *The Diving Bell and the Butterfly* by blinking his left eyelid for ten months.

Lewis Carroll and Ernest Hemingway both wrote most of their books standing up.

Before becoming a successful author of detective novels, Dashiell Hammett worked as a private detective. His first case was to track down a stolen Ferris wheel.

For inspiration, D.H. Lawrence used to climb mulberry trees naked.

Before becoming a writer, *Tarzan* author Edgar Rice Burroughs worked as a pencil-sharpener salesman for seven years.

Vladimir Nabokov, Russian author of *Lolita*, was a serious lepidopterologist, or student of butterflies.

Graphic novelist Neil Gaiman's first book was a biography of Duran Duran.

Hungarian-born Baroness Orczy, author of *The Scarlet Pimpernel*, could not speak a word of English until she was 15 but went on to write over 60 novels and short story collections in that language.

Mickey Spillane ordered 50,000 copies of his 1952 novel *Kiss Me, Deadly* to be destroyed because the comma had been left out of the title.

AUTOBIOGRAPHY TITLES

Open – tennis player Andre Agassi

Never Have Your Dog Stuffed and Other Things I've Learned – actor Alan Alda

It's All About a Ball – footballer Alan Ball

My Shit Life So Far – comedian Frankie Boyle

Coreyography – actor Corey Feldman

Wishful Drinking – actress Carrie Fisher

My Name Escapes Me – actor Alec Guinness

Don't Hassel the Hoff – actor David Hasselhoff

They Made a Monkee Out of Me – actor Davy Jones

Tall, Dark and Gruesome – horror actor Christopher Lee

All You Need Is Ears – Beatles producer George Martin

Born Standing Up – comedian Steve Martin

A View From a Broad – actress Bette Midler

It Sure Beats Working – actor Robert Mitchum

Me: Moir – comedian Vic Reeves, whose real name is Jim Moir

In the Time of Nick – broadcaster Nick Owen

Nerd Do Well – comedy actor Simon Pegg

Pryor Convictions – comedy actor Richard Pryor

Memoirs of a Professional Cad – actor George Sanders

Kiss and Make-Up – rock musician Gene Simmons

REJECTED AUTHORS

In 1944, American publishers Dial Press rejected George Orwell's political allegory *Animal Farm* on the grounds that it was impossible to sell animal stories in the USA.

John Creasey received 743 rejection letters before his first book was published. He went on to write 562 crime fiction novels that have sold more than 80 million copies worldwide.

When Jane Austen's novel *First Impressions* was initially rejected by a publisher, she made significant revisions to the manuscript and changed its title to *Pride and Prejudice*.

Harry Potter and the Philosopher's Stone was rejected by 12 publishers and J.K. Rowling was advised not to quit her day job.

Gone with the Wind by Margaret Mitchell was rejected 38 times before it was published.

Carrie by Stephen King was rejected 30 times.

Lord of the Flies by William Golding was rejected 20 times.

Zen and the Art of Motorcycle Maintenance by Robert S. Pirsig has sold over five million copies worldwide but only after it was rejected 121 times.

WHERE'S WALLY
AROUND THE WORLD

The little guy in the red and white stripes has
a number of international aliases …

UK: Wally	Hungary: Vili
USA: Waldo	Iceland: Valli
Afrikaans: Willie	Italy: Ubaldo
Croatia: Jura	Lithuania: Valdas
Czech Republic: Valdik	Norway: Willy
Denmark: Holger	Russia: Uolli
Estonia: Volli	Serbia: Gile
Finland: Vallu	Sweden: Waldo or Valle
France: Charlie	Turkey: Ali
Germany: Walter	Vietnam: Van Lang

LIKE A PIG IN LIT

FAMOUS SWINE IN LITERATURE

Babe (*The Sheep-Pig* by Dick King-Smith)

Empress of Blandings
(*Blandings Castle* novels by P.G. Wodehouse)

Gouger, Snouter, Rooter and Tusker
(*Discworld* by Terry Pratchett)

Gryllus (*The Pig Scrolls* by Paul Shipton)

Gub-Gub (*Doctor Dolittle* by Hugh Lofting)

Jodie (*The Amityville Horror* by Jay Anson)

Little Pig Robinson
(*The Tale of Little Pig Robinson* by Beatrix Potter)

Napoleon, Old Major, Snowball and Squealer
(*Animal Farm* by George Orwell)

Piglet (*Winnie-the-Pooh* by A.A. Milne)

Pigling Bland (*The Tale of Pigling Bland* by Beatrix Potter)

Sam Pig (*The Sam Pig Storybook* by Alison Uttley)

Wilbur (*Charlotte's Web* by E.B. White)

MR MEN AND LITTLE MISSES IN FRENCH

Monsieur Bing (Mr Bounce)

Monsieur Malchance (Mr Bump)

Monsieur Rapide (Mr Busy)

Monsieur Maladroit (Mr Clumsy)

Monsieur Glouton (Mr Greedy)

Monsieur Grincheux (Mr Grumpy)

Monsieur Endormi (Mr Lazy)

Monsieur Méli-Mélo (Mr Muddle)

Monsieur Silence (Mr Quiet)

Monsieur Mal-Élevé (Mr Rude)

Monsieur Étonnant (Mr Silly)

Monsieur Maigre (Mr Skinny)

Monsieur Atchoum (Mr Sneeze)

Monsieur Chatouille (Mr Tickle)

Monsieur Inquiet (Mr Worry)

Madame Farceuse (Little Miss Bad)

Madame Autoritaire (Little Miss Bossy)

Madame Je-sais-tout (Little Miss Brainy)

Madame Prudente (Little Miss Careful)

Madame Bavarde (Little Miss Chatterbox)

Madame Pourquoi (Little Miss Curious)

Madame Follette (Little Miss Dotty)

Madame Indécise (Little Miss Fickle)

Madame Dodue (Little Miss Greedy)

Madame Catastrophe (Little Miss Helpful)

Madame Tintamarre (Little Miss Loud)

Madame Canaille (Little Miss Naughty)

Madame Proprette (Little Miss Neat)

Madame Terreur (Little Miss Scary)

Madame Tête-en-l'air (Little Miss Scatterbrain)

Madame Moi-Je (Little Miss Show-Off)

Madame Timide (Little Miss Shy)

Madame Coquette (Little Miss Vain)

Madame Sage (Little Miss Wise)

UK POETS LAUREATE

John Dryden (1668–88)

Thomas Shadwell (1689–92)

Nahum Tate (1692–1715)

Nicholas Rowe (1715–18)

Laurence Eusden (1718–30)

Colley Cibber (1730–57)

William Whitehead (1757–85)

Thomas Warton (1785–90)

Henry James Pye (1790–1813)

Robert Southey (1813–43)

William Wordsworth (1843–50)

Alfred, Lord Tennyson (1850–92)

Alfred Austin (1896–1913)

Robert Bridges (1913–30)

John Masefield (1930–67)

Cecil Day-Lewis (1968–72)

John Betjeman (1972–84)

Ted Hughes (1984–98)

Andrew Motion (1999–2009)

Carol Ann Duffy (2009–2019)

Simon Armitage (2019–)

FIRSTS, SECONDS, ONLYS AND LASTS

FIRSTS

Buzz Aldrin was the first man to pee on the moon.

The first person to be killed by a robot was Robert Williams who was hit on the head by a mechanical arm at a Ford casting plant in Flat Rock, Michigan, on 25 January 1979.

The first telephone book was a single sheet, issued in New Haven, Connecticut, in 1878. It listed the names of about 50 subscribers but included no phone numbers.

The first mobile phone call was made by Motorola employee Martin Cooper on 3 April 1973 on Sixth Avenue in New York City. He called a friend who worked for rival company AT&T.

The first woman to model a bikini was 19-year-old French showgirl Micheline Bernardini at a fashion event in Paris on 5 July 1946.

The first person to survive going over Niagara Falls in a barrel was Annie Edson Taylor on 24 October 1901 – her sixty-third birthday.

The first BBC TV programme to be broadcast after the Second World War on 7 June 1946 was the same Mickey Mouse cartoon that had been cut short on 1 September 1939 when screens went blank for nearly seven years.

The first selfie was taken in 1839 by Robert Cornelius, an amateur chemist from Philadelphia.

In 1893, New Zealand became the first country to give women the vote.

On 10 June 1935, Dr Robert Holbrook Smith, of Akron, Ohio, became the first person to be cured by Alcoholics Anonymous.

The first person to vomit in space was Soviet cosmonaut Gherman Stepanovich Titov who suffered from space sickness while orbiting Earth aboard *Vostok 2* on 6 August 1961.

The world's first parking meter, known as Park-O-Meter No. 1, was installed in Oklahoma City on 16 July 1935.

In 2016, 42 years after inventing the Heimlich Manoeuvre, Dr Henry Heimlich performed it in person for the first time at the age of 96 to save a woman choking in his Cincinnati retirement home.

Mathematician and engineer Hero of Alexandria built the first vending machine as early as the first century AD. It was used to dispense holy water.

The first tweet was sent by Twitter co-creator Jack Dorsey on 21 March 2006. It read: 'just setting up my twttr'. Twttr was the service's original name.

The first singing telegram, a birthday greeting from a fan to singer Rudy Vallee, was delivered over the phone on 28 July 1933 by Western Union operator Lucille Lipps.

The first pedestrian to be killed by a car was Bridget Driscoll in the grounds of the Crystal Palace in London, on 17 August 1896. She was hit by a vehicle travelling at the 'reckless pace' of 4mph.

The world's first official nudist camp was Frei Sonnenland at Motzener See, Germany, which opened its doors in 1920.

The first speaking clock came into service in Paris on 14 February 1933, voiced by broadcasting personality Marcel Laporte.

The first supermarket (with self-service, checkouts and a turnstile entrance) was opened on 11 September 1916 by Clarence Saunders at his Piggly Wiggly store in Memphis, Tennessee.

The first bristle toothbrushes were used in China during the Tang Dynasty (AD 619–907), with bristles sourced from hogs.

In 1961, Terry Brooks appeared in a British TV commercial as the first Milkybar Kid.

The world's first jukebox was displayed and used at the Palais Royale Saloon in San Francisco on 23 November 1889.

The first escort agency, the S.O.S. Bureau, was run by Mrs Horace Farquharson and operated out of 31 Dover Street, London, from 1937. For £3 an evening, the impeccably connected Mrs Farquharson would provide a suitable companion for any social function.

The first launderette was the Washeteria, opened at Fort Worth, Texas, by J.F. Cantrell in 1934. It had four electric washing machines, but customers had to bring their own soap.

The first woman to run for President of the United States was Victoria Woodhull in 1872.

The world's first flight attendant was Germany's Heinrich Kubis who, in March 1912, looked after passengers on board the zeppelin *Schwaben*.

The first multi-storey car park appeared as early as May 1901 when the City and Suburban Electric Carriage Company opened a seven-floor building near London's Piccadilly Circus. It had space for 100 vehicles.

On 6 August 1890, convicted murderer William Kemmler, of Buffalo, New York, was the first person to be legally executed by electric chair.

The first motel was opened at San Luis Obispo, California, on 12 December 1925.

The first recorded strike took place in Egypt on 14 November 1152 BC when artisans working on the Royal Necropolis protested about poor working conditions and reduced grain rations.

On 26 September 1881, Godalming in Surrey became the first place in the world to have public electricity.

The first person to use an ATM was comedy actor Reg Varney when he performed the grand opening of the new invention at the Enfield branch of Barclays Bank on 27 June 1967.

In 1884, Phil Gilbert's shoe store in Vicksburg, Mississippi, became the first to sell shoes in boxed pairs. Previously each shoe was sold as an individual item.

SECONDS

American engineer Elisha Gray was the second person to invent the telephone. His application arrived at the US Patent Office on 14 February 1876, a few hours after Alexander Graham Bell's.

Australian athlete John Landy was the second man to run a mile in under four minutes. He clocked 3:57.9 in Finland on 21 June 1954 – six weeks after Roger Bannister's record-breaking run in Oxford.

The second US President to be assassinated – 16 years after Abraham Lincoln – was James Garfield who was fatally shot in Washington, D.C., on 2 July 1881 by Charles J. Guiteau – less than four months after being sworn in.

The world's second female prime minister was India's Indira Gandhi in 1966 – six years after Sirimavo Bandaranaike won power in Ceylon (modern day Sri Lanka).

On 23 May 1956 – three years after Edmund Hillary and Tenzing Norgay reached the summit of Everest – Switzerland's Ernst Schmied and Juerg Marmet became the second pair to climb the world's highest mountain.

American astronaut Alan Shepard was the second man in space, on 5 May 1961 – three weeks after Russian Yuri Gagarin.

The second band to perform at Live Aid at Wembley Stadium on 13 July 1985 – following on from opening act Status Quo – was The Style Council.

The second longest river in Africa, after the Nile, is the Congo.

The second person to fly solo across the Atlantic Ocean was Australian aviator Bert Hinkler who, in 1931, flew from Brazil to Africa – four years after Charles Lindbergh had flown from New York to Paris. In 1932, Amelia Earhart became the second person – and therefore the first woman – to fly solo across the North Atlantic, from Newfoundland to Ireland.

The horse that finished second to 100–1 outsider Foinavon in the infamous 1967 Grand National, when nearly half of the 44 runners came to grief at the twenty-third fence, was Honey End.

The second talkie film, *Tenderloin,* a crime thriller starring Dolores Costello, was released by Warner Brothers on 14 March 1928 – five months after *The Jazz Singer.*

ONLYS

George Bush is the only US President known to have vomited on a foreign dignitary. He threw up over the Japanese Prime Minister in 1992.

The only bone in the human body that is not connected to another is the hyoid, a horseshoe-shaped bone at the base of the tongue.

The only part of Britain that remained at war with Russia for 110 years after the end of the Crimean War was the small town of Berwick-upon-Tweed on the Scottish border. It was accidentally omitted from the 1856 Treaty of Paris, and so hostilities only officially ended when a Soviet official visited in 1966 to declare peace. The mayor of Berwick replied: 'Please tell the Russian people that at last they can sleep peacefully in their beds!'

Because of its S-shape, Panama is the only country in the world where you can watch the sun rise over the Pacific Ocean and set over the Atlantic.

The only six-letter word in the English language that contains all five vowels is 'eunoia', a rarely-used medical term to describe a state of normal mental health

Cimarron County is the only county in the United States that touches five states – Texas, Colorado, New Mexico, Kansas and its own, Oklahoma.

Australia is the only continent without an active volcano.

The only football competition in the world where the same two teams play each other every week is the Isles of Scilly Football League. The league only has two clubs – the Garrison Gunners and the Woolpack Wanderers.

The only film seen by fewer people than appeared in it was the 1945 Nazi epic *Kolberg*. It was released at a time when not many Berlin cinemas were still operating, so its total audience was considerably smaller than its vast cast of 187,000, which included 50,000 soldiers.

Hummingbirds are the only birds that can fly backwards as well as forwards.

The only British professional football team that contains the letter 'J' is Scottish club St Johnstone.

Elvis Presley made his only TV commercial in return for a box of hot glazed donuts.

The only prime minister who vanished never to be seen again was Australia's Harold Holt, who disappeared while taking an impromptu swim off a Melbourne beach in 1967. He was presumed drowned and declared dead, but his body has never been found.

The only American president to have been born on the 4 July was Calvin Coolidge, in 1872.

The only song to feature in the UK Top 20 with four different versions simultaneously is 'Unchained Melody'. In the week of 17 June 1955, Jimmy Young, Al Hibbler, Les Baxter and Liberace all had hits with the song, with Young at number one and Hibbler at number two.

There are more than 40 rivers in the state of Oklahoma but the only one that flows north is the Poteau River.

The only land reptile species native to Ireland is the common lizard.

Isaac Newton was elected as an MP in 1689 and served for exactly one year, during which the only time he ever spoke in Parliament was to ask for a window to be closed.

The only horse to win a race with a dead jockey is Sweet Kiss, whose rider, Frank Hayes, suffered a fatal heart attack long before the winning post but somehow managed to stay in the saddle to steer the 20–1 shot to victory in a steeplechase at Belmont Park, New York, on 4 June 1923.

The only former British Home Stores employee to have had a number one hit was George Michael.

Brazil is the only country that is crossed by both the equator and a tropic (Capricorn).

Mittwoch (Wednesday) is the only German day of the week that doesn't end in *tag* (day).

Nauru is the only country in the world without an official capital.

The only war known to have been started by a postage stamp was fought between Bolivia and Paraguay from 1932 to 1935 after first Bolivia and then Paraguay issued stamps proclaiming the disputed Gran Chaco territory to be theirs.

LASTS

Every year, the last inhabited territory to celebrate New Year is American Samoa (11 hours behind the UK).

The last *Titanic* survivor, Milvina Dean, died in Southampton in 2009 at the age of 97.

The last British monarch who could not speak English was George I. He was also the last British monarch to be buried outside the UK, being laid to rest in his native Hanover in 1727 after dying there on a visit.

The last line spoken by Marilyn Monroe on screen was 'How do you find your way back in the dark?' It is from the 1961 film *The Misfits* with Clark Gable.

The last two people to be hanged in the UK were Peter Allen and Gwynne Evans who were executed at prisons in Liverpool and Manchester respectively at 8:00 am on 13 August 1964.

The twenty-fourth and last letter of the Greek alphabet is omega.

The last major British TV drama series to be made in black and white was *The Forsyte Saga* in 1967.

Queen Lili'uokalani, the last royal ruler of Hawaii, was deposed in 1893.

Hawaii was the fiftieth and last state to join the United States, on 21 August 1959.

The last amateur footballer to play in an FA Cup final was Bill Slater for Blackpool in 1951.

Glenn Miller's last flight, on 15 December 1944, was from RAF Twinwood Farm in Clapham, Bedfordshire.

The last two prisoners to attempt to escape from Alcatraz were John Paul Scott and Darl Lee Parker on 16 December 1962. Parker was found just 100 yards away from the main island but Scott managed to swim to the mainland – the only inmate known to have done so – where he was discovered exhausted beneath the Golden Gate Bridge and returned to Alcatraz. The prison closed for good three months later.

The last surviving Munchkin from *The Wizard of Oz* was Jerry Maren, who died in 2018 aged 98.

The last sighting of a live great auk was off Newfoundland in 1852.

The last mainline steam passenger train in Britain ran from Liverpool to Carlisle and back on 11 August 1968. Four hundred and fifty enthusiasts paid the equivalent of £240 today for the experience.

Although they made an unannounced live appearance in January 1969 on the rooftop of the Apple building in London, The Beatles' last proper concert was at Candlestick Park, San Francisco, on 29 August 1966. The last song they played there was 'Long Tall Sally'.

In 1999, Bhutan became the last country on Earth to introduce television.

Bing Crosby's last golf score on the day he died – 14 October 1977 – was an 85. Because of his 13 handicap, he and his partner won by one shot.

After 5,531 episodes and 21 years, the last episode of British radio serial *Mrs Dale's Diary* (later *The Dales*) was broadcast on 25 April 1969.

On 24 June 2018, Saudi Arabia became the last country in the world to allow women to drive.

The *Hougoumont*, the last ship to take convicts from the UK to Australia, docked in Fremantle on 9 January 1868. About 168,000 prisoners had been transported to Australia since 1788.

Babe Ruth hit his 714th and last home run on 25 May 1935 at Forbes Field in Pittsburgh.

The last person in Britain to be tried and imprisoned under the 1735 Witchcraft Act was Scottish medium Helen Duncan in 1944. She was sentenced to nine months in jail.

SCIENCE AND
TECHNOLOGY

THE HUMAN BODY

The average speed of a sneeze is about 100mph.

Our ears and noses never stop growing.

The human nose can detect one trillion different smells.

The body heat produced by a human is similar to that from a 100-watt light bulb.

The human stomach lining replaces itself every three to four days.

Stomach acid is strong enough to dissolve razor blades.

The human stomach contains about 35 million digestive glands.

Twenty-five per cent of an adult human's bones are in their feet.

We have about 300 bones at birth, but only 206 as an adult. This is because as we grow, some of the bones fuse together.

Human bone is four times stronger than concrete.

There are more bacteria in the human mouth than there are people in the world.

We produce enough saliva in a lifetime to fill two swimming pools.

The two lines that connect our top lip to the bottom of our nose are known as the philtrum.

Although the sound of the average human snore measures 40 decibels, a loud snorer can manage over 110 — almost as loud as a chainsaw or a pneumatic drill.

One brow wrinkle is the result of around 200,000 frowns.

Like fingerprints, each human tongue has its own unique print.

The human tongue has 9,000 taste buds.

The skin is thickest on our feet (1.4mm) and thinnest on our eyelids (0.2mm).

We shed nearly nine pounds of skin a year.

The medical name for earwax is cerumen.

The h/h, or Bombay, blood group is the rarest in the world, present in only 0.0004 per cent of the world's population. In 2017, it was discovered that only one person in the whole of Colombia had that blood type, meaning that blood for a transfusion had to be imported from Brazil.

The human heart creates enough pressure when it pumps out to the body to squirt blood a distance of 30 feet.

The human heart beats about 100,000 times a day.

It only takes a minute for a blood cell to travel all the way around the body and back to the heart.

The total length of blood vessels in the human body is 62,000 miles — enough to stretch around the equator two and a half times.

The average person falls asleep at night in 15 minutes.

On average, we have four dreams every night, which works out at 1,460 a year.

We are about half an inch taller when we wake up in the morning than when we go to sleep at night. This is because pressure on the cartilage discs in the spine is relieved during sleep, allowing the discs to expand.

An adult small intestine is about 21 feet long. By contrast, the large intestine is only five feet long.

Each day on average, a pair of human feet lose half a pint of water in perspiration.

Perspiration is odourless. It is the bacteria on the skin which create the smell.

The average person has 67 different species of bacteria in their navel.

The liver is the only organ that can completely regenerate itself.

Men get hiccups twice as often as women.

The average human body contains enough fat to make seven bars of soap.

The medical term for nail biting is onychophagia.

Fingernails grow faster on the hand a person writes with.

The pop that we hear when we crack our knuckles is the sound of a bubble of gas bursting.

Water makes up more than 50 per cent of the average adult's body weight.

The average human body contains enough carbon to make 900 pencils.

The human brain has the capacity to store 4.7 billion books or 670 million web pages.

Messages from the human brain travel along nerves at up to 200mph.

There are so many nerve cells in the human brain that it would take almost 3,000 years to count them.

The brain is often more active when we're asleep than when we're awake.

Tooth enamel is the hardest substance in the human body.

The oldest known dental filling is 13,000 years old and made from bitumen, plants and hairs.

THE EYES HAVE IT

A human eye is composed of more than two million working parts.

Your eye muscles move more than 100,000 times a day.

Women blink almost twice as much as men.

In a single day, we may blink over 20,000 times.

The human eye can distinguish between approximately 10 million colours.

Newborn babies don't shed tears when they cry because their tear ducts haven't fully formed.

The cornea is the only living part of the body without a blood supply. Instead it gets its oxygen directly from the air.

Each eyelash has a life span of about five months. The combined length of all the eyelashes shed by a human in the course of a lifetime is over 98 feet.

PEOPLE WITH DIFFERENT COLOURED EYES

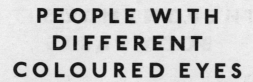

Alexander the Great	Michael Flatley
Gracie Allen	Josh Henderson
Dan Aykroyd	Tim McIlrath
Elizabeth Berkley	Simon Pegg
Kate Bosworth	Jane Seymour
David Bowie	Christopher Walken
Henry Cavill	Shane Warne
Alice Eve	

EPONYMOUS
BODY PARTS

Alcock's canal (in the pelvis, named after Irish anatomist Benjamin Alcock)

Bachmann's bundle (in the left atrium, after German physicist Jean George Bachmann)

Buck's fascia (in the penis, after American surgeon Gurdon Buck)

Cloquet's canal (in the eye, after French anatomist Jules Cloquet)

Cooper's suspensory ligaments (in the breast, after English surgeon Astley Cooper)

Descemet's membrane (in the eye, after French physician Jean Descemet)

Pouch of Douglas (behind the uterus, after Scottish anatomist James Douglas)

Eustachian tube (in the ear, after Italian anatomist Bartolomeo Eustachi)

Fallopian tube (in female genitalia, after Italian anatomist Gabriele Falloppio)

Giacomini vein (in the thigh, after Italian anatomist Carlo Giacomini)

Graafian follicle (in the ovaries, after Dutch anatomist Regnier de Graaf)

Gräfenburg Spot (or G-spot) (in the vagina, after German gynaecologist Ernst Gräfenburg)

Loop of Henle (in the kidney, after German pathologist F.G.J. Henle)

Hering's nerve (in the neck, after Austrian physician Heinrich Hering)

Hesselbach's triangle (in the abdomen, after German anatomist Franz Kaspar Hesselbach)

Houston's valves (in the rectum, after Irish anatomist John Houston)

Islets of Langerhans (in the pancreas, after German pathologist Paul Langerhans)

Lockwood's ligament (in the eye, after British surgeon Charles Barrett Lockwood)

McBurney's point (near the abdomen, after American surgeon Charles McBurney)

Glands of Montgomery (around the nipple, after Irish obstetrician William Montgomery)

Morison's pouch (near the liver, after British surgeon James Rutherford Morison)

Papez circuit (in the brain, after American neuroanatomist James Papez)

Peyer's patches (in the small intestine, after Swiss anatomist Johann Conrad Peyer)

Prussak's space (in the ear, after Russian otologist Alexander Prussak)

Purkinje fibres (in the heart, after Czech anatomist Jan E. Purkinje)

Duct of Santorini (near the pancreas, after Italian anatomist Giovanni Santorini)

Skene's gland (in the vagina, after Scottish gynaecologist Alexander Skene)

Circle of Willis (in the base of the brain, after English physician Thomas Willis)

Foramen of Winslow (near the abdomen, after French anatomist Jean-Jacques Winslow)

Zonule of Zinn (in the eye, after German anatomist Johann Zinn)

HUMAN BODY PARTS DISPLAYED IN MUSEUMS

When the Museum of Erotica opened in St Petersburg, Russia, in 2004, its prize exhibit was labelled as Rasputin's 13-inch-long penis.

Slim sections of Albert Einstein's brain are exhibited at the Mütter Museum in Philadelphia.

The head of Italian anatomist Antonio Scarpa is displayed in a glass box at the University of Pavia.

Three of Galileo's fingers are kept at the Galileo Museum in Florence.

The brain of Charles Babbage, inventor of the modern computer, can be found in London but at two different locations. One half is housed in the Science Museum while the other half sits in the Hunterian Museum.

After losing his right leg at the Battle of Gettysburg, American Civil War General Daniel Sickles ordered his surgeon to send the severed limb to what is now the National Museum of Health and Medicine in Maryland.

SPLIT ENDS

Humans have about the same number of hairs on our bodies as chimpanzees, but most of ours are so fine they're almost invisible.

The average person grows 590 miles of hair in a lifetime.

Combined, the hairs on an average human head could support the weight of two elephants.

Blondes have more hairs as well as more fun. On average, they have 140,000 hairs on their scalp, compared to 100,000 for brown or black hair and only 80,000 for redheads.

At any given time, 90 per cent of scalp hairs are growing – the others are resting.

The earliest combs date back over 5,000 years.

More than half of men have male pattern hair loss by the age of 50.

In the course of an average lifetime, we grow over six feet of nose hair. So keep those trimmers handy.

GETTING TO THE BOTTOM OF THINGS

Human poo is about 75 per cent water.

The average human produces two pounds of poo a day.

The foul smell is caused by the stool's bacteria that make sulphur-rich compounds.

The average poo requires six sheets of toilet paper.

Sixty per cent of toilet users look at the paper after they wipe.

Forty-nine per cent of men and 26 per cent of women read while sitting on the toilet.

Sweetcorn remains highly visible in poop because its outer layer is made up mostly of cellulose, which cannot be broken down by the human body when digested. So it comes out one end the same shape and colour as it went in at the other end.

The first sitting-type toilets were introduced in Egypt around 2500 BC, but most people still preferred to dig a hole in the ground.

The Romans were so intrigued by human faeces that they had their own god of dung, Stercutius.

In the 1990s, Romanians sent their old bank notes off to be recycled as toilet paper.

The average man releases enough farts each day to inflate a small balloon.

Neil Armstrong left four bags of poo behind on the moon.

In 2014, the Bath Bus Company began operating a bus that runs on fuel from human waste. The annual poo from five people produces one tank of gas.

Moulay Ismael, a seventeenth-century Sultan of Morocco known as Ismael the Bloodthirsty, presented samples of his bowel movements to the ladies of the court as a token of affection.

MINE'S BIGGER
THAN YOURS

In 2004, China's Xie Qiuping's hair was measured at 18ft 6in long.

When Norway's Hans Langseth died in 1927, his beard was 17ft 6in long.

Ram Singh Chauhan of India had a moustache that was 14 feet long in 2010.

Russia's Svetlana Pankratova has legs that are 51.9 inches long.

American Robert Wadlow, who, at 8ft 11in, was the tallest man in history, had feet to match. He wore US size 37AA shoes (UK 36) to accommodate his 18.5-inch-long feet.

Unsurprisingly, Robert Wadlow also had extraordinarily long hands that measured 12.75 inches from the wrist to the tip of his middle finger.

After growing them for nearly 30 years, Lee Redmond from Salt Lake City had individual fingernails that were 35 inches long. Together, they totalled over 28 feet by 2008. She then lost them in a car accident the following year.

Moustafa Ismail from Egypt had 31-inch biceps in 2013.

Annie Hawkins-Turner (aka Norma Stitz), from Atlanta, Georgia, boasts the world's largest natural breasts – cup size 102ZZZ. Each breast weighs 65 pounds … and they're still growing.

Anthony Victor, a retired headmaster from India, had an ear hair that was 7.1 inches long.

Jason Allen, of Tucson, Arizona, had a leg hair that was almost nine inches long in 2015.

In 2017, David Reed of Los Angeles had arm hair measured at 8.5 inches.

In 2016, Zheng Shusen of China was the proud owner of a 7.5-inch-long eyebrow hair.

Californian Nick Stoeberl has a four-inch tongue.

Mehmet Ozyurek from Turkey had a nose that measured 3.5 inches long.

Florida student Stuart Muller spent a year nurturing a single white eyelash until it reached a length of 2.75 inches in 2007.

Vernon Frenzel Sr, from Waynesville, Missouri, used tweezers to pluck an 18-mm-long hair from his left nostril in 2011.

SEX MATTERS

On average, men get 11 erections a day while awake and six more when they're asleep.

Twelve per cent of American women confess to using their mobile phones while having sex.

Forty-six per cent of American women think a good night's sleep is more important than sex.

The average Briton has sex 2,580 times in his or her lifetime.

In the course of an average lifetime, a man will produce 14 gallons of semen – enough to fill seven watering cans.

The speed of an ejaculation has been measured at 28mph.

Every day, 120 million acts of sexual intercourse take place in the world, resulting in 910,000 conceptions.

Sex lasts longest in Brazil (an average 30 minutes) and is quickest in Thailand (10 minutes).

Twenty-three per cent of Germans are stimulated by underarm odour.

The average age at which boys lose their virginity is 16.9 years and for girls 17.4 years.

Men have an average of seven sex partners during their lifetime; women four.

Seventy-fice per cent of men always reach orgasm during sex, but only 29 per cent of women do.

The average size of an erect human penis is 5.5 inches.

In ancient Egypt, men rubbed crocodile dung into their penis to try and make it bigger.

The first contraceptive diaphragms consisted of half an orange rind.

At the start of the Second World War, most condoms were imported into the UK from Germany. So British soldiers prepared for action stations wearing German condoms.

LIFE AS WE KNOW IT

(TIME SPENT DOING EVERYDAY THINGS IN AN AVERAGE LIFETIME)

Approximately five months of our lives are spent waiting in a car at red lights.

We spend 27 days waiting for trains.

We spend three years of our lives washing clothes.

We spend 375 days folding laundry.

We spend eight months laughing.

We spend five weeks arguing.

We spend 30 hours crying.

We spend six months queuing.

We spend ten weeks on hold listening to muzak while waiting to speak to a human at a call centre.

We spend eight years shopping.

We spend 11 years watching TV.

We spend nine years on our phones.

We spend two years in work meetings.

We spend five months complaining.

We spend over four months sitting on the toilet.

Men spend nine hours in a state of orgasm
whereas women only enjoy one hour.

Men spend four months shaving.

Women spend 480 days washing and blow-drying their hair.

Women spend one year deciding what to wear.

We spend 26 years sleeping.

We spend about five years of our lives eating.

OBSCURE PHOBIAS

Allodoxaphobia: fear of opinions

Atelophobia: fear of imperfection

Athazagoraphobia: fear of being forgotten

Aulophobia: fear of flutes

Automatonophobia: fear of ventriloquists' dummies

Barophobia: fear of gravity

Bathmophobia: fear of stairs

Bibliophobia: fear of books

Blennophobia: fear of slime

Bromidrophobia: fear of body odour

Cathisophobia: fear of sitting down

Chionophobia: fear of snow

Chorophobia: fear of dancing

Coprastasophobia: fear of constipation

Deipnophobia: fear of dinner parties

Dendrophobia: fear of trees

Emetophobia: fear of vomiting

Ephebiphobia: fear of teenagers

Epistaxiophobia: fear of nosebleeds

Genuphobia: fear of knees

Gerascophobia: fear of growing old

Haphephobia: fear of being touched

Ithyphallophobia: fear of seeing or having an erect penis

Jangelaphobia: fear of jelly/jell-o

Koumpounophobia: fear of buttons

Leukophobia: fear of the colour white

Lutraphobia: fear of otters

Macrophobia: fear of long waits

Nomatophobia: fear of names

Nomophobia: fear of being without mobile phone coverage

Omphalophobia: fear of the navel

Oneirogmophobia: fear of wet dreams

Papaphobia: fear of the pope

Phobophobia: fear of phobias

Podophobia: fear of feet

Pogonophobia: fear of beards

Porphyrophobia: fear of the colour purple

Pteronophobia: fear of being tickled with feathers

Quadraphobia: fear of things that come in fours

Rhypophobia: fear of defecation

Selenophobia: fear of the moon

Sesquipedalophobia: fear of long words

Sinistrophobia: fear of things to the left

Syngenesophobia: fear of relatives

Turophobia: fear of cheese

Trypophobia: fear of holes

Venustraphobia: fear of beautiful women

Wiccaphobia: fear of witches

Xenoglossophobia: fear of foreign languages

Zelophobia: fear of jealousy

PHOBIAS OF THE FAMOUS

Woody Allen – arachibutyrophobia, fear of
peanut butter sticking to the roof of the mouth

Pamela Anderson – eisoptrophobia, fear of mirrors

David Beckham – ataxophobia, fear of untidiness

Napoleon Bonaparte – ailurophobia, fear of cats

Johnny Depp – coulrophobia, fear of clowns

Queen Elizabeth I – anthophobia, fear of roses

Megan Fox – papyrophobia, fear of paper

Sigmund Freud – pteridophobia, fear of ferns

Alfred Hitchcock – ovophobia, fear of eggs

Scarlett Johansson – ornithophobia, fear of birds

Nicole Kidman – lepidopterophobia, fear of butterflies

Stephen King – triskaidekaphobia, fear of the number 13

Madonna – brontophobia, fear of thunder

Matthew McConaughey – entamaphobia,
fear of revolving doors

Kylie Minogue – suspendavestiphobia,
fear of coat hangers

Liam Payne – koutaliaphobia, fear of spoons

Keanu Reeves – nyctophobia, fear of darkness

Christina Ricci – botanophobia, fear of indoor plants

Billy Bob Thornton – furniturephobia,
fear of antique furniture

George Washington – taphephobia,
fear of being buried alive

Oprah Winfrey – chiclephobia, fear of chewing gum

Natalie Wood – hydrophobia, fear of water.
She died by drowning.

ACCIDENTS
WILL HAPPEN

*(Number of injuries caused per year in the UK
by seemingly innocuous household objects)*

Flip-flops: 200,000

Sofas: 43,173

Pouffes: 16,339

Armchairs: 15,355

Vegetables: 14,149

Putting on socks or tights: 11,788

Cotton buds: 8,569

Lawnmowers: 6,500

Trousers: 5,945

Flower pots: 5,300

Piles of ironing: 5,248

Garden pruners: 4,400

Garden spades: 3,600

Screwdrivers: 3,500

Clothes baskets: 3,421

Hedge trimmers: 3,100

Garden shears: 2,100

Opening jars: 2,000

Hoses and sprinklers: 1,900

Garden canes: 1,800

Hanging wallpaper: 1,500

Hairbrushes: 1,394

Chainsaws: 1,148

False teeth: 933

Sponges: 787

Deodorants: 431

Bird baths: 311

Bananas: 300

Toilet roll holders: 287

Kitchen cleaning pads: 226

Place mats: 165

Talcum powder: 123

Bread bins: 91

Tea cosies: 37

STRANGE
SYNDROMES

Alice in Wonderland Syndrome leads sufferers to believe that other people, animals or objects are much smaller than they really are.

People with Alien Hand Syndrome have one hand that behaves as if it is out of control and has a mind of its own.

Boanthropy is a delusional disorder where someone imagines that they are a cow or a bull.

Anyone with Capgras Delusion firmly believes that a close family member has been secretly replaced by an identical looking impostor.

People with Cotard's Syndrome are convinced that they are really dead. It is also known as Walking Corpse Syndrome.

Exploding Head Syndrome causes sufferers to hear loud bangs originating from inside their head.

People with Foreign Accent Syndrome suddenly start speaking in a foreign accent following a traumatic brain injury.

People with Genital Retraction Syndrome believe that either their penis or breasts are shrinking to the point of total disappearance.

In the 1990s, there were documented cases of Mary Hart Syndrome where people experienced seizures on hearing the voice of American TV personality Mary Hart.

Paris Syndrome is a mental disorder experienced by tourists who are overcome with excitement on visiting Paris for the first time. Around 20 Japanese tourists a year are affected by the syndrome.

Rapunzel Syndrome is an intestinal condition experienced by people who eat their own hair.

People with Stendhal Syndrome can experience rapid heartbeat, confusion and hallucinations just from looking at works of art or anything of beauty.

Stockholm Syndrome affects kidnap victims who, over time, become sympathetic towards their abductor.

Trimethylaminuria causes a person's sweat, urine and breath to smell of fish.

DREAMS AND
THEIR MEANINGS

Accordion playing – depression

Airport – new departure in life

Baking – desire to be pregnant

Beehive – well organised

Being late – anxiety about taking a different direction in life

Butterfly – romance, happiness

Cows – a need to slow down

Dart – sexual penetration

Dentist – doubt about an acquaintance

Dirty fingernails – disgrace

Eating lettuce – petty jealousy

Falling – insecurity and anxiety

Floods – unhappy marriage

Fog – business worries

Gun – penis

Hair turning grey – death

Harbour – womb

Honeysuckle – contentment

Horse – sexual prowess

Judge – guilt

Leather – successful sexual relationships

Limb amputation – loss of a friend

Lost cat – desire for freedom

Magpie – arguments

Naked in public – feeling wrongly accused of something

No shoes in public – low self-esteem

Plane crash – overambitious

Red underwear – hidden passions

Sailor – desire for adventure

Teeth falling out – concerns over appearance

Train – conformity

Unable to find a toilet – personal needs are not
being met because of putting others first

Unhappy dinner party – sexual frigidity

Unprepared for an exam – lack of confidence

Wolf – repressed sexual desires

Worm – fear of sex

FAMOUS HYPOCHONDRIACS

Hans Christian Andersen

Arnold Bennett

Otto von Bismarck

Charles Darwin

King George IV

Adolf Hitler

Howard Hughes

Dr Samuel Johnson

John Keats

Florence Nightingale

Niccolò Paganini

Marcel Proust

Percy Bysshe Shelley

Andy Warhol

Kenneth Williams

Tennessee Williams

EYE OF FROG AND OTHER MEDIEVAL REMEDIES

Binding the temples with a rope that has been used to hang a criminal relieves a headache.

Extracting a tooth from a live mole and wearing it eases toothache.

Urinating in an open grave cures incontinence.

Touching the hand of a corpse relieves a sore throat.

Throwing a dung beetle over your shoulder cures stomach ache.

Passing a child three times under the belly of a donkey cures whooping cough.

Drinking nine lice with ale every morning for a week eases the symptoms of jaundice.

Carrying a dead shrew in your pocket will ward off rheumatism.

Wearing a twig from an elder tree in your ear day and night will eventually cure deafness.

Carrying a child through a flock of sheep soothes respiratory problems.

Placing a cork under your pillow at night relieves cramp.

Wearing the eye of a frog as a necklace is an effective remedy for conjunctivitis.

Rubbing the grease from church bells into your body cures shingles.

Washing your hair in a man's urine kills ringworm.

Tying a hairy caterpillar in a bag around a child's neck cures whooping cough.

Decapitating an eel and rubbing its blood into your skin removes warts.

Boiling a red-haired dog in oil, then adding worms, pig's marrow and herbs and rubbing the mixture into the affected area works wonders for treating gout.

HISTORICAL BALDNESS CURES

The Ancient Egyptians recommended boiling porcupine hair in water and adding it to the scalp for four days. If porcupine was unavailable, the leg of a female greyhound sautéed in oil and added to the hoof of a donkey apparently did the trick.

Alternatively, the Egyptians would rub the fats of various creatures into their scalp – including hippos, lions, crocodiles, snakes and geese.

The ancient Greek physician Hippocrates devised a potion containing opium, horseradish, beetroot, spices, nettles and pigeon droppings.

The Chinese believed that eating rat flesh could halt a receding hairline.

In Tudor times, dog or horse urine was massaged into the scalp to reduce hair loss.

In Renaissance Europe, an application of cow saliva to the head was considered efficacious.

In Victorian Britain, people with thinning hair would rub cold tea and slices of lemon into their scalp.

In India, performing a headstand and meditating has long been considered a cure for baldness as it increases blood flow to the scalp.

Motor magnate Henry Ford used to wash his hair in water containing rusty razor blades in the hope that the iron would restore its virility.

ARE YOU SITTING COMFORTABLY?

FAMOUS PEOPLE WHO SUFFERED FROM PILES

Napoleon Bonaparte

Jimmy Carter

Casanova

Anton Chekhov

Charles Dickens

Fyodor Dostoevsky

Gerald Ford

George II

Ernest Hemingway

Whitney Houston

Karl Marx

Marilyn Monroe

Emperor Nero

Edgar Allan Poe

Cardinal Richelieu

Socrates

Elizabeth Taylor

Henri de Toulouse-Lautrec

Queen Victoria

Duke of Wellington

Kenneth Williams

William Wordsworth

BRISTOL STOOL SCALE

The Bristol Stool Scale is a diagnostic medical tool that classifies human poo into seven categories according to its appearance and consistency.

Type 1: separate hard lumps (severe constipation)

Type 2: lumpy and sausage like (mild constipation)

Type 3: a sausage shape with cracks in the surface (normal)

Type 4: like a smooth, soft sausage or snake (normal)

Type 5: soft blobs with clear-cut edges (lacking fibre)

Type 6: mushy consistency with ragged edges (mild diarrhea)

Type 7: Liquid consistency with no solid pieces (severe diarrhea)

THE EMBARRASSING TRUMPS

FARTS IN THE NEWS

While undergoing surgery at a hospital in Denmark in 2002 to remove a mole from his buttocks, a Danish man broke wind and set his genitals on fire. The personal gas reacted with a spark from the surgeon's electric knife and ignited the patient's genitals, which had previously been washed with surgical spirit.

Police who were called to a suspected domestic violence incident in Clawson, Michigan, in 2013 found that the cries of 'Stop! No!' were simply those of a woman imploring her boyfriend to cease farting.

In 2007, following a series of complaints from members, a Devon social club banned 77-year-old serial farter Maurice Fox from breaking wind indoors.

Ken Lawrence, an oboist with the Kansas City Symphony Orchestra, was suspended in 1994 after one of the horn players complained that he had farted loudly during a rehearsal for *The Nutcracker*, 'creating an overpowering smell'.

Police officers in Leicester, England, sniffed out a nearby cannabis farm after opening their patrol car windows because the officer in the back seat kept breaking wind.

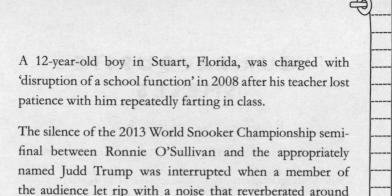

A 12-year-old boy in Stuart, Florida, was charged with 'disruption of a school function' in 2008 after his teacher lost patience with him repeatedly farting in class.

The silence of the 2013 World Snooker Championship semi-final between Ronnie O'Sullivan and the appropriately named Judd Trump was interrupted when a member of the audience let rip with a noise that reverberated around Sheffield's Crucible Theatre just as Trump was about to play his shot. When there was a second gas leak seconds later, someone shouted out by way of explanation: 'Weetabix!'

A 2006 American Airlines flight from Washington D.C. to Dallas was forced to divert to Nashville, Tennessee, after passengers smelled smoke on the plane. It turned out to be the fault of a woman lighting matches in the toilet to conceal the smell of her wind. She was banned from flying with the airline in future.

In 2018, a flight from Dubai to Amsterdam made an emergency landing in Vienna after a fight broke out because two men objected vehemently to another passenger's personal gas.

In 1665, doctors in London told people to store their farts in a jar and then inhale them to avoid being struck down by the Great Plague.

OUR FAVOURITE SMELLS

Freshly baked bread	A real Christmas tree
Bacon	Roses
Freshly cut grass	Vanilla
Coffee	Scented candles
Cakes baking in the oven	Log fires
The seaside	Lavender
Freshly washed clothes	Lemon
Sunday roast	Chocolate
Fish and chips	Barbecues
Fresh flowers	Cinnamon

WORST SMELLS
IN THE WORLD

Decomposing body

Sweaty crotch

Vomit

Garbage

Raw sewage

Teenage boy's bedroom

Skunk

Giraffe house at the zoo

Rotten eggs

Bad breath

Body odour

Durian fruit

Dog poo

Smelly feet

Stagnant water

Wet dog

Rotten fish

Someone else's farts

Cat urine

ODD ITEMS THAT HAVE BEEN REMOVED FROM THE HUMAN BODY

Seventy-eight items of cutlery (forks and spoons) were removed from the stomach of a Dutch woman, Margaret Daalman, in the 1970s.

In 2001, the British Dental Association reported that a 69-year-old man had had a toothbrush surgically removed from his rectum after he had inserted it there apparently to ease his itching haemorrhoids.

Following a robbery in China, Li Fuyan lived with a rusty, four-inch knife blade in his head for three years without knowing it.

Surgeons in Sicily removed 46 teaspoons, two cigarette lighters and a pair of tongs from a man's stomach.

A 37-year-old woman was admitted to hospital in Romania in 2009 with a large can of hairspray stuck up her backside.

In 2017, doctors in Satna, India, found 15 pounds of metal in Maksud Khan's stomach – 263 coins, 150 iron nails, dozens of razor blades, quilting needles, iron spikes and a six-inch strip of rusted iron shackle.

CIRCLING THE DRAIN

DOCTORS' ACRONYMS TO DESCRIBE PATIENTS

Doctors sometimes hide their true feelings about patients
in their notes by means of impolite acronyms.

AGA = Acute Gravity Attack (i.e. fell over)

AOB = Alcohol on Board

APTFRAN = Apply Pillow to Face, Repeat As Necessary
(for an annoying patient)

ATS = Acute Thespian Syndrome (i.e. hypochondriac)

BFH = Brat from Hell

BUNDY = But Unfortunately Not Dead Yet

BWS = Beached Whale Syndrome

CTD = Circling the Drain (i.e. expected to die soon)

DBI = Dirt Bag Index (number of tattoos x number of
missing teeth = days since patient last bathed)

DPS = Dumb Parent Syndrome

DTS = Danger to Shipping (i.e. obese)

FDSTW = Found Dead, Stayed That Way

FLK = Funny-Looking Kid

GOMER = Get Out of My Emergency Room
(an unwelcome patient)

GPO = Good For Parts Only

LMC = Low Marble Count (i.e. low intellect)

LOL = Little Old Lady

NFN = Normal For Norfolk

PAFO = Pissed and Fell Over

PBOO = Pine Box on Order (i.e. close to death)

PITA = Pain in the Arse

TAPS = Thick As Pig Shit

TEETH = Tried Everything Else, Try Homeopathy

TFTB = Too Fat to Breathe

TMB = Too Many Birthdays (i.e. very old)

UBI = Unexplained Beer Injury

WOMBAT = Waste of Money, Brains and Time

FAMOUS PEOPLE WITH DYSLEXIA

Muhammad Ali

Orlando Bloom

Richard Branson

Jim Carrey

Cher

Tom Cruise

Whoopi Goldberg

Duncan Goodhew

Susan Hampshire

Keith Harris
(but not Orville)

Magic Johnson

Mollie King

Keira Knightley

Steve Redgrave

Steven Spielberg

Jackie Stewart

Anthea Turner

Holly Willoughby

Henry Winkler

THE CHEMICAL ELEMENTS

1. Hydrogen

2. Helium

3. Lithium

4. Beryllium

5. Boron

6. Carbon

7. Nitrogen

8. Oxygen

9. Fluorine

10. Neon

11. Sodium

12. Magnesium

13. Aluminium

14. Silicon

15. Phosphorus

16. Sulphur

17. Chlorine

18. Argon

19. Potassium

20. Calcium

21. Scandium

22. Titanium

23. Vanadium

24. Chromium

25. Manganese

26. Iron

27. Cobalt

28. Nickel

29. Copper

30. Zinc

31. Gallium

32. Germanium

33. Arsenic

34. Selenium

35. Bromine

36. Krypton

37. Rubidium

38. Strontium

39. Yttrium

40. Zirconium

41. Niobium

42. Molybdenum

43. Technetium

44. Ruthenium

45. Rhodium

46. Palladium

47. Silver

48. Cadmium

49. Indium

50. Tin

51. Antimony

52. Tellurium

53. Iodine

54. Xenon

55. Caesium

56. Barium

57. Lanthanum

58. Cerium

59. Praseodymium

60. Neodymium

61. Promethium

62. Samarium

63. Europium

64. Gadolinium

65. Terbium

66. Dysprosium

67. Holmium

68. Erbium

69. Thulium

70. Ytterbium

71. Lutetium

72. Hafnium

73. Tantalum

74. Tungsten

75. Rhenium

76. Osmium

77. Iridium

78. Platinum

79. Gold	99. Einsteinium
80. Mercury	100. Fermium
81. Thallium	101. Mendelevium
82. Lead	102. Nobelium
83. Bismuth	103. Lawrencium
84. Polonium	104. Rutherfordium
85. Astatine	105. Dubnium
86. Radon	106. Seaborgium
87. Francium	107. Bohrium
88. Radium	108. Hassium
89. Actinium	109. Meitnerium
90. Thorium	110. Darmstadtium
91. Protactinium	111. Roentgenium
92. Uranium	112. Copernicium
93. Neptunium	113. Nihonium
94. Plutonium	114. Flerovium
95. Americium	115. Moscovium
96. Curium	116. Livermorium
97. Berkelium	117. Tennessine
98. Californium	118. Oganesson

AN ADVANCED
BREED OF MONKEYS

THE THOUGHTS OF
STEPHEN HAWKING

'People who boast about their IQ are losers.'

'Remember to look up at the stars and not down at your feet.'

'Without imperfection, you or I would not exist.'

'I regard the brain as a computer which will stop working when its components fail. There is no heaven or afterlife for broken-down computers; that is a fairy story for people afraid of the dark.'

'The downside of my celebrity is that I cannot go anywhere in the world without being recognised. It is not enough for me to wear dark glasses and a wig. The wheelchair gives me away.'

'We are just an advanced breed of monkeys on a minor planet of a very average star.'

[On the possibility of contact between humans and aliens] 'I think it would be a disaster. The extraterrestrials would probably be far in advance of us. The history of advanced races meeting more primitive people on this planet is not very happy, and they were the same species. I think we should keep our heads low.'

DECIBEL LEVELS

Rocket launch: 180dB

Howitzer cannon: 175dB

Shotgun: 160dB

Fighter jet launch: 150dB

Firecracker: 145dB

Aeroplane taking off: 140dB

Air raid siren: 135dB

Balloon popping: 130dB

Pneumatic drill: 120dB

Rock concert: 120dB

Thunderclap: 120dB

Chainsaw: 115dB

Emergency vehicle siren: 115dB

Pig's squeal: 115dB

Baby crying: 110dB

Car horn: 110dB

Motorcycle: 100dB

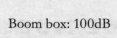

Boom box: 100dB

Food processor: 95dB

Electric drill: 95dB

Lawnmower: 90dB

Shouted conversation: 90dB

City traffic: 85dB

Hairdryer: 85dB

Toilet flush: 80dB

Doorbell: 80dB

Vacuum cleaner: 75dB

Dishwasher: 70dB

Electric shaver: 70dB

Conversational speech: 60dB

Electric toothbrush: 55dB

Coffee percolator: 55dB

Rainfall: 50dB

Whisper: 30dB

Normal breathing: 10dB

PRIME NUMBERS
UP TO 200

2, 3, 5, 7, 11, 13, 17, 19, 23, 29, 31, 37, 41, 43, 47, 53, 59, 61, 67, 71, 73, 79, 83, 89, 97, 101, 103, 107, 109, 113, 127, 131, 137, 139, 149, 151, 157, 163, 167, 173, 179, 181, 191, 193, 197, 199.

SPACE
ODDITIES

An astronaut orbiting Earth sees the sun rise and set 15 or 16 times a day.

An object weighing 100 pounds on Earth would only weigh 38 pounds on Mars. On Mars you would be able to jump three times as high as you could on Earth.

The Olympus Mons volcano on Mars is almost three times the size of Everest.

Although Mercury has daytime surface temperatures of over 400 degrees Celcius, it has ice at its poles.

A day on Mercury is longer than its year – because Mercury takes longer to spin on its axis than to orbit the Sun.

The Great Red Spot on Jupiter is a huge storm that has raged for at least 200 years. The storm is so big that three Earths could fit inside it.

The clouds on Venus rain sulphuric acid, but the acid drops never reach the ground due to evaporation.

Wind speeds on Neptune can reach over 1,200mph.

Travelling at 70mph, it would take almost 300 days to drive around one of Saturn's rings.

Saturn is so low in density that if the planet fell into a vast area of water it would float.

If you could fly a plane to Pluto, the journey would take over 800 years.

Only about 59 per cent of the moon is directly visible from Earth.

The biggest lunar crater is the Aitken basin, located on the far side of the moon. It measures 1,600 miles across — similiar to the distance from Paris to Moscow.

As there is no wind or rain on the moon to remove them (due to the lack of atmosphere), the footprints of the Apollo astronauts will probably remain visible for millions of years.

In an hour, the sun produces enough energy to power 2,880 trillion light bulbs — enough to give everybody on Earth a light bulb that would shine brightly for their entire lifetime.

Astronauts can't cry in space. Tears are unable to flow because of the lack of gravity.

There are more stars in the universe than grains of sand on all the beaches on Earth.

RAINING SPRATS
AND FROGS

WEIRD WEATHER

A shower of hundreds of live perch fell from the sky over Lajamanu, Australia, in 2010.

Live frogs were found inside two large hailstones which fell on Dubuque, Iowa, in 1882.

Several hundred dead sand eels landed on Sunderland in 1918 at the height of a storm.

Tangled clumps of wriggling worms fell from the sky at Jennings, Louisiana, in 2007.

A shower of dead birds – including ducks and woodpeckers – hit Baton Rouge, Louisiana, in 1896.

A shower of maggots accompanied a storm at Acapulco, Mexico, in 1968.

A crop of hard, green peaches fell from the sky at Shreveport, Indiana, in 1961.

Dozens of golf balls mysteriously landed on Punta Gorda, Florida, in 1969.

Lumps of meat fell from a cloudless sky in Bath County, Kentucky, in 1876. When examined, the meat proved to be lung and muscle tissue, either from a child or a horse.

MAIN CLOUD TYPES

Altocumulus – medium altitude, fluffy white cloud associated with settled weather

Altostratus – medium, featureless cloud that usually evolves from thickening layer of cirrostratus

Asperitas – only identified in 2015, consists of ominous, dark waves that tumble across the sky

Cirrocumulus – high, forms ripples which resemble scales of fish

Cirrostratus – high, creates a thin layer that covers much of the sky

Cirrus – high cloud, layered and tufty, like wisps in the sky

Cumulonimbus – low cloud with an anvil-shaped top, a sign of impending heavy rain and storms

Cumulus – low, fluffy, cauliflower-shaped white clouds that occasionally bear rain

Lenticularis – rare, smooth clouds that appear to hover in the sky; appear downwind of mountains

Mammatus – mammary-like clouds with hanging pouches; sign that worst of weather has passed

Nacreous – high clouds that glow with iridescent colours and form close to the poles in extreme cold

Nimbostratus – low altitude, rain or snow-bearing, grey cloud that develops from altostratus

Nimbus – low, dark cloud capable of releasing large amounts of precipitation

Stratocumulus – low cloud that forms white lines or waves in the sky; brings light precipitation

Stratus – low cloud that covers sky in blanket of dismal white or grey and is associated with drizzle

EXTREME WEATHER

There are more than three million lightning flashes a day worldwide – that's about 35 a second.

The temperature of a lightning bolt is 30,000 degrees Celsius – five times hotter than the surface of the sun. A single bolt of lightning contains enough energy to cook 100,000 pieces of toast.

The Empire State Building is struck by lightning on average 23 times a year.

Lightning kills about 2,000 people a year.

A tornado can produce a wind speed of 300mph.

In 1962, a cow in Iowa 'flew' nearly half a mile after being sucked up by a tornado.

The Tri-State Tornado, which hit parts of Missouri, Illinois and Indiana in 1925, lasted for over three hours and travelled 219 miles.

Around 1,200 tornadoes hit the US every year.

A dust tornado is called a 'willy-willy' in Australia.

UNDER MY UMBRELLA

EXTREMELY WET CITIES (BY INCHES OF RAINFALL PER YEAR)

Quibdó, Colombia (354in of rain and 304 wet days per year)

Buenaventura, Colombia (247in)

Mawlamyine, Myanmar (190in)

Monrovia, Liberia (182in)

Padang, Indonesia (175in)

Conakry, Guinea (171in)

Douala, Cameroon (162in)

Cayenne, French Guiana (147in)

Freetown, Sierra Leone (143in)

Ambon, Indonesia (139in)

Mangalore, India (137in)

Hilo, Hawaii (127in)

Kuala Terengganu, Malaysia (115in)

Belém, Brazil (113in)

Mobile, Alabama (67in)

Cardiff, Wales (38in – the UK's wettest city)

IG NOBEL
PRIZE WINNERS

This annual parody of the Nobel Prizes is awarded to genuine achievements that 'first make people laugh, and then make them think.' Past winners include:

1993: Mathematics – to Robert W. Faid, an American numerologist, who calculated the exact odds (710,609,175,188,282,000 to 1) that Mikhail Gorbachev is the Antichrist.

1995: Literature – to Americans David B. Busch and James R. Starling for their research study 'Rectal Foreign Bodies', and whose case reports included seven light bulbs, two flashlights, a knife sharpener, a frozen pig's tail and 11 different fruits and vegetables.

1997: Entomology – to Mark Hostetler of the University of Florida for his book *That Gunk on Your Car*, which identifies the insect splats that appear on car windows.

1999: Physics – to Australian scientist Dr Len Fisher for calculating the optimal way to dunk a biscuit.

2000: Computer Science – to American Chris Niswander for inventing PawSense, software that detects when a cat is walking across your computer keyboard.

2001: Medicine – to Peter Barss, of McGill University, Canada, for his impactful medical report 'Injuries Due to Falling Coconuts'.

2001: Literature – to the UK's John Richards, founder of the Apostrophe Protection Society, for his efforts to safeguard, promote and defend the differences between the plural and the possessive.

2001: Physics – to David Schmidt from the University of Massachusetts for his explanation of why a shower curtain tends to billow inwards while a shower is being taken.

2003: Physics – to a team of Australian scientists for their report: 'An Analysis of the Forces Required to Drag Sheep Over Various Surfaces'.

2004: Medicine – to American university researchers Steven Stack and James Gundlach for their groundbreaking report: 'The Effect of Country Music on Suicide'.

2005: Medicine – to Gregg Miller, American inventor of artificial testicles for dogs.

2005: Peace – to Clare Rind and Peter Simmons, of the University of Newcastle, UK, for monitoring the brain activity of a locust while it was watching selected highlights from *Star Wars*.

2006: Mathematics – to Australians Nic Svenson and Piers Barnes for calculating the number of photographs that must be taken to ensure that nobody in a group photo will have their eyes closed.

2008: Biology – to a team of French scientists for discovering that fleas living on dogs jump higher than fleas living on cats.

2009: Physics – to three US university scientists for analytically determining why pregnant women do not tip over.

2009: Veterinary medicine – to Catherine Douglas and Peter Rowlinson of Newcastle University, UK, for proving that cows with names give more milk than cows who are nameless.

2010: Physics – to a team of pioneering New Zealanders for demonstrating that, on icy footpaths in winter, people slip and fall less frequently if they wear socks on the outside of their shoes.

2012: Psychology – to Anita Eerland, Rolf Zwaan and Tulio Guadalupe for their insightful study: 'Leaning to the Left Makes the Eiffel Tower Seem Smaller'.

2013: Probability – to Scottish livestock researcher Dr Bert Tolkamp and his team for their report: 'Are Cows More Likely to Lie Down the Longer They Stand?'

2013: Psychology – to Brad Bushman of Ohio State University and his team for their study 'Beauty is in the Eye of the Beerholder', which conducted experiments to confirm that people who are drunk think they are more attractive.

2014: Physics – to a team of Japanese scientists for measuring the relative amounts of friction between a shoe and a banana skin, and between a banana skin and the ground, when a person steps on a banana skin that is on the ground.

2016: Medicine – to German neurologist Christolph Helmchen for discovering that if a person has an itch on the left side of the body, it can be relieved by looking into a mirror and scratching the right side of the body (and vice versa).

2016: Biology – to British designer Thomas Thwaites for creating prosthetic limb extensions that enabled him to move like, and spend time roaming hills with, goats.

2017: Anatomy – to Britain's James Heathcote for his medical research study 'Why Do Old Men Have Big Ears?'

2018: Literature – to an international team of researchers for documenting that most people who use complicated products do not read the instruction manual.

INVENTORS AND INVENTIONS

Liquid correction fluid (or Tippex) was invented in 1951 by Bette Nesmith Graham, the mother of future member of the Monkees, Mike Nesmith.

Robert Chesebrough, the American chemist who invented and marketed Vaseline petroleum jelly, ate a spoonful every day because he believed it contained tremendous health benefits. He lived to the age of 96.

The first roller skates were invented by Belgian musician Joseph Merlin who attempted to show them off while playing the violin at a London ball in the 1760s, but found himself unable to stop or change direction and ended up crashing into a full-length mirror and sustaining serious injuries.

The first ballpoint pens to go on sale in New York in 1945 cost $12.50 each – the equivalent of $170 in today's money.

Paul Winchell, the voice of Dick Dastardly in *Wacky Races* and Tigger in Disney's *Winnie-the-Pooh* films, invented one of the first artificial hearts with the assistance of Dr Henry Heimlich, creator of the Heimlich manoeuvre.

Edwin Beard Budding, English pioneer of the lawnmower, would only test his invention at night because he was worried his neighbours would think he was crazy.

Too shy to listen to a young lady's heartbeat by placing his ear next to her chest, young French physician René Laennec used a rolled up sheet of paper instead. Impressed to discover that the tubular shape magnified the sound, he went on to invent the stethoscope.

When King Camp Gillette's safety razor first went on sale in the United States in 1903, only 51 were sold that year. The following year he sold over 90,000.

Sylvan Goldman, owner of the Humpty-Dumpty supermarket chain, introduced the first shopping trolley at his Oklahoma City store in 1937 to encourage customers to buy more goods – but the trolley proved unpopular at first because men considered it effeminate and it reminded women of pushing a pram.

The ancient Etruscans of Italy were the first people to eat with false teeth – some 2,700 years ago. They used rows of animal teeth, fastened together with strips of gold.

Leo Fender, the inventor of the Telecaster and Stratocaster, could not play the guitar.

Wallace Carothers, the man who invented nylon, committed suicide two years before the first nylon products were introduced to the public.

The first electric kettles took 12 minutes to boil.

Hovercraft inventor Christopher Cockerell built his prototype model from an empty tin of cat food, a coffee tin and a vacuum cleaner.

When pre-gummed envelopes were first introduced at the end of the nineteenth century, they were unpopular with many people who thought it impolite to send their saliva to someone else.

The fax machine was invented before the telephone. Scottish clockmaker Alexander Bain patented the first fax machine in 1843 – around 30 years before fellow countryman Alexander Graham Bell devised the first telephone.

When Joseph Gayetty invented toilet paper in 1857, he had his name printed on every sheet.

Florida pharmacist Benjamin Green invented the first suntan cream in 1944 by cooking cocoa butter and other ingredients in a granite coffee pot on a stove and applying it to his bald head.

An early electric washing machine, the Magnet, was listed in the 1929 Harrods catalogue at a price of £42 and offered attachments so that it could also be used for making ice cream, mincing meat and sausage making.

Thomas Edison, inventor of the light bulb, was afraid of the dark.

Although he held over 1,000 patents by the time he died in 1931, Thomas Edison only had three months of formal schooling in his entire life.

Introduced in 1902, the first commercial vacuum cleaner was so bulky and noisy that it frightened passing horses and led to its inventor, Hubert Cecil Booth, being sued by cab proprietors.

The electric chair was the brainchild of Alfred P. Southwick, a dentist from Buffalo, New York.

Earl Silas Tupper's range of watertight, airtight, plastic containers called Tupperware struggled for sales at first because the revolutionary seal was so effective that store demonstrators were unable to open them. So he eventually took his products off the shelves and concentrated instead on direct selling via home demonstrations, which led to the creation of the Tupperware party.

The microwave oven was invented by accident after American engineer Percy Spencer, who was working in a laboratory testing magnetrons, the high-powered vacuum tubes used in radar systems, discovered that they had melted a peanut butter candy bar in his pocket.

When Kimberly-Clark introduced Kleenex as make-up removers in 1924 sales were slow until customers reported that the paper tissues were perfect for nose blowing.

At 16, Benjamin Franklin secretly submitted a series of articles to his brother's weekly newspaper, the *New England Courant*, under the name of Mrs Silence Dogood, a widow who offered views on everything from fashion and marriage to women's rights.

Charles Richter, who devised the Richter Scale for measuring earthquakes, was an enthusiastic naturist.

Venetian blinds were invented in Japan.

Velcro was invented by Georges de Mestral who, after walking his dog in his native Switzerland in 1950, was inspired by the way that burrs attached themselves to his clothing and to his dog's ears.

The idea for Pampers came about because Vic Mills, Director of Exploratory Development for Procter & Gamble in the US, hated changing the cloth nappies on his newborn grandchild.

Chester Greenwood, of Farmington, Maine, was only 15 when he invented ear muffs to stop his ears freezing while he was ice skating. He asked his grandmother to attach pads of beaver fur to a wire frame, and they proved such a hit with his friends that he patented them in 1877 when he was 18.

In 1900, long before the advent of the electric razor, Samuel L. Bligh of Pennsylvania attempted to mechanise the process of shaving with his 'beard grinder', a device that was operated by the shaver pedalling furiously.

The research papers of Marie Curie, who discovered radium, are still radioactive more than 100 years later and will be for at least another 1,500 years. Anyone wishing to access them must wear protective clothing and sign a liability waiver.

The can opener was invented 48 years after the can. British merchant Peter Durand devised the first tin can for preserving food in 1810 but it was not until 1858, as new manufacturing methods made the use of cans more widespread, that American Ezra Warner patented the first can opener.

Although it is believed that Frederick Graff invented the fire hydrant in 1801, there is no firm evidence to support this because the US Patent Office and its contents were destroyed by fire in 1836.

UNSUNG INVENTORS

George C. Beidler, American inventor
of the photocopier, 1903

Harry Brearley, English inventor of stainless steel, 1913

Dan Bricklin, American inventor of the
electronic spreadsheet, 1978

Alfred Butts, American inventor of Scrabble, 1938

Willis Carrier, American inventor of air conditioning, 1902

Marc Chavannes and Alfred Fielding,
American inventors of bubble wrap, 1957

Georges Claude, French inventor of neon lighting, 1910

Douglas Engelbart, American inventor
of the computer mouse, 1967

Adolphe E. Fick, German inventor of contact lenses, 1888

Fred Francis, English inventor of Scalextric, 1956

Erle Haas, American inventor of the tampon, 1931

Dr R.N. Harger, American inventor
of the breathalyser, 1938

Edwin T. Holmes, American inventor
of the burglar alarm, 1858

Walter Hunt, American inventor of the safety pin, 1849

Miller Reese Hutchinson, American inventor
of the hearing aid, 1901

Mary Phelps Jacob, American inventor
of the modern bra, 1913

Whitcomb L. Judson, American inventor of the zip, 1893

Carlton C. Magee, American inventor
of the parking meter, 1935

Jack Marks, English inventor of the boxer's gumshield, 1902

Edward Nairne, English inventor of the rubber eraser, 1770

James Naismith, Canadian inventor of basketball, 1891

Albert J. Parkhouse, American inventor
of the wire coat hanger, 1903

Eugene Polley, American inventor
of the TV remote control, 1955

Erik Rotheim, Norwegian inventor
of the aerosol spray, 1927

Percy Shaw, English inventor of the road catseye, 1935

John Shepherd-Barron, English inventor of the ATM, 1967

Frank Smith, English inventor of the
automatic tea-maker, 1902

Lucien B. Smith, American inventor of barbed wire, 1867

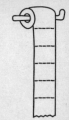

Charles P. Strite, American inventor
of the pop-up toaster, 1919

Johann Vaaler, Norwegian inventor of the paper clip, 1900

John Walker, English inventor of the safety match, 1826

Arthur Wynne, English inventor of
the crossword puzzle, 1913

Joseph L. Zimmerman, American inventor of
the telephone answering machine, 1949

PATENTLY
RIDICULOUS

In 1901, Thomas Ferry of Delaware invented a strap-on moustache guard 'designed to hold the moustache away from the lips and to prevent the lodgement of food thereon while eating.'

In 1902, Andrew Jackson Jr of Tennessee patented a pair of miniature goggles for chickens to stop them being hen-pecked.

In 1919, John Humphrey of Connecticut devised an alarm clock incorporating a mechanism that would rouse someone from their slumbers by hitting them with a hard rubber ball. He envisaged that it would be particularly useful for deaf people.

In 1923, Charles Purdy of Brooklyn patented his tooth and gum exercising device – two plates attached to a spring that are gripped between the teeth of two people in close proximity, allowing them to pull in opposite directions like a tug of war contest.

In 1937, Constance Honey of London patented a chocolate spoon for dispensing medicine to reluctant children, only to find that while they took their medicine they also ate all of her spoons.

In 1960, David Gutman of Philadelphia designed a pedestrian bumper for the front of a car that not only cushioned the impact in the event of a collision but also featured a pair

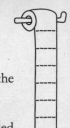

of giant claws which would grab the pedestrian around the waist and prevent him or her from falling on to the street.

In 1967, Harold W. Dahly of Chicago patented a solar-cooled hat, which operated via a solar-powered fan positioned discreetly inside the headgear.

In 1989, Moira and Frank Figone of California devised a foam-covered sound muffler for covering the mouth so that a frustrated person could scream without disturbing others. A microphone attachment activated a meter to give the user immediate visual feedback as to the intensity of sound produced.

In 1993, Raymond Norris of Oklahoma patented his combined camouflage and decoy service for duck hunters – a wearable cape with an attached hat in the shape of a stuffed duck resembling the kind to be hunted. He advised: 'The hunter can make head and body movements to increase the life-like nature of the decoy.'

In 1994, New Yorker Albert Cohen patented a spring-loaded high-five simulator for lone fans watching televised sporting events who have nobody with whom they can share their excitement.

Since the 1990s, Japan's Kenji Kawakami has been responsible for an entire range of useless inventions on his Chindogu label, including the banana case (a suitably shaped covering to stop bananas from bruising), the drymobile (a clothes line attached to a car), duster slippers for cats so that they can help with the housework, and the umbrella tie, an umbrella that can be worn around the neck like a tie if rain is forecast.

In 2007, London-based design consultant Tom Ballhatchet came up with a hamster-powered paper shredder – an environmentally friendly shredder powered by a hamster running on its wheel. It was calculated that to shred a single sheet of A4, the hamster would need to run flat out for 45 minutes.

In 2011, Londoner Dominic Wilcox designed the nose stylus, a strap-on, elongated clay nose with a stylus on the tip so that you can activate your mobile phone in cold weather without needing to take your gloves off.

INVENTORS KILLED BY THEIR OWN INVENTIONS

Attempting to prove that fresh meat could be preserved if frozen, in 1626 English scientist and philosopher Francis Bacon stuffed a chicken with snow and buried it, only to contract pneumonia from the refrigeration experiment and die.

Engineer Henry Winstanley built the first Eddystone Lighthouse off the south-west coast of England, but in 1703 a terrible storm destroyed the lighthouse with Winstanley and five other men inside.

American William Bullock perfected the rotary printing press but his foot was crushed during the installation of a new machine in Philadelphia. The foot developed gangrene and he died in 1867 in the course of the amputation.

Sylvester H. Roper invented the Roper steam velocipede, one of the world's first motorcycles, but was killed in 1896 near Cambridge, Massachusetts, when he fell off and suffered a head injury.

Polish-born French physicist Marie Curie invented the process to isolate radium but died in 1934 of aplastic anaemia as a result of prolonged exposure to radiation in the course of her research.

Stricken with polio, American engineer Thomas Midgley Jr devised an elaborate system of ropes and pulleys so that he could get out of bed, but one day in 1944 he became entangled in the ropes and died of strangulation.

Canadian stuntman Karel Soucek developed a shock-absorbent barrel, in which he went over the Niagara Falls in 1984. But he was killed in a stunt the following year when the barrel – with him inside – was dropped 180 feet from the roof of the Houston Astrodome.

WEIRD THINGS
SOLD ON EBAY

Lunch with American businessman Warren Buffett ($2.3 million)

The town of Bridgeville, California ($1.8 million)

The old Hollywood sign, which was replaced in 1978 ($450,400)

Australian man Ian Usher's entire life, including his house, car, motorcycle, introductions to his friends and a trial offer for his job ($384,000)

Princess Beatrice's distinctive royal wedding hat, likened by some to a giant pretzel ($131,648)

The 50,000-year-old skeleton of a woolly mammoth ($93,000)

A ghost in a jar ($55,992 was the winning bid but it was never paid)

Justin Bieber's hair clippings ($40,668)

Zoe Pemberton's 'cuddly but annoying' grandmother Marion Goodall ($30,000 was bid before eBay shut it down)

A grilled cheese sandwich with the face of the Virgin Mary ($28,000)

William Shatner's kidney stone ($25,000)

A false fingernail lost on stage by Lady Gaga in 2012 ($13,000)

Utah mother Kari Smith's forehead for advertising space ($10,000)

A paper tissue that actress Scarlett Johansson used for blowing her nose on TV ($5,300)

Justin Timberlake's half-eaten French toast ($3,154)

Grateful Dead singer Jerry Garcia's former toilet ($2,550)

An unwanted Brussels sprout left over from British man Leigh Knight's Christmas dinner ($2,100)

Four golf balls surgically removed from a python's stomach ($1,401)

A cornflake shaped like the state of Illinois ($1,350)

A Dorito shaped like the Pope's hat ($1,209)

A suit of armour for a guinea pig ($1,150)

A jar purportedly containing the breath of Brad Pitt and Angelina Jolie ($530)

A wad of bubble gum allegedly chewed by Britney Spears ($514)

Water from a cup that Elvis Presley supposedly once drank from ($455)

A haunted rubber duck ($107.50)

Jeremy Corbyn's paper cup ($66.30)

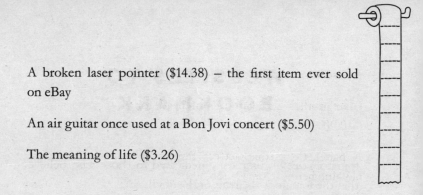

A broken laser pointer ($14.38) – the first item ever sold on eBay

An air guitar once used at a Bon Jovi concert ($5.50)

The meaning of life ($3.26)

WEBSITES TO BOOKMARK

tomatoesareevil.com: a site dedicated to those who believe that the tomato is the fruit of the devil.

catsthatlooklikehitler.com: dozens of photos of cats that bear an uncanny resemblance to the Fuhrer.

boxwars.net: the go-to site for people who like to re-enact historical battles wearing suits of armour made from cardboard.

isitchristmas.com: self-explanatory site that gives the simple answer 'NO' for every day of the year but one. Ideal for those with no access to a calendar, diary, phone, brain …

mauricebennett.co.nz: illustrates the New Zealander's unique ability to create lifelike images of the Mona Lisa, Elvis or Barack Obama from slices of toast.

eelslap.com: allows you to use your computer mouse to slap a complete stranger around the face with a virtual eel.

bedbugger.com: offers invaluable tips on how to combat an infestation of bed bugs.

furnitureporn.com: shows pictures of chairs, tables and sun loungers behaving badly when your back is turned.

zombiepassions.com: a dating site for zombies, zombie lovers and zombie survivalists.

TWITTERATI

CELEBRITIES WITH THE MOST TWITTER FOLLOWERS (AS OF JANUARY 2019)

Katy Perry – 107 million

Justin Bieber – 105 million

Barack Obama – 104 million

Rihanna – 89 million

Taylor Swift – 83 million

Lady Gaga – 77 million

EllenDeGeneres – 77 million

Cristiano Ronaldo – 76 million

Justin Timberlake – 65 million

Ariana Grande – 60 million

Kim Kardashian – 59 million

Demi Lovato – 57 million

Selena Gomez – 56.9 million

Donald Trump – 56.7 million

Britney Spears – 56.5 million

VAGUELY INTERESTING TWITTER STATISTICS

500 million tweets are sent each day – that's 6,000 every second.

A day's worth of tweets would fill a book with 10 million pages.

The country with the most Twitter users is the United States, followed by Brazil, Japan and Mexico.

The average Twitter user has 707 followers.

Over 1.3 billion Twitter accounts have been created, of which 391 million have no followers at all.

Ninety-two per cent of world leaders use Twitter.

Pope Francis has 18 million followers on Twitter.

Queen Elizabeth II sent her first tweet in 2014 to launch an Information Age exhibition at London's Science Museum.

The most popular emoji on Twitter is the face with tears of joy.

One in 13 tweets contains a swear word.

HOLLYWOOD STARS WHO SHUN SOCIAL MEDIA

Jennifer Aniston	Jake Gyllenhaal
Emily Blunt	Scarlett Johansson
Sandra Bullock	Mila Kunis
George Clooney	Jennifer Lawrence
Bradley Cooper	Daniel Radcliffe
Daniel Craig	Julia Roberts
Benedict Cumberbatch	Kristen Stewart
Ralph Fiennes	Emma Stone
Martin Freeman	Kate Winslet

THERE'S AN APP
FOR EVERYTHING

Bowel Mover: the number one app for tracking the regularity of your number twos.

Carrr Matey: an app that tells you where you've parked your car – in a pirate voice.

Fake-An-Excuse: offers over 45 realistic excuses (plus sound effects) to give you a valid reason for ending a phone call.

Hold On: see how long you can keep pressing on a coloured square without lifting your finger.

iShaver Pro: gives men a virtual electric razor shave, complete with virtual falling bristles.

Milk the Cow: download the app, squeeze the udders and fill the bucket with milk in the fastest time possible.

Paper Racing: a game to see who can spin off a roll of toilet paper the fastest.

Pimple Popper: a game that tests your technique at squeezing whiteheads, blackheads and scabs on eight screen faces.

Places I've Pooped: helps you keep track of every location in the world where you've had a dump.

RunPee: tells you the best time to go for a pee during a movie without missing any key action.

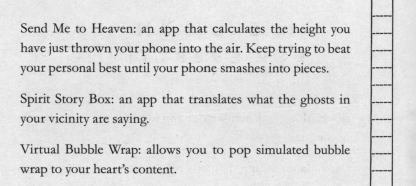

Send Me to Heaven: an app that calculates the height you have just thrown your phone into the air. Keep trying to beat your personal best until your phone smashes into pieces.

Spirit Story Box: an app that translates what the ghosts in your vicinity are saying.

Virtual Bubble Wrap: allows you to pop simulated bubble wrap to your heart's content.

FOOD AND DRINK

FOOD AND DRINK NAMED AFTER REAL PEOPLE

Omelette Arnold Bennett (an unfolded omelette with smoked haddock invented at London's Savoy Hotel for English writer Arnold Bennett)

Bartlett pear (the English Williams pear variety was renamed by Massachusetts nurseryman Enoch Bartlett)

Battenberg cake (reportedly named in honour of the marriage of Queen Victoria's granddaughter Victoria to Prince Louis of Battenberg in 1884)

Béchamel sauce (after seventeenth-century French financier Louis de Béchamel who was also chief steward to Louis XIV)

Bellini (cocktail named after Italian Renaissance artist Giovanni Bellini because its distinctive shade of pink reminded its inventor, Giuseppe Cipriani, founder of Harry's Bar in Venice, of a toga in a painting by Bellini)

Eggs Benedict (most likely after New York stockbroker Lemuel Benedict who went to the Waldorf Hotel for breakfast in 1894 while suffering from a hangover and asked for a restorative involving bacon, a poached egg and hollandaise sauce)

Bramley apple (after butcher Matthew Bramley who, in 1846, bought a cottage in Southwell, Nottinghamshire, where the first apple tree of its type had grown from pips planted by the previous owner)

Caesar salad (after Caesar Cardini who created it at his restaurant in Tijuana, Mexico, in 1924)

Carpaccio (after Italian painter Vittore Carpaccio because the colour of the thinly sliced raw beef was similar to the red that the artist was renowned for)

Chateaubriand (steak cut named after nineteenth-century French writer François René de Chateaubriand)

Clementine (after Clément Rodier, a French monk, who created a new species of mandarin while working at an orphanage in Algeria)

Veuve Clicquot (brand of champagne named after Barbe-Nicole Ponsardin, the widow (French *veuve*) of François Clicquot, and the head of his champagne house following his death)

Cox's Orange Pippin (apple variety named after its creator, Richard Cox, a retired Buckinghamshire brewer)

Frangipane (almond tart named after Italian Marquis Muzio Frangipani)

Greengage (after Sir William Gage, who first imported the fruit into England from France in 1724)

Garibaldi biscuits (after Italian patriot Giuseppe Garibaldi)

Earl Grey tea (after Charles Grey, 2nd Earl Grey, who was British Prime Minister 1830–34)

Coquille St Jacques (scallop dish named after St James the Great, first martyred apostle and noted fisherman)

Chicken à la King (after its creator, William King, chef at the Bellevue Hotel, Philadelphia)

Kneipp bread (wholewheat bread named after Bavarian priest Sebastian Kneipp)

Lamingtons (small Australian cakes named after Charles Cochrane-Baillie, 2nd Baron Lamington, who was governor of Queensland 1896–1901)

Loganberry (blackberry/raspberry hybrid created by chance in 1883 by American horticulturalist James Harvey Logan)

Margarita (possibly named after Dallas socialite Margarita Samas who said she invented the cocktail for a party in 1948, but others claim it was created in Tijuana, Mexico, for actress Rita Hayworth, whose real name was Margarita Cansino)

Pizza Margherita (after Queen Margherita of Savoy who was presented with the pizza in the colours of the Italian flag on a visit to Naples)

Bloody Mary (after the nickname of Queen Mary I of England, 1553–58)

Peach Melba (when Savoy Hotel chef Auguste Escoffier heard Australian opera singer Dame Nellie Melba perform at London's Covent Garden he was inspired to create a dessert for her)

Mornay sauce (probably after Frenchman Philippe de Mornay, a member of the court of Henri IV)

Nachos (after their creator, Mexican restaurant maître d' Ignacio 'Nacho' Anaya)

Potatoes Parmentier (after Antoine-Augustin Parmentier who almost single-handedly convinced his fellow Frenchmen that potatoes were not poisonous)

Pavlova (meringue-based dessert named after Russian ballerina Anna Pavlova)

Dom Pérignon (after Dom Pérignon, seventeenth-century French Benedictine monk and winemaker)

Praline (after César de Choiseul, Count du Plessis-Praslin, seventeenth-century French diplomat)

Oysters Rockefeller (after American business magnate John D. Rockefeller)

Tournedos Rossini (after Italian composer Gioachino Rossini, a renowned gourmet)

Sachertorte (chocolate cake invented by Austrian Franz Sacher in Vienna in 1832)

Sandwich (after John Montagu, 4th Earl of Sandwich, who did not invent it but certainly helped popularise it in the eighteenth century)

Granny Smith (apple that originated in Australia from a seedling propagated by Maria Ann 'Granny' Smith)

Beef Stroganoff (possibly named after Russian military commander Count Pavel Alexandrovich Stroganov)

Victoria sponge (after Queen Victoria)

Beef Wellington (after Arthur Wellesley, 1st Duke of Wellington)

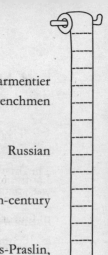

KNOW YOUR ONIONS

VEGETABLE FACTS

The first frozen food to go on sale in Britain, in 1936, was aparagus.

Eating a stick of celery burns more calories than the celery itself contains.

The ancient Greeks awarded celery to their sporting champions.

The onion is a member of the lily family.

Before the seventeenth century, nearly all cutivated carrots were purple.

The Jerusalem artichoke is a native of North America.

Chicago is named after the Native American word for wild garlic, which grew in the area.

Potatoes were the first food to be grown in space, when plants were taken on board the 1995 shuttle Columbia.

The potato belongs to the same family as deadly nightshade.

The Egyptian workers who constructed the Pyramids were paid in radishes.

ALL THINGS FRUIT

A strawberry is not an actual berry but a banana is.

Apple pips contain cyanide.

7,500 varieties of apple are grown in the world, which means that if you tried a new variety every day, it would take 20 years to taste them all.

Until 1830, tomatoes were believed to be poisonous.

Ninety per cent of pumpkins grown in the United States are cultivated within a 90-mile radius of Peoria, Illinois.

You can speed up the ripening of a pineapple by standing it upside down.

A kiwifruit contains nearly twice as much vitamin C as an orange.

A single pomegranate can contain as many as 1,400 seeds.

In 2018, a pair of Yubari melons – prized for their rarity and sweetness – sold for $27,000 at auction in Japan.

The durian fruit is so pungent that it is banned on public transport in south-east Asia. American chef Anthony Bourdain said that eating one will make your breath 'smell as if you'd been French-kissing your dead grandmother'.

FEELING FRUITY

APHRODISIAC FOODS

Apricots	Honey
Asparagus	Oysters
Avocado	Parsnips (when young)
Bananas	Pig's trotters
Basil	Pine nuts
Chillies	Pomegranate
Chocolate	Rattlesnake
Figs	Snails
Garlic	Truffles
Ginger	Watermelon

SCOVILLE HEAT SCALE OF SPICES AND CHILLI PEPPERS

Named after its creator, American pharmacist Wilbur Scoville, the scale measures the heat contained in spicy foods. The measurements are recorded in Scoville Heat Units (SHUs).

Pure Capsaicin – 16.0 million Scoville Heat Units (SHUs)

Police Grade – Pepper Spray 5.3 million

Pepper – X 3.1 million

Dragon's Breath Pepper – 2.4 million

Carolina Reaper Pepper – 2.2 million

Trinidad Moruga Scorpion – 2.1 million

Standard Pepper Spray – 2.0 million

Naga Viper Pepper – 1.3 million

New Mexico Scorpion – 1.2 million

Naga Jolokia – 1.1 million

Bhut Jolokia (Ghost Pepper) – 1.0 million

Raja Mirch – 900,000

Trinidad Yellow Scorpion – 600,000

Piri Piri – 300,000

Scotch Bonnet – 250,000

Yellow Thai – 150,000

Cayenne Pepper – 50,000

Chipotle Pepper – 15,000

Jalapeno Pepper – 8,000

Tabasco Sauce – 3,750

Pimento Pepper – 500

GOUDA TO KNOW

WEIRD CHEESE FACTS

The world's most expensive cheese, pule, is made from the milk of the endangered Balkan donkey. Produced on a single farm in Serbia, it costs over $600 per pound. In 2012, Serbian tennis player Novak Djokovic bought the entire annual production of pule for his restaurant chain.

Cornish Yarg cheese is served coated in nettle leaves. It originates from an old recipe found in their attic by farmers Alan and Jenny Gray (Yarg is Gray spelt backwards).

The Dutch makers of Leyden cheese used to wash their feet in the whey.

A farm in Bjurholm, Sweden, makes moose cheese.

Casu Marzu cheese from Sardinia contains live maggots.

Cheese was a form of currency in sixteenth-century Denmark.

Although the village of Stilton is in Cambridgeshire, the cheese that bears its name is only licensed to be made in Derbyshire, Leicestershire and Nottinghamshire. So Stilton cheese made in Stilton is illegal.

In the twelfth century, Blanche of Navarre tried to win the heart of French King Philippe Auguste by sending him 200 cheeses each year.

Contrary to popular belief, mice prefer chocolate to cheese.

EXOTIC ICE CREAM FLAVOURS

Avocado (France)

Blue Cheese (London)

Carrot Cake (London)

Cheeseburger (Venezuela)

Cloudwater Stout (Manchester)

Corn on the Cob (New York)

Cow Tongue (Japan)

Creole Tomato (New Orleans)

Crocodile Egg (Philippines)

Foie Gras (France)

Garlic (New York)

Ghost Pepper (Delaware)

Gin (Ireland)

Horseradish (New York)

Lobster (Maine)

Mamushi Snake (Japan)

Mushy Peas and Fish (Whitby, North Yorkshire)

Octopus (Japan)

Pickled Mango (Ohio)

Raw Horse Flesh (Japan)

MOST POPULAR
ICE CREAM FLAVOURS

Vanilla

Chocolate

Strawberry

Mint choc chip

Choc chip cookie dough

Rocky road (chocolate ice cream,
nuts and marshmallows)

Cookies and cream

Butterscotch

Coconut

Raspberry ripple

Banana

Rum and raisin

Coffee

Tutti frutti

Pistachio

FOOD FOR THOUGHT

Cornflakes were introduced by Michigan physician John Harvey Kellogg to combat masturbation. He believed that plain foods, such as cereals, would curb unwelcome sexual desire.

More than half the labour force in Thailand is involved in rice production.

There are more than 40,000 varieties of rice and it is grown on every continent except Antarctica.

In the nineteenth century, tomato ketchup was used to treat diarrhea.

The oldest soup dates back to around 6000 BC and was made from hippopotamus and sparrow meat.

Castoreum, which is used as vanilla flavouring, is a secretion from the anal glands of beavers.

Kangatarians in Australia refuse to eat any meat that isn't from a kangaroo.

Honey is the only food that does not spoil. It can last for up to 3,000 years.

You could buy tickets to watch George II and the royal family eat Sunday dinner at Hampton Court.

If not prepared properly, fugu, or pufferfish, can kill you as it contains a toxin 1,200 times deadlier than cyanide.

Peanuts are one of the ingredients in dynamite.

It takes about 50 gallons of maple sap to make one gallon of maple syrup.

The ice lolly, or popsicle, was invented in 1905 by an 11-year-old Californian boy, Frank Epperson.

Marmite was recommended for treating cases of scrotal dermatitis among British soldiers serving in the Far East.

Although it had been around for over 3,000 years, most of Europe did not adopt the table fork until the eighteenth century. This was partly because church leaders argued that only human fingers, created by God, should touch God's bounty and also because the use of a fork by men was considered effeminate.

Only about a third of the world's population eats with a knife and fork.

Popcorn was banned in most American cinemas in the 1920s because it was too noisy.

British serial killer Rose West won first prize in a prison baking contest with a Victoria sponge at HMP Low Newton.

When the Prussian army encircled Paris in 1870, cutting off food supplies, 70,000 horses were slaughtered for their meat. When that ran out, French restaurant chefs turned to vermin and pets and finally to the city zoo, where even the two elephants ended up on the dinner table. Ironically, most diners declared that elephant meat was instantly forgettable.

CHOCOLATE CHIPS

When Mars Bars were first exported to the Soviet Union in 1991, the queues were so long that no customer was allowed to buy more than four.

One hundred pounds of chocolate are eaten in the US every second.

Louis XVI of France was such a chocoholic that he employed a special courtier whose principal duty was to keep the king supplied with chocolate.

The average chocolate bar contains eight insect parts. Anything less than 60 insect pieces per 100 grams of chocolate (two bars) is deemed safe for consumption in the US.

Enough jars of Nutella are sold each year to cover the Great Wall of China eight times.

The original Flake bar was created by chance after an employee at the Cadbury's factory in Bournville, Birmingham, noticed that the streams of excess chocolate which fell from the moulds formed flaky ripples as they cooled.

M&Ms were created in 1941 so that American soldiers could enjoy chocolate without it melting. More than 400 million M&Ms are produced every day in the US.

The light brown Smartie was axed by Nestlé Rowntree in 1989 – after 52 years of loyal service – to accommodate the blue Smartie that had recently been introduced in Germany.

In 2014, French inventor Christian Poincheval created a pill that makes farts smell like chocolate.

So many Toblerones are sold each year that, laid end to end, they would stretch one and a half times around the Earth.

White chocolate isn't technically chocolate, because it contains no cocoa solids.

During the Second World War, a shortage of milk forced Rowntree's to make KitKats with plain instead of milk chocolate. To signify the switch, the wrapper changed from red to blue.

Japan has 200 flavours of KitKat, including corn, green bean and soy sauce.

In 1930, American chef Ruth Wakefield mixed a broken piece of Nestlé chocolate into her cookie dough and invented chocolate chip cookies. She later sold the idea to Nestlé in return for a lifetime supply of chocolate.

In 2013, Belgium issued a limited edition of stamps that smelled and tasted of chocolate.

BRITAIN'S FAVOURITE CHOCOLATE BARS

1. Mars Bar

2. Galaxy

3. Snickers

4. Twix

5. Dairy Milk

6. Wispa

7. KitKat

8. Twirl

9. Crunchie

10. Double Decker

11= Picnic

11= Boost

13. Bounty

WHEN SWEET BRANDS WERE INTRODUCED

Rowntree's Fruit Pastilles – 1881

Rowntree's Fruit Gums – 1893

Liquorice Allsorts – 1899

Hershey Bar – 1900

Flake – 1920

Crunchie – 1929

Mars Bar – 1932

Fry's Five Centres – 1934, discontinued 1992

KitKat – 1935

Parma Violets – 1946

Polo mints – 1948

Spangles – 1948, discontinued 1984

Bounty – 1951

Love Hearts – 1954

Refreshers – 1955

Caramac – 1959

Opal Fruits – 1960, now known as Starburst

Revels – 1967

Twix – 1967

Curly Wurly – 1970

SPAM, SPAM, SPAM, SPAM

Spam was introduced by Hormel Foods in 1937. The precise origin of the name is shrouded in secrecy but it is short for either 'spiced ham' or 'shoulder pork and ham'.

The US military bought over 150 million pounds of Spam during the Second World War. And Russian leader Nikita Khrushchev admitted that 'without Spam we wouldn't have been able to feed our army'.

In the 1990s, 3.8 cans of Spam were consumed every second in the United States, totalling nearly 122 million cans annually.

A six-year-old boy from Dorset, England, developed an allergy to all meats except Spam and ate his way through six cans of Spam every week for three years.

In Hawaii, Spam is so popular that it is sometimes referred to as 'the Hawaiian steak'.

In 2012, the eight billionth can of Spam was sold worldwide.

When *Monty Python's Flying Circus* performed the Spam song, Hormel were so thrilled with the publicity that they offered to send the Pythons free supplies of Spam. The offer was politely declined.

There is a Spam Museum in Austin, Minnesota, which displays, among other things, Spam recipes from around the world.

FAST FOOD

On average, you will consume 12 pubic hairs in your fast food every year.

Americans eat 100 acres of pizza a day.

Uniquely the McDonald's in Sedona, Arizona, has turquoise not golden arches because the trademark yellow was considered too garish next to the local sandstone.

The first McDonald's mascot was a chef named Speedee. Ronald McDonald replaced him in 1963.

McDonald's operates around 37,000 restaurants worldwide, serving 69 million customers every day.

The Hawaiian pizza was invented in 1962 by a Greek who ran a restaurant in Canada.

In 2001, Pizza Hut delivered a six-inch salami pizza to the International Space Station – the first pizza delivered to outer space.

Because a small restaurant called Burger King in Mattoon, Illinois, registered the name first, no outlet of the huge chain is allowed to open within 20 miles of it.

FAVOURITE PIZZA TOPPINGS WORLDWIDE

Australia – ham and egg

Brazil – green peas

Britain – mushroom

Costa Rica – coconut

Finland – Berlusconi (smoked reindeer, mushroom and onion)

France – tarte flambée (bacon, onion and fresh cream)

Germany – canned tuna

Greece – feta cheese, olives, oregano, tomato and green pepper

India – pickled ginger, minced mutton and paneer

Italy – Margherita (basil, mozzarella and tomato)

Japan – eel and squid

Netherlands – Double Dutch (double meat, double cheese, double onion)

Pakistan – curry

Portugal – chorizo

Russia – mockba (a mix of fish and onion)

Sweden – chicken, peanuts, banana, pineapple and curry powder

United States – pepperoni

FUSSY EATERS

Don Gorske from Wisconsin ate his 30,000th Big Mac in 2018. He has eaten two Big Macs almost every day since 1972.

Samantha Archer from London gets through 100 bottles of tomato ketchup every year, putting it on everything from salad to curries and even eating spoonfuls of it as a snack.

Dave Nunley from Cambridgeshire only eats cheese and gets through 238 pounds of grated mild cheddar every year.

Jiang Musheng from China ate live tree frogs for over 40 years to ward off abdominal pains.

Debbie Taylor from Essex has eaten nothing but crisps for over ten years, her favourite meal being beef flavour Monster Munch.

Andy Park from Wiltshire has eaten Christmas dinner almost every day since 1993.

Julie Tori from Hampshire ate at least four pounds of carrots every day bar one for over ten years. On the day she missed out on her favourite vegetable, she suffered a panic attack.

Natalie Swindells from Cheshire lives on four bowls of Rice Krispies a day and has not eaten a vegetable in 20 years.

Adele Edwards, of Bradenton, Florida, was diagnosed with the medical disorder Pica after revealing that she had been eating the foam inside sofa cushions for 21 years. In 2011, she confessed: 'In the last year I've eaten seven sofas.'

Gary Watkinson from Huddersfield has eaten beans on toast for every meal for 20 years.

Sophie Ray from Wrexham ate nothing but cheese and tomato pizza for eight years.

Hans Raj, from Uttar Pradesh, India, has eaten a plate of gravel and sand every day for over 25 years. By way of a change, he occasionally snacks on rocks and pieces of brick.

RESTAURANTS WITH
A DIFFERENCE

There is a chain of toilet-themed restaurants in China where diners sit on toilet seats and eat from bowls shaped like bidets.

The New Lucky Restaurant in Ahmedabad, India, is built in the middle of an old cemetery. The tables sit alongside visible graves.

At the El Diablo restaurant on Lanzarote, food is cooked over the heat of an active volcano.

A decommissioned Indonesian Boeing 737 jet aeroplane has opened as a restaurant in Wuhan, China. It features a flight simulation system to make customers think they are airborne.

The CaliBurger restaurant in Pasadena, California, employs a robot, Flippy, to flip its burgers.

At a prison-themed restaurant in Jilin, China, customers eat basic prison food in mocked up cells.

Twins Restaurant, a 1990s New York eatery, was owned by identical twin sisters Lisa and Debbie Ganz and staffed by 37 sets of identical twins.

Ithaa, an underwater restaurant in the Maldives, is located 16 feet below the ocean surface with a transparent roof so that customers can see their potential meal swim past.

At O'Naturel, a restaurant in Paris, France, customers leave their clothes in a cloakroom and dine naked.

In 2016, Ginger's Grill in Prestatyn, Wales, announced a 20 per cent discount to any customer with genuine red hair.

The West Lake Restaurant in Changsha, China, can seat 5,000 customers. It employs 1,000 people, including 300 chefs.

The Solo Per Due restaurant in Vacone, Italy, only has room for two customers.

At Dans Le Noir, a restaurant in London, diners eat in total darkness (even mobile phones and digital watches must be left outside) and are served by visually impaired staff.

Instead of using waiters, the Vytopna Restaurant in Prague delivers drinks to customers via a 1,300-foot-long model train set.

Muru, a restaurant in Helsinki, is located nearly 300 feet underground in a mining museum. Diners wear safety helmets for the descent.

The Methane Gas Canteen, a restaurant in Semarang, Indonesia, is located at a landfill and allows customers to pay for their food with recyclable plastic garbage.

ACQUIRED TASTES

Guolizhuang, a restaurant in Beijing, specialises in serving animal penises, including water buffalo, deer, donkey, goat, dog, seal and yak.

The Filipino delicacy balut consists of a partially developed duck embryo. It is eaten directly from the shell, just before the chick is old enough to have grown a beak and feathers.

A still-beating heart of a dead snake is a popular appetiser in Vietnam. At some establishments the waiter will kill and gut the snake – usually a cobra – at your table.

A word of caution when ordering Rocky Mountain Oysters or Prairie Oysters in North America – they are deep-fried bull's testicles.

Fried tarantula is considered a tasty snack in Cambodia.

Raw puffin heart is one of the national dishes of Iceland.

The trademark starter in Dongyang, China, is virgin boy eggs – eggs that are boiled in the urine of prepubescent schoolboys.

In remote areas of Canada and Alaska, you might find jellied moose nose among your cold meat platter.

The Romans used to dine out on such delights as flamingo's tongue, stuffed thrush, boiled cow's womb, and calf brain custard.

In Malawi, roadside vendors sell mouse kebabs – towers of roasted field mice impaled on sticks.

The traditional Inuit dish kiviak is a dead auk that has been left to ferment inside a rotten seal skin for seven months. It is particularly popular at birthdays, weddings and Christmas.

In Mexico, the appearance of escamoles on the menu denotes ant eggs.

Seal flipper pie – made with real flippers from real seals – is an Easter treat in Newfoundland.

On the island of Lewis off the west coast of Scotland, look out for guga on the menu. It is boiled baby gannet.

65 million guinea pigs – or cuy – are eaten annually in Peru, usually roasted.

The chief component of the Norwegian dish smalahove is a sheep's head.

The Chinese dessert ingredient hasma is made from the fatty tissue found near the fallopian tubes of female snow frogs.

Dormouse stew has been a popular dish in Slovenia for over 500 years.

Surströmming is a fermented Baltic sea herring which possesses such a foul stench that if a can of it smashes to the floor in a Swedish supermarket, the store is usually evacuated.

In Thailand, the dish mok huak is tadpole casserole.

The Korean dish sannakji is live baby octopus. Even though it has been chopped into small pieces, the suction cups on the tentacles are still active and can cling to your tongue and throat as you try to swallow.

LESSER KNOWN PASTAS

There are over 600 different types of pasta.
Here are some that may have escaped your attention:

Anelli – small rings

Bucatini – hollow straws

Cavatappi – corkscrew shapes

Cencioni – flower petal shapes

Conchiglie – seashell shapes

Creste di galli – cock's comb shapes

Ditali – thimbles

Farfalle – bow tie or butterfly shapes

Mafalde – long, flat, rectangular ribbons with ruffled sides

Orecchiette – 'little ears'

Radiatori – radiator-like shapes

Riccioli – curls

Rotelle – little wheels

Stelle – star shapes

SPEED EATERS

Patrick Bertoletti of Chicago ate 72 cupcakes in six minutes. He has also eaten 38 Mars Bars in five minutes.

Darron Breedon of Virginia ate 480 oysters in eight minutes.

Joey Chestnut of California ate 141 hard boiled eggs in eight minutes. He has also eaten 74 hot dogs and buns in ten minutes.

Carmen Cincotti from New Jersey ate 61.75 ears of sweetcorn in 12 minutes.

Geoffrey Esper from Massachusetts ate 83 slices of 10-inch pizza in ten minutes.

Bob Shoudt of Philadelphia ate 36 peanut butter and banana sandwiches in ten minutes.

Matt Stonie from California ate 182 strips of bacon in five minutes.

Sonya Thomas of Virginia ate 80 chicken nuggets in five minutes.

In 2018, ex-boxer Mario Melo choked to death during a televised croissant-eating contest in Argentina.

ROADKILL RATINGS

British roadkill enthusiast Jonathan McGowan described the taste of various dead creatures that he had scraped off the road and cooked:

Adder: a bit like bacon rind.

Badger: not very nice on its own, but okay in a stew.

Fox: delicious and lean; young foxes taste rather like chicken. Fox lasagne is a favourite.

Frog: it really does taste like chicken, excellent in a stir-fry.

Hedgehog: very fatty.

Heron: adds something to a spaghetti bolognese.

Mouse: weird, with a very bitter flavour.

Mole: horrible, with a rancid taste.

Owl: works well in a curry.

Pheasant: tastes like turkey.

Rat: delicious, like pork but salty.

Squirrel: good firm meat, similar to rabbit and with a distinctly nutty flavour.

SOUND BITES

'I will not eat oysters. I want my food dead. Not sick. Not wounded. Dead' – Woody Allen

'Seize the moment. Remember all those women on the *Titanic* who waved off the dessert cart' – Erma Bombeck

'I wouldn't give someone my last Rolo if they were in a diabetic coma' – Jo Brand

'It's impossible to eat a Toblerone without hurting yourself' – Billy Connolly

'Unlike European mustards that bring out the subtle flavours of food, English mustard makes your nose bleed' – Jack Dee

'Rice is great when you're hungry and want 2,000 of something' – Mitch Hedberg

'You never know where to look when eating a banana' – Peter Kay

'Chopsticks are one of the reasons the Chinese never invented custard' – Spike Milligan

'Anything you have to acquire a taste for was not meant to be eaten' – Eddie Murphy

'I was a vegetarian until I started leaning toward the sunlight' – Rita Rudner

'You don't eat Mexican food, you just rent it' – Alexei Sayle

'Training is everything; cauliflower is nothing but cabbage with a college education' – Mark Twain

'The first time I tried organic wheat bread, I thought I was chewing on roofing material' – Robin Williams

'Why do people who work in health food shops always look so unhealthy?' – Victoria Wood

LAST MEALS OF FAMOUS PEOPLE

John Belushi – bowl of lentil soup

Napoleon Bonaparte – liver and bacon chops, sautéed kidneys, eggs, garlic toast and tomatoes

Bing Crosby – cup of chicken broth and a ham, lettuce and tomato sandwich

James Dean – apple pie

Ernest Hemingway – steak, baked potato and salad

Jimi Hendrix – tuna sandwich

Adolf Hitler – pasta

Whitney Houston – burger and fries

Saddam Hussein – boiled chicken and rice

Michael Jackson – chicken and spinach salad

John F. Kennedy – two boiled eggs, toast and marmalade

John Lennon – corned beef sandwich

Abraham Lincoln – mock turtle soup, roast Virginia fowl, baked yams and cauliflower cheese

Elvis Presley – four scoops of ice cream and six chocolate chip cookies

Frank Sinatra – grilled cheese sandwich

LOST IN TRANSLATION

AMUSING ITEMS ON FOREIGN MENUS

Toes with butter and jam (Bali)

Stewed dork with minced garlic (China)

Cold shredded children and sea blubber in spicy sauce (China)

Fillet Streak, Chocolate Mouse (China)

Husband and wife lung slice (China)

Dreaded veal cutlet with potatoes in cream (China)

Homemade graves with onions (Czech Republic)

French fried ships (Egypt)

Prawn cock and tail (Egypt)

Sweet lime soda, Red Bull, Diet cock (India)

Battered soul (India)

Pimps no 1 or Pimps no 2 (Iraq)

Martini & nipples (Italy)

Crotch steamed dish (Korea)

Roasted duck let loose (Poland)

Beef rashers beaten up in the country peoples fashion (Poland)

Sausage in the father-in-law (Russia)

Ice cream in the ass (Russia)

Kidneys of the chef (Spain)

Chicken gordon blue, pork shops, eggs scrambling (Thailand)

Muchroom soup (Thailand)

Pork with fresh garbage (Vietnam)

BARS AROUND THE WORLD

The Beer Wall in Bruges, Belgium, sells 1,600 different beers.

At the Timber Lounge in Halifax, Nova Scotia, customers can relieve the stress of the working day by hurling axes.

The Kid Mai Death Café in Bangkok, Thailand, has a funeral theme. If customers can lie down in a full-size coffin with the lid on for three minutes, they get a discount on their food and drink.

The Kayabukiya Tavern near Tokyo employs two macaque monkeys as waiters.

The 3440 café is located at 3,440 metres up a mountain in the Austrian Alps and is accessed via a ski lift.

At the Black Rat Café, a pop-up business that opened in San Francisco in 2017, visitors sipped their coffee surrounded by live rats.

BRITAIN'S OLDEST PUBS

Many pubs claim to be the oldest in Britain, so these dates might need to be taken with a larger pinch of salt than you would find in a bag of plain crisps:

The Old Ferryboat Inn, Holywell, Cambridgeshire (c.560)

Ye Olde Fighting Cocks, St Albans, Hertfordshire (c.795)

The Bingley Arms, Leeds (c.905)

Porch House, Stow-on-the-Wold, Gloucestershire (c.947)

Royal Standard of England, Forty Green, Buckinghamshire (c.1086)

The Skirrid Mountain Inn, Abergavenny, Monmouthshire (c.1110)

Ye Olde Trip to Jerusalem, Nottingham (c.1189)

White Hart Inn, Drury Lane, London (c.1216)

Ye Olde Salutation Inn, Nottingham (c.1240)

The Adam and Eve, Norwich, Norfolk (c.1241)

Ye Olde Man and Scythe, Bolton, Greater Manchester (c.1251)

The Sheep Heid Inn, Edinburgh (c.1360)

The Bell Inn, Nottingham (c.1437)

The Prospect of Whitby, Wapping, London (c.1520)

MOST COMMON
BRITISH PUB NAMES

1. Red Lion

2. Crown

3. Royal Oak

4. White Hart

5. Swan

6. Plough

7. Railway

8. White Horse

9. Ship

10. New Inn

11. Kings Arms

12. George

13. Rose and Crown

14. Bell

15. Kings Head

16. Wheatsheaf

17. Queens Head

18. Victoria

19. Black Horse

20. Castle

21. Star

22. Cross Keys

23. Anchor

24. Prince of Wales

25. White Lion

26. Greyhound

27. Station

28. Rising Sun

29. Coach and Horses

30. Chequers

UNUSUAL BRITISH PUB NAMES

The Actress and Bishop, Birmingham

The Ape and Apple, Manchester

The Bear's Paw, Warmingham, Cheshire

The Bettle and Chisel, Delabole, Cornwall

The Blazing Donkey, Ham, Kent

The Bleeding Heart Tavern, City of London

The Bleeding Wolf, Stoke-on-Trent, Staffordshire

The Bucket of Blood, Phillack, Cornwall

The Bull and Spectacles, Blithbury, Staffordshire

The Bunch of Carrots, Hampton Bishop, Herefordshire

The Butt and Oyster, Ipswich, Suffolk

The Case Is Altered, Pinner, Middlesex

The Cat and Custard Pot Inn, Paddlesworth, Kent

Dewdrop Inn, Loughborough, Leicestershire

The Dirty Habit, Maidstone, Kent

The Dirty Onion, Belfast

The Drunken Duck, Ambleside, Cumbria

The Fat Cat, Norwich, Norfolk

The Fawcett Inn, Portsmouth, Hampshire

The Flying Saucer, Gillingham, Kent

The Frog and Orange, Wingham, Kent

The Gate Hangs Well, Syston, Leicestershire

The Goat and Tricycle, Bournemouth

The Hanging Bat, Edinburgh

The Hung Drawn and Quartered, City of London

The Jolly Taxpayer, Portsmouth, Hampshire

The Kremlin, Clee Hill, Shropshire

The Lad in the Lane, Birmingham

The Leg of Mutton and Cauliflower, Ashtead, Surrey

The Legend of Oily Johnnies, Winscales, Cumbria

The Moody Cow, Upton Bishop, Herefordshire

The Moon and Sixpence, Whitby, North Yorkshire

The Mousetrap Inn, Bourton-on-the-Water, Gloucestershire

My Father's Moustache, Louth, Lincolnshire

The Newt and Cucumber, Cardiff

The Nobody Inn, Doddiscombsleigh, Devon

The Old Mother Redcap, Blackburn, Lancashire

The Old Thirteenth Cheshire Astley Volunteer Rifleman
Corps Inn, Stalybridge, Tameside

The Only Running Footman, Mayfair, London

The Poacher's Pocket, Chatham, Kent

Poosie Nansie's, Mauchline, Ayrshire

The Pub with No Name, Brighton, East Sussex

The Pyrotechnist's Arms, Nunhead, London

The Quiet Woman, Buxton, Derbyshire

The Roaring Donkey, Clacton-on-Sea, Essex

The Rusty Bicycle, Oxford

The Scran and Scallie, Edinburgh

The Skiving Scholar, Plymouth, Devon

The Smoking Dog, Malmesbury, Wiltshire

The Snooty Fox, Tetbury, Gloucestershire

The Swan and Cemetery, Bury, Greater Manchester

The Swan with Two Necks, Blackbrook, Staffordshire

The Three-Legged Mare, York

The Unruly Pig, Woodbridge, Suffolk

The Vat and Fiddle, Nottingham

The Walrus and the Carpenter, City of London

The Who'd a Thought It, Marlborough, Wiltshire

The World Turned Upside Down, Reading, Berkshire

Ye Olde Cheshire Cheese, City of London

LIQUID
REFRESHMENTS

165 million cups of tea are consumed every day in the UK.

China is the world's largest tea-producing country, followed by India and Kenya.

Ninety-six per cent of tea in Britain is made using a tea bag. Packing tea in paper dates back to eighth-century China, but the modern tea bag was not invented until the early twentieth century.

In Italian, the word 'espresso' does not mean 'quick' but 'forced out'.

Beethoven was very particular about his coffee and insisted that it made be made with exactly 60 coffee beans.

Coca-Cola was originally sold as a medicine. Its inventor, John Pemberton, claimed that it cured many diseases, including morphine addiction, nerve disorders and impotence.

Since 1973, visitors to a bar in Dawson City in Canada's Yukon Territory have taken part in the Sourtoe Cocktail Challenge, which involves drinking from a glass containing a real severed human toe. The rules state that the drinker's lips must touch the toe but not swallow it.

It is estimated that, at any given time, 0.7 per cent of the world's population are drunk.

A raisin dropped in a glass of champagne will bounce up and down continuously because the bubbles in the champagne become trapped in the raisin's wrinkles.

On a royal hunting trip to Egypt, Edward VII's entourage took 7,000 bottles of wine.

The special ingredient of Ttongsul, a medicinal rice wine from Korea, is the fermented faeces of a child. According to local medicine men, children around the age of six are best because their poo does not smell. Obviously these people have never been to a children's birthday party.

BEERS AND THEIR COUNTRY OF ORIGIN

Amstel: Netherlands

Angkor: Cambodia

Asahi: Japan

Bintang: Indonesia

Brahma: Brazil

Budweiser: United States

Carlsberg: Denmark

Castlemaine XXXX: Australia

Cobra: India

Coors: United States

Corona: Mexico

Erdinger: Germany

Estrella: Spain

Foster's: Australia

Goldstar: Israel

Grolsch: Netherlands

Guinness: Ireland

Heineken: Netherlands

Hoegaarden: Belgium

Karlovacko: Croatia

Kingfisher: India

Kronenbourg: France

Krusovice: Czech Republic

Labatt: Canada

Paulaner: Germany

Peroni: Italy

Red Stripe: Jamaica

San Miguel: Spain

Singha: Thailand

Staropramen: Czech Republic

Stella Artois: Belgium

Tiger: Singapore

Tusker: Kenya

Ursus: Romania

Zywiec: Poland

INTERESTINGLY NAMED BEERS

Arrogant Bastard Ale (Stone Brewing Company, California)

Beard of Zeus (Short's, Michigan)

Belligerent Ass (Portneuf Valley, Idaho)

Bishop's Finger (Shepherd Neame, Kent – known locally as Nun's Delight)

Blind Pig (Russian River, California)

Blithering Idiot (Weyerbacher, Pennsylvania)

Buttface Ale (Ram Brewery, Washington State)

The Dog's Bollocks (Wychwood, Oxfordshire)

Fiddler's Elbow (Wychwood, Oxfordshire)

Ginger Tosser (Skinners, Cornwall)

He'Brew (Schmaltz, New York)

Homo Erectus (Walking Man, Washington State)

Hoptimus Prime (Ruckus, New York)

Human Blockhead (Coney Island, New York)

Kiltlifter (Four Peaks, Arizona)

MILF (Mother's Brewing Company, Missouri)

Moose Drool (Big Sky, Montana)

My Wife's Bitter (Burleigh, Queensland)

Nipple Mountain (Pagosa, Colorado)

Old Leghumper (Thirsty Dog, Ohio)

Old Peculier (Theakston, North Yorkshire)

Old Slapper (Bank Top, Lancashire)

Old Speckled Hen (Morland/Greene King, Suffolk)

Panty Peeler (Midnight Sun, Alaska)

Piddle in the Hole (Wyre Piddle, Worcestershire)

Polygamy Porter (Wasatch, Utah – why have just one?)

Purple Monkey Dishwasher (Evil Genius, Pennsylvania)

Seriously Bad Elf (Ridgeway, Oxfordshire)

Sheepshagger (Cairngorm, Inverness-shire)

Sick Duck (Flyers, Washington State)

Skull Splitter (Orkney, Scotland)

Smooth Hoperator (Stoudts, Pennsylvania)

Tactical Nuclear Penguin (BrewDog, Aberdeenshire)

Yellow Snow (Rogue Ales, Oregon)

DEAR BEER

MOST EXPENSIVE CITIES
IN WHICH TO BUY A PINT

1. Dubai (£9) ($11.52)

2. Oslo (£7) ($8.96)

3. Hong Kong (£6) ($7.68)

4. Singapore (£5.94) ($7.60)

5= New York (£5.32) ($6.81)

5= Paris (£5.32) ($6.81)

7. Boston (£5.20) ($6.65)

8. London (£5.19) ($6.64)

9. Stockholm (£5.14) ($6.58)

10. Dublin (£5.05) ($6.46)

11= Zurich (£5.00) ($6.40)

11= Melbourne (£5.00) ($6.40)

13. Shanghai (£4.88) ($6.25)

14. Auckland (£4.85) ($6.21)

15. Copenhagen (£4.81) ($6.16)

16. Helsinki (£4.70) ($6.02)

17. San Francisco (£4.65) ($5.95)

18= Milan (£4.62) ($5.91)

18= Wellington (£4.62) ($5.91)

20. Los Angeles (£4.58) ($5.86)

21. Rome (£4.50) ($5.76)

CHAMPAGNE BOTTLE SIZES

(NUMBER OF GLASSES PER BOTTLE IN BRACKETS)

Piccolo (1)

Demi (3)

Bottle (6)

Magnum (12)

Jeroboam (24)

Rehoboam (36)

Methuselah (48)

Salmanazar (72)

Balthazar (96)

Nebuchadnezzar (120)

Solomon (144)

Sovereign (200)

Primat/Gloiath (216)

Melchizedek (240)

COUNTRIES THAT CONSUME MOST ALCOHOL PER CAPITA

1. Belarus
2. Moldova
3. Lithuania
4. Russia
5. Romania
6. Ukraine
7. Andorra
8. Hungary
9. Czech Republic
10. Slovakia
11. Portugal
12. Serbia
13. Grenada
14. Poland
15. Latvia
16. Finland
17. South Korea
18. France
19. Australia
20. Croatia
21. Ireland
22. Luxembourg
23. Germany
24. Slovenia
25. United Kingdom
26. South Africa
27. New Zealand
28. Canada
29. United States

LEADING COFFEE PRODUCING COUNTRIES

1. Brazil

2. Vietnam

3. Colombia

4. Indonesia

5. Ethiopia

6= Honduras

6= India

8. Uganda

9. Mexico

10. Guatemala

11. Peru

12. Nicaragua

13. China

14. Ivory Coast

15. Costa Rica

16. Kenya

17= Papua New Guinea

17= Tanzania

19. El Salvador

20. Ecuador

SPORT
AND
GAMES

SPORTING FAILURES

Running in the 1979 Pan-American Games marathon, Wallace Williams of the Virgin Islands was so slow that by the time he reached the stadium it was locked and everyone had gone home.

Preparing for a bout at the 1992 New York Golden Gloves Championships, boxer Daniel Caruso psyched himself up by pounding his gloves into his face. In doing so, he broke his nose and was declared unfit to box.

Goalkeeper Isadore Irandir of Brazilian team Rio Preto was still on his knees in the goalmouth saying his traditional pre-match prayers when opponents Corinthians kicked off. Three seconds later, just as he was concluding his beseechments to the Almighty, a 60-yard shot from Roberto Rivelino flew past his ear and into the net.

At Wincanton in 2008, 44-year-old amateur Anthony Knott – unkindly dubbed 'British horse racing's worst jockey' – finally won his first race after 28 years of trying.

American golfer Maud McInnes took 166 shots on the 130-yard sixteenth hole at the 1912 Shawnee Invitational for Ladies in Pennsylvania – 163 over par. She drove into a river and pursued the ball downstream in a boat while making frequent unsuccessful attempts to pitch the ball back onto dry land. It took her two hours to complete the hole.

Cuban postman Felix Carvajal was denied bronze at the 1904 Olympic marathon because in the closing stages he stopped

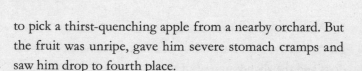

to pick a thirst-quenching apple from a nearby orchard. But the fruit was unripe, gave him severe stomach cramps and saw him drop to fourth place.

Russian tennis player Mikhail Youzhny was so disappointed with his performance at the 2008 Sony Ericsson Open in Miami that he whacked himself three times on the head with his racket and then needed a timeout because he had cracked his skull open.

Incompetent marshalling at the 1988 Liège-Bastogne-Liège cycle race in Belgium sent the entire field of 200 riders speeding down a hill straight into roadworks. The ensuing crash brought down more than 50 competitors.

During the 1930 World Cup football semi-final between Argentina and the United States, the American team trainer, Jock Coll, ran on to the pitch to treat an injured player. Still fuming over a disputed Argentine goal, Coll threw down his medical bag in a fit of pique, but in doing so he broke a bottle of chloroform, accidentally anaesthetised himself and had to be carried off by his own team.

After travelling over 3,500 miles from New York to Sandwich, Kent, for the 1937 Amateur Golf Championship, Brigadier-General Critchley arrived six minutes late and was disqualified.

In 1960, Wym Essajas became the first person to be chosen to represent Suriname at the Olympics when he was sent to Rome to take part in the 800 metres. Unfortunately a breakdown in communications meant that he was told the heats were in the afternoon instead of the morning so by the time he reached the stadium his race had been run ... without him. He thus returned home without competing.

In April 1995, a black cat found its way on to Belfast greyhound track in the middle of a race, causing a pile up of dogs and the abandonment of the race.

As South Africa's Johannes Coleman stormed across the finishing line of the 1938 Natal Marathon, he was convinced he had set a new world record by at least three minutes – but he found to his horror that all of the timekeepers were drinking tea in the refreshment room because they hadn't expected any of the runners back so soon. Consequently his time could not be ratified.

At the 2012 London Olympics, organisers had to apologise to North Korea's women footballers after their pictures were displayed on a giant screen next to the flag of South Korea.

At the 1929 Rose Bowl, confused University of California centre Roy Riegels ran nearly half the length of the field with the ball – in the wrong direction, towards his own goal. 'Wrong-Way Riegels' became an overnight celebrity, even receiving an offer of marriage in which he and his bride would walk up the aisle instead of down!

Israeli athlete Lonah Salpeter celebrated what she thought was a silver medal in the women's 5,000 metres final at the 2018 European Championships in Berlin, only to realise that there was still another lap to go. Her mistake caused her to lose momentum and she finished only fourth.

Selected to play for the French rugby team against Scotland in 1911, Gaston Vareilles travelled to the game by train with his new team-mates. When the train pulled into Lyon, he jumped off to buy a sandwich but by the time he returned the train was disappearing into the distance. He missed the game and was never picked again for his country.

Mexico's Roberto Alvarez languished so far behind the other competitors in the 50-kilometre cross-country skiing at the 1988 Winter Olympics that worried officials despatched a search party to look for him.

After finishing a creditable fourth in the 1989 500cc United States Grand Prix at Laguna Seca, Australian motorcyclist Kevin Magee waved to the crowds on his lap of honour, fell off his machine and broke a leg.

American boxer Ralph Walton was still adjusting his gumshield when he was knocked out by Al Couture just half a second into their 1946 bout at Lewiston, Maine.

Voted Leicester City's 1995–96 Player of the Year for his safe hands, goalkeeper Kevin Poole was presented with a cut-glass rose ball … which he then dropped.

Eighteen-year-old Soviet rower Vyacheslav Ivanov celebrated winning the single sculls at the 1956 Melbourne Olympics by throwing his gold medal into the air. Alas, he failed to catch it and it sank into the depths of Lake Wendouree never to be seen again.

After beating 1,000 rivals in a 500-mile race, Percy the champion racing pigeon flopped down exhausted in his Sheffield loft and was promptly eaten by an opportunistic cat. To add insult to injury, the 90-minute delay in finding his remains and handing his identification tag to the judges relegated Percy from a posthumous first to third place.

WEIRD SPORTING EVENTS

At the annual cheese rolling event in Gloucestershire, runners tumble down a steep hill in pursuit of a large cheese. Paramedics and ambulances wait at the foot of the hill.

A wife carrying race has been part of the Finnish sporting calendar since 1992.

At the Darwin Beer Can Regatta in Australia, competitors take to the sea in boats made from hundreds of beer cans that have been taped together.

The Afghan sport of buzkashi is similar to polo, but the 'ball' is the headless, gutted carcass of a dead goat.

Every August Bank Holiday at Stacksteads in Lancashire, competitors wrestle each other in a huge pool of gravy.

Each year, over 600 runners take part in a race up the 1,576 stairs of the Empire State Building.

Gumboot throwing is all the rage in New Zealand.

At the Great Knaresborough Bed Race in North Yorkshire, runners wheel beds along a 2.4-mile course that includes crossing the icy waters of the River Nidd.

There is an annual 12-hour lawnmower race in West Sussex.

The Indonesian game of sepak bola api is like football except that the players are barefoot and the ball is on fire.

At the World Black Pudding Throwing Championships in Lancashire, competitors hurl black puddings at a pile of Yorkshire puddings with the aim of knocking down as many as possible.

The South African sport of bokdrol spoeg determines who can spit pellets of kudu or impala dung the furthest.

The World Worm Charming Championships are held each year in the Cheshire village of Willaston.

In Japan, competitors race around city streets riding regular office chairs.

The World Toe Wrestling Championships take place at a Derbyshire pub.

Bog snorkelling in Wales sees participants from across the globe snorkel two lengths of a 60-yard-long, four-foot-deep trench that runs through a weed-infested peat bog.

At the Pig-N-Ford Races in Tillamook, Oregon, drivers speed around a dirt track in a stripped-down Model T Ford while carrying a live pig under one arm.

FREAK SPORTING INJURIES

Shortly after Manchester United's Champions League victory over Lyon in 2008, midfielder Darren Fletcher was sitting on the toilet when the door came off its hinges and hit him on the head, leaving him requiring stitches.

Toronto Blue Jays' baseball player Glenallen Hill sustained serious cuts after falling out of bed and crashing into a glass table while having a nightmare about spiders.

After scoring a goal in the Swiss Soccer League in 2004, Servette midfielder Paulo Diogo jumped into the crowd to celebrate, but in doing so caught his wedding ring on the perimeter fence and ripped off the top half of his finger. Despite his pain, he was then booked by the referee for excessive celebration.

Detroit Tigers baseball pitcher Joel Zumaya missed three games in 2006 through playing the video game *Guitar Hero* too energetically.

Liverpool striker Robbie Fowler suffered a knee injury when stretching to pick up the TV remote.

England cricketer Derek Pringle once injured his back while writing a letter.

Mike Tereui, a weightlifter from the Cook Islands, saw his medal chances at the 1990 Commonwealth Games evaporate after he seriously injured his hand while attempting to punch a pig that was raiding his vegetable patch.

English snooker player Stephen Lee had to withdraw from the 1999 British Open after twisting a neck muscle while answering the phone.

Chicago Cubs baseball player Sammy Sosa sprained a ligament in his back in 2004 while sneezing.

Glasgow Rangers defender Kirk Broadfoot suffered minor burns when a microwaved egg exploded in his face.

In 2008, St Louis Blues ice hockey player Erik Johnson tore his knee while getting out of a golf cart.

Norwegian footballer Svein Grondalen had to withdraw from an international fixture because he ran into a moose while out jogging.

Scottish sprinter Euan Clarke missed a number of races in 1991 after cutting his eyeball while trying to wipe sweat from his forehead with a crisp packet.

Atlanta Braves baseball player Ryan Klesko missed several games with a strained back after injuring himself while picking up his lunch tray.

Former Leicestershire cricketer Nigel Briers sprained his thumb after catching it in his trouser pocket.

Chelsea goalkeeper Dave Beasant missed the start of the 1993–94 season after dropping a jar of salad cream on his big toe.

Boston Red Sox baseball player Wade Boggs hurt his back while pulling on his cowboy boots.

When Australian rugby league player Jamie Ainscough complained of an infection in his arm, an X-ray showed he had another player's tooth embedded in it.

SURPRISING SPORTS STARS

Fidel Castro was an enthusiastic baseball pitcher at the University of Havana and was rumoured to have attracted interest from American professional teams.

George Clooney was such a good baseball player at high school that he was invited to try out for the Cincinnati Reds.

In the late 1980s, Daniel Craig played rugby union for Hoylake RFC on the Wirral.

While at Kennett High School, Missouri, Sheryl Crow was an all-star track athlete, winning a medal in the 75-metre hurdles.

Geena Davis almost qualified for the 2000 US Olympic archery team, finishing twenty-fourth out of 300.

Sir Arthur Conan Doyle played soccer as a goalkeeper for Portsmouth, using the pseudonym 'A.C. Smith'. He also played cricket for the MCC, bowling out the great W.G. Grace for his only first-class wicket.

Before his political career, Gerald Ford played football for the University of Michigan and helped his team win national titles in both 1932 and 1933.

Jamie Foxx was an accomplished footballer at Terrell High School in Texas and was the first person in the school's history to pass over 1,000 yards.

Julio Iglesias was the goalkeeper with Real Madrid's reserve team until a car crash left him unable to walk for two years and ended his football career.

Billy Joel was a talented amateur boxer in his younger days, winning his first 22 bouts, but quit the sport after his nose was broken in his twenty-fourth fight.

Mollie King, once of girl band The Saturdays, was selected for the Great Britain children's skiing team when she was 11.

Hugh Laurie rowed for the unsuccessful Cambridge crew in the 1980 University Boat Race.

At the age of ten, Avril Lavigne was playing ice hockey in a boys' league in Napanee, Ontario, earning Most Valuable Player honours two years in a row.

Broadcaster Gabby Logan represented Wales at the 1990 Commonwealth Games in Auckland, finishing eleventh in the rhythmic gymnastics.

In 1955, Johnny Mathis was ranked joint eighty-fifth in the world for the high jump.

Entertainer Des O'Connor was a tricky winger with Northampton Town Football Club shortly after the Second World War.

Ryan O'Neal boxed in Golden Gloves contests as a teenager.

Sarah Palin helped lead the Wasilla High School basketball team to a 1982 Alaska state championship.

The 19-year-old Stephen Hawking was a rowing cox at Oxford University in 1961.

Edgar Allan Poe was an accomplished long jumper and an excellent swimmer, holding the record for swimming six miles up the James River in Virginia.

Actor Jason Statham represented Great Britain as a diver at the 1990 Commonwealth Games, his best finish being eighth in the one-metre springboard.

At 16, Rod Stewart signed as a professional footballer with Brentford but only lasted three weeks.

TV presenter Bradley Walsh was a professional footballer with Brentford for two years in the 1970s but never made the first team.

SPORTS STARS'
NICKNAMES

Martin Adams, darts: 'Wolfie'

Shoaib Akhtar, cricket: 'The Rawalpindi Express'

Muhammad Ali, boxing: 'The Louisville Lip/The Greatest'

Martin Allen, football: 'Mad Dog'

Nicolas Anelka, football: 'The Incredible Sulk'

Charles Barkley, basketball: 'The Round Mound of Rebound'

John Barnes, football: 'Digger'

Franz Beckenbauer, football: 'Der Kaiser'

Nigel Benn, boxing: 'The Dark Destroyer'

Jerome Bettis, American football: 'The Bus'

Nigel Bond, snooker: 'Basildon'

Ian Botham, cricket: 'Beefy'

Eric Bristow, darts: 'The Crafty Cockney'

Kobe Bryant, basketball: 'The Black Mamba'

Maria Bueno, tennis: 'The Sao Paulo Swallow'

Emilio Butragueño, football: 'The Vulture'

Johnny Byrne, football: 'Budgie'

Shane Byrne, motorcycling: 'Shaky'

Primo Carnera, boxing: 'The Ambling Alp'

Steve Cauthen, horse racing: 'The Kentucky Kid'

Craig Chalmers, rugby union: 'Judith'

Wilt Chamberlain, basketball: 'The Stilt'

John Charles, football: 'The Gentle Giant'

Eddie Charlton, snooker: 'Steady Eddie'

Jack Charlton, football: 'The Giraffe'

Allan Clarke, football: 'Sniffer'

Maureen Connolly, tennis: 'Little Mo'

James J. Corbett, boxing: 'Gentleman Jim'

Fred Couples, golf: 'Boom Boom'

John Daly, golf: 'Wild Thing'

Edgar Davids, football: 'The Pitbull'

Steve Davis, snooker: 'The Nugget'

Andre Dawson, baseball: 'The Hawk'

Jack Dempsey, boxing: 'The Manassa Mauler'

Joe DiMaggio, baseball: 'Joltin''

Allan Donald, cricket: 'White Lightning'

Mick Doohan, motorcycling:
'The Thunder from Down Under'

Dale Earnhardt Sr, motor racing: 'The Intimidator'

Ernie Els, golf: 'The Big Easy'

Eusebio, football: 'The Black Panther'

Chris Evert, tennis: 'The Ice Maiden'

Brett Favre, American football: 'The Gunslinger'

Duncan Ferguson, football: 'Duncan Disorderly'

Tom Finney, football: 'The Preston Plumber'

Andy Fordham, darts: 'The Viking'

Joe Frazier, boxing: 'Smokin' Joe'

Wayne Gardner, motorcycling: 'The Wollongong Whiz'

Garrincha, football: 'Little Bird'

Vitas Gerulaitis, tennis: 'The Lithuanian Lion'

Harold Grange, American football: 'The Galloping Ghost'

Fitz Hall, football: 'One Size' (as in 'one size fits all')

Anthony Hamilton, snooker: 'The Sheriff of Pottingham'

Ron Harris, football: 'Chopper'

Leon Haslam, motorcycling: 'The Pocket Rocket'

Thomas Hearns, boxing: 'Hitman'

Javier Hernandez, football: 'The Little Pea'

Alex Higgins, snooker: 'Hurricane'

John Higgins, snooker: 'The Wizard of Wishaw'

Graham Hill, motor racing: 'Mr Monaco'

Martina Hingis, tennis: 'The Swiss Miss'

Ben Hogan, golf: 'The Hawk'

Michael Holding, cricket: 'Whispering Death'

Evander Holyfield, boxing: 'The Real Deal'

Emlyn Hughes, football: 'Crazy Horse'

Mark Hughes, football: 'Sparky'

James Hunt, motor racing: 'Hunt the Shunt'

Norman Hunter, football: 'Bites Yer Legs'

Joe Jackson, baseball: 'Shoeless'

James Jeffries, boxing: 'The Boilermaker'

Miguel Angel Jimenez, golf: 'The Mechanic'

Earvin Johnson, basketball: 'Magic'

Andrew Johnston, golfer: 'Beef'

Daryl Johnston, American football: 'Moose'

Jimmy Johnstone, football: 'Jinky'

Kevin Keegan, football: 'Mighty Mouse'

Toni Kukoč, basketball: 'The Croatian Sensation'

Rod Laver, tennis: 'The Rocket'

Tommy Lawrence, football: 'The Flying Pig'

Colin Meads, rugby union: 'The Pine Tree'

Nat Lofthouse, football: 'The Lion of Vienna'

John Lowe, darts: 'Old Stone Face'

Karl Malone, basketball: 'The Mailman'
(because he always delivered)

Stanley Matthews, football: 'The Wizard of the Dribble'

Jason McAteer, football: 'Trigger'

Willie McCovey, baseball: 'Stretch'

John McEnroe, tennis: 'Superbrat'

Phil Mickelson, golf: 'Lefty'

Helen Wills Moody, tennis: 'Little Miss Poker Face'

Jose Mourinho, football: 'The Special One'

Gerd Müller, football: 'Der Bomber'

Joe Namath, American football: 'Broadway Joe'

Jack Nicklaus, golf: 'The Golden Bear'

Greg Norman, golf: 'The Great White Shark'

Tazio Nuvolari, motor racing: 'The Flying Mantuan'

Martin Offiah, rugby league: 'Chariots'

Shaquille O'Neal, basketball: 'Diesel'

Ronnie O'Sullivan, snooker: 'The Rocket'

Ray Parlour, football: 'The Romford Pele'

Walter Payton, American football: 'Sweetness'

Stuart Pearce, football: 'Psycho'

William Perry, American football: 'The Refrigerator'

Michael Phelps, swimming: 'The Baltimore Bullet'

Lester Piggott, horse racing: 'The Long Fellow'

Gary Player, golf: 'The Black Knight'

Alain Prost, motor racing: 'The Professor'

Ferenc Puskas, football: 'The Galloping Major'

Kimi Raikkonen, motor racing: 'The Iceman'

Claudio Ranieri, football: 'The Tinkerman'

Ray Reardon, snooker: 'Dracula'

Carlos Reutemann, motor racing: 'The Bull'

Luigi Riva, football: 'The Rumble of Thunder'

Gianni Rivera, football: 'The Golden Boy'

Larry Robinson, ice hockey: 'Big Bird'

Dennis Rodman, basketball: 'The Worm'

Valentino Rossi, motorcycling: 'The Doctor'

Pete Sampras, tennis: 'Pistol Pete'

Doug Sanders, golf: 'The Peacock of the Fairways'

Gene Sarazen, golf: 'The Squire'

Mark Selby, snooker: 'The Jester from Leicester'

Harbhajan Singh, cricket: 'The Turbanator'

Kenny Smith, basketball: 'The Jet'

Stan Smith, tennis: 'The Leaning Tower of Pasadena'

Ole Gunnar Solskjaer, football: 'The Baby-Faced Assassin'

Craig Stadler, golf: 'The Walrus'

Joe Swail, snooker: 'The Outlaw'

Phil Taylor, darts: 'The Power'

Sachin Tendulkar, cricket: 'The Little Master'

Frank Thomas, baseball: 'Big Hurt'

Cliff Thorburn, snooker: 'The Grinder'

Ian Thorpe, swimming: 'Thorpedo'

Lee Trevino, golf: 'Super Mex'

Fred Trueman, cricket: 'Fiery'

Phil Tufnell, cricket: 'The Cat'

Frank Tyson, cricket: 'Typhoon'

Mike Tyson, boxing: 'Iron Mike'

Marco van Basten, football: 'The Swan of Utrecht'

Robin van Persie, football: 'The Flying Dutchman'

Wolfgang von Trips, motor racing: 'Taffy'

Tom Weiskopf, golf: 'The Towering Inferno'

Jimmy White, snooker: 'The Whirlwind'

Bobby Windsor, rugby union: 'The Iron Duke'

Keith Wood, rugby union: 'The Raging Potato'

SPORTSPEOPLE WITH UNFORTUNATE NAMES

Jean Condom (French rugby union player)

Johnny Dickshot (American baseball player)

Fair Hooker (American footballer)

Misty Hyman (American swimmer)

Rusty Kuntz (American baseball player)

Ralf Minge (German footballer)

Gaylord Silly (Seychelles runner)

Yoshie Takeshita (Japanese volleyball player)

Dick Trickle (American motor racing driver)

Andreas Wank (German ski jumper)

SUMMER OLYMPICS
HOST CITIES

1896 Athens	1968 Mexico City
1900 Paris	1972 Munich
1904 St. Louis	1976 Montreal
1908 London	1980 Moscow
1912 Stockholm	1984 Los Angeles
1920 Antwerp	1988 Seoul
1924 Paris	1992 Barcelona
1928 Amsterdam	1996 Atlanta
1932 Los Angeles	2000 Sydney
1936 Berlin	2004 Athens
1948 London	2008 Beijing
1952 Helsinki	2012 London
1956 Melbourne	2016 Rio de Janeiro
1960 Rome	2020 Tokyo
1964 Tokyo	

WINTER OLYMPICS HOST VENUES

1924 Chamonix, France

1928 St. Moritz, Switzerland

1932 Lake Placid, United States

1936 Garmisch-Partenkirchen, Germany

1948 St. Moritz, Switzerland

1952 Oslo, Norway

1956 Cortina d'Ampezzo, Italy

1960 Squaw Valley, United States

1964 Innsbruck, Austria

1968 Grenoble, France

1972 Sapporo, Japan

1976 Innsbruck, Austria

1980 Lake Placid, United States

1984 Sarajevo, Yugoslavia

1988 Calgary, Canada

1992 Albertville, France

1994 Lillehammer, Norway

1998 Nagano, Japan

2002 Salt Lake City, United States

2006 Turin, Italy

2010 Vancouver, Canada

2014 Sochi, Russia

2018 PyeongChang, South Korea

2022 Beijing, China

COUNTRIES WITH MOST OLYMPIC MEDALS PER CAPITA

1. Liechtenstein

2. Norway

3. Finland

4. Sweden

5. Hungary

6. Switzerland

7. Austria

8. Bahamas

9. Denmark

10. East Germany

11. Estonia

12. Bulgaria

13. Jamaica

14. New Zealand

15. Netherlands

16. Australia

17. Cuba

18. Slovenia

19. Grenada

20. Romania

21. Bermuda

22. Trinidad and Tobago

23. Canada

24. Great Britain

25. Belgium

OLYMPIC HEROES

American gymnast George Eyser won three gold medals at the 1904 Olympics despite having a wooden left leg.

Italian runner Dorando Pietri missed out on gold in the 1908 marathon in London because after he had collapsed 10 yards from the finish, over-anxious officials helped him across the line.

Japanese runner Shizo Kanakuri was officially declared a missing person after failing to finish the 1912 Olympic marathon in Stockholm. On the fiftieth anniversary of the race, a Swedish journalist tracked him down to a school in Tamana, where he was teaching geography, blissfully unaware of his cult status back in Scandinavia. In 1967, at the age of 76, Kanakuri returned to Stockholm's Olympic Stadium and jogged across the finish line to complete the race that he had started 55 years earlier.

After his right hand was shattered by a grenade, Hungarian Károly Takács taught himself to shoot left-handed and went on to win the Olympic rapid-fire pistol event in 1948 and 1952.

Competing in the 2000 Sydney Olympics, Eric Moussambani from Equatorial Guinea swam the 100 metres freestyle in the slowest ever Olympic time of 1min 52.7sec. He finished the two lengths over a minute slower than the winners of the other heats and more than seven seconds outside the world record for the 200 metres, but his dogged determination earned him international affection as 'Eric the Eel'. He had taken up swimming only eight months before and had practised in a crocodile-infested river and a hotel swimming pool.

SOME DISCONTINUED
OLYMPIC SPORTS

(LAST YEAR STAGED)

Cricket (1900)

Croquet (1900)

Horse long jump (1900)

Live pigeon shooting (1900)

Underwater swimming (1900)

Plunge for distance (1904)

Lacrosse (1908)

Motorboating (1908)

Rackets (1908)

Duelling pistols (1912)

Tug of war (1920)

Rope climb (1932)

Polo (1936)

Solo synchronised swimming (1992)

MISCELLANEOUS OLYMPIANS

John B. Kelly, father of Grace Kelly, won two rowing golds for the United States at the 1920 Olympics.

Before playing Tarzan, Johnny Weissmuller won five Olympic gold medals for swimming.

Twelve years after surviving the sinking of the *Titanic*, Richard Williams partnered Hazel Wightman to win gold for the United States in the tennis mixed doubles at the 1924 Olympics.

Harold Sakata, who went on to play the villainous Oddjob in *Goldfinger*, won a silver medal at the 1948 Olympics in weightlifting.

Bob Anderson, who was the stuntman for Darth Vader's fight scenes in the original *Star Wars* trilogy, represented Great Britain in fencing at the 1952 Olympics.

Noel Harrison, son of Rex Harrison and later a successful actor in his own right, was a member of the British ski team at the Winter Olympics in 1952 and 1956.

Menzies 'Ming' Campbell, former leader of the Liberal Democrats, competed for Great Britain in the 200 metres and the 4x100 metres relay at the 1964 Olympics.

One-time teenage violin prodigy Vanessa-Mae represented Thailand under the name Vanessa Vanakorn in the giant slalom skiing event at the 2014 Winter Olympics.

A GOOD WALK
SPOILED

PITHY QUOTES ABOUT GOLF

'It took me 17 years to get 3,000 hits in baseball. I did it in one afternoon on the golf course' – Hank Aaron

'I don't enjoy playing videogame golf because there is nothing to throw' – Paul Azinger

'Although golf was originally restricted to wealthy, overweight Protestants, today it's open to anybody who owns hideous clothing' – Dave Barry

'Golf is played by 20 million mature American men whose wives think they are out having fun' – Jim Bishop

'Golf is a game whose aim is to hit a very small ball into an even smaller hole, with weapons singularly ill-designed for the purpose' – Winston Churchill

'The reason the pro tells you to keep your head down is so you can't see him laughing' – Phyllis Diller

'They call it golf because all the other four-letter words were taken' – Raymond Floyd

'The only time my prayers are never answered is on the golf course' – Billy Graham

'By the time a man can afford to lose a golf ball, he can't hit it that far' – Lewis Grizzard

'I'll always remember the day I broke 90. I had a few beers in the clubhouse and was so excited I forgot to play the back nine' – Bruce Lansky

'The only useful putting advice I ever got from my caddie was to keep the ball low' – Chi Chi Rodriguez

'You've just one problem: you stand too close to the ball – after you've hit it' – Sam Snead

'Why am I using a new putter? Because the last one didn't float too well' – Craig Stadler

'If there's a thunderstorm on a golf course, walk down the middle of the fairway holding a one-iron over your head. Even God can't hit a one-iron' – Lee Trevino

'Golf is a good walk spoiled' – Mark Twain

'Golf, like measles, should be caught young' – P.G. Wodehouse

EXTREME
GOLF HOLES

The single hole at Elfego Baca, New Mexico, is 7,000 feet above sea level and the tee is three miles from a 50-foot green. The best recorded score is a nine.

The 14th green at the Coeur d'Alene Resort in Idaho is on a man-made floating island in the middle of a lake. The green moves with the current.

The 15th hole at Carbrook, Queensland, has sharks swimming in the water hazard.

The green for hole 3B at the Four Seasons Punta Mita course in Mexico sits on a natural island in the Pacific Ocean. At high tide, it can only be reached in an amphibious golf cart.

The 15th hole at Cape Kidnappers, Hawke's Bay, New Zealand, is known as the Pirate's Plank because there is a 460-foot cliff drop on one side and a deep cavern on the other.

The tee at the Extreme 19th at the Legend Golf and Safari Resort in South Africa is located at the top of a mountain and is accessible only by helicopter. The green is 1,400 feet below. Each player is given six balls with tracking devices.

CHALLENGING
ROUNDS OF GOLF

The 18-hole Nullarbor Links is the longest golf course in the world, stretching over 800 miles along the Eyre Highway from Kalgoorlie, Western Australia, to Ceduna, South Australia. Seven of the holes, which are up to 50 miles apart, are in existing golf courses. The tees and greens of the remaining 11 have artificial grass but the land in between is rough desert terrain with plenty of wombat holes. The par-72 course can be completed in four days.

In 1939, stockbroker Richard Sutton won a bet by putting his way along 3.5 miles of London streets in under 200 strokes. He approached his destination – the steps of White's Club near Piccadilly – in 102 but it then took him another 40 to putt out of the gutter and onto the pavement.

Scott Base Country Club, run by the New Zealand Antarctic Programme, is located just 13 degrees from the South Pole. As the course is made of solid ice, players use orange golf balls and are required to wear full survival gear.

Rufus Stewart, the club professional at Kooyonga, South Australia, played the 18-hole course in total darkness one night in 1931, going round in 77 and not losing a single ball.

In 1912, actor Harry Dearth won a bet by defeating opponent Graham Margeston over nine holes at Bushey Hall Golf Club in Hertfordshire while wearing a suit of armour.

In 2017, Northern Ireland golfer Adam Rolston played a 1,256-mile-long 'hole' across Mongolia – through desert, swamps and rivers – taking 80 days, 20,093 shots and using 135 balls. He had calculated that it would take 14,000 shots to complete, so his final score was 6,093 over par.

CELEBRITIES AND THEIR FAVOURITE FOOTBALL TEAMS

Adele – Tottenham Hotspur

Kate Adie – Sunderland

Damon Albarn – Chelsea

Ant and Dec – Newcastle United

Bill Bailey – Queens Park Rangers

Sean Bean – Sheffield United

Danny Boyle – Bury

Jo Brand – Crystal Palace

Russell Brand – West Ham United

Gordon Brown – Raith Rovers

Jake Bugg – Notts County

Gerard Butler – Celtic

Jenson Button – Bristol City

David Byrne – Dumbarton

Paul Chuckle – Rotherham United

Tom Courtenay – Hull City

Daniel Craig – Liverpool

Craig David – Southampton

Judi Dench – Everton

Will Ferrell – Chelsea

Stephen Fry – Norwich City

Noel Gallagher – Manchester City

Michael Grade – Charlton Athletic

Hugh Grant – Fulham

Tom Hanks – Aston Villa

Prince Harry – Arsenal

Eddie Izzard – Crystal Palace

Hugh Jackman – Norwich City

Mick Jagger – Arsenal

Elton John – Watford

Vernon Kay – Bolton Wanderers

Lorraine Kelly – Dundee United

John Kettley – Burnley

Keira Knightley – West Ham United

Jude Law – Tottenham Hotspur

David 'Bumble' Lloyd – Accrington Stanley

Rory McIlroy – Manchester United

Bob Mortimer – Middlesbrough

Alison Moyet – Southend United

Mike Myers – Liverpool

Michael Parkinson – Barnsley

Jeremy Paxman – Leeds United

Suzi Perry – Wolverhampton Wanderers

Robert Plant – Wolverhampton Wanderers

Daniel Radcliffe – Fulham

Gordon Ramsay – Rangers

Rachel Riley – Manchester United

Seth Rogen – AFC Bournemouth

Ed Sheeran – Chelsea

Frank Skinner – West Bromwich Albion

Jeff Stelling – Hartlepool United

Shakin' Stevens – Cardiff City

Jack Straw – Blackburn Rovers

Sylvester Stallone – Everton

Patrick Stewart – Huddersfield Town

Rod Stewart – Celtic

Pete Waterman – Walsall

Josh Widdicombe – Plymouth Argyle

Prince William – Aston Villa

Robbie Williams – Port Vale

Catherine Zeta-Jones – Swansea City

BRITISH FOOTBALL TEAMS' ORIGINAL NAMES

Abbey United (Cambridge United)

Ardwick (Manchester City)

Belmont (Tranmere Rovers)

Black Arabs (Bristol Rovers)

Christ Church (Bolton Wanderers)

Dial Square (Arsenal)

Excelsior (Airdrieonians)

Ferranti Thistle (Livingston)

Headington United (Oxford United)

New Brompton (Gillingham)

Newton Heath Lancashire and Yorkshire Railway
(Manchester United)

Pine Villa (Oldham Athletic)

Riverside (Cardiff City)

St Domingo (Everton)

St Jude's (Queens Park Rangers)

St Luke's (Wolverhampton Wanderers)

Singers FC (Coventry City)

Small Heath Alliance (Birmingham City)

Thames Ironworks (West Ham United)

BRITISH FOOTBALL TEAMS' NICKNAMES

(PREMIER LEAGUE, EFL AND SCOTTISH LEAGUE)

England and Wales:

Accrington Stanley – Stanley

AFC Bournemouth – the Cherries

AFC Wimbledon – the Dons, the Wombles

Arsenal – the Gunners

Aston Villa – the Villans

Barnsley – the Tykes

Birmingham City – the Blues

Blackburn Rovers – Rovers

Blackpool – the Seasiders, the Tangerines

Bolton Wanderers – the Trotters

Bradford City – the Bantams

Brentford – the Bees

Brighton & Hove Albion – the Seagulls

Bristol City – the Robins

Bristol Rovers – the Gas, the Pirates

Burnley – the Clarets

Burton Albion – the Brewers

Bury – the Shakers

Cambridge United – the U's

Cardiff City – the Bluebirds

Carlisle United – the Cumbrians

Charlton Athletic – the Addicks, the Robins, the Valiants

Chelsea – the Blues, the Pensioners

Cheltenham Town – the Robins

Colchester United – the U's

Coventry City – the Sky Blues

Crawley Town – the Red Devils

Crewe Alexandra – the Railwaymen

Crystal Palace – the Eagles, the Glaziers

Derby County – the Rams

Doncaster Rovers – Donny, the Vikings

Exeter City – the Grecians

Everton – the Toffees

Fleetwood Town – the Cod Army

Forest Green Rovers – Rovers, the Green Devils

Fulham – the Cottagers

Gillingham – the Gills

Grimsby Town – the Mariners

Huddersfield Town – the Terriers

Hull City – the Tigers

Ipswich Town – the Tractor Boys

Leeds United – the Whites, the Peacocks

Leicester City – the Foxes

Lincoln City – the Imps

Liverpool – the Reds

Luton Town – the Hatters

Macclesfield Town – the Silkmen

Manchester City – the Sky Blues

Manchester United – the Red Devils

Mansfield Town – the Stags

Middlesbrough – Boro

Millwall – the Lions

MK Dons – the Dons

Morecambe – the Shrimps

Newcastle United – the Magpies, the Toon

Newport County – the Exiles, the Ironsides

Northampton Town – the Cobblers

Norwich City – the Canaries

Nottingham Forest – the Reds, the Tricky Trees

Notts County – the Magpies

Oldham Athletic – the Latics

Oxford United – the U's

Queens Park Rangers – the Hoops, the R's

Peterborough United – the Posh

Plymouth Argyle – the Pilgrims

Portsmouth – Pompey

Port Vale – the Valiants

Preston North End – the Lilywhites

Reading – the Royals, the Biscuitmen

Rochdale – Dale

Rotherham United – the Millers

Scunthorpe United – the Iron

Sheffield United – the Blades

Sheffield Wednesday – the Owls

Shrewsbury Town – the Shrews

Southampton – the Saints

Southend United – the Shrimpers

Stevenage – Boro

Stoke City – the Potters

Sunderland – the Black Cats

Swansea City – the Swans

Swindon Town – the Robins

Tottenham Hotspur – Spurs, the Lilywhites

Tranmere Rovers – Rovers

Walsall – the Saddlers

Watford – the Hornets

West Bromwich Albion – the Baggies, the Throstles

West Ham United – the Hammers, the Irons

Wigan Athletic – the Latics

Wolverhampton Wanderers – the Wolves

Wycombe Wanderers – the Chairboys

Yeovil Town – the Glovers

Scotland:

Aberdeen – the Dons

Airdrieonians – the Diamonds

Albion Rovers – the Wee Rovers

Alloa Athletic – the Wasps

Annan Athletic – the Galabankies

Arbroath – the Red Lichties

Ayr United – the Honest Men

Berwick Rangers – the Borderers, the Wee Gers

Brechin City – the Hedgemen

Celtic – the Bhoys, the Hoops

Clyde – the Bully Wee

Cowdenbeath – the Blue Brazil

Dumbarton – the Sons

Dundee – the Dee

Dundee United – the Terrors, the Tangerines

Dunfermline Athletic – the Pars

East Fife – the Fifers

Edinburgh City – the Citizens, the Lilywhites

Elgin City – the Black and Whites

Falkirk – the Bairns

Forfar Athletic – the Loons

Greenock Morton – the Ton

Hamilton Academical – the Accies

Hearts – the Jam Tarts, the Jambos

Hibernian – the Hibees

Inverness Caledonian Thistle – Caley Thistle

Kilmarnock – Killie

Livingston – Livi, the Lions

Montrose – the Gable Endies

Motherwell – the Steelmen

Partick Thistle – the Jags

Peterhead – the Blue Toon

Queen of the South – the Doonhamers

Queen's Park – the Spiders

Raith Rovers – the Rovers

Rangers – the Gers, the Light Blues

Ross County – the Staggies

St Johnstone – the Saints

St Mirren – the Buddies

Stenhousemuir – the Warriors

Stirling Albion – the Binos

Stranraer – the Blues

FOOTBALLERS WITH FAMOUS NAMES

Michael Ball, singer
and Everton defender (1996–2001)

Alan Bennett, playwright
and Cheltenham Town defender (2011–13)

James Brown, godfather of soul
and Hartlepool United midfielder (2004–12)

Jimmy Carter, US President
and Millwall winger (1987–91)

Adam Clayton, U2 bass guitarist
and Leeds United midfielder (2010–12)

Thomas Cruise, actor
and Torquay United midfielder (2012–15)

James Dean, actor
and Bury striker (2007–08)

Lee Evans, comedian
and Wolverhampton Wanderers midfielder (2013–18)

Scott Fitzgerald, author
and Wimbledon defender (1989–97)

Danny Glover, actor
and Port Vale striker (2007–10)

David Gray, musician
and Stevenage defender (2012–14)

Michael Jackson, singer
and Blackpool defender (2006–08)

Chris Martin, singer
and Norwich City striker (2006–13)

Paul McKenna, hypnotist
and Preston North End midfielder (1996–2009)

Daniel O'Donnell, Irish singer
and Crewe defender (2007–10)

John Osborne, playwright
and West Bromich Albion goalkeeper (1966–77)

Matt Smith, *Doctor Who*
and Oldham Athletic striker (2011–13)

Mickey Spillane, crime novelist
and Brentford midfielder (2010–12)

Joe Walsh, guitarist
and Crawley Town defender (2012–15)

Paul Weller, musician
and Burnley midfielder (1993–2004)

Andy Williams, singer
and Doncaster Rovers striker (2015–18)

Robbie Williams, singer
and Huddersfield Town defender (2004–07)

ON THE BALL

To prevent the World Cup trophy from falling into the hands of the Nazis, FIFA's Italian Vice-President, Dr Ottorino Barassi, kept it hidden in a shoe box under his bed throughout the Second World War.

Referee Henning Erikstrup was about to blow the final whistle at a 1960 Danish League match between Norager and Ebeltoft when his dentures fell out. As he scrambled around on the pitch looking for them, Ebeltoft equalised. But Mr Erikstrup disallowed the goal, replaced his teeth and blew for full-time.

The first club to play at Anfield, from 1884 to 1891, was not Liverpool, but city rivals Everton.

Following a series of controversial World Cup qualifiers between the two countries in 1969, Honduras and El Salvador embarked on a four-day war in which 3,000 civilians died.

When Hartlepool beat Notts County 2–1 in 2013, their goalscorers were Hartley and Poole.

A 1979 Scottish Cup tie between Falkirk and Inverness Thistle was postponed 29 times because of bad weather.

Stopping off en route to Iceland, the Albanian national team was thrown out of England in 1990 after going on a shopping spree at Heathrow Airport. They had thought 'duty free' meant help yourself.

Bolton Wanderers arrived for a match at Middlesbrough in the 1940s without any shin pads. So their trainer went out and bought 22 paperback romantic novels as temporary replacements.

At the age of 52, Pedro Gatica cycled from his home in Argentina to Mexico for the 1986 World Cup, only to find on arrival that he couldn't afford to get into the stadium. While he was haggling for a ticket, a thief stole his bike.

Italian giants Juventus owe their famous black and white striped shirts to English minnows Notts County. In 1903, Juventus were tired of their pink shirts fading, so they asked John Savage, an English player in their side, to help. He had links to Notts County and arranged for a set of their black and white striped shirts to be sent out to Turin.

An East German junior player was once sent off for flirting with the referee. The official, 20-year-old Marita Rall, ordered him off when he tried to arrange a date with her while the game was in progress.

FIFTEEN HOOLIGANS

RUGBY UNION NUMBERS AND POSITIONS

15. Full back

14. Right wing

13. Outside centre

12. Inside centre

11. Left wing

10. Fly half

9. Scrum half

8. Number 8

7. Openside flanker

6. Blindside flanker

5. Number 5 lock / Second row

4. Number 4 lock / Second row

3. Tighthead prop

2. Hooker

1. Loosehead prop

QUICK SINGLES

CRICKET TRIVIA

The first-ever Test match – between Australia and England in Melbourne in 1877 – ended in a win for the home side by 45 runs. One hundred years later, a special Centenary Test was played in Melbourne to mark the occasion, and again Australia won by exactly 45 runs.

'Chuck' Fleetwood-Smith, an Australian Test cricketer of the 1930s, used to perform bird impressions as he came in to bowl.

A 1939 Test match between England and South Africa at Durban was finally declared a draw after ten days because the England players had to catch their ship home.

Former England fast bowler John Snow had two volumes of his poetry published in the 1970s.

Playing against Australia at Adelaide in 1947, England wicketkeeper Godfrey Evans batted for 97 minutes without scoring.

Alec Stewart was born on 8 April 1963 (8/4/63) and he went on to score precisely 8,463 Test runs for England.

The opposing captains in the 1905 Ashes series – England's the Hon. F.S. Jackson and Australia's Joe Darling – were born on the same day, 21 November 1870.

Former England wicketkeeper Jack Russell is a talented artist whose paintings have sold for over £25,000.

When South African Daryll Cullinan hit a six for Border against Boland in 1995, the ball landed in a frying pan containing hot calamari, causing play to be halted for ten minutes while the ball cooled down.

The oldest English first-class county cricket club is Sussex, formed in 1839.

Warwickshire County Cricket Club souvenir mugs for England bowler Ashley Giles were mistakenly printed in 2004 with the label 'King of Spain' instead of 'King of Spin'.

As well as playing cricket for England, Johnny Douglas won a boxing gold medal at the 1908 Olympics.

Australia's Clem Hill scored 99, 98 and 97 in successive Test matches in the 1901–02 Ashes series.

During a Test match against the West Indies before a crowd of 20,000 at Edgbaston in 2004, England's Andrew Flintoff hit an enormous six into the top tier of the stand ... where the ball was dropped by his father Colin.

Andrew Flintoff used to play chess for Lancashire.

Batting at Kalgoorlie, Australia, in the 1970s, Stan Dawson was struck by a ball which set light to a box of matches in his trouser pocket. He was run out as he tried to beat down the flames.

When Pakistan batsman Abdul Aziz was injured in the first innings of a match in Karachi in 1959, the scorecard read: 'Abdul Aziz retired hurt ... 0'. However the injury proved to be fatal, so for the second innings the scorer wrote: 'Abdul Aziz did not bat, dead ... 0.'

BOXING WEIGHT CLASSES

Unlimited: Heavyweight

200 pounds: Cruiserweight

175 pounds: Light heavyweight

168 pounds: Super middleweight

160 pounds: Middleweight

154 pounds: Super welterweight

147 pounds: Welterweight

140 pounds: Super lightweight

135 pounds: Lightweight

130 pounds: Super featherweight

126 pounds: Featherweight

122 pounds: Super bantamweight

118 pounds: Bantamweight

115 pounds: Super flyweight

112 pounds: Flyweight

108 pounds: Light flyweight

INDOOR SPORTS

Basketball was invented in 1891, but the first basketball hoops were peach baskets with the bottoms intact. So officials had to retrieve the ball after each basket. Open ended nylon nets were not introduced until 1912.

Early basketball games used footballs. Players would often rub coal dust on their hands to grip the ball better. The modern orange basketball was only introduced in the late 1950s.

Manute Bol, at 7ft 7in, and Muggsy Bogues, 5ft 3in, were the tallest and shortest players in National Basketball Association history at the time, and were team-mates with the Washington Bullets in 1987.

Basketball players sometimes run three miles during a game.

A bowling pin only needs to tilt 7.5 degrees to fall down.

Badminton shuttlecocks are made from the feathers of a goose, ideally from the left wing because the right wing has a different curvature and, when smashed, will spin anti-clockwise instead of clockwise. There are 16 feathers in each shuttle.

Whiff whaff and gossima were early versions of ping pong.

The sport of rackets, which is similar to squash, was first played in the eighteenth century by inmates of London debtors' prisons who used to hit a ball against the prison walls for exercise.

When Englishman Joe Davis became the first world snooker champion in 1927, his prize money was £6 10s 0d (about $10). Today's winner pockets over £425,000 ($545,000).

Under the rules of snooker, if a player is colourblind the referee is permitted to inform him or her of the colour of a particular ball.

Nearly 80 per cent of the world's billiard balls are made in Belgium.

Mary, Queen of Scots owned one of the world's first billiard tables. When she was executed in 1587, her headless body was wrapped in the cloth from her billiard table.

FORMULA ONE GRAND PRIX CIRCUITS SINCE 1950

Emirati (Yas Marina, Abu Dhabi)

Argentine (Autodromo José Carlos Pace, Buenos Aires)

Australian (Adelaide; Albert Park, Melbourne)

Austrian (Zeltweg Airfield; Red Bull Ring,
previously known as A-1 Ring and Osterreichring)

Azerbaijani (Baku)

Bahraini (Bahrain International)

Belgian (Spa-Francorchamps; Zolder; Nivelles-Baulers)

Brazilian (Autodromo Internacional Nelson Piquet,
Rio de Janeiro; Interlagos, Sao Paulo)

British (Aintree; Brands Hatch; Silverstone)

Caesars Palace (Las Vegas)

Canadian (Circuit Gilles Villeneuve, Montreal;
Mont-Tremblant, Quebec; Mosport
International Raceway, Ontario)

Chinese (Shanghai)

Dallas (Dallas, Texas)

Detroit (Detroit Street Circuit)

Dutch (Zandvoort)

European (Donington Park, UK; Brands Hatch, UK; Nürburgring, Germany; Jerez, Spain; Valencia, Spain; Baku, Azerbaijan)

French (Le Mans; Clermont-Ferrand; Reims; Magny-Cours; Dijon; Rouen-Les Essarts; Paul Ricard)

German (AVUS, Berlin; Hockenheim; Nürburgring)

Hungarian (Hungaroring)

Indian (Buddh International, Greater Noida)

Italian (Monza; Imola)

Japanese (Fuji Speedway, Oyama; Suzuka)

Korean (Korea International Circuit, Yeongam)

Luxembourg (Nürburgring, Germany)

Malaysian (Sepang)

Mexican (Autodromo Hermanos Rodriguez, Mexico City)

Monaco (Monaco)

Moroccan (Ain-Diab, Casablanca)

Pacific (Okayama, Japan)

Pescara (Pescara, Italy)

Portuguese (Estoril; Monsanto, Lisbon; Boavista, Porto)

Russian (Sochi)

San Marino (Imola)

Singaporean (Marina Bay Street Circuit)

South African (Kyalami; Prince George Circuit,
East London)

Spanish (Catalunya, Barcelona; Jerez; Circuito del Jarama,
San Sebastian; Montjuic Street Circuit, Barcelona;
Pedralbes Street Circuit, Barcelona)

Swedish (Anderstorp)

Swiss (Bremgarten, Bern; Dijon, France)

Turkish (Istanbul Park)

United States (Watkins Glen, New York; Phoenix, Arizona;
Sebring, Florida; Indianapolis; Riverside International
Raceway, California; Circuit of the Americas, Austin, Texas)

United States West (Long Beach, California)

EXCUSE ME WHILE I INTERRUPT MYSELF

WORDS OF WISDOM FROM MURRAY WALKER

Legendary British Formula One commentator Murray Walker had a unique style at the microphone, described by TV critic Clive James as sounding 'like a man whose trousers are on fire'. At his most excitable, he also had a knack for tying himself in verbal knots and stating the obvious.

'We now have exactly the same situation as we had at the start of the race, only exactly the opposite.'

'He's in front of everyone in this race except for the two in front of him.'

'There's nothing wrong with the car except that it's on fire.'

'Either that car is stationary or it's on the move.'

'With half of the race gone, there is half of the race still to go.'

'This is lap 54, after that it's 55, 56, 57, 58.'

'The lead is now 6.9 seconds. In fact it's just under seven seconds.'

'The gap between the cars is 0.9 of a second, which is less than one second.'

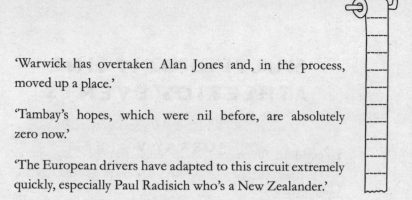

'Warwick has overtaken Alan Jones and, in the process, moved up a place.'

'Tambay's hopes, which were nil before, are absolutely zero now.'

'The European drivers have adapted to this circuit extremely quickly, especially Paul Radisich who's a New Zealander.'

'I imagine that the conditions in those cars today are totally unimaginable.'

'I make no apologies for their absence; I'm sorry they're not here.'

'This is an interesting circuit because it has inclines – and not just up but down as well.'

'Knowing exactly where Nigel Mansell is because he can see him in his earphones.'

'You can see now that the gap between Mansell and Piquet is rather more than just visual.'

'Do my eyes deceive me, or is Senna's Lotus sounding rough?'

'I've just stopped my startwatch.'

'And now excuse me while I interrupt myself.'

'A sad ending, albeit a happy one.'

MULTI-DISCIPLINE
ATHLETICS EVENTS

Decathlon: 100 metres, long jump, shot put, high jump, 400 metres, 110 metres hurdles, discus, pole vault, javelin, 1500 metres

Heptathlon: 100 metres hurdles, high jump, shot put, 200 metres, long jump, javelin, 800 metres

Indoor pentathlon: 60 metres hurdles, high jump, shot put, long jump, 800 metres

Modern pentathlon: Shooting, swimming, fencing, equestrian, cross country running

Triathlon: Swimming, cycling, running

Biathlon: Cross-country skiing, rifle shooting

GAME, SET AND MATCH

In 1932, Britain's Henry 'Bunny' Austin became the first tennis player to wear shorts instead of long trousers at Wimbledon.

The tiebreak was introduced at Wimbledon in 1971.

A first-round men's singles match at Wimbledon in 2010 saw American John Isner beat France's Nicolas Mahut in a game that lasted 11 hours and five minutes, spread over three days. Isner won the final set 70–68.

Twenty-eight tons of strawberries are eaten each year at Wimbledon. Over 54,000 balls are used during the fortnight.

Since 2002, Rufus, a Harris hawk, has been stationed at Wimbledon to keep the sky clear of pigeons. Rufus has over 10,000 followers on Twitter.

The French Open is played at Stade Roland Garros, named after a First World War fighter pilot.

Maria Sharapova's grunt has been measured at 105 decibels – louder than a motorbike.

'Federer' can be typed entirely with the left hand.

US CITIES WITH TEAMS FROM FOUR MAJOR LEAGUE SPORTS

NFL (American football), MLB (baseball), NBA (basketball) and NHL (ice hockey) – including metropolitan area of city.

Boston (New England Patriots, Boston Red Sox, Boston Celtics, Boston Bruins)

Chicago (Chicago Bears, Chicago Cubs and Chicago White Sox, Chicago Bulls, Chicago Blackhawks)

Dallas–Fort Worth (Dallas Cowboys, Texas Rangers, Dallas Mavericks, Dallas Stars)

Denver (Denver Broncos, Colorado Rockies, Denver Nuggets, Colorado Avalanche)

Detroit (Detroit Lions, Detroit Tigers, Detroit Pistons, Detroit Red Wings)

Los Angeles (Los Angeles Chargers and Los Angeles Rams; Los Angeles Angels and Los Angeles Dodgers; Los Angeles Clippers and Los Angeles Lakers; Anaheim Ducks and Los Angeles Kings)

Miami (Miami Dolphins, Miami Marlins, Miami Heat, Florida Panthers)

Minneapolis–St. Paul (Minnesota Vikings, Minnesota Twins, Minnesota Timberwolves, Minnesota Wild)

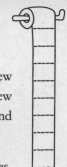

New York City (New York Giants and New York Jets; New York Mets and New York Yankees; Brooklyn Nets and New York Knicks; New Jersey Devils, New York Islanders and New York Rangers)

Philadelphia (Philadelphia Eagles, Philadelphia Phillies, Philadelphia 76ers, Philadelphia Flyers)

Phoenix (Arizona Cardinals, Arizona Diamondbacks, Phoenix Suns, Arizona Coyotes)

San Francisco Bay Area (Oakland Raiders and San Francisco 49ers; Oakland Athletics and San Francisco Giants; Golden State Warriors, San Jose Sharks)

Washington, D.C. (Washington Redskins, Washington Nationals, Washington Wizards, Washington Capitals)

CURRENT MAJOR LEAGUE BASEBALL STADIUMS

Angel Stadium, Anaheim (Los Angeles Angels)

AT&T Park (San Francisco Giants)

Busch Stadium (St. Louis Cardinals)

Chase Field, Phoenix (Arizona Diamondbacks)

Citi Field (New York Mets)

Citizens Bank Park (Philadelphia Phillies)

Comerica Park (Detroit Tigers)

Coors Field, Denver (Colorado Rockies)

Dodger Stadium (Los Angeles Dodgers)

Fenway Park (Boston Red Sox)

Globe Life Park, Arlington (Texas Rangers)

Great American Ball Park (Cincinnati Reds)

Guaranteed Rate Field (Chicago White Sox)

Kauffman Stadium (Kansas City Royals)

Marlins Park (Miami Marlins)

Miller Park (Milwaukee Brewers)

Minute Maid Park (Houston Astros)

Nationals Park (Washington Nationals)

Oakland–Alameda County Coliseum (Oakland Athletics)

Oriole Park (Baltimore Orioles)

Petco Park (San Diego Padres)

PNC Park (Pittsburgh Pirates)

Progressive Field (Cleveland Indians)

Rogers Centre (Toronto Blue Jays)

SunTrust Park, Cumberland (Atlanta Braves)

Target Field, Minneapolis (Minnesota Twins)

T-Mobile Park (Seattle Mariners)

Tropicana Field, St Petersburg (Tampa Bay Rays)

Wrigley Field (Chicago Cubs)

Yankee Stadium (New York Yankees)

THE SUPER BOWL
BY NUMBERS

Americans eat 1.33 billion chicken wings during Super Bowl weekend.

Over 20 million Americans attend a Super Bowl party.

A 30-second TV advertising slot during the Super Bowl costs $5 million.

Around 7 million Americans fail to show up for work on the Monday following the game. This absenteeism is estimated to cost employers $3 billion.

28.4 million tweets were sent during the 2015 Super Bowl.

A last-minute ticket for the Super Bowl will cost you at least $7,000.

Twenty-six per cent of Americans believe that God plays a role in determining the outcome of the game.

DEFUNCT UK RACECOURSES

(WITH YEAR CLOSED)

Aldershot (1927)

Alexandra Park, North London (1970)

Anglesey (1903)

Blackpool (1915)

Bogside, Ayrshire (1965)

Bournemouth (1928)

Bromford Bridge, Birmingham (1965)

Buckfastleigh (1960)

Cardiff (Ely) (1939)

Colwall Park, Worcestershire (1949)

Derby (1939)

Folkestone (2012)

Gatwick (1940)

Hambleton, North Yorkshire (1911)

Hawthorn Hill, Surrey (1939)

Hethersett, Norfolk (1939)

Hooton Park, Cheshire (1915)

Hull (1909)

Hurst Park, Surrey (1962)

Ipswich (1911)

Keele Park, Staffordshire (1906)

Lanark (1977)

Lewes (1964)

Lincoln (1965)

Manchester (1963)

Newport, Wales (1948)

Northampton (1904)

Northolt Park, West London (1940)

Pershore, Worcestershire (1939)

Plymouth (1930)

Portsmouth (1939)

Rothbury, Northumberland (1965)

Shincliffe, County Durham (1914)

Shirley Park, Birmingham (1940)

Southend (1931)

Stockton (1981)

Tenby (1936)

Totnes (1939)

Woore, Shropshire (1963)

Wye, Kent (1974)

A GAME OF
TWO HALVES

When ice hockey was first played in Canada in the mid nineteenth century, the earliest pucks were pieces of frozen cow dung.

If US swimmer Michael Phelps was a country, his career total of 23 Olympic golds would put him in thirty-ninth place in the all-time Summer Olympics medal table – ahead of the likes of India, Argentina and Mexico.

Cheetah racing was staged in London in 1937.

Every ball used in Major and Minor League Baseball is first coated in mud from the Delaware River so that pitchers can obtain a better grip.

During the 1970s, American golfer Jack Nicklaus played all 40 majors and finished in the top 10 in 35 of them.

When 17-year-old Dutch racing driver Max Verstappen made his Formula One debut at the 2015 Australian Grand Prix, he was not yet old enough to drive legally on the road in his home country.

Because it is customary for any Japanese golfer who gets a hole-in-one to buy celebratory gifts for friends, many players take out hole-in-one insurance.

The men's world long jump record has been broken only once since 1968 – by Mike Powell in 1991.

In the 1905 American Football season, 18 players were killed and 159 seriously injured.

Former British 400 metres champion Roger Black – winner of two Olympic silver medals – was not allowed to run as a schoolboy because of a serious heart defect.

In 1965, when golfer Jack Nicklaus won his second Masters title, jockey Willie Shoemaker won the Kentucky Derby, the Boston Celtics won the NBA championship, and the Montreal Canadiens won ice hockey's Stanley Cup. In 1986, Nicklaus won his final Masters – and the other three events occurred again, too.

Belgian racing driver Camille Jenatzy was shot on a hunting trip with friends in 1913 while impersonating a wild boar. Jenatzy hid behind a bush and made grunting sounds, but the prank backfired when Alfred Madoux, believing it was a wild animal, shot him fatally.

TOY STORIES

The Barbie doll's full name is Barbara Millicent Roberts. She was introduced in 1959 but sales were slow at first because mothers were reluctant to buy a doll with breasts.

In 2003, Barbie was declared a threat to public morality in Saudi Arabia.

After a 43-year-long romance, Barbie and her boyfriend Ken broke up in 2004 but reunited seven years later on Valentine's Day.

Introduced in 1961, Barbie's British counterpart Sindy had clothes designed by the likes of Mary Quant and Vivienne Westwood, but did not own a bath until 1972.

Lego is the world's biggest tyre manufacturer, producing 306 million a year.

Six eight-studded Lego bricks fit together in 915,103,765 different combinations.

It took Canadians Chris Haney and Scott Abbott just 45 minutes to conceive Trivial Pursuit in 1982.

Monopoly owes its origins to *The Landlord's Game*, which was created in 1903 by Elizabeth Magie to educate users about Georgism, an economic philosophy.

Reinvented in 1933 by unemployed heating engineer Charles Darrow and based on the streets of Atlantic City, Monopoly was initially rejected by US games manufacturer Parker Brothers for having '52 fundamental playing errors'.

Table football game Subbuteo takes its name from inventor Peter Adolph's favourite bird, the hobby (Latin name: *Falco subbuteo*).

Cluedo (Clue in North America) was invented by Birmingham musician Anthony Pratt in 1944. His original idea featured several features that were subsequently axed – characters (Mr Brown, Mr Gold, Miss Grey and Mrs Silver), rooms (the gun room and the cellar) and weapons (bomb, syringe, poker and shillelagh).

One in four adults still have their childhood teddy bear. A person who collects, or is fond of teddy bears, is called an arctophile.

Bear hugs predate teddy bears by 60 years. The term 'bear hug' was first recorded in 1846.

After the *Titanic* sank in 1912, German toy company Steiff honoured the victims by creating 500 'mourning' teddy bears that were black with red-rimmed eyes.

The frisbee was modelled on a pie tin made by the Frisbie bakery in Bridgeport, Connecticut. Students from nearby Yale University used to eat the pies at lunchtime and then throw the empty tins to one other.

The slinky was invented by accident. During the Second World War, US naval engineer Richard James was trying to invent a spring that could keep sensitive nautical instruments stable while on rough seas. When he knocked one of his experimental springs off a shelf, he was fascinated to see how it 'walked' in a series of arcs and thought it would make a great toy.

The yo-yo was based on a sixteenth-century Filipino weapon.

Miniatur Wunderland, a model railway in Hamburg, has 10 miles of track, over 1,000 trains, 260,000 figures, 1,380 signals, 385,000 LEDs, 9,250 cars, over 4,000 buildings and 130,000 trees.

Spirograph was invented in 1962 by electronics engineer Denys Fisher while researching a new design for NATO bomb detonators.

The Super Nintendo Entertainment System was initially shipped in secrecy at night to avoid it being intercepted by the Yakuza, a Japanese organised crime syndicate.

FOREIGN NAMES FOR CLASSIC CLUEDO CHARACTERS

Miss Scarlett

Mademoiselle Rose (Belgium, France)

Fraulein Ming (Germany)

Evelyne Rose (Switzerland)

Menina Isobel (Portugal)

Señora Amapola (Spain)

Dis. Floga (Greece)

Fröken Röd (Denmark, Finland, Sweden)

Colonel Mustard

Colonel Moutarde (Belgium, France)

Oberst von Gatow (Germany)

Madame Curry (Switzerland)

Marqués de Marina (Spain)

Si. Mustardas (Greece)

Överste Senap (Denmark, Finland, Sweden)

Oberst Gulin (Norway)

Mrs White

Madame Leblanc (Belgium, France)

Frau Weiss (Germany)

Signora Bianchi (Italy)

Senhora Ana (Portugal)

Señora Prada (Spain)

Ka. Aspru (Greece)

Fru. Vit (Denmark, Finland, Sweden)

Dona Branca (Brazil)

Reverend Green

Dr Olive (Belgium, France)

Herr Grün (Germany)

Dottor Verde (Italy)

Dr Pacheco (Portugal)

Señor Pizarro (Spain)

Ald. Prasinos (Greece)

Pastor Grön (Denmark, Finland, Sweden)

Senhor Marinho (Brazil)

Mrs Peacock

Madame Pervenche (Belgium, France)

Baronin von Porz (Germany)

Capitano Azurro (Switzerland)

Signora Pavone (Italy)

Profesora Rubio (Spain)

Fru Blå (Denmark, Finland, Sweden)

Baronesse von Blauw (Norway)

Dona Violeta (Brazil)

Professor Plum

Prof. Violet (Belgium, France)

Prof. Bloom (Germany)

Dr Dunkel (Switzerland)

Dr Mandarino (Spain)

Kath. Damaskinos (Greece)

Prof. Plommen (Denmark, Finland, Sweden)

SOME GOOD
SCRABBLE WORDS

Bezique: a card game

Caziques: native chiefs

Chutzpah: supreme self-confidence

Muzjiks: Russian peasants

Oryx: an Arabian antelope

Qanat: an irrigation tunnel

Qi: the circulating life energy in Chinese philosophy

Quartzy: resembling quartz

Vizcacha: a burrowing rodent from South America

Wagyu: a Japanese breed of cattle

Xebec: a sailing boat

Xeme: a fork-tailed gull

Xi: fourteenth letter of Greek alphabet

Xu: a Vietnamese coin, equal to
one hundredth of a dong

Xylem: plant tissue

Xyster: a surgical instrument

Za: slang for pizza

Zax: a small axe for cutting roof slates

Zebu: a humped ox

Zouk: a Caribbean musical style

STREETS IN CLASSIC AUSTRALIAN EDITION MONOPOLY

(CLOCKWISE FROM 'GO')

Darwin: Todd Street, Smith Street

Hobart: Salamanca Place, Davey Street, Macquarie Street

Perth: William Street, Barrack Street, Hay Street

Adelaide: North Terrace, Victoria Square, Rundle Mall

Brisbane: Stanley Street, Petries Bight, Wickham Terrace

Melbourne: Collins Street, Elizabeth Street, Bourke Street

Sydney: Castlereagh Street, George Street, Pitt Street

Canberra: Flinders Way, Kings Avenue

Stations (clockwise from 'Go'): Perth Station, Adelaide Station, Flinders Street Station (Melbourne), Sydney Station

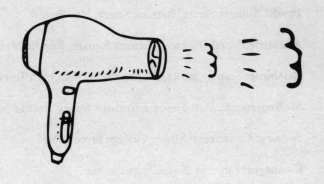

PLANET
EARTH

CAPITALS OF
THE WORLD

Afghanistan: Kabul

Albania: Tirana

Algeria: Algiers

Andorra: Andorra la Vella

Angola: Luanda

Anguilla: The Valley

Antigua and Barbuda: Saint John's

Argentina: Buenos Aires

Armenia: Yerevan

Aruba: Oranjestad

Ascension Island: Georgetown

Australia: Canberra

Austria: Vienna

Azerbaijan: Baku

Bahamas: Nassau

Bahrain: Manama

Bangladesh: Dhaka

Barbados: Bridgetown

Belarus: Minsk

Belgium: Brussels

Belize: Belmopan

Benin: Porto-Novo

Bermuda: Hamilton

Bhutan: Thimphu

Bolivia: La Paz

Bonaire: Kralendijk

Bosnia and Herzegovina: Sarajevo

Botswana: Gaborone

Brazil: Brasília

British Virgin Islands: Road Town

Brunei: Bandar Seri Begawan

Bulgaria: Sofia

Burkina Faso: Ouagadougou

Burundi: Gitega

Cambodia: Phnom Penh

Cameroon: Yaoundé

Canada: Ottawa

Cape Verde: Praia

Cayman Islands: George Town

Central African Republic: Bangui

Chad: N'Djamena

Chile: Santiago

China: Beijing

Colombia: Bogotá

Comoros: Moroni

Congo: Brazzaville

Congo, Democratic Republic of: Kinshasa

Cook Islands: Avarua

Costa Rica: San José

Côte d'Ivoire: Yamoussoukro

Croatia: Zagreb

Cuba: Havana

Cyprus: Nicosia

Czech Republic: Prague

Denmark: Copenhagen

Djibouti: Djibouti

Dominica: Roseau

Dominican Republic: Santo Domingo

Ecuador: Quito

Egypt: Cairo

El Salvador: San Salvador

Equatorial Guinea: Ciudad de la Paz

Eritrea: Asmara

Estonia: Tallinn

Eswatini: Mbabane, Lobamba

Ethiopia: Addis Ababa

Falkland Islands: Stanley

Faroe Islands: Tórshavn

Fiji: Suva

Finland: Helsinki

France: Paris

French Guiana: Cayenne

Gabon: Libreville

Gambia: Banjul

Georgia: Tbilisi

Germany: Berlin

Ghana: Accra

Greece: Athens

Grenada: St George's

Greenland: Nuuk

Guadeloupe: Basse-Terre

Guatemala: Guatemala City

Guernsey: St Peter Port

Guinea: Conakry

Guinea-Bissau: Bissau

Guyana: Georgetown

Haiti: Port-au-Prince

Honduras: Tegucigalpa

Hungary: Budapest

Iceland: Reykjavik

India: New Delhi

Indonesia: Jakarta

Iran: Tehran

Iraq: Baghdad

Ireland: Dublin

Isle of Man: Douglas

Israel: Jerusalem

Italy: Rome

Jamaica: Kingston

Japan: Tokyo

Jersey: St Helier

Jordan: Amman

Kazakhstan: Astana

Kenya: Nairobi

Kiribati: South Tarawa

Kosovo: Pristina

Kuwait: Kuwait City

Kyrgyzstan: Bishkek

Laos: Vientiane

Latvia: Riga

Lebanon: Beirut

Lesotho: Maseru

Liberia: Monrovia

Libya: Tripoli

Liechtenstein: Vaduz

Lithuania: Vilnius

Luxembourg: Luxembourg

Macedonia: Skopje

Madagascar: Antananarivo

Malawi: Lilongwe

Malaysia: Kuala Lumpur

Maldives: Malé

Mali: Bamako

Malta: Valletta

Marshall Islands: Majuro

Martinique: Fort-de-France

Mauritania: Nouakchott

Mauritius: Port Louis

Mayotte: Mamoudzou

Mexico: Mexico City

Micronesia: Palikir

Moldova: Chisinau

Monaco: Monaco

Mongolia: Ulaanbaatar

Montenegro: Podgorica

Montserrat: Plymouth, Brades

Morocco: Rabat

Mozambique: Maputo

Myanmar: Naypyidaw

Namibia: Windhoek

Nauru: No official capital – Yaren District: de facto

Nepal: Kathmandu

Netherlands: Amsterdam

New Zealand: Wellington

Nicaragua: Managua

Niger: Niamey

Nigeria: Abuja

Northern Ireland: Belfast

North Korea: Pyongyang

Norway: Oslo

Oman: Muscat

Pakistan: Islamabad

Palau: Ngerulmud

Palestine: East Jerusalem

Panama: Panama City

Papua New Guinea: Port Moresby

Paraguay: Asunción

Peru: Lima

Philippines: Manila

Pitcairn Islands: Adamstown

Poland: Warsaw

Portugal: Lisbon

Puerto Rico: San Juan

Qatar: Doha

Réunion: Saint-Denis

Romania: Bucharest

Russia: Moscow

Rwanda: Kigali

Saint Helena: Jamestown

Saint Kitts and Nevis: Basseterre

Saint Lucia: Castries

Saint Vincent and the Grenadines: Kingstown

Samoa: Apia

San Marino: San Marino

São Tomé and Principe: São Tomé

Saudi Arabia: Riyadh

Scotland: Edinburgh

Senegal: Dakar

Serbia: Belgrade

Seychelles: Victoria

Sierra Leone: Freetown

Singapore: Singapore

Sint Maarten: Philipsburg

Slovakia: Bratislava

Slovenia: Ljubljana

Solomon Islands: Honiara

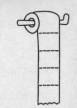

Somalia: Mogadishu

Somaliland: Hargeisa

South Africa: Cape Town, Pretoria, Bloemfontein

South Korea: Seoul

South Sudan: Juba

Spain: Madrid

Sri Lanka: Sri Jayawardenepura Kotte

Sudan: Khartoum

Suriname: Paramaribo

Sweden: Stockholm

Switzerland: Bern

Syria: Damascus

Taiwan: Taipei

Tajikistan: Dushanbe

Tanzania: Dodoma

Thailand: Bangkok

Timor-Leste: Dili

Togo: Lomé

Tonga: Nuku'alofa

Trinidad and Tobago: Port of Spain

Tunisia: Tunis

Turkey: Ankara

Turkmenistan: Ashgabat

Turks and Caicos Islands: Cockburn Town

Tuvalu: Funafuti

Uganda: Kampala

Ukraine: Kiev

United Arab Emirates: Abu Dhabi

United Kingdom: London

United States of America: Washington, D.C.

United States Virgin Islands: Charlotte Amalie

Uruguay: Montevideo

Uzbekistan: Tashkent

Vanuatu: Port Vila

Vatican City: Vatican City

Venezuela: Caracas

Vietnam: Hanoi

Wales: Cardiff

Yemen: Sana'a

Zambia: Lusaka

Zimbabwe: Harare

PLACE NAMES AND THEIR MEANINGS

Accra (Ghana): ants

Addis Ababa (Ethiopia): new flower

Algiers (Algeria): the islands

Baghdad (Iraq): God's gift

Baku (Azerbaijan): wind-pounded city

Bangkok (Thailand): wild plum village

Beijing (China): northern capital

Belgrade (Serbia): white city

Brussels (Belgium): buildings on a marsh

Buenos Aires (Argentina): fair winds

Cairo (Egypt): victorious

Canberra (Australia): meeting place

Copenhagen (Denmark): merchants' harbour

Croydon (England): valley where wild saffron grows

Dublin (Ireland): black pool

Florence (Italy): the flourishing

Glasgow (Scotland): green hollow

Gothenburg (Sweden): great stronghold

Hanoi (Vietnam): between rivers

Jakarta (Indonesia): place of victory

Khartoum (Sudan): end of an elephant's trunk

Kuala Lumpur (Malaysia): mud-yellow estuary

La Paz (Bolivia): the peace

Lagos (Nigeria): lakes

Luxembourg (Luxembourg): little castle

Montevideo (Uruguay): I saw a mountain

Nairobi (Kenya): the place of cool waters

Ottawa (Canada): traders

Philadelphia (United States): brotherly love

Porto-Novo (Benin): new port

Pyongyang (North Korea): flat land

Rabat (Morocco): fortified place

Rangoon (Myanmar): end of strife

Reykjavik (Iceland): smoky bay

Rio de Janeiro (Brazil): January river

Riyadh (Saudi Arabia): gardens

San Salvador (El Salvador): holy saviour

Sofia (Bulgaria): wisdom

Tbilisi (Georgia): warm springs

Tehran (Iran): warm place

Tel Aviv (Israel): spring mound

Tokyo (Japan): eastern capital

Toronto (Canada): place where trees stand in the water

Tripoli (Libya): three cities

Ulaanbaatar (Mongolia): the red hero

WORLD CURRENCIES

Afghanistan: afghani

Albania: lek

Algeria: Algerian dinar

Andorra: euro

Angola: kwanza

Anguilla: East Caribbean dollar

Antigua and Barbuda: East Caribbean dollar

Argentina: Argentine peso

Armenia: dram

Aruba: Aruban florin

Ascension Island: Saint Helena pound

Australia: Australian dollar

Austria: euro

Azerbaijan: manat

Bahamas: Bahamian dollar

Bahrain: Bahraini dinar

Bangladesh: taka

Barbados: Barbadian dollar

Belarus: Belarusian ruble

Belgium: euro

Belize: Belize dollar

Benin: West African CFA franc

Bermuda: Bermudian dollar

Bhutan: ngultrum

Bolivia: boliviano

Bonaire: United States dollar

Bosnia and Herzegovina: convertible mark

Botswana: pula

Brazil: real

British Virgin Islands: United States dollar

Brunei: Brunei dollar

Bulgaria: lev

Burkina Faso: West African CFA franc

Burundi: Burundi franc

Cambodia: riel

Cameroon: Central African CFA franc

Canada: Canadian dollar

Cape Verde: Cape Verde escudo

Cayman Islands: Cayman Islands dollar

Central African Republic: Central African CFA franc

Chad: Central African CFA franc

Chile: Chilean peso

China: yuan renminbi

Colombia: Colombian peso

Comoros: Comorian franc

Congo: Central African CFA franc

Congo, Democratic Republic of: Congolese franc

Cook Islands: New Zealand dollar

Costa Rica: colón

Côte d'Ivoire: West African CFA franc

Croatia: kuna

Cuba: Cuban convertible peso

Cyprus: Cypriot pound

Czech Republic: koruna

Denmark: Danish krone

Djibouti: Djiboutian franc

Dominica: East Caribbean dollar

Dominican Republic: Dominican peso

Ecuador: United States dollar

Egypt: Egyptian pound

El Salvador: United States dollar

Equatorial Guinea: Central African CFA franc

Eritrea: nakfa

Estonia: euro

Eswatini: Swazi lilangeni

Ethiopia: birr

Falkland Islands: Falkland pound

Faroe Islands: Danish krone

Fiji: Fijian dollar

Finland: euro

France: euro

French Guiana: euro

Gabon: Central African CFA franc

Gambia: dalasi

Georgia: lari

Germany: euro

Ghana: cedi

Gibraltar: Gibraltar pound

Greece: euro

Greenland: Danish krone

Grenada: East Caribbean dollar

Guadeloupe: euro

Guam: United States dollar

Guatemala: quetzal

Guinea: Guinean franc

Guinea-Bissau: West African CFA franc

Guyana: Guyanese dollar

Haiti: gourde

Honduras: lempira

Hong Kong: Hong Kong dollar

Hungary: forint

Iceland: Icelandic krona

India: Indian rupee

Indonesia: rupiah

Iran: Iranian rial

Iraq: Iraqi dinar

Ireland: euro

Israel: new shekel

Italy: euro

Jamaica: Jamaican dollar

Japan: yen

Jordan: Jordanian dinar

Kazakhstan: tenge

Kenya: Kenyan shilling

Kiribati: Australian dollar

Kosovo: euro

Kuwait: Kuwaiti dinar

Kyrgyzstan: som

Laos: kip

Latvia: euro

Lebanon: Lebanese pound

Lesotho: loti

Liberia: Liberian dollar

Libya: Libyan dinar

Liechtenstein: Swiss franc

Lithuania: euro

Luxembourg: euro

Macau: pataca

Macedonia: denar

Madagascar: ariary

Malawi: Malawian kwacha

Malaysia: ringgit

Maldives: rufiyaa

Mali: West African CFA franc

Malta: euro

Marshall Islands: United States dollar

Martinique: euro

Mauritania: ouguiya

Mauritius: Mauritian rupee

Mayotte: euro

Mexico: Mexican peso

Micronesia: United States dollar

Moldova: Moldovan leu

Monaco: euro

Mongolia: tugrik

Montenegro: euro

Montserrat: East Caribbean dollar

Morocco: Moroccan dirham

Mozambique: metical

Myanmar: kyat

Namibia: Namibian dollar

Nauru: Australian dollar

Nepal: Nepalese rupee

Netherlands: euro

New Caledonia: French Pacific franc

New Zealand: New Zealand dollar

Nicaragua: córdoba

Niger: West African CFA franc

Nigeria: naira

North Korea: North Korean won

Norway: Norwegian krone

Oman: Omani rial

Pakistan: Pakistan rupee

Palau: United States dollar

Palestine: Egyptian pound, Jordanian dinar,
Israeli new shekel

Panama: balboa, United States dollar

Papua New Guinea: kina

Paraguay: guaraní

Peru: nuevo sol

Philippines: Philippine peso

Pitcairn Islands: New Zealand dollar

Poland: zloty

Portugal: euro

Puerto Rico: United States dollar

Qatar: Qatari riyal

Réunion: euro

Romania: Romanian leu

Russia: Russian ruble

Rwanda: Rwandan franc

Saint Helena: Saint Helena pound

Saint Kitts and Nevis: East Caribbean dollar

Saint Lucia: East Caribbean dollar

Saint Vincent and the Grenadines: East Caribbean dollar

Samoa: tālā

San Marino: euro

São Tomé and Principe: dobra

Saudi Arabia: Saudi Arabian riyal

Senegal: West African CFA franc

Serbia: Serbian dinar

Seychelles: Seychellois rupee

Sierra Leone: leone

Singapore: Singapore dollar

Sint Maarten: Netherlands Antillean guilder

Slovakia: euro

Slovenia: euro

Solomon Islands: Solomon Islands dollar

Somalia: Somali shilling

Somaliland: Somaliland shilling

South Africa: rand

South Korea: South Korean won

South Sudan: South Sudanese pound

Spain: euro

Sri Lanka: Sri Lankan rupee

Sudan: Sudanese pound

Suriname: Suriname dollar

Sweden: Swedish krona

Switzerland: Swiss franc

Syria: Syrian pound

Taiwan: New Taiwan dollar

Tajikistan: Tajikistani somoni

Tanzania: Tanzanian shilling

Thailand: baht

Timor-Leste: United States dollar

Togo: West African CFA franc

Tonga: pa'anga

Trinidad and Tobago: Trinidad and Tobago dollar

Tunisia: Tunisian dinar

Turkey: Turkish lira

Turkmenistan: manat

Turks and Caicos Islands: United States dollar

Tuvalu: Australian dollar

Uganda: Ugandan shilling

Ukraine: hryvnia

United Arab Emirates: United Arab Emirates dirham

United Kingdom: pound sterling

United States of America: United States dollar

United States Virgin Islands: United States dollar

Uruguay: Uruguayan peso

Uzbekistan: Uzbekistani som

Vanuatu: vatu

Vatican City: euro

Venezuela: bolívar

Vietnam: dong

Yemen: Yemeni rial

Zambia: Zambian kwacha

Zimbabwe: Zimbabwean dollar

PEOPLE WHO HAVE FEATURED ON CURRENCIES OF THE WORLD

Hans Christian Andersen, writer
(front, Danish 10 krone, 1952–75)

Jane Austen, novelist
(back, British £10, from 2017)

Béla Bartók, composer
(front, Hungarian 1,000 forint, 1983–99)

Alexander Graham Bell, inventor
(back, Scottish £1, 1997 commemorative)

Ingmar Bergman, film director
(front, Swedish 200 krona, from 2015)

Hector Berlioz, composer
(both sides, French 10 franc, 1972–78)

Niels Bohr, physicist
(front, Danish 500 krone, 1997–2011)

Paul Cézanne, artist
(front, French 100 franc, 1997–2002)

Frédéric Chopin, composer
(front, Polish 20 zloty, 2010 commemorative)

Captain James Cook, explorer
(back, Australian £1, 1953–66)

Marie Curie, chemist
(front, Polish 20 zloty, 2011 commemorative)

Charles Darwin, naturalist (back, British £10, 2000–2018)

René Descartes, philosopher
(front, French 100 franc, 1942–44)

Viola Desmond, anti-racism campaigner
(front, Canadian $10, from 2018)

Charles Dickens, author (back, British £10, 1992–2003)

Gustave Eiffel, engineer
(front, French 200 franc, 1996–2002)

Sir Edward Elgar, composer (back, British £20, 1999–2010)

Sir John Franklin, explorer (back, Australian £5, 1953–66)

Sigmund Freud, psychoanalyst
(front, Austrian 50 schilling, 1987–2001)

Elizabeth Fry, social reformer
(back, British £5, 2001–2017)

Greta Garbo, actress (front, Swedish 100 krona, from 2016)

Jacob and Wilhelm Grimm, fairy tale authors
(front, German 1,000 Deutsche mark, 1992–2002)

Che Guevara, revolutionary
(both sides, Cuban 3 pesos, from 2004)

Frans Hals, artist (front, Dutch 10 gulden, 1971–77)

Sir Edmund Hillary, mountaineer
(front New Zealand $5, from 1990)

Arthur Honegger, composer
(front, Swiss 20 franc, from 1996)

Victor Hugo, novelist
(both sides, French 500 franc, 1954–58)

James Joyce, author (front, Irish £10, 1993–2002)

Genghis Khan, warlord
(front, Mongolian 20,000 tugrik, from 2006)

Henry Lawson, poet (back, Australian $10, 1966–93)

Le Corbusier, architect (front, Swiss 10 franc, from 1997)

Gabriel Garcia Marquez, writer
(front, Colombian 50,000 pesos, from 2015)

Karl Marx, philosopher
(front, East German 100 mark, 1975–90)

Dame Nellie Melba, opera singer
(front, Australian $100, from 1996)

Old Tom Morris, golfer
(back, Scottish £5, 2004 commemorative)

Wolfgang Amadeus Mozart, composer
(front, Austrian 5,000 schilling, 1989–2001)

Edvard Munch, artist
(front, Norwegian 1,000 krone, from 2001)

Sir Isaac Newton, scientist (back, British £1, 1978–88)

Florence Nightingale, nurse
(back, British £10, 1975–94)

Paavo Nurmi, distance runner
(back, Finnish 10 mark, 1986–92)

Louis Pasteur, chemist
(both sides, French 5 franc, 1966–70)

Eva Peron, First Lady (front, Argentine $100, from 2012)

Raphael, artist (front, Italian 500,000 lira, 1997–2002)

Ernest Rutherford, physicist
(front, New Zealand $100, from 1990)

Sir Walter Scott, novelist (front, Scottish £20, from 1999)

Jean Sibelius, composer
(back, Finnish 100 mark, 1986–2002)

Adam Smith, economist (back, British £20, from 2007)

Robert Louis Stevenson, novelist
(back, Scottish £1, 1994 commemorative)

Nikola Tesla, electrical engineer
(both sides, Serbian 100 dinar, from 2006)

James Watt, inventor (back, British £50, from 2011)

Lev Yashin, goalkeeper
(front, Russian 100 ruble, 2018 commemorative)

UNLUCKY EVENTS THAT HAPPENED ON FRIDAY THE THIRTEENTH

Professional stuntman Sam Patch died after trying to jump from the Genesee River's High Falls, New York state, on Friday 13 November 1829. His remains were discovered four months later, seven miles downstream.

British racing driver Sir Henry Segrave was killed on Friday 13 June, 1930 on Lake Windermere while attempting to break the world water speed record.

Devastating bushfires swept through the Australian state of Victoria on Friday 13 January 1939, causing 71 fatalities and destroying nearly 4,000 buildings.

Five Nazi bombs were dropped on Buckingham Palace on Friday 13 September 1940, killing one person.

On Friday 13 October 1972, an aeroplane carrying 45 people came down in the Andes. Only 16 survived – and they did so by eating the flesh of the dead passengers and crew.

The British Museum had to cancel a lecture entitled 'Good and Bad Luck in the Ancient World' that was scheduled for Friday 13 November 1981 because the lecturer was taken ill.

Gravedigger John Giblin ended up in hospital on Friday 13 March 1987 after falling into an open grave and breaking his leg on the coffin.

A stock market crash on Friday 13 October 1989 wiped 6.9 per cent off the value of the Dow Jones index.

An earthquake in eastern Turkey killed around 500 people on Friday 13 March 1992.

On Friday 13 August 2004, a swarm of wasps attacked guests waiting for the wedding of Michelle and Gary Docherty at East Kilbride Register Office, Scotland. The bride's aunt, Mary Strachan, broke an expensive camera trying to fend off the insects and when Michelle finally arrived, a wasp flew up her dress, sparking a panic attack. After the ceremony, two minibuses booked to transport guests to the reception failed to turn up and the couple lost their wedding video.

Freak weather led to 27 inches of snow falling on upstate New York on Friday 13 October 2006, leaving 400,000 people without power that day.

At 13.13 on Friday 13 August 2010, a 13-year-old boy was struck by lightning while watching an air show in Lowestoft, Suffolk.

The liner *Costa Concordia* hit a rock off the coast of Italy on Friday 13 January 2012, killing 32 people.

North Wales bus driver Bob Renphrey suffered repeated mishaps on Friday the thirteenth over the years, including four car crashes, losing his job, falling into a river, walking through a plate-glass door and crashing his motorcycle. When he died in 1998, his wife tried to book his funeral for Friday 13 March, but all of the local undertakers were too busy that day.

RIVER DEEP

CITIES AND THE RIVERS THAT FLOW THROUGH THEM

Accra – Odaw

Adelaide – Torrens

Amsterdam – Amstel

Antwerp – Scheldt

Baghdad – Tigris

Bangkok – Chao Phraya

Belfast – Lagan

Bern – Aare

Boston – Charles

Brussels – Zenne

Bucharest – Dambovita

Budapest – Danube

Buenos Aires – Plate

Cairo – Nile

Calcutta – Hooghly/Hugli

Caracas – Guaire

Cardiff – Taff

Cologne – Rhine

Dallas – Trinity

Damascus – Barada

Dublin – Liffey

Edmonton – North Saskatchewan

Glasgow – Clyde

Helsinki – Vantaa

Hong Kong – Pearl

Jakarta – Ciliwung

Kiev – Dnieper

La Paz – Choqueyapu

Lima – Rimac

Lisbon – Tagus

London – Thames

Madrid – Manzanares

Melbourne – Yarra

Montreal – St Lawrence

Moscow – Moskva

New Delhi – Yamuna

New York – Hudson

Oslo – Akerselva

Paris – Seine

Perth – Swan

Prague – Vltava

Pretoria – Apies

Riga – Daugava

Rome – Tiber

St. Louis – Mississippi

St. Petersburg, Russia – Neva

Santiago – Mapocho

Sarajevo – Miljacka

Seoul – Han

Shanghai – Huangpu

Sheffield – Don

Skopje – Vardar

Strasbourg – Ill

Sydney – Parramatta

Tokyo – Sumida

Vienna – Danube

Warsaw – Vistula

Washington, D.C. – Potomac

Wellington – Hutt

Zagreb – Sava

MOUNTAIN HIGH

SOME COUNTRIES AND
THEIR HIGHEST PEAKS

Afghanistan – Noshaq, 24,580ft

Albania – Korab, 9.068ft

Algeria – Mount Tahat, 9,852ft

Angola – Mount Moco, 8,596ft

Argentina – Aconcagua, 22,835ft

Armenia – Mount Aragats, 13,419ft

Australia – Mount Kosciuszko, 7,310ft

Austria – Grossglockner, 12,461ft

Azerbaijan – Mount Bazardüzü, 14,715ft

Bahrain – Mountain of Smoke, 400ft

Barbados – Mount Hillaby, 1,102ft

Belgium – Signal de Botrange, 2,277ft

Bhutan – Gangkhar Puensum, 24,836ft

Bolivia – Sajama, 21,463ft

Bosnia and Herzegovina – Maglić, 7,828ft

Brazil – Pico da Neblina, 9,826ft

Bulgaria – Musala, 9,596ft

Cambodia – Phnom Aural, 5,938ft

Canada – Mount Logan, 19,551ft

Chad – Emi Koussi, 11,302ft

Chile – Ojos del Salado, 22,615ft

China – Mount Everest, 29,029ft

Croatia – Dinara, 6,007ft

Cuba – Pico Turquino, 6,476ft

Czech Republic – Sněžka, 5,259ft

Denmark – Møllehøj, 561ft

Ecuador – Chimborazo, 20,561ft

Egypt – Mount Catherine, 8,625ft

El Salvador – Cerro El Pital, 8,957ft

Estonia – Suur Munamägi, 1,043ft

Ethiopia – Ras Dejen, 14,928ft

France – Mont Blanc, 15,781ft

Germany – Zugspitze, 9,718ft

Greece – Mount Olympus, 9,577ft

Haiti – Pic la Selle, 8,793ft

Hungary – Kekes, 3,327ft

Iceland – Hvannadalshnukur, 6,921ft

India – Kangchenjunga, 28,169ft

Iran – Damavand, 18,406ft

Ireland – Carrauntoohil, 3,406ft

Italy – Monte Bianco, 15,781ft

Jamaica – Blue Mountain Peak, 7,402ft

Japan – Mount Fuji, 12,388ft

Kazakhstan – Khan Tengri, 22,999ft

Kenya – Mount Kenya, 17,057ft

Liechtenstein – Grauspitz, 8,527ft

Luxembourg – Kneiff, 1,837ft

Macedonia – Golem Korab, 9,068ft

Malawi – Mount Mulanje, 9,849ft

Maldives – Mount Villingili, 17ft

Mexico – Pico de Orizaba, 18,491ft

Morocco – Jbel Toubkal, 13,665ft

Mozambique – Monte Binga, 7,992ft

Netherlands – mainland – Vaalserberg, 1,058ft

New Zealand – Mount Cook, 12,218ft

Nigeria – Chappal Waddi, 7,936ft

Norway – Galdhøpiggen, 8,100ft

Pakistan – K2, 28,251ft

Peru – Huascarán, 22,205ft

Philippines – Mount Apo, 9,692ft

Poland – Rysy, 8,199ft

Portugal – mainland – Torre, 6,539ft

Romania – Moldoveanu, 8,346ft

Russia – Mount Elbrus, 18,510ft

San Marino – Monte Titano, 2,477ft

Saudi Arabia – Jabal Sawda, 9,843ft

Serbia – Midžor, 7,116ft

Sierra Leone – Mount Bintumani, 6,391ft

Slovenia – Triglav, 9,396ft

South Africa – Mafadi, 11,319ft

Spain – mainland – Mulhacén, 11,413ft

Sweden – Kebnekaise, 6,880ft

Switzerland – Dufourspitze, 15,203ft

Tajikistan – Ismoil Somoni Peak, 24,590ft

Tanzania – Kilimanjaro, 19,331ft

Thailand – Doi Inthanon, 8,415ft

Turkey – Mount Ararat, 16,854ft

Uganda – Margherita Peak, 16,762ft

Ukraine – Hoverla, 6,762ft

United Kingdom – Ben Nevis, 4,413ft

United States – Denali, 20,310ft

Uruguay – Cerro Catedral, 1,685ft

Venezuela – Pico Bolivar, 16,332ft

Vietnam – Fan Si Pan, 10,312ft

Zambia – Mafinga Central, 7,641ft

Zimbabwe – Mount Nyangani, 8,504ft

MOST COMMON
US PLACE NAMES

(NUMBER OF PLACES
WITH THAT NAME)

1. Washington (88)

2. Springfield (41)

3. Franklin (35)

4. Lebanon (34)

5. Greenville (31)

6= Clinton (30)

6= Georgetown (30)

8. Bristol (29)

9. Fairview (28)

10. Salem (26)

11= Madison (25)

11= Milton (25)

13= Arlington (23)

13= Ashland (23)

13= Dover (23)

13= Manchester (23)

13= Oxford (23)

18. Jackson (22)

19= Burlington (21)

19= Newport (21)

LONG OVERDUE

A book of short stories titled *Forty Minutes Late* was returned to a San Francisco library 100 years late. Eighty-three-year-old Phoebe Webb had borrowed the book in 1917 but died a week before the due date, and it was finally returned by her great-grandson Webb Johnson a century later.

A copy of *The Siege of Troy and the Wanderings of Ulysses* was borrowed from Armley Library in Leeds by Rusholme Hutton in 1883 and returned by his grandson Stephen 133 years later. If the overdue book fine had been imposed, it would have totalled £10,679 ($13,621).

A 1916 postcard sent by English soldier Alfred Arthur to his sister Ellen as he was about to leave for the First World War was finally delivered by Royal Mail in 2010 – 94 years late and long after both parties had died. It was also delivered to the wrong address in Norwich.

In 2015, Thérèse Pailla received a letter placing an order of yarn that was intended for her great-grandfather 138 years earlier. The 1877 letter was sent from Sains-du-Nord, France, to Trélon, just six miles away.

A message in a bottle that was dropped into the sea off Devon in 1908 washed up on the Frisian Islands off the north coast of Germany 108 years later. The card inside the bottle, which was released as part of a marine research experiment, promised the finder one shilling. This was duly paid in 2016 to retired German postal worker Marianne Winkler.

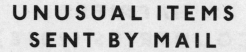

UNUSUAL ITEMS
SENT BY MAIL

When athlete Reg Spiers found himself in London unable to afford the plane fare home to Australia for his daughter's birthday in 1964, he decided to post himself to Perth in a wooden crate. He survived the 63-hour journey via Paris, Bombay and Singapore by living on fruit juice, two tins of spaghetti, a packet of biscuits, a bar of chocolate and a tube of fruit gums.

In 1913, Mr and Mrs Jessie Beauge, of Glen Este, Ohio, mailed their 10-pound baby son to his grandmother's house at a cost of 15 cents in stamps because it was cheaper to send him via the US Postal Service's new parcel post than it was to buy a rail ticket. They even insured him for $50.

For the construction of a bank in Vernal, Utah, in 1916, William H. Coltharp arranged for more than 15,000 bricks to be mailed to the town via parcel post. To keep within the permitted 50-pound weight limit per package, the bricks were individually wrapped in paper and divided into crates of ten.

Friends Janet Brittain and Lesley Charlton have exchanged the same birthday card for over 50 years. They grew up together in Hertfordshire but have since moved to North Yorkshire and Cambridgeshire respectively, with the result that the card has travelled more than 9,000 miles in the post.

HAPPIEST COUNTRIES (2018)

1. Finland
2. Norway
3. Denmark
4. Iceland
5. Switzerland
6. Netherlands
7. Canada
8. New Zealand
9. Sweden
10. Australia

11. Israel
12. Austria
13. Costa Rica
14. Ireland
15. Germany
16. Belgium
17. Luxembourg
18. United States
19. United Kingdom
20. United Arab Emirates

MOST POPULATED CITIES

1. Chongqing, China (30.2 million)

2. Shanghai, China (24.2 million)

3. Beijing, China (21.8 million)

4. Istanbul, Turkey (15.1 million)

5. Karachi, Pakistan (15.0 million)

6. Dhaka, Bangladesh (14.4 million)

7. Guangzhou, China (13.1 million)

8. Shenzhen, China (12.5 million)

9. Mumbai, India (12.4 million)

10. Moscow, Russia (13.2 million)

11. São Paulo, Brazil (12.0 million)

12. Kinshasa, Democratic Republic of the Congo (11.4 million)

13. Tianjin, China (11.2 million)

14. Lahore, Pakistan (11.1 million)

15. Delhi, India (11.0 million)

16. Jakarta, Indonesia (10.62 million)

17. Dongguan, China (10.61 million)

18. Seoul, South Korea (9.8 million)

19. Foshan, China (9.3 million)

20. Tokyo, Japan (9.2 million)

21. Chengdu, China (9.0 million)

22. Lima, Peru (8.89 million)

23. Mexico City, Mexico (8.87 million)

24. London, England (8.84 million)

25. Tehran, Iran (8.7 million)

26. New York, USA (8.6 million)

27. Bangalore, India (8.4 million)

28. Shenyang, China (8.1 million)

29. Wuhan, China (8.0 million)

30. Bogotá, Colombia (7.9 million)

WEIRD LAWS

It is illegal to get a fish drunk in Ohio.

Reincarnation in China is illegal without government permission.

In the UK, a pregnant woman can legally relieve herself wherever she wants – even, if she so requests, in a policeman's helmet.

It is illegal to bring a rocket launcher to council meetings in Billings, Montana.

It is against the law to disrupt a wedding in South Australia.

In Wyoming, it is illegal to take a picture of a rabbit from January to April without an official permit.

It is illegal to throw your couch at your neighbour in Warsaw, Indiana.

You are not allowed to make people laugh in Alabama by wearing a false moustache in church.

In the UK, it is an offence to let your dog mate with any dog belonging to the Royal Family.

It is illegal to take a selfie with tigers or any other big cats in New York.

It is against Australian law to dress up as Batman and Robin.

In California, it is illegal to threaten a butterfly.

It is unlawful to swear in front of a corpse in the US state of Georgia.

Flushing the toilet after 10pm is illegal in Switzerland.

Women in Vermont must obtain their husband's written permission before getting false teeth.

In Chicago, it is against the law to eat in a restaurant or any other place that is on fire.

It is an offence to be drunk while in charge of cattle in England and Wales.

It is illegal to fall asleep in a cheese shop in Illinois.

In Indiana, it is against the law to catch fish with your bare hands.

It is against the law to display a hypnotised person in a store window in Everett, Washington.

In Sarasota, Florida, it is illegal to sing in public while wearing a swimsuit.

It is illegal for an MP to wear a suit of armour in the UK Parliament.

In Oxford, Ohio, it is unlawful for a woman to remove her clothes if she is standing in front of a picture of a man.

It is illegal to dust any building in Clarendon, Texas, with a feather duster.

In the UK, placing a postage stamp bearing the monarch's head upside down on an envelope is an act of treason.

You cannot play more than ten hours of bingo a week in North Carolina.

In Little Rock, Arkansas, it is illegal to sound a vehicle horn at any place where cold drinks or sandwiches are served after 9pm.

Under the Metropolitan Police Act of 1839, it is still illegal to beat or shake a carpet or rug in any London street, although it is permissible to shake a doormat before 8am.

It is illegal to wake a sleeping fireman in Racine, Wisconsin.

Anyone in Oklahoma caught making weird facial expressions at a dog risks a fine or jail.

In Scotland, it is illegal to turn someone away if they knock on your door and ask to use your toilet.

In Huron, South Dakota, it is unlawful to cause static between the hours of 7am and 11pm.

Dog owners in Turin, Italy, are liable to be fined if they do not walk their pets at least three times a day.

In Topeka, Kansas, it is illegal to sing the alphabet on the streets at night.

It is an offence to interfere with a homing pigeon in the Australian state of Victoria.

It is illegal to erect a washing line across any thoroughfare in the City of London.

It is unlawful to whistle underwater in Vermont.

Eating while sitting on church steps is banned in Florence, Italy.

In Salem, Massachusetts, it is still illegal for a married couple to sleep naked in a rented room.

Humming in public on a Sunday is forbidden in Cicero, Illinois.

Under Oklahoma law, it is forbidden to make glue out of dead skunks.

A 2004 Act states that, 'No person shall import into England potatoes which he knows to be or has reasonable cause to suspect to be Polish potatoes.'

In Canton, Ohio, anyone seeking to play leap frog with a friend in a park must first obtain permission from the park superintendent.

The Salmon Act of 1986 makes it illegal for anyone in the UK to handle a salmon in suspicious circumstances.

If intending to sell a wheelbarrow in Des Plaines, Illinois, you must not chain it to a tree.

It is illegal to be in possession of more than 50kg of potatoes in Western Australia.

Worrying or harassing squirrels is unlawful in La Crosse, Wisconsin.

In the UK, it is illegal to ride in a taxi if you have the plague.

It is still technically illegal for a man in Hartford, Connecticut, to kiss his wife in public on a Sunday.

In Waterloo, Nebraska, barbers are prohibited from eating onions between the hours of 7am and 7pm.

In Samoa, it is against the law for a man to forget his wife's birthday.

It is illegal for unmarried women in Florida to go parachuting on a Sunday.

In France, it is illegal to name a pig Napoleon.

It is illegal to give your dog a lighted cigar in Zion, Illinois.

It is strictly illegal to set off a nuclear bomb in a city park in Destin, Florida.

SOME CRIMES THAT WERE PUNISHABLE BY DEATH IN EIGHTEENTH-CENTURY BRITAIN

Damaging Westminster Bridge

Impersonating a Chelsea Pensioner

Cutting down young trees

Malicious maiming of cattle

Being in the company of gypsies for a month

Poaching

Begging without a licence
(if you were a soldier or a sailor)

Being out at night with a blackened face

Horse theft

Pickpocketing

An unmarried mother concealing a stillborn child

Forgery

Destroying turnpike roads

Writing a threatening letter

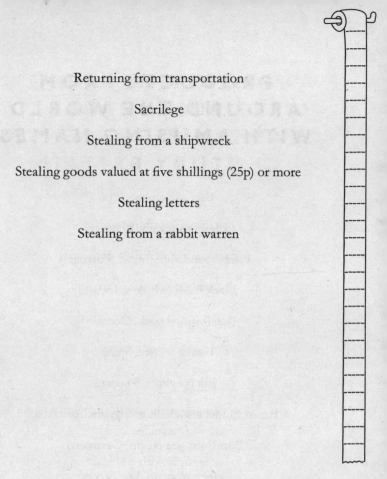

Returning from transportation

Sacrilege

Stealing from a shipwreck

Stealing goods valued at five shillings (25p) or more

Stealing letters

Stealing from a rabbit warren

PRODUCTS FROM AROUND THE WORLD WITH AMUSING NAMES

Barf (detergent, Iran)

Big Nuts (candy, Belgium)

Bimbo Sandwich (bread, Portugal)

Black Bush (whiskey, Ireland)

Bog (canned pork, Denmark)

Bonka (coffee, Spain)

Bra (yoghurt, Sweden)

Breast Munchies (chicken nuggets, Australia)

BumBum (ice cream, Germany)

Cemen (tomato dip, Turkey)

Cock Soup (soup, Jamaica)

Dickmilch (milk drink, Germany)

Erektus (energy drink, Czech Republic)

Fart (chocolate bar, Poland)

Finger Marie (biscuit, Sweden)

JussiPussi (dinner rolls, Finland)

Krapai (pickled dill, Turkey)

Noblice (cakes, Serbia)

Nutkick (chocolate bar, Finland)

Only Puke (food snack, China)

Pee Cola (soft drink, Ghana)

Plopp (chocolate bar, Sweden)

Poo (food snack, Indonesia)

Seigneurie d'Arse (wine, France)

Shitto (pepper sauce, Ghana)

Soup for Sluts (ramen noodles, Japan)

Urinal (hot drink, Romania)

PUNDERFUL SHOP AND BUSINESS NAMES

Alan Cartridge – printer ink refill shop in Leeds, England

Alexander the Grate – fireplace retailer in Belfast, Northern Ireland

Back to the Fuchsia – flower shop in Milton Keynes, England

Bapman – sandwich shop in York, England

Bar Humbug – inn in Bristol, England

Bits & PCs – computer business in Biggar, Scotland

Bonnie Tiler – wall and floor tiling business in Newcastle upon Tyne, England

Brim Full of Rasher – mobile snack business in England

Cash 22 – credit and finance business in London, England

Codrophenia – fish and chip shop in Sheffield, England

Curl Up & Dye – hair salon in Norfolk, Virginia

Cycloanalysts – bicycle shop in Oxford, England

Farther Treads – tyre shop in Liverpool, England

Floral 'n' Hardy – flower shop in Lanark, Scotland

Florist Gump – flower business in Bunbury, Western Australia

Get Stuffed – taxidermist in London, England

Hairy Pop-Ins – barber in Wokingham, England

Jack the Stripper – wood stripping company in London, England

Jason Donervan – fast food truck in Bradford-on-Avon, England

Jean-Claude Van Man – removal company in Southport, England

Knit Wit   clothing store in Philadelphia, Pennsylvania

Kumquat Mae – vegetarian restaurant in Sheffield, England

Let's Fascia It – home repairs business, Nottingham, England

Lord of the Fries – restaurant in Melbourne, Australia

Melon Cauli – fruit and vegetable seller in Birmingham, England

Men at Wok – Chinese restaurant in Williston, Vermont

Mowsart – garden maintenance business in Humberside, England

Old Volks Home – Volkswagen repair business in Soquel, California

Only Food & Sauces – café in Blackburn, Lancashire

Our Soles – safety and workplace supplies business in Southampton, England

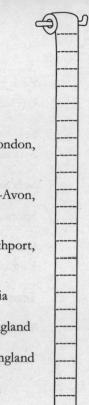

Pane in the Glass – double glazing company in Ashford, Greater London

Sew Materialistic – textile company in Nipawin. Saskatchewan, Canada

Sofa So Good – furniture store in Vancouver, Canada

Specs Appeal – optical shop in Winnipeg, Canada

Spruce Springclean – carpet cleaning business in Cornwall, England

Temple of Vroom – driving school in Aylesbury, England

Top Bun – mobile food truck in Des Moines, Iowa

Wash Up, Doc? – laundry service in Pangasinan, Philippines

SIGNS OF THE TIMES

ODD SIGNS FROM AROUND THE WORLD

CUSTOMERS GIVING ORDERS WILL BE PROMPTLY EXECUTED – tailor's shop in Mumbai

BUDDY'S STORE: EAT HERE, GET GAS – roadside in Maine

OPEN SEVEN DAYS A WEEK AND WEEKENDS TOO – restaurant in New Zealand

SAFETY LADDER, CLIMB AT OWN RISK – dock in Alaska

CAUTION SLOW KIDS ON ROADS WITH NO SHOULDERS – on a road in Cairns, Australia

SPECIALIST IN WOMEN AND OTHER DISEASES – doctor's office in Rome

BEWARE! TO TOUCH THESE WIRES IS INSTANT DEATH ANYONE FOUND DOING SO WILL BE PROSECUTED – railroad station in the US

LADIES MAY HAVE A FIT UPSTAIRS – Hong Kong clothing shop

TO STOP THE DRIP, TURN COCK TO RIGHT – washroom in Finland

RESTRICTED BREEDING AREA. ZOO EMPLOYEES ONLY! – zoo in Virginia

LADIES ARE REQUESTED NOT TO HAVE CHILDREN IN THE BAR – cocktail bar in Norway

THIS TOILET IS A DISPLAY MODEL. PLEASE ASK A MEMBER OF STAFF IF YOU WOULD LIKE TO WATCH A DEMONSTRATION – the London Boat Show

NO DUMPING – TRESPASSERS WILL BE VIOLATED – street in Oklahoma City

I SLAUGHTER MYSELF TWICE DAILY – butcher's shop in Israel

WE SELL GAS TO ANYONE IN A GLASS CONTAINER – gas station in Santa Fe, New Mexico

GUARD DOGS OPERATING – UK hospital

TRESPASSERS WILL BE PROSECUTED TO THE FULL EXTENT OF THE LAW – SISTERS OF MERCY – on the wall of a Baltimore estate

TEETH EXTRACTED BY THE LATEST METHODISTS – Hong Kong dentist's office

MEMBERS AND NON-MEMBERS ONLY – club in Mexico

NO TRESPASSING WITHOUT PERMISSION – grounds of a Nairobi school

15 MEN'S WOOL SUITS, $10 THEY WON'T LAST AN HOUR! – men's clothing store in Tacoma, Washington

THE NEXT MATINEE FILM SCREENING IN SUPPORT OF HALESWORTH DEMENTIA TRUST WILL BE LA LA LAND – on the board at a hall in Sussex

PERSONS ARE PROHIBITED FROM PICKING FLOWERS FROM ANY BUT THEIR OWN GRAVES – cemetery in Pennsylvania

PARKING IN BACKSIDE – a sign in Dubai directing motorists to the rear of the building

IN SHORT

TRADE NAMES YOU MAY NOT KNOW ARE ABBREVIATIONS

3M (Minnesota Mining and Manufacturing)

Adidas (from company founder Adolf 'Adi' Dassler)

Aldi (from Albrecht, the surname of founders Karl and Theo, and *diskont*, German for 'discount')

Britvic (British Vitamin Products)

Brylcreem (brilliantine and cream)

Castrol (castor oil)

Disprin (dissolve aspirin)

Drambuie (from the Gaelic *dram* (drink) and *buidh* (pleasing))

Durex (durability, reliability, excellence)

Elastoplast (elastic plaster)

Findus (from Swedish company Fruit, Wine and Liqueur Industries)

Flymo (flying mower)

Hovis (from the Latin *hominis vis* (strength of man))

Ikea (an acronym from the name of founder Ingvar Kamprad, Elmtaryd (the farm where he grew up) and Agunnaryd (his home village))

Lego (from the Danish *leg godt*, play well)

Lufthansa (from *luft*, German for 'air', and the Hanseatic League, a Northern European merchants' confederation during the Middle Ages)

Nikon (from Nippon Kogaku, which means Japanese Optical)

Pez (from *pfefferminz*, the German word for 'peppermint', which was the sweet's original flavour)

Radox (radiated oxygen)

SPAR (an acronym of *Door Eendrachtig Samenwerken Profiteren Allen Regelmatig*, Dutch for 'Through united co-operation everyone regularly profits')

Velcro (from the French *velours* (velvet) and *croché* (hooked))

PHONETIC ALPHABETS

NATO: Alfa, Bravo, Charlie, Delta, Echo, Foxtrot, Golf, Hotel, India, Juliet, Kilo, Lima, Mike, November, Oscar, Papa, Quebec, Romeo. Sierra, Tango, Uniform, Victor, Whiskey, X-ray, Yankee, Zulu.

NEW YORK POLICE: Adam, Boy, Charlie, David, Edward, Frank, George, Henry, Ida, John, King, Lincoln, Mary, Nora, Ocean, Paul, Queen, Robert, Sam, Tom, Union, Victor, William, X-ray, Yellow, Zebra.

FRENCH: Anatole, Berthe, Célestin, Désiré, Eugène, François, Gaston, Henri, Irma, Joseph, Kléber, Louis, Marcel, Nicolas, Oscar, Pierre, Quintal, Raoul, Suzanne, Thérèse, Ursule, Victor, William, Xavier, Yvonne, Zoé.

GERMAN: Anton, Berta, Charlotte, Dora, Emil, Friedrich, Gustav, Heinrich, Ida, Julius, Kaufmann, Ludwig, Martha, Nordpol, Otto, Paula, Quelle, Richard, Siegfried, Theodor, Ulrich, Viktor, Wilhelm, Xanthippe, Ypsilon, Zeppelin.

ITALIAN: Ancona, Bologna, Como, Domodossola, Empoli, Firenze, Genova, Hotel, Imola, Jesolo, Kursaal, Livorno, Milano, Napoli, Otranto, Padova, Quarto, Roma, Salerno, Torino, Udine, Venezia, Washington, Xeres, Yacht, Zara.

SPANISH: Antonio, Barcelona, Carmen, Dinamarca, Enrique, Francia, Guadalupe, Huelva, Inés, Jueves, Kilo, Lorenzo, Madrid, Navarra, Oviedo, Paris, Querido, Ramón, Sábado, Tango, Uruguay, Valencia, Washington, Ximena, Yegua, Zapata.

IMPORTANT DATES FOR YOUR DIARY

2 January: Run It Up the Flagpole
and See If Anyone Salutes Day

4 January: Spaghetti Day

11 January: Learn Your Name in Morse Code Day

14 January: Dress Up Your Pet Day

21 January: Squirrel Appreciation Day

23 January: Measure Your Feet Day

28 January (or last Monday of the month):
Bubble Wrap Appreciation Day

4 February: Pass the Buck Day

10 February: Umbrella Day

11 February: Don't Cry Over Spilled Milk Day

17 February: Random Acts of Kindness Day

23 February: International Dog Biscuit Appreciation Day

28 February: Tooth Fairy Day

1 March: Peanut Butter Lovers' Day

3 March: If Pets Had Thumbs Day

10 March: Middle Name Pride Day

26 March: Spinach Day

28 March: Something on a Stick Day

31 March: Bunsen Burner Day

4 April: World Rat Day

7 April: No Housework Day

11 April: Barbershop Quartet Day

13 April: Scrabble Day

14 April: Look Up at the Sky Day

16 April: Wear Pyjamas to Work Day

17 April: Blah, Blah, Blah Day

18 April: International Jugglers Day

19 April: Garlic Day

26 April: Hug an Australian Day

30 April: Hairstyle Appreciation Day

5 May: World Naked Gardening Day

9 May: Lost Sock Memorial Day

10 May: Clean Up Your Room Day

14 May: Dance Like a Chicken Day

16 May: Hug a Tree Day

22 May: World Goth Day

29 May: Learn About Composting Day

1 June: Doughnut Day

4 June: Hug Your Cat Day

6 June: Yo-Yo Day

9 June: Donald Duck Day

10 June: Ballpoint Pen Day

17 June: Eat Your Vegetables Day

19 June: World Sauntering Day

28 June: International Body Piercing Day

29 June: International Mud Day

1 July: International Joke Day

6 July: International Kissing Day

15 July: Cow Appreciation Day

17 July: World Emoji Day

27 July: Take Your Houseplants For a Walk Day

5 August: Underwear Day

6 August: Wiggle Your Toes Day

8 August: Sneak Some Zucchini Onto
Your Neighbour's Porch Day

13 August: Left Handers' Day

18 August: Bad Poetry Day

20 August: World Mosquito Day

25 August: Kiss and Make Up Day

5 September: Be Late For Something Day

13 September: Positive Thinking Day

19 September: International Talk Like a Pirate Day

21 September: Miniature Golf Day

28 September: Ask a Stupid Question Day

1 October: World Vegetarian Day

2 October: Name Your Car Day

5 October (or first Friday of the month): World Smile Day

10 October (or second Wednesday of the month):
Take Your Teddy Bear to Work Day

12 October: World Egg Day

14 October: Be Bald and Free Day

17 October: Wear Something Gaudy Day

25 October: Punk For a Day Day

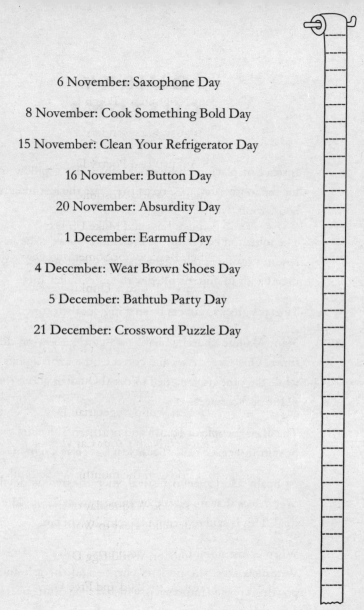

6 November: Saxophone Day

8 November: Cook Something Bold Day

15 November: Clean Your Refrigerator Day

16 November: Button Day

20 November: Absurdity Day

1 December: Earmuff Day

4 December: Wear Brown Shoes Day

5 December: Bathtub Party Day

21 December: Crossword Puzzle Day

QUIRKY
CUSTOMS

Instead of placing children's teeth under a pillow to wait for the tooth fairy, in Greece they toss the lost molars onto house roofs.

The initiation ceremony of the Satare-Mawe tribe in Brazil requires young boys to demonstrate their courage by placing their hands in mittens filled with angry bullet ants.

Tibetans greet strangers by sticking out their tongues.

Many Maltese churches have two clocks showing different times. One face shows the correct time for religious locals while the other is designed to confuse Satan about the time of the next service.

The Masai people of Kenya and northern Tanzania say hello by spitting at each other because it is seen as a sign of respect.

At Spain's El Colacho festival, men dressed as devils leap over babies that are placed on a mattress in the middle of the road. This is said to cleanse the children of sin.

When a member of the Yanomami tribe of Brazil and Venezuela dies, the body is burned and the ash and bone powder is turned into a soup, which is then drunk by relatives.

NAMES FOR SANTA
AROUND THE WORLD

Albania: Babadimri

Armenia: Gaghant Baba

Austria: Christkind

Belgium and France: Père Noël

Brazil: Papai Noel

Bulgaria: Dyado Koleda

Chile: Viejo Pascuero

China: Shengdan Laoren

Croatia: Sveti Nikola

Denmark: Julemanden

Finland: Joulupukki

Germany: Weihnachtsmann

Greece: Agios Vasilis

Hawaii: Kanakaloka

Hungary: Mikulas

Iceland: Jólasveinarnir

Italy: Babbo Natale

Japan: Hoteiosho

Lithuania: Kaledu Senelis

Netherlands: Sinterklass/Kerstman

Norway: Julenissen ('Christmas Gnome')

Poland: Swiety Mikolaj

Portugal: Pai Natal

Romania: Moş Crăciun

Russia: Ded Moroz ('Grandfather Frost')

Spain: Papa Noel

Sweden: Jultomten

Turkey: Noel Baba

NATIONAL SUPERSTITIONS

The number four is considered unlucky in China because it sounds similar to the Chinese word for death.

Cutting your nails on a Sunday in Croatia is thought to bring bad luck.

Killing a spider in Finland is said to bring rain the next day.

In France, if you step in dog poo with your left foot, good luck (and probably a bad smell) will follow.

If you sneeze three times before breakfast on a Sunday in Iceland, you will receive some reward that week.

If you meet a funeral procession on a road in Ireland, you should turn and walk with it for at least four steps to keep misfortune at bay.

In Japan, picking up a comb with its teeth facing your body is believed to bring bad luck.

When a hearse passes by in Japan, you are advised to tuck your thumbs in to protect your parents. This is because the Japanese word for thumb translates as 'parent-finger' and so by hiding it you are safeguarding your parents from death.

If you eat fish in Latvia on New Year's Eve and put the scales inside your wallet, it means that money will keep flowing into it throughout the year.

In Lithuania, an unmarried person who sits at the corner of a table won't marry for seven years.

In Mexico, if you stare at a dog while it poos, it is believed you will develop a pimple on your eye.

A man hit with a broom in Nigeria becomes impotent unless he retaliates seven times with the same broom.

It is considered bad luck for a young Norwegian lady to knit a sweater for her boyfriend, because it means he will end the relationship.

In Poland, it is considered bad luck to have a wedding in May.

Spilling wine on the table in Portugal brings happiness to the entire house.

If a bird poos on you or your car in Russia, it is considered good luck. Indeed, if a whole flock of birds is involved, you could be a future lottery winner.

Scottish fishermen will consider not heading out to sea if they have passed a church minister on the way to their boats.

In Serbia, if you bite your tongue it means that your grandmother plans to bake a cake for you.

The Spanish believe that eating 12 grapes at midnight on New Year's Eve will guarantee 12 months of good luck

Leaving your keys on a table in Sweden will bring bad luck.

In Turkey, anyone who chews gum at night is believed to be chewing the flesh of the dead.

Before entering a new house in Ukraine, homeowners are urged to send a cat in first to greet the house spirit.

NOT THE PLACE TO KEEP A SAUSAGE

NATIONAL PROVERBS

The river won't get dirty just by the dog's bark – Afghan

You cannot catch a flea with gloves – Albanian

Good fences make good neighbours – American

The bride who doesn't know how to dance says the floor is slanted – Armenian

Experience is the comb that nature gives us when we are bald – Belgian

A one-eyed uncle is better than no uncle at all – Bengali

A dried fish cannot be used as a cat's pillow – Chinese

Flies never visit an egg that has no crack – Chinese

He who must die must die in the dark, even though he sells candles – Colombian

He who wins the first hand leaves with only his pants – Corsican

Don't sail out farther than you can row back – Danish

The dog's kennel is not the place to keep a sausage – Danish

Carefulness is the mother of the porcelain cabinet – Dutch

A handful of patience is worth a bushel of brains – Dutch

Fine words butter no parsnips – English

Don't dig your grave with your own knife and fork – English

When spiders unite, they can tie down a lion – Ethiopian

When the mouse is full, the flour tastes bitter – Faroese

A herring barrel will always smell of herring – French

There is no pillow so soft as a clear conscience – French

With patience and spit one gets the mosquito – German

A lean agreement is better than a fat lawsuit – German

When the fox preaches, look to the geese – German

Everything has an ending, only a sausage has two – German

When the frog is eating his chillies, why should the lizard sweat? – Ghanaian

Observe your enemies, for they first find your faults – Greek

The dead do not know the value of white sheets – Haitian

If you want your eggs hatched, sit on them yourself – Haitian

When an elephant is in trouble, even a frog will kick him – Hindi

You can't straighten a dog's tail by putting it in a hosepipe – Indian

Never bolt your door with a boiled carrot – Irish

Bare walls make giddy housekeepers – Irish

After the game, the king and the pawn go into the same box – Italian

Below the navel there is neither religion nor truth – Italian

The best armour is to keep out of range – Italian

If you go to a donkey's house, don't talk about ears – Jamaican

Fall seven times, stand up eight – Japanese

The crow that mimics a cormorant is drowned – Japanese

Don't think there are no crocodiles because the water is calm – Malaysian

The shrimp that sleeps gets carried by the tide – Mexican

Turn your face to the sun and the shadows will fall behind you – New Zealand

A humble calf will feed from two mothers – Polish

A guest sees more in an hour than the host in a year – Polish

It's when it's small that the cucumber gets warped – Portuguese

Better a mouse in the pot than no meat at all – Romanian

The only free cheese is in the mousetrap – Russian

Gossip needs no carriage – Russian

A thistle is a fat salad for an ass's mouth – Scottish

Never draw your dirk when a blow will do it – Scottish

The badger is not aware of its own blaze – Siberian

Don't shake the tree when the pears fall off themselves – Slovakian

He who has scalded himself on milk weeps when he sees a cow – Spanish

A large chair does not make a king – Sudanese

In the shallowest waters, the ugliest fish swim – Swedish

The afternoon knows what the morning never suspected – Swedish

When one shuts one eye, one does not hear everything – Swiss

The night rinses what the day has soaped – Swiss

Never squat with your spurs on – Texan

Nobody lifts the dog's tail when it defecates – Thai

In a battle between elephants, the ants get squashed – Thai

Who keeps company with the wolf will learn to howl – Vietnamese

A spoon does not know the taste of soup nor a learned fool the taste of wisdom – Welsh

MADE IN BRITAIN

Britain exports over 50,000 boomerangs to Australia every year.

Nowhere in the UK is more than 70 miles from the sea. The furthest point from any coast is Church Flatts Farm, located outside the Derbyshire village of Coton in the Elms.

Nothing officially happened in Britain between 3 and 13 September 1752, because the country was switching from the old Julian calender to the Gregorian calendar. As the Julian calendar was 11 days behind, those 11 days were eliminated so that 2 September was immediately followed by the fourteenth.

The Shetland island of Foula still uses the Julian calendar and therefore celebrates Christmas Day on 6 January.

Eleven per cent of British people do not wash their hands after going to the toilet.

A 1571 Act of Parliament stipulated that all Englishmen over six years of age, except for nobles and 'persons of degree', must wear a flat cap on Sundays and public holidays or be fined three farthings (three quarters of a penny) per day. The measure was introduced to boost the wool trade but was repealed in 1597.

There are seashells on the summit of Mount Snowdon, the tallest mountain in England and Wales, because thousands of years ago the area that makes up Snowdonia National Park was at the bottom of the ocean.

The town of Beverley, near Hull, is named after the beaver population that once lived in the area.

During the First World War, British secret service agents used semen as invisible ink.

London's Big Ben refers to the Great Bell rather than the tower or the clock. The tower is officially the Elizabeth Tower and the clock is known as the Great Clock of Westminster.

On 12 August 1949, a flock of starlings landed on the minute hand of the Great Clock of Westminster and put the time back by four and a half minutes.

Thirty-nine per cent of British people read on the toilet.

Under the laws of ninth-century King Alfred the Great, anyone caught fighting in the presence of a bishop had to pay 100 shillings in compensation. The fine rose to 150 shillings if an archbishop was present.

The 1884 London Telephone Directory included the names of W.S. Gilbert and Sir Arthur Sullivan.

When Directory Enquiries was introduced in Britain, the first operators were boys but these were considered 'too high-spirited' and were replaced by demure ladies. Applicants had to be single and were expected to resign if they got married.

Almost one in five British women have gone to work not wearing any underwear.

King Henry III kept a polar bear as part of the royal menagerie at the Tower of London. The bear – a gift from King Haakon IV of Norway – used to go fishing in the Thames.

Attempting to commit suicide was a punishable crime in England and Wales until 1961.

Twenty per cent of British teenagers think Winston Churchill was a fictional character.

The Dorset/Somerset border runs through the middle of the White Post pub at Rimpton Hill. The pub used to have one bar in each county, and when the two counties had different licensing hours, customers had to leave the Dorset bar at 10.30pm and move into the Somerset bar so that they could drink for another half-hour.

The reigning monarch owns all the sturgeons, porpoises, whales and dolphins in the waters around the UK.

In 1800, almost a quarter of all British women were named Mary.

At least 2,000 castles have been listed in Scotland past and present, which works out at one castle every 15 square miles.

Although the Great Fire of London destroyed much of the city in 1666, only six deaths were officially recorded.

More British people believe in ghosts than in God.

THE AMERICAN WAY

Around 100 US firefighters are convicted of arson every year.

Montana allows double-proxy weddings, where neither marriage partner is required to be present at the ceremony.

There is one lawyer for every 300 people in the US.

Mount Whitney, the highest point in the contiguous United States, and Badwater Basin in Death Valley, the lowest point in the US, are less than 85 miles apart.

One in eight US workers has been employed by McDonald's, ranging from Amazon founder Jeff Bezos to singer Pink.

It takes 90 days for a drop of water to travel the entire length of the Mississippi River from northern Minnesota to the Gulf of Mexico.

More than 6,000 shipwrecks lie at the bottom of the Great Lakes.

Sixty-one per cent of Americans admit to peeing in the shower and 41 per cent say they have peed in swimming pools.

The Kobuk Valley National Park in northern Alaska has 100-foot-high sand dunes.

The first rollercoaster in the US – the Switchback Railway, which opened in Coney Island, New York, in 1884 – had a top speed of only 6mph.

Twenty-five times more people are bitten by New Yorkers than by sharks.

The town of Colma, California, has around 1,800 living residents but more than 1.5 million bodies are buried in its cemeteries.

There are 17.5 miles of corridor in the Pentagon.

The highest point in Pennsylvania is lower than the lowest point in Colorado.

Medical error is the third leading cause of death in the United States.

Visitors to the shrine at the Saint Roch Chapel in New Orleans, Louisiana, leave as an offering their old prosthetic body parts, including glass eyes, dental plates, crutches and false limbs.

Seven per cent of Americans believe the moon landings were faked. A similar number also believe that Elvis is still alive.

ROMAN TOWN NAMES IN BRITAIN

Ad Pontes (Staines-upon-Thames)

Alaunodunum (Maidenhead)

Aquae Arnemetiae (Buxton)

Aquae Sulis (Bath)

Caesaromagus (Chelmsford)

Camulodunum (Colchester)

Concangis (Chester-le-Street)

Condate (Northwich)

Corinium Dobunnorum (Cirencester)

Danum (Doncaster)

Deva (Chester)

Dubris (Dover)

Durnovaria (Dorchester)

Durocobrivis (Dunstable)

Durocornovium (Swindon)

Duroliponte/Cantabrigia (Cambridge)

Durovernum Cantiacorum (Canterbury)

Eboracum (York)

Glevum (Gloucester)

Hortonium (Halifax)

Isca Dumnoniorum (Exeter)

Isca Augusta (Caerleon)

Lactodorum (Towcester)

Lagentium (Castleford)

Leodis (Leeds)

Lindum Colonia (Lincoln)

Londinium (London)

Luguvalium (Carlisle)

Moridunum (Carmarthen)

Noviomagus Reginorum (Chichester)

Olicana (Ilkley)

Pons Aelius (Newcastle upon Tyne)

Portus Felix (Filey)

Ratae Corieltauvorum (Leicester)

Segontium (Caernarfon)

Venta Belgarum (Winchester)

Verulamium (St Albans)

SOME BRITISH PLACE NAMES IN CANADA

Aldershot (Nova Scotia)

Aylesbury (Saskatchewan)

Bingley (Alberta)

Bolton (Ontario)

Brighton (Newfoundland)

Bury (Quebec)

Canterbury (New Brunswick)

Carlisle (Ontario)

Derby (British Columbia)

Edmonton (Alberta)

Elgin (Quebec)

Grantham (Alberta)

Grimsby (Ontario)

Halifax (Nova Scotia)

Maidstone (Saskatchewan)

Matlock (Manitoba)

Montrose (British Columbia)

Morden (Manitoba)

Nelson (British Columbia)

Oldham (Nova Scotia)

Southampton (Ontario)

Wakefield (Quebec)

Wembley (Alberta)

Weymouth (Nova Scotia)

Windsor (Ontario)

Woking (Alberta)

UK CITIES

Aberdeen, Armagh, Bangor (Wales), Bath, Belfast, Birmingham, Bradford, Brighton & Hove, Bristol, Cambridge, Canterbury, Cardiff, Carlisle, Chelmsford, Chester, Chichester, Coventry, Derby, Derry, Dundee, Durham, Edinburgh, Ely, Exeter, Glasgow, Gloucester, Hereford, Hull, Inverness, Lancaster, Leeds, Leicester, Lichfield, Lincoln, Lisburn, Liverpool, City of London, Manchester, Newcastle upon Tyne, Newport, Newry, Norwich, Nottingham, Oxford, Perth, Peterborough, Plymouth, Portsmouth, Preston, Ripon, St Albans, St Asaph, St Davids, Salford, Salisbury, Sheffield, Southampton, Stirling, Stoke-on-Trent, Sunderland, Swansea, Truro, Wakefield, Wells, City of Westminster, Winchester, Wolverhampton, Worcester, York

US NATIONAL PARKS

Acadia (Maine)

Arches (Utah)

Badlands (South Dakota)

Big Bend (Texas)

Biscayne (Florida)

Black Canyon of the Gunnison (Colorado)

Bryce Canyon (Utah)

Canyonlands (Utah)

Capitol Reef (Utah)

Carlsbad Caverns (New Mexico)

Channel Islands (California)

Congaree (South Carolina)

Crater Lake (Oregon)

Cuyahoga Valley (Ohio)

Death Valley (California, Nevada)

Denali (Alaska)

Dry Tortugas (Florida)

Everglades (Florida)

Gates of the Arctic (Alaska)

Gateway Arch (Missouri)

Glacier (Montana)

Glacier Bay (Alaska)

Grand Canyon (Arizona)

Grand Teton (Wyoming)

Great Basin (Nevada)

Great Sand Dunes (Colorado)

Great Smoky Mountains (Tennessee, North Carolina)

Guadalupe Mountains (Texas)

Haleakalā (Hawaii)

Hawaii Volcanoes (Hawaii)

Hot Springs (Arkansas)

Isle Royale (Michigan)

Joshua Tree (California)

Katmai (Alaska)

Kenai Fjords (Alaska)

Kings Canyon (California)

Kobuk Valley (Alaska)

Lake Clark (Alaska)

Lassen Volcanic (California)

Mammoth Cave (Kentucky)

Mesa Verde (Colorado)

Mount Rainier (Washington)

North Cascades (Washington)

Olympic (Washington)

Petrified Forest (Arizona)

Pinnacles (California)

Redwood (California)

Rocky Mountain (Colorado)

Saguaro (Arizona)

Sequoia (California)

Shenandoah (Virginia)

Theodore Roosevelt (North Dakota)

Voyageurs (Minnesota)

Wind Cave (South Dakota)

Wrangell-St. Elias (Alaska)

Yellowstone (Wyoming, Montana, Idaho)

Yosemite (California)

Zion (Utah)

UNESCO WORLD HERITAGE SITES IN THE UK

Blaenavon Industrial Landscape (Wales)

Blenheim Palace (Oxfordshire)

Canterbury Cathedral, St Augustine's Abbey
and St Martin's Church (Kent)

Castles and Town Walls of King Edward I
(including Conwy, Caernarfon, Harlech and
Beaumaris, Isle of Anglesey and Gwynedd, Wales)

City of Bath

Cornwall and West Devon Mining Landscape

Derwent Valley Mills (Derbyshire)

Dorset and East Devon Coast

Durham Castle and Cathedral

English Lake District (Cumbria)

Forth Bridge (Edinburgh, Inchgarvie
and Fife, Scotland)

Frontiers of the Roman Empire
(including Hadrian's Wall and the Antonine Wall,
northern England and southern Scotland)

Giant's Causeway and Causeway Coast
(County Antrim, Northern Ireland)

Heart of Neolithic Orkney (Orkney, Scotland)

Ironbridge Gorge (Shropshire)

Liverpool Maritime Mercantile City

Maritime Greenwich (London)

New Lanark (Scotland)

Old and New Towns of Edinburgh

Palace of Westminster and Westminster Abbey (London)

Pontcysyllte Aqueduct and Canal
(Wrexham, Wales and Shropshire)

Royal Botanical Gardens (Kew, London)

St Kilda (Scotland)

Saltaire (Shipley, West Yorkshire)

Stonehenge and Avebury (Wiltshire)

Studley Royal Park, including Fountains Abbey
(North Yorkshire)

Tower of London

BRITONS' FAVOURITE HOLIDAY DESTINATIONS

1. Majorca

2. Tenerife

3. Algarve

4. Ibiza

5. Lanzarote

6. Orlando

7. Gran Canaria

8. Benidorm

9. Crete

10. Disneyland Paris

GOING POTTY

THE WORLD OF TOILETS

The Bell Inn at Ticehurst, East Sussex, has tubas as urinals in the men's toilet.

The Goldman Hotel in Frankfurt, Germany, has men's urinals in the shape of Mick Jagger's lips.

A small wooden outside toilet located on the shoreline of Haida Gwaii, British Columbia, features an automatic flush powered by the moon, which washes away all waste twice a day.

An outside toilet in Siberia's Altai Mountains is perched on the edge of a cliff 8,500 feet above sea level. It serves five workers at a nearby weather station and is so remote that new toilet roll is delivered once a month by helicopter.

Directly above the men's toilet at Rheinfels Castle in Germany is a razor-sharp guillotine. To flush the toilet, you pull a lever but fortunately the blade does not drop.

FLAGS

The flag of the Philippines is flown with the blue band uppermost in times of peace and with the red band on top to indicate a state of war.

Denmark's flag is the oldest design that is still in use, having debuted in 1219.

The flag of Belize is the only one to feature human beings as a major design element.

The flags of Chad and Romania are almost identical with blue, red and yellow vertical stripes.

The flag of Nepal is the only national flag that is not rectangular.

The flags of Australia and New Zealand are so similar that when Australian Prime Minister Bob Hawke visited Canada in 1984, he was greeted with the New Zealand flag.

If you turn an Indonesian flag upside down, it becomes a Polish flag.

The original Olympic flag went missing for 77 years after the 1920 Games until American diver Hal Haig Prieste revealed that he had stolen it as a dare and had kept it in his suitcase ever since.

COUNTRIES WITH MOST NOBEL PRIZE WINNERS PER CAPITA

1. Faroe Islands

2. Saint Lucia

3. Luxembourg

4. Switzerland

5. Sweden

6. Iceland

7. Denmark

8. Norway

9. Austria

10. United Kingdom

11. Timor-Leste

12. Ireland

13. Israel

14. Hungary

15. Germany

US STATE NICKNAMES

Alabama – Yellowhammer State

Alaska – The Last Frontier

Arizona – Grand Canyon State

Arkansas – Natural State

California – Golden State

Colorado – Centennial State

Connecticut – Constitution State

Delaware – First State

Florida – Sunshine State

Georgia – Peach State

Hawaii – Aloha State

Idaho – Gem State

Illinois – Prairie State

Indiana – Hoosier State

Iowa – Hawkeye State

Kansas – Sunflower State

Kentucky – Bluegrass State

Louisiana – Pelican State

Maine – Pine Tree State

Maryland – Old Line State

Massachusetts – Bay State

Michigan – Great Lakes State

Minnesota – North Star State

Mississippi – Magnolia State

Missouri – Show Me State

Montana – Treasure State

Nebraska – Cornhusker State

Nevada – Silver State

New Hampshire – Granite State

New Jersey – Garden State

New Mexico – The Land of Enchantment

New York – Empire State

North Carolina – Tar Heel State

North Dakota – Peace Garden State

Ohio – Buckeye State

Oklahoma – Sooner State

Oregon – Beaver State

Pennsylvania – Keystone State

Rhode Island – Ocean State

South Carolina – Palmetto State

South Dakota – Mount Rushmore State

Tennessee – Volunteer State

Texas – Lone Star State

Utah – Beehive State

Vermont – Green Mountain State

Virginia – Old Dominion

Washington – Evergreen State

West Virginia – Mountain State

Wisconsin – Badger State

Wyoming – Equality State

WHO SAYS THERE ARE NO FAMOUS BELGIANS?

Leo Baekeland, inventor of bakelite

Rudy Beckers, inventor of the parking sensor

Plastic Bertrand, punk singer who had 1978 hit with 'Ça Plane Pour Moi'

Jean-Marc Bosman, footballer who changed the transfer rules

Jacques Brel, singer/songwriter who wrote 'If You Go Away'

Albert Claude, the first biochemist to isolate a cancer cell

Kim Clijsters, tennis player, winner of four Grand Slam singles titles

Nicolas Colsaerts, golfer and Ryder Cup winner

Pierre Culliford (aka Peyo), creator of the Smurfs

Jeannine Deckers (aka the Singing Nun), who had a 1963 hit with 'Dominique'

Edward De Smedt, chemist and inventor of modern day road asphalt

Louis Hennepin, who, in 1680, became the first European to explore the Upper Mississippi

Justine Henin, tennis player who spent 117 weeks as world number one

Jacky Ickx, Formula One racing driver (1966–79) and six-time winner of the Le Mans 24-Hour Race

Sandra Kim, 13-year-old winner of the 1986 Eurovision Song Contest

Georges Lemaître, astronomer who first put forward the Big Bang Theory

Jean Joseph Étienne Lenoir, inventor of the internal-combustion engine

Constant Loiseau, nineteenth-century inventor of the optometer

Maurice Maeterlinck, author who was awarded the Nobel Prize for Literature in 1911

René Magritte, twentieth-century surrealist artist

Eddy Merckx, racing cyclist who won the Tour de France five times

John Joseph Merlin, inventor of roller skates

Lambert Adolphe Quetelet, inventor of the Body Mass Index for measuring obesity

Georges Remi (aka Hergé), creator of Tintin

Peter Paul Rubens, early seventeenthth-century painter

Adolphe Sax, inventor of the saxophone in 1846

Georges Simenon, author and creator of fictional detective Jules Maigret

Jean 'Toots' Thielemans, celebrated harmonica player

Jean-Claude Van Damme, martial artist and actor

Charles Van Depoele, engineer and pioneer in electric railway technology

Anthony van Dyck, seventeenth-century painter, famous for his portraits of Charles I

Jan van Eyck, influential fifteenth-century painter

Andreas Vesalius, founding father of modern human anatomy

MAD HOUSES

ARCHITECTURALLY
DIFFERENT BUILDINGS

A terraced house in Oxford has a 25-foot-long, fibreglass shark sculpture buried nose-down in the roof.

The Mercure Kakadu Crocodile Hotel in Jabiru, Australia, is built in the shape of a giant crocodile. The rooms run along the body to the tail and the swimming pool is in the croc's alimentary canal.

Everything in Sir Thomas Tresham's sixteenth-century Triangular Lodge at Rushton, Northamptonshire, relates to the number three in honour of the Holy Trinity. It has three sides, each of which measure 33 feet; three gables on each side; three storeys and triangular or hexagonal rooms decorated with trefoils or triangles in groups of three. All of the Latin inscriptions have 33 letters.

The old Longaberger Company building in Newark, Ohio, is the shape of a maple wood basket. Constructed in the 1990s, the seven-storey edifice was designed as a 160 times replica of one of the company's signature products, the Medium Market Basket.

Built in 1922 by Elis F. Stenman, the Paper House in Rockport, Massachusetts, is made entirely from recycled newspaper. The walls have 215 reinforced layers of newsprint while the furniture – including chairs, desks and even a piano – is all made from paper.

A summer house in Dunmore, Scotland, is topped with a 53-foot-high stone pineapple.

A shoe repair shop in Bakersfield, California, is housed in a 30-foot-long, 20-foot-high building shaped like a 1947 shoe, complete with black lace, white low top roof and an orthopedic heel. The entrance is in the toe.

Everything inside and out is turned on its head in the Upside Down House at Szymbark, Poland. Entry is through a window in the roof and visitors walk on the ceilings.

A 335-foot-high office block in Bangkok, Thailand, is shaped like an elephant.

The Winchester Mystery House in San Jose, California, reflects former rifle heiress Sarah Winchester's obsession with the number 13. She ordered the house to built with 13 bathrooms, 13 windows in the rooms, 13 steps on staircases, with 13 hooks in every cupboard, 13 drain holes in the sinks and 13 candles in every chandelier.

ALARM THE
HALL PORTER

HOTEL INSTRUCTIONS

You are requested to take advantage of the chambermaid (Tokyo)

The lift is being fixed for the next day. During that time we regret that you will be unbearable (Romania)

In case of fire, please do your utmost to alarm the hall porter (Austria)

Please do not lock the door as we have lost the key (Ireland)

Please leave your values at the front desk (Paris)

Depositing the room key into another person is prohibited (Tokyo)

All fire extinguishers must be examined at least ten days before any fire (London)

No consummation whatever may take place in this foyer (Baghdad)

Visitors are expected to complain at the office between the hours of 9 and 11am daily (Athens)

Guests are requested not to smoke or do other disgusting behaviours in bed (Tokyo)

It is our intention to pleasure you every day (Hamburg)

If you telephone for room service you will get the answer you deserve (Canary Islands)

If service is required, give two strokes to the maid and three to the waiter (Italy)

If you wish breakfast, lift the telephone and our waitress will arrive. This will be enough to bring up your food (Tel Aviv)

You are welcome to visit the cemetery where famous Russian and Soviet composers, artists and writers are buried daily except Thursday (Moscow)

UNUSUAL CAUSES OF DEATH IN THE US

(ON AVERAGE, PER YEAR)

Falling out of bed (450)

Autoerotic asphyxiation (150)

Constipation (144)

Choking on ballpoint pen caps (100)

Falling from trees (94)

Lawnmower accidents (75)

Victims of serial killers (67)

Struck by lightning (31)

Dog bites (30)

Trampled by cows (20)

Nightwear catching fire (6)

Snake bites (5)

Roller coasters (4)

Selfie-related accidents (3)

Crushed by vending machines (2)

Shot dead accidentally by toddlers (2)

NICHE MUSEUMS

Barney Smith's Toilet Seat Art Museum, The Colony, Texas

Brain Museum, Lima, Peru

British Lawnmower Museum, Southport, Merseyside

Burlingame Museum of Pez Memorabilia,
Burlingame, California

Burnt Food Museum, Arlington, Massachusetts

Carrot Museum, Berlotte, Belgium

Chez Galip Hair Museum, Avanos, Turkey

Cumberland Pencil Museum, Keswick, Cumbria

Disgusting Food Museum, Malmo, Sweden

Dog Collar Museum, Leeds Castle, Kent

French Fry Museum, Bruges, Belgium

Gherkin Museum, Lehde, Germany

Good Vibrations Antique Vibrator Museum,
San Francisco, California

Hammer Museum, Haines, Alaska

Icelandic Phallological Museum, Reykjavik, Iceland

International Banana Museum, Mecca, California

Kansas Barbed Wire Museum, La Crosse, Kansas

Lunch Box Museum, Columbus, Georgia

Milk Bottle Museum, Malvern, Worcestershire

Moist Towelette Museum, East Lansing, Michigan

Momofuku Ando Instant Ramen Museum, Ikeda, Japan

Mousetrap Museum, Neroth, Germany

Museum of Bad Art, Somerville, Massachusetts

Museum of Broken Relationships, Zagreb, Croatia

Museum of Failure, Helsingborg, Sweden

Museum of Funeral Carriages, Barcelona, Spain

Museum of Witchcraft and Magic, Boscastle, Cornwall

National Leprechaun Museum, Dublin, Ireland

New Zealand Beer Can Museum, Galatea, New Zealand

Paris Sewer Museum, Paris, France

Rezola Cement Museum, San Sebastian, Spain

Salt and Pepper Shaker Museum, Gatlinburg, Tennessee

Sock World and Sock-Knitting Machine Museum,
Hokitika, New Zealand

Sulabh International Museum of Toilets, New Delhi, India

Umbrella Cover Museum, Peaks Island, Maine

SPECIALISED SOCIETIES

Bagpipe Society

British Boomerang Society

British Sausage Appreciation Society

British Water Tower Appreciation Society

Cheese of the Month Club

Cloud Appreciation Society

Crossroads Appreciation Society

Cummerbund Society

Flat Earth Society

George Formby Society

Pylon Appreciation Society

Richard III Society

Roundabout Appreciation Society

Sheffield Omnibus Enthusiasts Society

The Society of Bearded Gentlemen

Ugly Animal Preservation Society

Wallpaper History Society

Writing Equipment Society

US STATE CAPITALS

Alabama – Montgomery

Alaska – Juneau

Arizona – Phoenix

Arkansas – Little Rock

California – Sacramento

Colorado – Denver

Connecticut – Hartford

Delaware – Dover

Florida – Tallahassee

Georgia – Atlanta

Hawaii – Honolulu

Idaho – Boise

Illinois – Springfield

Indiana – Indianapolis

Iowa – Des Moines

Kansas – Topeka

Kentucky – Frankfort

Louisiana – Baton Rouge

Maine – Augusta

Maryland – Annapolis

Massachusetts – Boston

Michigan – Lansing

Minnesota – Saint Paul

Mississippi – Jackson

Missouri – Jefferson City

Montana – Helena

Nebraska – Lincoln

Nevada – Carson City

New Hampshire – Concord

New Jersey – Trenton

New Mexico – Santa Fe

New York – Albany

North Carolina – Raleigh

North Dakota – Bismarck

Ohio – Columbus

Oklahoma – Oklahoma City

Oregon – Salem

Pennsylvania – Harrisburg

Rhode Island – Providence

South Carolina – Columbia

South Dakota – Pierre

Tennessee – Nashville

Texas – Austin

Utah – Salt Lake City

Vermont – Montpelier

Virginia – Richmond

Washington – Olympia

West Virginia – Charleston

Wisconsin – Madison

Wyoming – Cheyenne

NUMBER ONES

Afghanistan is the largest producer of heroin.

Andorra has the highest consumption of tobacco per capita.

Australia is the largest producer of wool.

Belgium has the highest divorce rate.

Bolivia is the largest exporter of Brazil nuts.

Brazil is the largest producer of oranges.

Bulgaria is the largest producer of lavender oil.

Cambodia has the most public holidays.

Canada is the largest producer of lentils.

China is the largest producer of sex toys.

Colombia is the largest producer of emeralds.

Costa Rica is the largest producer of pineapples.

Denmark is the least corrupt country, according to the organisation Transparency International.

Ecuador is the biggest exporter of bananas.

Finland has the most Mensa geniuses per capita.

France has the most tourists per year.

Germany is the largest hop producer.

Honduras has the highest homicide rate.

Iceland is the most peaceful country, according to the Global Peace Index.

Indonesia is the country with the largest number of active volcanoes.

Iran is the largest producer of pistachio nuts.

Ireland has the highest consumption of milk per capita.

Italy is the largest wine producer.

Japan has the longest life expectancy.

Libya has the most road traffic fatalities per capita.

Martinique has the highest female-to-male ratio.

Mexico is the largest avocado producer.

Monaco is the most densely populated.

Niger has the highest birth rate.

Palau has the highest prevalence of obesity.

Qatar has the most doctors per capita.

Romania has the highest home ownership rate.

Russia has the most chess grandmasters.

San Marino has the most cars per capita.

South Korea has the highest plastic surgery rate.

Sri Lanka has the highest suicide rate.

Sweden is the most generous country in terms of
international aid by per centage of national income.

Switzerland has the largest number
of millionaires per capita.

Turkey is the largest cherry producer.

The United States is the biggest exporter
of human hair extensions.

THE LARGEST
GREEK ISLANDS

1. Crete

2. Euboea

3. Lesbos

4. Rhodes

5. Chios

6. Kefalonia

7. Corfu

8. Samos

9. Lemnos

10. Naxos

11. Zakynthos

12. Thassos

13. Andros

14. Lefkada

15. Karpathos

16. Kos

17. Kythira

18. Icaria

19. Skyros

20. Paros

ODD PLACE NAMES

Accident, Maryland

Anus, France

Arse, Indonesia

Backside, Scotland

Bald Knob, Arkansas

Ballplay, Alabama

Banana, Kiribati

Bastardo, Italy

Batman, Turkey

Beaverlick, Kentucky

Belchertown, Massachusetts

Bell End, England

Bitche, France

Blubberhouses, England

Boring, Oregon (twinned with Dull, Scotland)

Brokenwind, Scotland

Brown Willy, England

Bumbum, Papua New Guinea

Burrumbuttock, Australia

Butt of Lewis, Scotland

Cape Foulwind, New Zealand

Climax, Canada

Cockburn, Australia

Condom, France

Crapstone, England

Darling, South Africa

Desire, Pennsylvania

Diapur, Australia

Dildo, Canada

Droop, West Virginia

Eggs and Bacon Bay, Australia

Embarrass, Minnesota

Erect, North Carolina

Fanny Barks, England

Flushing, Netherlands

Fucking, Austria

Great Snoring, England (neighbour to Little Snoring)

Happy Bottom, England

Hell, Norway

Hose, England

Humpybong, Australia

Intercourse, Pennsylvania

Jimcumbilly, Australia

Kissing, Germany

Knob Lick, Missouri

Koolyanobbing, Australia

Le Grand Sex, Switzerland

Minge, Haiti

Mount Buggery, Australia

Muck, Scotland

Mudford Sock, England

Muff, Ireland

North Piddle, England

Nowhere, Oklahoma

Peculiar, Missouri

Pensioners Bush, Australia

Pimpinbudgie, Australia

Poop, Mexico

Pratt's Bottom, England

Pussy, France

Queen Camel, England

Rectum, Netherlands

Rottenegg, Austria

Scratchy Bottom, England

Shag Point, New Zealand

Shitterton, England

Shush, Iran

Silly, Belgium

Six Mile Bottom, England

Sleepy Eye, Minnesota

Smug, Poland

Sodom, Wales

Splatt, England

Squirrel, Idaho

Sugartit, Kentucky

Surprise, Arizona

Swastika, Canada

Thong, England

Tightsqueeze, Virginia

Tightwad, Missouri

Tittybong, Australia

Twatt, Scotland

Ugley, Essex, England

Wankers Corner, Oregon

Wet Beaver Creek, Arizona

Wetwang, England

Whakapapa, New Zealand

Windpassing, Austria

STRANGE PLACES

Point Nemo in the South Pacific Ocean is located so far from land that the nearest humans are often astronauts orbiting Earth on the International Space Station.

An underground coal seam fire on Australia's Mount Wingen has been burning for 6,000 years.

Due to an iron-rich underground lake, a 50-foot-high waterfall on Antarctica's Taylor Glacier is blood red.

Because it straddles three states and therefore three time zones, the small Australian town of Cameron Corner celebrates New Year three times – first in New South Wales, then half an hour later in South Australia and finally 30 minutes after that in Queensland.

The Tonlé Sap River in Cambodia usually runs south from Tonlé Sap Lake to the Mekong River, but during the monsoon season the Mekong River rises and its floodwaters force the Tonlé Sap to reverse its course and flow north.

The area of northwestern Venezuela, where the Catatumbo River meets Lake Maracaibo, experiences 1.2 million lightning strikes per year. The natural light show crackles through the sky for up to 160 nights a year for as long as ten hours at a time.

CITY INHABITANTS

Aberdeen – Aberdonian

Albuquerque – Burqueño

Alexandria – Alexandrine

Amalfi – Amalfitan

Amsterdam – Amsterdammer

Armagh – Armachian

Asunción – Asunceno

Beirut – Beiruti

Bergamo – Bergamasque

Birmingham, UK – Brummie

Bologna – Bolognese

Bordeaux – Bordelais

Bremen – Bremer

Brisbane – Brisbanite

Brussels – Bruxellois

Buenos Aires – Bonaerense

Buffalo – Buffalonian

Cadiz – Gaditano

Cairns – Cairnsitte

Cairo – Cairene

Cambridge – Cantabrigian

Caracas – Caraquenian

Cheltenham – Cheltonian

Chester – Cestrian

Christchurch – Cantabrian

Damascus – Damascene

Dundee – Dundonian

Edinburgh – Edinburger

Florence – Florentine

Frankfurt – Frankfurter

Galway – Galwegian

Genoa – Genovese

Glasgow – Glaswegian

Grenoble – Grenoblois

Guadalajara – Tapatio

The Hague – Haguer

Halifax, Canada – Haligonian

Indianapolis – Hoosier

La Paz – Paceño

Las Vegas – Las Vegan

Leeds – Loiner

Lima – Limeño

Limassol – Lemesouti

Limerick – Limerickman

Lisbon – Lisboeta

Liverpool – Liverpudlian, Scouser

Los Angeles – Angeleno

Madrid – Madrilenian

Manchester – Mancunian

Manila – Manileño

Marseille – Marsellais

Medellin – Paisa

Memphis – Memphian

Mexico City – Chilango

Minneapolis – Minneapolitan

Monaco – Monegasque

Monterrey – Regiomontano

Moose Jaw – Moose Javian

Moscow – Muscovite

Mumbai – Mumbaikar

Munich – Münchner

Naples – Neapolitan

Nazareth – Nazarene

Newcastle upon Tyne – Novocastrian, Geordie

Nice – Niçois

Oxford – Oxonian

Parma – Parmesan

Quebec City – Québécois

Rio de Janeiro – Carioca

Rouen – Rouennais

Sacramento – Sacrementan

St Albans – Albanian

Shrewsbury – Salopian

Southampton – Sotonian

Strasbourg – Strasbourgeois

Sunderland – Mackem

Sydney – Sydneysider

Warsaw – Varsovian

Wolverhampton – Wulfrunian

HARD YAKKA

AUSTRALIAN SLANG WORDS

Arvo: afternoon

Bitzer: mongrel dog

Bludger: lazy person

Bonzer: great

Cark it: die

Cobber: friend

Coldie: beer

Crook: sick

Dag: nerd

Daks: trousers

Dunny: toilet

Fair dinkum: genuine

Liquid laugh: vomit

Mongrel: despicable person

Ocker: unsophisticated person

Rack off!: get lost!

Ripper: brilliant, fantastic

Root rat: somebody constantly on the lookout for sex

Shonky: underhanded

Spunk: good looking person

Stonkered: defeated

Tinny: can of beer

Tucker: food

Wowser: spoilsport

Yabber: talk a lot

Yakka: work

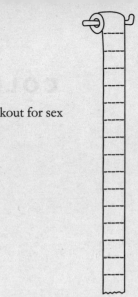

COLLECTIVE NOUNS

An ambush of widows

An audience of squid

A bask of crocodiles

A bazaar of guillemots

A business of ferrets

A cete of badgers

A chine of polecats

A circus of puffins

A condescension of actors

A conflagration of arsonists

A conspiracy of lemurs

A deceit of lapwings

A descent of woodpeckers

A disguising of tailors

An enchantment of nightingales

An equivocation of politicians

An exaltation of larks

A flange of baboons

A loveliness of ladybirds

A mischief of mice

A murder of crows

A murmuration of starlings

An obstinacy of buffalo

An ostentation of peacocks

A parliament of owls

A piteousness of doves

A poverty of pipers

A promise of barmen

A rhumba of rattlesnakes

A shiver of sharks

A shrewdness of apes

A siege of bitterns/herons

A smack of jellyfish

A sneer of butlers

A tabernacle of bakers

An unkindness of ravens

SOUFFLES BROKE OUT

UNFORTUNATE NEWSPAPER MISPRINTS

The bride, who was given away by her father, wore a dress of white figured brocade with a trailing veil held in place by a coronet of pearls. She carried a bouquet of rose buds and goods vehicles, leaving free access to all private vehicles not built for more than seven passengers – *Atherstone News and Herald*

Londonderry Development Commission has plans to spend about £24,000 within the next few months on improving the standard of street fighting in the city centre – *Belfast Telegraph*

If the motion were passed, no strike action would be taken by NALGO without a ballet of all its members – *Bristol Evening Post*

There will be plenty of fun and games, including a beer tent, homemade teas and a dog show, with proceeds going to Hearing Dogs for the Dead – *Bucks Examiner*

The ballet travels with its own symphony orchestra which is directed by Mrs Goberman. The orchestra contains 20 virtuous performers – *Clemson College Tiger,* South Carolina

Landlords: We have ten ants looking for good-quality homes – *County Down Spectator*

Douglas Carswell became the second elected UKIP MP last month when he won the Clacton by-election, after defecating from the Tories – *Daily Mail*

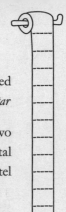

Sid Scott made his debut at a reggae concert – and stopped a riot when souffles broke out in the huge crowd – *Daily Star*

The constable now preferred a further charge against the two girls of stealing a carving knife, a fork and two ornamental judges which he found on top of a wardrobe in the hotel bedroom – *Dublin Evening Mail*

Traffic tailed back as far as Hemel Hempstead from the contra-flow system near the Berry Grove junction at Bushey where a bride is being repainted at night and during weekends – *Evening Echo*, Hertfordshire

'They've been suggesting that for some time, it's all rubbish. It's fiction.' His comments followed claims that the Prince has been secretly Mrs Parker-Bowles for more than a decade, and as often as once a week – *Evening Gazette*, Middlesbrough

It wasn't the proper doctor – just a young locust taking his place while he was away – *Evening News*, London

The skeleton was believed to be that of a Saxon worrier – *Express and Echo*, Exeter

For sale: 83 Ford Grandad – *Express and Star*, Wolverhampton

Belcoo police seized twenty cattle and thirty small pigs on suspicion of having been smuggled, assisted by Miss K. McDermott (violin) and Mrs. P. O'Rourke (percussion and effects) – *Fermanagh Herald*

Among the most outrageous demands of employers was a request for details of one secretary's menstrual cycle so that her boss could give her a wide birth – *Guardian*

We could put chlorine in vast quantities into water and apart from bleaching your heir, it would have no effect – *Guardian*

On orders from the White Mouse, the FBI last night sealed off the offices of the ousted special Watergate prosecutor Archibald Cox and his staff – *International Herald Tribune*

The bride was very upset when one of her little attendants accidentally stepped on her brain and tore it – *Kent Messenger*

For Sale. Lovely rosewood piano. Owner going abroad with beautiful twisted legs – *North Wales Advertiser*

Oxford City Council is to press the Thames Water Authority to help improve sanity facilities along the riverbanks – *Oxford Times*

Dressed in a suit and wearing the familiar red rose in his bottom hole, Lt General Afrifa appeared for the last time – *The Pioneer*, Ghana

God has blessed us with many riches, In Heaven and in Earth, So we follow the example of the wise men, Who gave golf, frankincense and myrrh – *Portsmouth Daily Times*, Ohio

Julia Roberts Finds Life And Her Holes Get Better With Age – headline, *Post-Journal*, New York

The degenerative manifestations of 'old age' have included memory loss, disorientation, confusion, perceptional difficulties, speech loss, disorientation, confusion, perceptional difficulties, speech problems – *Richmond Register*, Kentucky

Hafen is an enthusiastic reader and claims 'Lame is Rob' by Victor Hugo as her favorite book – *The Scroll*, Idaho

The decision to shut Ringinglow fire station has angered many including the 6,900 residents who singed a petition against the closure – *Sheffield Weekly Gazette*

Best man was Mr Martin Gasson. A reception was held at Langford's Hotel, Hove. The couple are honeymooning in grease – *Shoreham Herald*

The strike leaders had called a meeting that was to have been held in a bra near the factory, but it was found to be too small to hold them all – *South London Press*

His mother died when he was seven years old, while his father lived to be nearly a centurion – *Wallasey and Wirral Chronicle*

Men's and Ladies' Singles, Pairs and Triples as well as Mixed Pairs are invited to the Yarmouth Bowling Green to compete for £5,000 of prize money at the Great Yarmouth Open Bowels Festival – *Where and When in East Anglia*

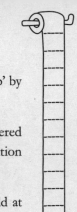

OXFORD DICTIONARIES' WORDS OF THE YEAR

2004: chav

2005: sudoku

2006: bovvered

2007: carbon footprint

2008: credit crunch

2009: simples

2010: big society

2011: squeezed middle

2012: omnishambles

2013: selfie

2014: vape

2015: 'face with tears of joy' emoji

2016: post-truth

2017: youthquake

2018: toxic

SINGLE-WORD PALINDROMES

(FOUR LETTERS OR MORE)

Alula, Boob, Civic, Deed, Degged, Deified, Denned, Detartrated, Dewed, Evitative, Kayak, Kook, Level, Madam, Marram, Minim, Naan, Noon, Peep, Poop, Pullup, Racecar, Radar, Redder, Redivider, Refer, Reifier, Repaper, Reviver, Revver, Rotator, Rotavator, Rotor, Sagas, Sees, Sememes, Semes, Seres, Sexes, Shahs, Solos, Spacecaps, Stats, Succus, Tenet, Terret, Toot.

SOME RARELY
USED WORDS

Abomasum (n): the fourth stomach of a ruminant, such as a cow or sheep.

Anguilliform (adj): shaped like an eel.

Bardolatry (n): finding the humour in Shakespeare funnier than it really is.

Blatherskite (n): someone who talks at great length without making much sense.

Borborygmus (n): a rumbling noise in the intestines.

Callipygian (adj): possessing shapely buttocks.

Clinomania (n): an overwhelming desire to lie down.

Crepuscular (adj): relating to twilight.

Dendrochronology (n): the study of tree rings.

Fipple (n): the mouthpiece of a wind instrument such as a recorder.

Floccinaucinihilipilification (n): the habitual tendency to estimate something as worthless.

Gynotikolobomassophile (n): someone who likes to nibble a woman's earlobes.

Hypercatalectic (adj): having an extra syllable at the end of a verse.

Juglandaceous (adj): pertaining to walnuts.

Kenspeckle (adj, Scottish): easily recognisable.

Liripipe (n): the long dangling tail of a medieval academic hood.

Monorchid (adj): having only one testicle.

Mubblefubbles (pl. n): feelings of despondency.

Nephelodometer (n): instrument for calculating the speed of clouds.

Omphalopsychite (n): one who meditates by staring at their navel.

Pavonine (adj): resembling a peacock.

Petrichor (n): the pleasant smell that accompanies the first rain after a dry spell.

Quiddle (vb): to waste time on trivial matters.

Quockerwodger (n): puppet-like politician whose strings are pulled by someone else.

Rhinotillexomania (n): compulsive nose picking.

Scurryfunge (vb): to rush around the house tidying up before visitors arrive.

Snollygoster (n): a person without principles, especially a politician.

Stercoraceous (adj): dung-like.

Struthious (adj): related to an ostrich.

Throttlebottom (n): inept person in public office.

Wittol (n): a man who knows of and tolerates his wife's infidelities.

Xenodocheionology (n): the study of hotels and inns.

Zalambdotont (adj): having molar teeth with v-shaped ridges.

ORIGINS OF PHRASES

Bite the bullet: Before the days of effective anaesthetics, military surgeons used to make wounded soldiers bite on a bullet to ease the pain.

Butter someone up: Ancient Indians sought favour by throwing balls of clarified butter at statues of the gods.

Cool as a cucumber: Even in hot weather, the inside of a cucumber is up to 20 degrees Fahrenheit cooler than the outside air.

Get out the wrong side of bed: In Roman times, it was considered bad luck to get out of bed on the left side.

Hair of the dog: Medieval medicine dictated that if you were bitten by a mad dog you should lay one of its hairs across the wound to heal it.

Let your hair down: In the seventeenth century, women were expected to wear their hair up in public, only letting it down to be washed or when they were alone at home and could relax.

Like chalk and cheese: In the foureenth century, cheese was the same colour as chalk and unscrupulous shopkeepers would sometimes try to pass off chalk as cheese.

Pull out all the stops: A pipe organ has stops that control the airflow and thus the volume. To play the instrument as loudly as possible, all the stops need to be pulled out.

Show your true colours: Warships used to fly multiple flags to confuse the enemy, but the rules of warfare stated that a ship had to hoist its true flag before opening fire.

Spill the beans: In ancient Greece, secret votes were cast by placing white or black beans in a jar but if the container was knocked over, the beans would fall out and the secret would be revealed early.

Wear your heart on your sleeve: If a medieval knight chose to defend a woman's honour in a horseback joust, he would show his loyalty to her by tying a cloth in her colours around his arm.

LONG WORDS IN THE GERMAN DICTIONARY

Betäubungsmittelverschreibungsverordnung (n): regulation requiring a prescription for an anaesthetic

Bezirksschornsteinfegermeister (n): head district chimney sweep

Donaudampfschiffahrtsgesellschaftskapitän (n): Danube steamship company captain

Freundschaftsbezeigungen (pl. n): demonstrations of friendship

Generalstaatsverordnetenversammlungen (pl. n): general states representatives meetings

Handschuhschneeballwerfer (n): a person who wears gloves to throw snowballs

Höchstgeschwindigkeitsbegrenzung (n): maximum speed limit

Nahrungsmittelunverträglichkeit (n): a food intolerance

Niederschlagswahrscheinlichkeit (n): likelihood of rain

Parkzeitüberschreitung (n): exceeding the permitted parking time

Rechtsschutzversicherungsgesellschaften (pl. n): legal protection insurance companies

To the dismay of many, *Rindfleischetikettierungsüberwachungsaufgabenübertragungsgesetz* ('law for the delegation of monitoring beef labelling') was officially dropped from the German language in 2013.

ENGLISH WORDS WITH FOREIGN PARENTS

Addenda (Latin)

Aficionado (Spanish)

Alcohol (Arabic)

Alfresco (Italian)

Amok (Malay)

Angst (German)

Avatar (Hindi)

Balcony (Italian)

Bandana (Hindi)

Bangle (Hindi)

Bazaar (Persian)

Bonanza (Spanish)

Bravura (Italian)

Bungalow (Hindi)

Cameo (Italian)

Canyon (Spanish)

Catalogue (French)

Catamaran (Tamil)

Cheetah (Hindi)

Chutney (Hindi)

Chutzpah (Yiddish)

Cot (Hindi)

Cummerbund (Persian)

Dinghy (Hindi)

Doppelganger (German)

Dungarees (Hindi)

Fiasco (Italian)

Flamingo (Portuguese)

Galleon (Spanish)

Gingham (Malay)

Guru (Hindi)

Gymkhana (Hindi)

Hoi polloi (Greek)

Incommunicado (Spanish)

Intelligentsia (Russian)

Jodhpurs (Hindi)

Juggernaut (Hindi)

Jungle (Sanskrit)

Kamikaze (Japanese)

Karaoke (Japanese)

Karma (Hindi)

Ketchup (Malay)

Kitsch (German)

Kowtow (Cantonese)

Loot (Hindi)

Mannequin (French)

Mantra (Hindi)

Massage (French)

Mogul (Hindi)

Mosquito (Spanish)

Motto (Italian)

Patio (Spanish)

Poltergeist (German)

Prairie (French)

Pundit (Hindi)

Pyjamas (Hindi)

Quisling (Norwegian)

Regret (French)

Rendezvous (French)

Robot (Czech)

Rodeo (Spanish)

Safari (Swahili)

Satsuma (Japanese)

Shampoo (Hindi)

Sherbet (Turkish)

Ski (Norwegian)

Slalom (Norwegian)

Smorgasbord (Swedish)

Sofa (Turkish)

Tattoo (Samoan)

Terror (French)

Thug (Hindi)

Tobacco (Spanish)   Veranda (Hindi)

Tsunami (Japanese)   Victim (Latin)

Tycoon (Japanese)   Yacht (Dutch)

Typhoon (Urdu)   Zeitgeist (German)

Vendetta (Italian)

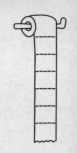

WORDS WITH MOST MEANINGS IN THE OXFORD ENGLISH DICTIONARY

1. Run (645)

2. Set (464)

3. Go (368)

4. Take (343)

5. Stand (334)

6. Get (289)

7. Turn (288)

8. Put (268)

9. Fall (264)

10. Strike (250)

COMMON LATIN
PHRASES IN ENGLISH

Ad hoc – for this purpose

Ad infinitum – without end

Ad nauseam – to a sickening extent

Bona fide – in good faith, genuine

Carpe diem – seize the day/moment

Caveat emptor – let the buyer beware

Coitus interruptus – sexual intercourse which is stopped before ejaculation

Compos mentis – of sound mind

De facto – in fact

Et alia – and others

Et cetera – and the rest

Ex gratia – done as a favour

Habeas corpus – writ requiring a person to be brought before a judge, usually to determine the legality of detention

In absentia – in their absence

In extremis – at the point of death or in a very difficult situation

In flagrante delicto – caught red-handed, literally 'in blazing offence'

In loco parentis – in place of a parent

In memoriam – in memory of

In situ – in position

Ipso facto – by the fact itself

Mea culpa – through my own fault

Non sequitur – a conclusion that does not logically follow

Per annum – by thc year

Per capita – by head

Per se – in itself

Persona non grata – an unacceptable person

Post mortem – after death

Prima facie – on the face of it

Pro rata – proportionately

Quid pro quo – one thing for another

Rigor mortis – the stiffness of death

Sine die – without a specified date

Status quo – the existing state of affairs

Tempus fugit – time flies

Terra firma – on dry land

Vice versa – the other way round

10-LETTER WORDS THAT CAN BE WRITTEN USING ONLY THE TOP ROW OF A KEYBOARD

Pepperroot

Pepperwort

Perpetuity

Pewterwort

Pirouetter

Prerequire

Pretorture

Proprietor

Repertoire

Repetitory

Tetterwort

Typewriter

MOST WIDELY SPOKEN LANGUAGES IN THE WORLD

1. Mandarin (1,030 million)

2. English (890 million)

3. Arabic (560 million)

4. Spanish (420 million)

5. Hindi (380 million)

6. Bengali (210 million)

7. Portuguese (200 million)

8. Russian (170 million)

9= French (160 million)

9= Urdu (160 million)

CALIFORNIA DREAMING

'In California, everyone thinks fat is something you can catch, and therefore is to be avoided' – Roseanne Barr

'I'd move to Los Angeles if Australia and New Zealand were swallowed by a huge tidal wave, if there was a bubonic plague in Europe, and if Africa disappeared from some Martian attack' – Russell Crowe

'In Los Angeles, everyone has perfect teeth. It's crocodile land' – Gwyneth Paltrow

'You can't smoke in a restaurant in Los Angeles, which is mildly ironic when you consider the fact that you can't breathe outside a restaurant in Los Angeles' – Greg Proops

'People in LA are deathly afraid of gluten. I swear to God, you could rob a liquor store in this city with a bagel' – Ryan Reynolds

'In California, handicapped parking is for women who are frigid' – Joan Rivers

FIGLIO DI PUTTANA!

FOREIGN SWEAR WORDS AND INSULTS

Äitisi nai poroja! – your mother copulates with reindeer! (Finnish)

Anavy sikim – motherfucker (Azerbaijani)

Bangsat – bastard (Indonesian)

Ben zonah – son of a bitch (Hebrew)

Butoh – asshole (Malaysian)

Cào ni zuzong shiba dài! – fuck your ancestors to the eighteenth generation! (Mandarin Chinese)

Choodmarani – motherfucker (Bengali)

Coochka – bitch (Bulgarian)

Da-te-n pula mea! – go fuck yourself (Romanian)

Debil – idiot (Albanian)

Do prdele! – up yours! (Czech)

Drittsekk – scumbag (Norwegian)

Eem vorigas bacheek doer! – kiss my ass! (Armenian)

Escroto – asshole (Portuguese)

Figlio di puttana – son of a whore (Italian)

Foder a mona! – piss off! (Portuguese)

Gloopan – idiot (Croatian)

Haramjada – bastard (Bengali)

Hlandbrenndu! – screw you! (Icelandic)

Hoerenjong – son of a bitch (Dutch)

Ik laat een scheet in jouw richting – I fart in your direction (Dutch)

Ja-schuck! – you bastard! (Korean)

Jebem ti mamu – I shag your mother (Slovenian)

Jiao ni sheng háizi zhang zhi chuang! – may your child be born with haemorrhoids! (Mandarin Chinese)

Kuksuger – cocksucker (Norwegian)

Lech mich am Arsch! – lick my ass! (German)

Leeghoofd – airhead (Dutch)

Malaka – wanker (Greek)

Mardar sag – your mother is a dog (Persian)

Metete un palo por el culo! – shove a stick up your arse! (Spanish)

Mine vittu! – go fuck yourself! (Estonian)

Molopää – dickhead (Finnish)

Ngentot – fart (Indonesian)

Onara atama – fart head (Japanese)

Poephol – asshole (Afrikaans)

Plá ar do theach! – a plague on your house! (Gaelic)

Rend mig! – fuck you! (Danish)

Schlemeil – clumsy idiot (Yiddish)

Shoopchino – asshole (Croatian)

Siktir! – get lost! (Turkish)

Skurwysyn – son of a bitch (Polish)

Ta dig i röven! – up yours! (Swedish)

Teef – bitch (Afrikaans)

Vaffanculo! – go fuck yourself! (Italian)

Va te branler! – go play with yourself! (French)

Verpiss dich! – get lost! (German)

Vilket arsle han är! – what an asshole he is! (Swedish)

Wajab zibik! – an infection to your dick! (Arabic)

Zhopa – asshole (Russian)

TOASTS

Cheers (English)

Chok dee (Thai)

Fenékig (Hungarian)

Iechyd da (Welsh)

Kanpai (Japanese)

Kippis (Finnish)

Mabuhay (Filipino)

Na zdravi (Czech)

Na zdrowie (Polish)

Noroc (Romanian)

Proost (Dutch)

Prost (German)

Salud (Spanish)

Salute (Italian)

Santé (French)

Saúde (Portuguese)

Şerefe (Turkish)

Skål (Danish, Norwegian, Swedish)

Sláinte (Irish Gaelic)

Terviseks (Estonian)

Živjeli (Croatian)

FANCY THAT!

Notorious English-born highwayman Black Bart, who robbed at least 28 Wells Fargo stagecoaches in northern California between 1875 and 1883, was afraid of horses and carried out all his robberies on foot.

A 1958 earthquake in Lituya Bay, Alaska, created a megatsunami with waves 1,720 feet high – taller than the Empire State Building.

Two million dollars worth of gold and silver float through Switzerland's sewer systems every year.

Bruce Lee failed his US Army physical exam.

In Yap, Micronesia, people still use giant limestone discs as currency. There are about 13,000 currently in circulation, some weighing more than a car.

Despite lasting for around three hours, the actual playing time in a Major League Baseball game is under 18 minutes.

The 1918 Spanish flu outbreak killed more people than the First World War.

The Greek national anthem has 158 verses, but only the first two are usually played.

The letter z used to be called an izzard.

US park ranger Roy C. Sullivan survived being struck by lightning seven times.

The Eiffel Tower was originally intended for Barcelona but was rejected for being too ugly.

27 July is National Sleepy Head Day in Finland, when the last person in a house to get out of bed that day is thrown into a lake, a river or the sea.

On average, we check our phones 150 times a day.

Every Olympic gold medal-winning US men's ice hockey team has included a player from the small town of Warroad, Minnesota.

There are so many local dialects in Norway that people can buy Norwegian-to-Norwegian dictionaries.

The amount a computer mouse moves is measured in mickeys.

The wealth of Nauru was built on bird poo. Tons of natural droppings on the Pacific island were used to make fertiliser, which was exported to sustain the Australian agriculture industry.

Debbie McGee was a member of the Iranian National Ballet.

The Austrian town of Saalfelden employs an official hermit.

Neil Armstrong's NASA application was a week late. If his friend Dick Day had not secretly added his letter to the pile, Armstrong would have been rejected.

The word 'huh' appears in more than 400 languages around the world.

The Anna Creek Station cattle ranch in South Australia covers an area bigger than Israel.

Saddam Hussein's 2002 campaign anthem was Whitney Houston's 'I Will Always Love You'.

When Iceland's football team beat England at Euro 2016, the match was watched by 99.8 per cent of Icelandic TV viewers.

When counting in English, your lips won't touch until you reach one million.

The Amazon River has 1,100 tributaries.

Tonga once issued a postage stamp in the shape of a banana.

Each year, 100 people in Russia are killed by icicles.

The Sami people of northern Finland use a unit of measure called a poronkusema, based on the distance a reindeer can walk before it needs to urinate. It is approximately 4.7 miles.

'Dump', 'wipe' and 'floater' are all terms used in volleyball.